Industrializing
THE ROCKIES

Mining the American West

Boomtown Blues: Colorado Oil Shale
Andrew Gulliford

High Altitude Energy: A History of Fossil Fuels in Colorado
Lee Scamehorn

*Industrializing the Rockies: Growth, Competition,
and Turmoil in the Coalfields of Colorado and Wyoming*
David A. Wolff

Silver Saga: The Story of Caribou, Colorado, Revised Edition
Duane A. Smith

Wesley Earl Dunkle: Alaska's Flying Miner
Charles Caldwell Hawley

Yellowcake Towns: Uranium Mining Communities in the American West
Michael A. Amundson

Series Editors

Duane A. Smith
Robert A. Trennert
Liping Zhu

Industrializing
THE ROCKIES

GROWTH,
COMPETITION,
AND TURMOIL
IN THE COALFIELDS OF COLORADO
AND WYOMING,
1868–1914

DAVID A. WOLFF

UNIVERSITY PRESS OF COLORADO

© 2003 by the University Press of Colorado

Published by the University Press of Colorado
5589 Arapahoe Avenue, Suite 206C
Boulder, Colorado 80303

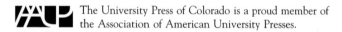 The University Press of Colorado is a proud member of
the Association of American University Presses.

The University Press of Colorado is a cooperative publishing enterprise supported, in part, by
Adams State College, Colorado State University, Fort Lewis College, Mesa State College,
Metropolitan State College of Denver, University of Colorado, University of Northern
Colorado, and Western State College of Colorado.

The paper used in this publication meets the minimum requirements of the American National
Standard for Information Sciences—Permanence of Paper for Printed Library Materials. ANSI
Z39.48-1992

Library of Congress Cataloging-in-Publication Data

Wolff, David A.
  Industrializing the Rockies : growth, competition, and turmoil in the coalfields of Colorado
and Wyoming / David A. Wolff.
    p. cm. — (Mining the American West)
Includes bibliographical references and index.
  ISBN 0-87081-747-7 (hardcover : alk. paper)
  1. Coal miners—Colorado—History. 2. Coal miners—Wyoming—History. 3. Strikes and
lockouts—Coal mining—Rocky Mountains Region—History. 4. Coal Strike, Colo., 1913–
1914. 5. Rock Springs Massacre, Rock Springs, Wyo., 1885. 6. Coal miners—Labor unions—
Colorado—History. 7. Coal miners—Labor unions—Wyoming—History. 8. Industrial
relations—Rocky Mountains Region—History. 9. Coal industry—Rocky Mountains Region—
History. I. Title. II. Series.
  HD8039.M62 U697 2003
  338.2'724'0978709034—dc21

                                                                            2003010958

Design by Daniel Pratt

12 11 10 09 08 07 06 05 04 03   10 9 8 7 6 5 4 3 2 1

For
Sarah, Shana, and Anne

CONTENTS

PREFACE

TWO TRAGIC EVENTS SEEMINGLY DEFINE THE ROCKY MOUNTAIN COAL INDUSTRY: the Rock Springs Massacre of 1885 and the Ludlow Massacre of 1914. At Rock Springs, Wyoming, twenty-eight Chinese coal miners died at the hands of racist and rebellious white coal diggers, and nearly thirty years later the deaths of thirteen women and children at the Ludlow tent colony in southern Colorado punctuated months of violence as coal managers and miners fought for an advantage. Both incidents indicate a massive breakdown in relations between company operators and miners. But they also share something else. These events involved the West's largest coal operations: the Union Pacific Railroad's coal mines in Wyoming and the Colorado Fuel and Iron's openings in Colorado. From this coincidence two questions arose that inspired this study. Did something about these two companies cause these violent eruptions? And was there any connection between the two events?

The drama of these episodes has drawn the interest of several scholars. Among them, noted western historian T. A. Larson coauthored two articles on the Rock Springs Massacre, and others, such as Dudley Gardner and Verla

Flores in *Forgotten Frontier: A History of Wyoming Coal Mining,* have examined the massacre to a greater or lesser degree. The Ludlow Massacre drew the attention of presidential nominee George McGovern, and his work has been followed by many other fine authors such as Barron Beshoar and Zesse Papanikolas. More recently, Priscilla Long has written extensively about Ludlow, and she focuses a large part of her monograph *Where the Sun Never Shines: A History of America's Bloody Coal Industry* on that incident.[1]

These writers made the massacres the defining moments in coalfield labor relations, and they also seemingly offer two possible answers to the questions posed earlier. The first is that violence connected the two events. In fact, the impression develops that turmoil was continual during the nearly thirty years that separated the two massacres. And second, the companies did have something in common: they both ruthlessly oppressed their workers as they denied freedoms and banished any hint of unionization. These impressions, however, cannot and do not tell the whole story. They belie the complexities involved in labor relations and coal mining. Long's *Where the Sun Never Shines* explores the coal industry in some detail, but labor relations in her view still boils down to bad companies crushing good workers.

The present study expands the understanding of coalfield labor relations and places the conflicts in the fuller context of a developing Rocky Mountain coal industry. Beyond the periodic violent outbursts, nearly every aspect of the coal industry affected labor relations. Three elements emerge as the most critical. The first involved who controlled the coal companies and what operating philosophy they applied. On the one hand, if a person entered the coal business for purely speculative reasons and quick profit, poor labor relations often resulted. On the other hand, some operators wanted to bring more stability to the coalfield, which often meant better relations with workers. The second feature that affected labor relations involved the workers and their workplace environment. As obvious as this seems, miners came at different times with different expectations. Plus, after their arrival in the coalfields, their thinking changed. Their original expectations and how they changed contributed significantly to the way miners interacted with the company. And third, the business environment, meaning the ups and downs of the business cycle and competition among companies, had a major impact on companies and consequent worker relations. During bad economic times, company managers often tried to make money by cutting wages. This action spread hardship and misery throughout the coalfields. The way these three variables came together determined labor relations.

As much as the interaction between labor and management is a major part of this story, it also covers the growth of the coal industry in Colorado and Wyoming from inception to maturity. Industrial mining first came to the West with the arrival of the Union Pacific Railroad and the opening of the first mines at Carbon, Wyoming, in 1868. Other operations soon followed, and southwestern Wyoming developed into one of the West's most important coal-producing regions. In Colorado, industrial mining started in the Denver Basin of northern Colorado with the coming of the Denver Pacific Railroad in 1870. Although these mines northwest of Denver dominated Colorado's early production, William Jackson Palmer changed this dynamic when he built the Denver and Rio Grande Railroad along the Front Range and opened new coal regions in central and southern Colorado. These locations soon outclassed those in northern Colorado. In fact, the coalfield around Trinidad rapidly became Colorado's most important producer, and these mines eventually allowed the Colorado Fuel and Iron Company to dominate the West's coal business.

This study is organized chronologically, with chapters generally centered around economic periods. This allows for an examination of what happens in times of prosperity and periods of recession. During good times, mines and companies expanded—often dramatically—whereas economic slowdowns meant stagnation but seldom shrinkage. More important, the chronological approach exposes change over time. For instance, the first coal developers came as speculators, whereas later arrivals brought a maturing business philosophy. One example of this mentality was seen in the evolution of coal towns. Early locations such as Carbon were unplanned and unkept, built mostly by miners. Eventually, coal operators saw an advantage in developing full company towns where rental houses and a store could provide extra revenue and some element of control. These new towns often went hand in hand with a changing workforce. The first arrivals were often skilled miners from the British Isles, but company managers soon replaced them with unskilled workers from a variety of places. Although the miners changed, the job did not, and the later arrivals became just as resistant to company machinations as those who came earlier. The way these changes unfolded cannot be fully appreciated unless they are seen over time.

This study ends in 1914 for three reasons. First and most obviously, the Ludlow Massacre happened that year. With this event the goal of examining the continuity in labor relations through that violent episode is accomplished. Second, after the Ludlow Massacre business philosophies and labor relations changed dramatically. John D. Rockefeller Jr. adopted the Employee Representation Plan for his miners, and John C. Osgood—an old labor nemesis—finally accepted the union. These modifications would need many more pages to explain. And third, by 1914 the era of expansion in Colorado and Wyoming coalfields had come to an end. Coal production began stagnating by the time of Ludlow, and this situation brought new problems.

This work started as an examination of the Colorado Fuel and Iron Company (CF&I) and the Union Pacific Coal Company (UPCC), but it grew beyond those bounds. It became readily apparent that to understand the large companies, some small operations also needed to be included. This became especially relevant when market dynamics appeared as an important force in company behavior. The smaller operations had to worry about losing their coal markets during strikes; consequently, they settled with their workers quite readily. The UPCC and CF&I did not have the same market concerns.

To fully analyze the market forces, this study examines four major coalfields—one in the western half of southern Wyoming and three along the Colorado Front Range. The three Colorado fields can be associated with nearby towns: Denver, Cañon City, and Trinidad. These four locations allow for a broad overview of labor interactions and expose the subtle differences caused by markets and different ownerships. Plus, the areas' proximity means the workers and companies shared similar problems. The CF&I and the UPCC may have been the largest coal operations in the area, but a variety of other companies need to be considered to gain a good understanding of the markets at that time.

This study thus crosses state lines as it discusses the different operations, which may cause confusion. Saying mines are in Colorado or Wyoming is handy for locating them, but state boundaries are arbitrary. These coal companies often worked and competed across state lines. Considering them together regardless of state boundaries makes the most sense. But as the coal business developed, each state passed different legislation that affected the coalfields. The variety of laws made the political boundaries more important. This narrative uses the reference labels of Colorado and Wyoming and then moves back and forth between the states as the story advances. This technique is essential for a comparison of changes over time. It is hoped that the subtitles will limit confusion on the part of the reader.

Other coalfields existed in Colorado, Wyoming, and the West beyond those discussed here. At times, operations on the Western Slope of Colorado and in northern Wyoming enter the narrative. The fact that these operations and those in Montana and Utah are not discussed more thoroughly does not infer unimportance; simply, the mines along the Front Range and in southern Wyoming had the conditions necessary for this study. These areas contained the region's first industrial mines and coal miners and the West's largest coal companies. Around these companies and their miners swirled all the problems of coal mining: financial speculation, economic uncertainty, struggles for control, and labor strife.

In the end, the happenings at Ludlow and Rock Springs were connected; both incidents grew out of a struggle for control. The white miners at Rock Springs were trying to maintain their traditional positions against a company policy of racial diversification. The rioters lost in 1885, but in a little more than two decades the workers managed to bring the United Mine Workers of

America (UMWA) to the Wyoming coalfield. When the Union Pacific Coal Company signed the union contract in 1907, it relinquished some of its control and also gave the miners some of the highest coal wages in the country. Victory came for the workers because the UMWA instilled a solidarity that overcame the company's diversification policies and the company changed its attitude toward the union. The Union Pacific Railroad needed coal to keep its trains running, and working with UMWA made more sense than threatening the railroad's operations.

In southern Colorado, the battle at Ludlow was also about control. The workers wanted more say over their lives and jobs, as they felt company domination everywhere. The operators, led by the Colorado Fuel and Iron Company, had adopted a number of policies to maintain a hold over their workers—which included never yielding to UMWA. In part, this reflected the implacable antiunionism of John D. Rockefeller Jr. and John C. Osgood, but it also stemmed from the fact that these allied companies had a fuel monopoly. They worried little about losing markets when a strike threatened, and they knew they could outlast the union. But in 1913 and 1914 the hostility and tension between the two sides exploded into the violence surrounding Ludlow.

A number of people deserve hearty thanks for helping me with this project. First and foremost, I thank my family, Sarah, Shana, and Anne, for their ongoing support. I also thank those who read the manuscript and made critical comments. Peter Iverson did the most to help, and I thank him very much. Dale Martin, Jay Fell, and Janeen Larsen also contributed significantly, and I greatly appreciate their help. Finally, I thank Bob Trennert, Duane Smith, Phil VanderMeer, and Venessa Adcock for their comments. I am lucky to be associated with such fine mining historians as Duane, Bob, Jay, and Dale.

Many librarians and archivists also helped. I enjoyed the time I spent at the Union Pacific Historical Museum in Omaha, the Nebraska State Historical Society in Lincoln, the American Heritage Center in Laramie, the Wyoming State Archives in Cheyenne, the Colorado School of Mines in Golden, the Colorado Research Library of the Colorado Historical Society in Denver, and the Denver Public Library. I particularly want to thank Rick Ewig in Laramie, Ann Nelson in Cheyenne, Barbara Dey in Denver, and Bob Sorgenfrei in Golden.

I also thank the Black Hills State University Committee of the Chiesman Foundation for Democracy for helping fund the research on the Knights of Labor in Chapter 4.

NOTES

1. Paul Crane and Alfred Larson, "The Chinese Massacre," *Annals of Wyoming* 12 (January 1940): 47–55; Paul Crane and Alfred Larson, "The Chinese Massacre, Part II," *Annals of Wyoming* 12 (April 1940): 153–161; Craig Storti, *Incident at Bitter*

Creek: The Story of the Rock Springs Chinese Massacre (Ames: Iowa State University Press, 1991); A. Dudley Gardner and Verla R. Flores, Forgotten Frontier: A History of Wyoming Coal Mining (Boulder: Westview, 1989); George S. McGovern and Leonard F. Guttridge, The Great Coalfield War (Boston: Houghton Mifflin, 1972); Barron B. Beshoar, Out of the Depths: The Story of John R. Lawson, a Labor Leader (Denver: Golden, 1942); Zeese Papanikolas, Buried Unsung: Louis Tikas and the Ludlow Massacre (Salt Lake City: University of Utah Press, 1982); Priscilla Long, Where the Sun Never Shines: A History of America's Bloody Coal Industry (New York: Paragon House, 1989).

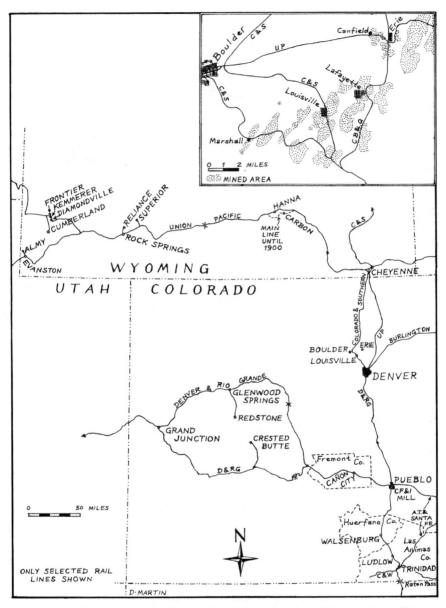

Selected coalfields, towns, and rail lines in Colorado and southern Wyoming. Inset: Towns, rail lines, and coal deposits in the northern Colorado coalfield.

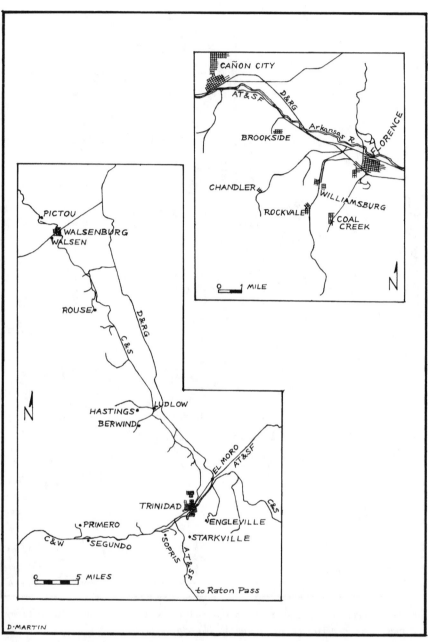

Above right: *Cañon City, Colorado coalfield.* Lower left: *southern Colorado coalfield.*

CHAPTER ONE

MINING BEGINS, 1868-1873

A HEAVY MIST HUNG OVER DENVER as the steam engine pulled two passenger cars away from the Denver Pacific depot in January 1871. But the winter weather could not dampen the spirits of those onboard. A number of Denver luminaries had been invited along to celebrate a significant achievement. Seventeen miles of the Boulder Valley Railroad had been completed, and the railroad's contractors, David H. Moffat Jr. and Robert E. Carr, wanted to show off the new line. The forty guests represented nearly all of Denver's leading businesses, including the Board of Trade; Wells, Fargo & Co.; Western Union; First National Bank; and the *Rocky Mountain News*. As the train moved north the sky cleared, and the passengers' enthusiasm only increased as they took in the beauty of the mountains and plains.

The Boulder Valley line terminated at the new town of Erie. Here the excursionists toured the town site and the Boulder Valley coal mine. Once back on the train, they toasted Moffat, Carr, and their railroad. In reporting the event, the *Rocky Mountain News* called the line's completion historic and raved about its importance to Denver. Yet the line connected no established communities and provided no link between existing rail lines. Its importance came from coal. The fuel had been mined in the Erie area for some time but only on a small scale, limited by transportation costs. The new rail line greatly reduced the expense of haulage and suddenly made coal an economically viable fuel for Denver businesses and residents. Since Denver's founding and the development of the mountain West, people had sought coal as an alternative to wood. The Boulder Valley Railroad finally made that alternative a reality for northern Colorado.[1]

The existence of coal in and around the Rocky Mountains had long been recognized. Native Americans, fur trappers, explorers, and government surveyors all encountered it. The most important discoveries came with the surveys of Howard Stansbury in 1849 and the Gunnison-Beckwith party in 1853. Ordered by the Bureau of Topographical Engineers to conduct a reconnaissance of possible transcontinental rail routes, Stansbury moved along the Platte River Road to Salt Lake City, locating coal across the western half of southern Wyoming. The Gunnison-Beckwith party inspected southern Colorado, finding coal along the Front Range. In the 1850s these discoveries had little value, but when railroad companies moved west after the Civil War, they became very significant. The railroads needed coal for fuel, and a market existed in homes and industries. When railroads arrived, southwestern Wyoming and the Front Range of Colorado became the largest coal-producing regions in the West.[2]

Those who moved west before the railroads had little interest in coal. If emigrants, military posts, or early settlers happened to be close to an outcropping, they used the coal they found. For instance, to supply the blacksmith shop at Fort Bridger, the army established a Military Coal Reservation in southwest Wyoming in 1859. In southern Colorado, Hispanic farmers and ranchers along the Purgatoire River dug coal from the numerous outcroppings, but most people ignored the fuel.[3]

The Colorado gold rush of 1859 brought a greater potential demand for coal. Prospectors discovered gold along the banks of Dry Creek, and the subsequent rush created a number of prominent communities. Denver rose at the confluence of Cherry Creek and the South Platte River, Golden developed to the west of Denver, and Central City, Black Hawk, and Nevadaville emerged in the mountains. Ninety miles south of Denver entrepreneurs platted Cañon City on the Arkansas River in an attempt to challenge Denver's preeminent position as the gold rush service center. After just one year, the gold rush had brought 34,277 people to Colorado.[4]

The rush, however, brought neither sustained development nor a market for coal. As Rodman Wilson Paul states, "Colorado's life started with a curious contradiction." The discovery of gold caused people to search the width and breadth of the Colorado Rockies looking for placer gold, but they found little.

As Paul emphasizes, "[T]he output was small, very small, if compared with the early years of California or Nevada."[5] Prospectors did find gold ore, but the precious metal could not be easily extracted from the country rock. The failure to find immediate wealth caused many fortune hunters to move on soon after they arrived in Colorado.[6]

Disillusionment continued throughout the 1860s. The untreatable ore, Indian wars, years of bad crops, and a breakdown of communication with the East during the Civil War created economic depression in the mid-1860s. From the 34,277 people counted in 1860, a special territorial census taken in 1861 showed that Colorado's population had slipped to 25,329. A decade later Colorado had rebounded to 39,864 residents, but many of those counted in 1870 were not the same as those listed in the 1860 census. Contemporary observer Frank Fossett estimated that perhaps 100,000 people had tried to make Colorado their home between 1858 and 1870, but most had departed. Without economic stability and with a high population turnover, little coal development was undertaken.[7]

Most in the region, however, understood the value of coal, and some entrepreneurs searched the Front Range foothills for promising outcroppings. Potential coal developers had two motives. First, they wanted to profit from marketing coal, and second, they hoped to use the discovery of coal to entice future economic expansion—to turn their mining camp into an industrial center. To the latter end, the *Rocky Mountain News* eagerly published news of coal-prospecting tours around Denver. As early as August 1859, the paper reported coal locations found within miles of town. Attention soon focused on coal lands that became known as the Denver Basin, later the Northern Coal Field. This coal region, roughly twenty miles northwest of Denver, ran from the southwest to the northeast for more than twenty miles. By September, coal from this area was selling in Denver for twenty-five dollars per ton— six times its value if purchased at the mine. The inflated price reflected the product's bulky nature and the lack of railroads to haul it.[8]

Although sales were limited, developers remained active in the coal banks northwest of Denver. Without rail connections, these small mines were appropriately called "wagon mines." The most prominent operator in the field, Joseph Marshall, opened a mine on South Boulder Creek in 1863, eighteen miles from Denver. He wanted to supply the Denver market, but he also had grander visions. Marshall erected a small iron blast furnace in 1864, with little success. The coal apparently did not work well in the furnace, causing Marshall to turn to charcoal. He discovered what others would come to recognize— that the coal deposits varied in quality from subbituminous to lignite. These two lower grades of coal have less heat value and more moisture than bituminous and anthracite coals. That made the Denver Basin product suitable for domestic uses but not the best fuel for industrial or railroad use. Nevertheless, the Marshall coal bank and the entire Northern Coal Field would eventually become a prominent coal provider for the Denver domestic market.[9]

Similarly, early gold rush entrepreneurs tried digging coal at Cañon City, ninety miles south of Denver. Beginning a few miles east of Cañon City, coal abounded along the eastern slope of the Wet Mountains. This field ran to the southeast for about fourteen miles, encompassing nearly forty-four square miles. Developers first came to the location in 1860, and they believed they had an advantage over the Denver Basin, for this was a good grade of bituminous coal. It worked well in steam engines and proved an excellent domestic coal. The limited market at Cañon City and the ninety-mile haul to Denver, how-ever, made sales difficult. Prior to the arrival of the railroad, only the Musser mine operated. The *Rocky Mountain News* reported in 1870 that its product sold in Denver for forty dollars a ton.[10]

These flirtations with coal mining amounted to little in the first years of white encroachment into Colorado. Although the U.S. Geological Survey pinpointed 1864 as the year "coal mining as an industry" began in Colorado, only 500 tons were produced that year—a very small amount compared with the millions of tons that would be produced in later years. The 500 tons produced in 1864 came from the Denver Basin, primarily from the Marshall Mine. The mine had a capacity of 20 to 30 tons of coal a day, and it sold at the mine for four dollars per ton. But coal mining still remained insignificant in Colorado. The 1870 census found only five men claiming to be coal miners in the entire territory.[11]

In 1868, as the Colorado depression continued, Denverites looked appre-hensively to the north as the Union Pacific built its line across what would become southern Wyoming, bypassing their city. The situation looked grim as Denver residents began moving to the new boomtown of Cheyenne. In an attempt to save their community, prominent Denver citizens such as William Byers and David Moffat formed the Denver Board of Trade to build their own railroad connecting "Denver to the Pacific." To prove their scheme's viability, the board investigated the availability of coal for fuel and announced that "enough of this article exists on the present line to warrant no further fear on this subject."[12] Denverites did not build their road to the Pacific. Instead, Moffat and his associates would build an extension to Cheyenne to meet the Union Pacific in 1870. By that time, however, substantial coal mining had already begun in Wyoming.

Unlike Colorado, which developed in response to a gold rush and without a railroad, the Union Pacific preceded significant white settlement in Wyo-ming. Some non–Native Americans did live in Wyoming before the Union Pacific built through in 1868, around forts and at stage stations along the various trails. In particular, a number of stops sat along the Overland Trail, which connected Denver and Salt Lake City. This trail paralleled much of the

Union Pacific's future line, crossing the various coalfields that stretched from the center to the western edge of Wyoming. At such stops as Point of Rocks and Bitter Creek, local stage agents dug coal out of outcroppings for use in their stoves. The fuel existed at several different locations across southern Wyoming, but when the Union Pacific arrived, it connected all the coalfields to work as one.[13]

INDUSTRIAL COAL MINING COMES TO WYOMING

The Union Pacific Railroad brought industrial coal mining to Wyoming and the West. Built as the eastern portion of the transcontinental railroad, the Union Pacific provided an immediate market for coal for its locomotives, and the rail line provided connections to markets elsewhere. Thanks to the U.S. Congress, the railroad dominated Wyoming's coal industry. The Pacific Railway Acts of 1862 and 1864 gave the railroad a right-of-way through public lands, twenty square miles of federal land for every mile of track built, and federal bonds to help finance construction. The land grant also included the coal deposits beneath the surface. The existence of coal in southern Wyoming helped persuade location engineers to build along that route, ignoring other possibilities such as the easier South Pass. Federal generosity eliminated any fuel concerns for the railroad and put it in a commanding position over the region's resources. In return, the government mandated a variety of concessions, including placing two presidentially appointed "government directors" on the company's board.[14]

Despite government oversight, loans, and land grants that seemingly guaranteed profitability, the Union Pacific became embroiled in one of the worst financial scandals in U.S. history. Led by Thomas Durant, some of Union Pacific's primary investors created the construction company Credit Mobilier of America, taking the name from a similar French concern. Durant and his associates then hired Credit Mobilier to build the rail line for the Union Pacific at greatly exaggerated costs. This setup allowed the railroad's key promoters to gain large, immediate profits from construction, whereas revenue from general railroad operations might be slow in coming. Although such associated companies had been used before in the United States, Credit Mobilier's fame came not only from the excess profits it garnered but also from the apparent bribery that accompanied those profits. Directors Oliver and Oakes Ames used Credit Mobilier stock to win favor with Congress. The resultant congressional investigation tarnished the railroad's reputation for years.[15]

President Oliver Ames and other railroad directors sought a similar money-making scheme from the company's coal lands. They initially signed a contract with Cyrus O. Godfrey and Thomas Wardell of Missouri to begin mining and selling coal in 1868. Shortly thereafter, the railroad men created a new enterprise, the Wyoming Coal and Mining Company, to take over the contract. Ames and five other Union Pacific directors owned nine-tenths of the new firm's stock, and Wardell held one-tenth. A new associated company had been born, and as with Credit Mobilier the operating agreement promised substantial returns to the primary investors. The contract allowed Wyoming Coal and Mining to mine on Union Pacific lands and sell the coal to the railroad. Not only would the railroad buy its own coal, but the contract set a price three times higher than it should have been: six dollars a ton for the first two years of the contract, then gradually decreasing to three dollars a ton over the fifteen years of the agreement. The railroad also promised to reduce its freight rates by 25 percent on coal the company shipped to other customers. The Union Pacific directors not only wanted to profit handsomely from sales to themselves, but the last provision would also limit competition along the line, giving the new concern a significant advantage in the region's coal market.[16]

Unaware of the directors' intentions, some early Wyoming entrepreneurs hoped to capitalize on the Union Pacific's need for coal. As the railroad built west, these people began opening small mines along the right-of-way. Archibald and Duncan Blair started a mine near their Overland route stage station on Bitter Creek. They soon learned, however, that the railroad's drive for a monopoly made it an unreliable customer. The railroad purchased coal from them only when its own mines failed to meet the demand. Even this limited patronage disappeared as Wyoming Coal and Mining expanded, forcing operators such as the Blair brothers to close.[17]

Ames and the other directors needed Wardell to make the new coal company work. The railroad men knew little about coal mining, and Wardell had experience in that area. Wardell had operated coal mines in Missouri and sold coal to the railroad. To attract him to Wyoming, the board gave him part ownership of the company and control of day-to-day operations. Wardell came to the new coalfield with the knowledge, experience, and manpower to open the mines. He soon became the primary figure in Wyoming coal mining.[18]

As the railroad built west in 1868 and 1869, Wardell opened mines at three locations across a 250-mile stretch of southern Wyoming: Carbon in south-central Wyoming, Rock Springs 150 miles to the west, and Almy in the extreme southwestern corner. Wardell opened mines at different locations for a number of reasons. First, money was saved by shipping coal to the markets closest to a particular mine. As the easternmost location, Carbon attempted to provide for the Union Pacific's needs to the east. It became the coal company's largest producer, with 142 of the 223 employees in 1870. Carbon produced well over half of the company's total output for the first seven years of operation. Rock Springs and Almy were initially smaller locations, supplying more local markets.[19]

Second, as a good manager, Wardell understood the utility of opening multiple mines. He needed to worry about production, expense, and safety. Each mine could produce only so many tons per day, and having several mines gave him the flexibility to expand or contract output as needed. Expansion was necessary with increased rail traffic or when a mine disaster closed another mine. For example, in 1871, Mine No. 1 at Carbon caught fire and had to be abandoned for a year; during that time coal production was increased at the other mines. Danger and expenses also increased as coal mines went deeper into the ground. The expense came from the longer underground hauls, and the danger resulted from a greater chance of cave-ins and the increased possibility of trapping explosive coal gas. Operating several shallow mines limited these problems. Well-run coal companies always tried to spread production over a number of mines.[20]

Wardell also knew the value of experienced workers. He brought most of his employees from coal mines in Missouri, the majority of whom had previously worked as miners in the British Isles. Great Britain led the world in coal use and development, and as the industry spread to the United States, skilled coal miners immigrated. Of the 142 coal miners at Carbon, 93—65.5 percent—had been born in England, Scotland, Ireland, or Wales. Of those, 55 were from England. Territory-wide, people from the British Isles made up only 21.6 percent of Wyoming's population. Forty of the miners, or 28.2 percent, had been born in the United States, and the majority of them had parents from the British Isles. These men had the skills Wardell needed, and he got them to move west by promising top pay.[21]

Wardell and his recruits came to Wyoming to open mines. Most gave little thought to building houses or creating towns. The three Wyoming Coal and Mining Company camps—Carbon, Rock Springs, and Almy—took shape with little planning. At each of the sites, crude, primitive camps grew. The only substantial structures were company offices and the tipple where coal was transferred to railroad cars. The company built few houses, with most miners arranging their own living situations. Some dug caves into the sides of nearby ravines and gulches, covering the fronts with boards and earth, and others built soddies and shacks. Adding to the camps' irregular appearance, the dwellings were scattered between the mine portals and the designated center of town. Rock Springs was notably diffuse. In 1870 the census taker found fewer than 150 people scattered around three separate locations.[22]

Carbon stands out as the West's first coal town, but it had the atmosphere of a frontier town. Men predominated: of the 244 people living in Carbon in 1870, 173 were adult males—over 70 percent of the population. The town had 32 women, 31 of whom were married. Most of the women worked as housewives, caring for the town's 35 children. Many of the single men lived together in about fifty log buildings scattered near the mines. Although small

1.1 Carbon, Wyoming. Developed by Thomas Wardell of the Wyoming Coal and Mining Company in 1868, Carbon was the first coal town along the Union Pacific Railroad. The town grew with little coal company control, and its appearance reflected that fact. It lasted until 1902. Courtesy, Wyoming State Archives 13253.

and seemingly unorganized, Carbon had some order, as residents settled where they wanted. The Irish lived near one another, as did the Scotch, Welsh, and English. Wardell built a company store that dominated business the first few years, but the town soon attracted two more general merchandise stores, six saloons, and two hotels. The preponderance of saloons gave the town notoriety, generating stories of lawlessness and outlaws. Even Calamity Jane reportedly stopped there for a drink.[23]

Carbon also gained fame for its esprit de corps. Many of the skilled miners who first came to the town remained in Carbon, taking pride in working and living there. They built schools and churches and served as the core of the community even as the town changed over the years. By 1880, 365 people lived in Carbon—nearly a 50 percent increase from ten years before—and with this growth came more ethnic diversity. Yet the original miners from the British Isles still predominated. The coal company built more company housing, but Carbon retained its independent nature, allowing the citizens to in-

1.2 Coal tipple at Rock Springs Coal Mine No. 1. The Wyoming Coal and Mining Company opened Rock Springs in 1868, and by 1871, Mine No. 1 was a substantial producer, making Rock Springs one of the West's most important mining towns. Courtesy, Wyoming State Archives 1446.

corporate the town in 1890. This community spirit persisted until the Union Pacific relocated the rail line and closed the mines in 1902, causing the town to vanish slowly.[24]

Despite resembling frontier towns, camps such as Carbon did have a few company town characteristics. The miners did not buy land but built on railroad property. Wardell ran company stores, and the company owned a few rental houses. The Wyoming Coal and Mining Company did not want to be in the company town business; it had a contract to mine coal on Union Pacific land. A company town that involved building and renting housing would fall under railroad purview, and the railroad initially had little interest. The few rentals that did exist were built to attract key personnel. Wardell built the company stores because he knew the profit they could return. For a time he had a monopoly, but before long the Union Pacific rented town lots to other businesses. Nevertheless, Wardell's business remained strong. In these first

Wyoming coal towns, the Union Pacific held the land, Wardell ran the company stores, but the workers still enjoyed fairly independent lives.[25]

Some authors argue that coal companies had to build towns and provide services to attract workers to remote mining regions. In Wyoming, miners moved to the barren sage plain without company housing or even a developed camp. Wardell just promised good money. He did open stores, and their operations may initially have been essential, as competing stores did not open for a few years because business entrepreneurs preferred to establish stores at railroad division points such as Cheyenne and Laramie where the markets seemed more promising than those in coal camps. Once the camps grew, however, businesses came to the coalfields. Coal companies then did not need company towns to operate in isolated regions.[26]

Wardell and the Wyoming Coal and Mining Company prospered from the start. From 1868 through 1872, he and his associates opened five mines at the three locations that produced over 350,000 tons of coal during that time. Rival companies shipped more than 100,000 tons of coal during the same period. One coal operator in southwest Wyoming, the Central Pacific Railroad's Rocky Mountain Coal and Iron Company, did not compete directly with Wardell. The firm opened a mine at Almy in 1869, working closely with the Union Pacific and the Wyoming Coal and Mining Companies. The Central Pacific gained little coal from its land grant, and as the western end of the transcontinental rail link, it needed Wyoming fuel. Union Pacific management understood the importance of keeping its sister road running, so it allowed Rocky Mountain Coal and Iron to develop neighboring mines, including some on Union Pacific land. Rocky Mountain Coal and Iron remained relatively small, shipping its product to western Utah and California and never competing with Wardell's operation. Along the Union Pacific line, Wardell had a near monopoly.[27]

INDUSTRIAL COAL MINING COMES TO COLORADO

As in Wyoming, true industrial mining came to Colorado with railroad development. Unlike Wyoming where the Union Pacific Railroad dominated, in Colorado at least six major railroads and a number of coal companies eventually competed for business. But in the late 1860s most Coloradans remained concerned about the lack of rail connections. Denver business leaders saw two possibilities for railroad construction—Union Pacific Eastern Division, better known as the Kansas Pacific, and the Denver Pacific.

Congress created the Kansas Pacific as part of the Pacific Railway Acts to serve as a southern branch of the primary transcontinental line. Although the initial ordinance had this southern line connect with the Union Pacific several hundred miles east of Denver, Denverites successfully lobbied to have the connecting point moved westward to Denver in 1866. This step seemed to promise success, but disaster hit when the road stopped construction for lack of capital.[28]

Denver's business elite, led by former governor John Evans, would not be deterred by this setback. They organized the Denver Pacific Railroad and Telegraph Company to build the rail line from Denver to Cheyenne. To start, the Denver Pacific needed to acquire the financial support and land grant the government had promised the Kansas Pacific for this portion of the line. Evans lobbied Congress extensively for the transfer, and in 1869 the lawmakers agreed. These negotiations encouraged Kansas Pacific president Robert E. Carr and some associates to help David H. Moffat Jr. and Walter S. Cheesman of Denver finance the road. This cooperation guaranteed that the two railroads would work together closely.[29]

To build the Denver Pacific, the developers used an associated construction company—a mechanism similar to the Union Pacific's Credit Mobilier. Under the direction of Evans and William J. Palmer, the company completed the line in June 1870. Two months later a reinvigorated Kansas Pacific reached Denver. Shortly after these successes, Carr and Moffat organized yet another construction company to build the Boulder Valley Railroad west from the Denver Pacific's main line to the town of Erie and the Northern Colorado Coal Field. Its completion instigated the January 1871 celebration described at the start of this chapter. By then Denver had a rail connection to the east, a tie to the transcontinental line to the north, and a coal mine spur to the west—all reasons to celebrate.[30]

If these rail promoters had continued to follow the Union Pacific model, they would next have organized a coal company to exploit the coal under the land grant. Instead they hired a promotion company to sell their grant lands for "settlement and improvement," including, as they advertised, approximately 40,000 acres of coal lands. The reason Evans, Moffat, and Carr chose not to enter the coal business is unclear. After the railroad construction, they may have lacked the capital to organize a mining company, or they may have wanted a number of mines to open. Several competing operations would have lowered the price for coal and perhaps stimulated more traffic for the railroad. Unlike Wardell and the Union Pacific directors, Moffat, Carr, and associates did not seek a monopoly. Instead they allowed the free market to reign in the Northern Coal Field, a situation that lasted for years.[31]

By the time the Boulder Valley Railroad reached Erie, coal developers had already formed a new mining company. New York investors Ransom Balcom and E. C. Kattel had joined with some "Denver capitalists"—reportedly with the Kansas Pacific Railroad—to buy one of the small operations already in the area, the Briggs's Mine, named after its original owner, Henry Briggs. The operation was renamed the Boulder Valley Coal Company, and the promoters' Kansas Pacific connections may have ensured it the rail line. Nevertheless,

Balcom, Kattel, and associates bought Briggs's operation instead of the Denver Pacific's undeveloped coal lands for two reasons. First, although a small producer, Briggs's Mine had a physical plant and work crew in place. The promoters did not need to find an experienced coal contractor as the Union Pacific had. Second, Briggs's Mine had already exposed and developed a paying vein of coal, allowing for immediate coal production. Much of the land grant coal lay hidden underground, and exploration and preliminary development needed to be done before a suitable mine location could be found. The Boulder Valley investors knew they had purchased four veins of coal and a 500-foot sloping shaft ready for operation.[32]

The construction of the Boulder Valley Railroad and the consequent expansion of the Boulder Valley Mine brought true industrial mining to Colorado. Although the Marshall Mine had been Colorado's first consistent producer, the new operation rapidly outpaced it. Boulder Valley coal went to the Denver Pacific, the Kansas Pacific, and the Denver market. Coal production in Colorado increased from just under 16,000 tons in 1871 to over 68,500 tons in 1872, with 79 percent of the 1872 product coming from the enlarged Boulder Valley Mine.[33]

Near the mine, Balcom and Kattel, with the apparent help of railroad officials, platted the town of Erie in 1871. The developers did not see Erie as a company town but envisioned it as an independent community, with great potential for growth. With Erie serving as the end of track for two years and then as a station stop on the extended railroad, the town founders attempted to prosper by selling lots and attracting businesses. They laid out the town in a neat grid pattern, naming the streets after the primary promoters, including Balcom, Kattel, Carr, and Moffat. Residents soon constructed homes, hotels, and a variety of other establishments. Within two years nearly 100 homes had been constructed, and in 1874 community leaders incorporated the community. The Boulder Valley Coal Company did not build houses or open a store. Miners who came to Erie chose where they lived, and some acquired small farms. The generally favorable climate and soil in northern Colorado allowed for successful agriculture, and farming proved a great benefit to many miners. Coal mining was seasonal; domestic coal sales diminished in the summer, causing many operators to shorten working time or close their mines. The mines in the Northern Coal Field relied on the Denver domestic market, and when coal sales fell and work time shortened, the miners could farm to survive. The farming influence gave Erie the ambiance of an agricultural prairie town.[34]

Erie, however, attracted the same type of miners as Carbon, Rock Springs, and Almy in Wyoming. Miners of British ancestry predominated. Nearly 65 percent of Erie's miners were born in Great Britain, with over 60 percent of that number from England—percentages very similar to Carbon's. Unlike the Wyoming Coal and Mining operation, the Boulder Valley firm did not need to go far to recruit people with the proper skills. Many had already come to Colorado to try their hand at hard-rock mining. Some experienced miners moved back and forth between metal and coal mines, depending on wages and conditions. Although less common than in the coal mines, men from the British Isles were prevalent in the early metal mines. After a stint in the mountains, miners saw Erie as an attractive alternative. The men who came— many of whom had families—often stayed. Sixty percent of the miners were married, and in 1880, 166 children lived in town—accounting for over 45 percent of the total population. Additionally, a number of people were employed in business activities unrelated to coal. Although Colorado's first coal town did not physically resemble the coal camps in Wyoming, its ethnic mix strongly resembled those earlier camps. And whereas Carbon looked like it belonged on the western frontier and Erie on the midwestern prairie, residents of both towns were intensely proud of their communities.[35]

Construction of the Boulder Valley Railroad brought industrial coal mining to Erie, and when the promoters extended the line to Boulder in 1873, new markets and mines opened. Unlike the Union Pacific developers who only wanted to market and handle their coal, the investors in the Kansas Pacific, Denver Pacific, and Boulder Valley lines encouraged other mines to open. They wanted as much traffic as possible. Mines such as the Rob Roy and the Star soon opened near Erie, and a few miles west of Erie the town of Canfield developed. Before long at least seven mines were operating in the Denver Basin, and the northern Colorado mines dominated the territory's coal output during the 1870s.[36]

INDUSTRIAL COAL MINING MOVES TO CENTRAL COLORADO

Although they enjoyed a head start, the Denver Basin mines did not continue to control the Colorado coal market. Mines south of Denver, in central and southern Colorado, would soon come into prominence. These, too, required railroad connections. Although some Colorado railroad promoters saw the Denver-to-Cheyenne connection as the region's best bet for success, other railroad entrepreneurs had different ideas. In particular, William Jackson Palmer envisioned a line that would run along the Front Range of the Rocky Mountains, connecting Denver with Santa Fe and then Mexico. Palmer had become familiar with the American Southwest when he surveyed possible routes for the Kansas Pacific. He saw potential rail traffic coming from the Rio Grande Valley, New Mexico, and the mountain mining communities in Colorado. When the Kansas Pacific opted not to build through the region, Palmer organized his own company to capture these markets—the Denver and Rio Grande Railway Company—on October 27, 1870.[37]

Although he was only thirty-four when he started the railroad, Palmer already had years of railroad experience. He began his career at age seventeen in Pennsylvania, taking a brief hiatus in England to study the use of coal in steam locomotives. When he returned to the United States, Palmer worked for the Pennsylvania Railroad until he joined the Fifteenth Pennsylvania Volunteer Cavalry during the Civil War, quickly rising to the rank of brevet brigadier general. When the war ended, Palmer returned to railroading with the Kansas Pacific. He served as director of surveys and then coordinated construction of the line into Denver. These experiences prepared Palmer well for his Colorado endeavors.[38]

Palmer had also developed business ideas seemingly contrary to nineteenth-century American norms. He wanted his railroad run in a scrupulous fashion, and he hoped for good relations with the workers. In part, Palmer saw himself as a social planner, believing he could create a better society. Yet he knew the realities of competition might prevent him from achieving these goals. Palmer also tried to change western railroading. He believed a railroad that ran primarily north and south could work; most other major railroads in the nation extended east and west. In addition, he adopted a different gauge for the railroad's track. Nearly all rail lines had 4 feet, 8½ inches between the rails, known as standard gauge. The Denver and Rio Grande rails were set at 3 feet, known as narrow gauge. This configuration saved money on construction and was easier to build in rough terrains. Palmer's vision for the future overrode the constraints of tradition.[39]

Palmer encouraged a number of associates from his Civil War and earlier railroad days to join him, as well as eastern and European investors. The board of directors included Robert Henry Lamborn who had served with Palmer during the war, former Colorado governor Alexander C. Hunt, and New York financier William P. Mellen. Other men important to the railroad were William S. Jackson, the secretary and treasurer, and Dr. William A. Bell, who sought to raise money abroad.[40]

Palmer and these associates initially hoped to gain the same federal largesse of land and money as the Union Pacific had, but by the early 1870s, Congress had become suspicious of railroad machinations. The railroad was only given a 100-foot right-of-way through public lands and small acreages for stations and shops. The Denver and Rio Grande (D&RG) would have to rely on private capital, and the promoters had to be creative to find it. They often used ancillary or associated companies—including coal-mining operations—to attract investors, build the railroad, and guarantee profits. The chronic lack of capital, however, led to constant financial struggles.[41]

The rail line also connected few established markets. The Union Pacific and the Kansas Pacific could anticipate immediate transcontinental traffic; Palmer's railroad could not. The D&RG board members knew they had to create markets to make the road successful. They did not expect business to develop automatically as the railroad approached. Consequently, the railroad

1.3 William Jackson Palmer. One of Colorado's leading developers and capitalists, Palmer organized the Denver and Rio Grande Railway in 1870 and then established a series of land and town development companies that opened mines near Cañon City, Walsenburg, and Trinidad. Courtesy, *Denver Public Library, Western History Collection Z-310.*

backers anticipated developing towns, promoting agriculture, harvesting timber, and digging coal. If successful, twin streams of revenue would follow—one from the new enterprises, and the other from railroad traffic.[42]

To acquire the land and start development, Palmer and his associates created a series of land companies: the Mountain Base Investment Fund, the National Land and Improvement Company, and the Central Colorado Improvement Company. Each venture essentially succeeded and absorbed the previous company. These enterprises sold stocks and bonds and, with the cash thus obtained, purchased the desired lands. In this era of railroad fraud and failures, land companies seemed like sounder investments, but the D&RG promoters also encouraged investors to buy their railroad securities. To Palmer and his associates, such a purchase seemed logical because the ventures were intertwined: land values increased as the railroad approached, and railroad profitability advanced as land was developed. Plus, diversity reduced risk. The companies were not part of the railroad organization in any legal sense; they were independently organized and operated, but they worked closely together. Palmer, however, needed the land company revenue for further extensions of the railroad.[43]

Although the railroad and associated land companies promised investors a potential long-term return, the railroad's board of directors also created the Union Contract Company to construct the line. Much as the Union Pacific's Credit Mobilier had done, the Union Contract Company greatly overestimated the cost of construction and then received payment in the form of railroad securities. Reportedly, the contract company received stocks and bonds worth at par value four times the actual cost of building the road; if the construction company sold the bonds at 80 percent of their value, it would gain a sum "several hundred thousand dollars in excess of the cost of construction." Palmer, Bell, and other officials wanted the guarantee of early profits.[44]

Construction began on the Denver and Rio Grande in March 1871, reaching the promoters' first land development project—Colorado Springs—in October 1871. Soon after, they extended the line south to Pueblo and then up the Arkansas Valley for thirty-six miles to the company town of Labran. Constructed in late 1872, Labran sat just a few miles below the Cañon City coalfields at a location where the railroad promoters felt the proper mix of ingredients for an ironworks existed—coal, iron ore, and water. Although this vision for Labran was never realized, access to coal remained important. Up to this point the railroad had used coal from the Erie mines, which Palmer and the railroad executives denounced as inferior. They anxiously anticipated using the bituminous coal at Cañon City in their locomotives, as well as selling it on the domestic market.[45]

The promoters needed first to acquire coal lands, and in the Cañon City area they purchased over 1,100 acres from previous claimants, including the already opened Musser property. Keeping with the announced development policy, the acquisition should have been made by an associated land company. Palmer and his associates, however, were not that straightforward. Instead, a few of the main operatives—including Governor Hunt—arrived in the area in advance of the railroad and, without explaining their intent, bought the land. Next they sold it to their own land company—the National Land and Improvement Company—at a profit in 1871. Then as the railroad approached in 1872, they again transferred it to the recently formed Central Colorado Improvement Company. At each step of the way, the Palmer insiders hoped to profit.[46]

The Central Colorado Improvement Company (CCI) became an important tool for the railroad promoters. Palmer, Mellen, and Lamborn created this concern in November 1871, giving it a sweeping mandate: acquire land along the Arkansas Valley, increase the value of the holdings, make Pueblo and Cañon City grow, colonize agricultural tracts, stimulate the iron business, create traffic for the railroad, and supply the ever-increasing demand for coal. Further, the CCI was to help complete the Denver and Rio Grande Railway up the Arkansas Valley by buying railroad bonds. In exchange, the railroad company agreed to haul CCI's coal at a 15 percent discount for thirty years.[47]

The maze of companies and contracts continued to grow as the Denver and Rio Grande Railway built toward Cañon City. The railroad's Arkansas Valley branch did not build to the coal deposits but ended three miles below. Continuing to form a pyramid of companies, Palmer incorporated a subsidiary—the Cañon City Railway—to build to the coalfield. After doing some initial work in the coal mines, the CCI decided to contract out the coal operations. In August 1872 the improvement company ran advertisements in area publications calling for proposals to produce 200 tons of coal daily. The selected contractor would furnish all necessary mining equipment while the improvement company retained the physical plant. The bid winner would mine coal and sell it to the CCI. The lowest price per ton would win the contract. With this tactic the company relieved itself of the expense and concern of running a mine while obtaining low-cost coal. The CCI planned to profit by reselling the product to the railroad and on the domestic market.[48]

The Central Colorado Improvement Company awarded the contract to two men known as Jones & Burdess, who organized the Cañon City Coal Mining Company. They offered to provide coal for $2.25 a ton, and by December 1872 they anticipated working two mines that could provide 100 to 120 tons of coal a day. They won the bid at a price deemed excessive in the Denver Basin region. The CCI accepted the higher cost because it reflected the more difficult mining conditions in the Cañon City field. The coal veins in that region varied from 3 feet 4 inches to 4 feet thick, whereas the seams in northern Colorado ran up to 14 feet. Narrow coal veins presented more of a challenge to mine than thicker veins, and miners could demand more pay for the more difficult work. These conditions required the experienced miners from the British Isles.[49]

The town of Coal Creek began to develop around the mine. It resembled the coal communities in southern Wyoming, basically independent of company control but with some company town features. Like the Wyoming Coal and Mining Company, the CCI managers put limited effort toward community development. They built ten houses, but most miners had to find their own dwellings and build Coal Creek without direction. It became an "irregularly laid out" community situated along cattle trails through the Wet Mountains. The improvement company did not initially establish a company store. Throughout its mining history, Coal Creek basically remained an independent coal camp.[50]

By the end of 1872, conditions looked promising at Coal Creek. The contractors had worked the mines for only a few months, but they had produced nearly 5,000 tons of coal. A third of the production went to Denver where the improvement company sold it for nine dollars per ton—nearly twice the price of the lower-grade northern Colorado coal. The rest went to the Rio Grande for locomotive fuel, and the Colorado Improvement Company made from 75 cents to a dollar a ton profit. Palmer, Mellen, Lamborn, and the other investors saw good things and expected more to come, as they had a monopoly on the production and transportation of central Colorado coal. The Kansas Pacific and the Atchison, Topeka & Santa Fe Railroads had announced plans to build toward the region, but Palmer and his associates did not immediately fear the competition. They looked forward to providing for those companies' fuel needs, and they anticipated completing a line to the mountains where they could supply the mining communities with coal. The future looked bright.[51]

Palmer and the other investors in the Denver and Rio Grande Railway and associated improvement companies brought industrial coal mining to central Colorado. By 1873 the Coal Creek area remained the lowest-producing region in the Rocky Mountains, yet the good-quality coal portended growth—especially as other rail lines approached. The Rio Grande spawned this mining activity but passed the venture off to an associated company and then to a contractor. This setup allowed the mine and mining town to develop with little control from the parent company. The railroad men were more concerned about fuel and profit. Western railroads could not guarantee a return, but coal could. In this environment the railroad men did not establish an operating philosophy beyond the drive for financial returns; in contrast, the miners had a strong sense of what their work meant.

COALFIELD CULTURE

Whereas the parent companies established little control over the coalfields, the workers who came west were steeped in a work tradition and a mine culture. This spirit grew out of their shared backgrounds, common work experiences, and the nature of the workplace. Underground miners generally worked independently; thus they controlled the quality and quantity of the work. The mining companies in Wyoming and Colorado initially developed their mines by the room-and-pillar method. In this process miners drove a tunnel into the coal vein, and at right angles off of this tunnel they opened individual "rooms," or work areas. Two men generally worked in each room. The rooms averaged twenty-four feet in width and extended into the coal for several hundred feet, stopping when it became impractical to work further. Between the work areas large pillars of coal, sometimes a hundred feet wide, were left in place to support the roof of the mine. This technique dispersed the men throughout the mine and consequently prevented the underground foreman from having much contact with them. The miners made most of the mining decisions and set the pace of work. In some instances the men could leave the workplace whenever they wished. Further, the amount the miners produced determined their earnings. The company paid by the ton of coal produced, called a tonnage rate, which led the miner to see himself as an independent contractor. In essence, the men controlled the workplace, and this underground independence has been called the "miner's freedom."[52]

Along with controlling the workplace, many miners took great pride in their skills. Their job required a high level of knowledge, experience, and dexterity; and they gained the necessary training by serving an apprenticeship. Many miners had entered the mines as boys—working on coal tipples, tending the animals, or helping their fathers load coal. Gradually, they learned to cut and blast coal and became true miners. In a typical mine the majority of workers were not fully trained miners but people working toward that position. Despite the hierarchy within the mine, the laborers and miners shared a craft attitude toward their job. Further, they experienced the same dangers underground and viewed the coal company with general contempt. This caused a unity among many of the men, and they fought to defend their job's craft status.[53]

Many miners had been active in labor movements. The British miners were seasoned trade unionists and were the center of organizing activity in the United States. In combination with American miners, they formed a number of labor organizations over the years. In the 1860s and early 1870s they created the American Miners' Association, followed by the Workingmen's Benevolent Association and the Miners' National Association—all designed to fight wage reductions, improve mine conditions, and preserve traditional freedoms on the job.[54]

The British and American coal miners brought a strong work culture with them. The location of the coal mine, be it Missouri or Wyoming, made little difference. They wanted full control of their jobs, work environment, and lives. The high wages paid in Wyoming and Colorado further emboldened the

1.4 Miners' tools. A miner required picks, augers, powder, shovels, forks, and bar-down rods for his job. Courtesy, Collection of Joseph R. Douda.

workers. They recognized coal as the fuel of the Industrial Revolution and believed it had significant social value. They had little problem with coal selling at a high price as long as they received a fair portion of the money. The high-priced western coal market allowed them to receive what they wanted— a just share of coal's value.

1.5 *Mule hauling coal out of entries. Mules were essential for the underground movement of coal. This mule worked in the Rock Springs mines. Courtesy, American Heritage Center Collections 25356, American Heritage Center, University of Wyoming.*

Miners' desire to protect their craft and high wages contrasted sharply with the interest of owners and operators in the industrializing West. Entrepreneurs like Wardell and Palmer paid well when opening properties, but the drive for profit in a highly competitive world, coupled with the need to support railroad development, drove them to seek greater efficiency everywhere. The coal companies thus sought to gain increasing control over workers and to reduce costs. Because wages accounted for about two-thirds of production costs, the two sides found themselves on a collision course. The tight labor market, however, generally prevented owners from reducing compensation as much as they wanted.[55]

LABOR RELATIONS IN THE EARLY COALFIELDS

In Wyoming, Wardell and his colleagues quickly ran into problems. Labor shortages and concerns over money haunted the early years of Wyoming Coal and Mining. The growth of traffic along the Union Pacific Railroad outstripped

the company's ability to supply fuel, and Wardell had too few workers to expand the mines. These shortages forced the railroad to turn continually to
outside sources such as the Blair brothers for extra coal. In 1869 railroad
officials fretted over these problems, including the high wages, but rational-
ized them by calling Wyoming a "wild uncultured country." To relieve the
labor shortage they provided free passes for travel to Carbon, but few came. To
make the situation worse, the railroad fell behind in coal payments, causing
Wardell to fall behind in wages. In July 1869 a railroad official reported that
the men were close to "turning out" for past-due pay.[56]

The miners soon formed a union in Carbon and became involved in what
the coal company history calls "a succession of labor troubles." These troubles
involved jurisdictional strikes and workers protesting company practices, but
they also had economic overtones. In 1871 the union took a stand against the
operation of the company store. The men felt overcharged for goods and especially disliked the implicit threat of discharge if they did not shop there. When
Wardell refused to alter the practice, the miners went on strike. They added a
wage increase for some underground occupations to their demands.[57]

The miners saw themselves as defending their rights, especially freedom
of choice. Wardell, however, may have intentionally used store policies to
instigate the strike. He felt pressure from the Union Pacific to stabilize labor
relations and reduce the payroll, and destroying the union probably seemed
logical. The idea became even more important since the labor movement had
recently spread to Rock Springs, and the miners there walked out in support
of the Carbon strike.[58]

Wardell and railroad officials had seemingly worked out a plan to break
the union. Initially, Wardell did little as the miners walked off the job and
reportedly deserted the town in protest. When an opening presented itself,
though, Wardell moved to gain control and end the workers' solidarity. That
moment came when five men broke ranks and resumed work. Feeling confident of their authority, the remaining strikers demanded that Wardell discharge
the strikebreakers. He refused. The strikers responded by arming themselves,
intending to confront the traitors as they emerged from the mine.[59]

Wardell was ready. Claiming that the miners' actions endangered the
nation's transcontinental communications link, he requested federal troops to
protect the mines. The government dispatched soldiers from nearby Fort Steele
to both Carbon and Rock Springs. The militarily imposed peace allowed Wardell
to crush the striking miners. He fired key union men at both camps and began
hiring new workmen. With the help of the railroad, Wardell imported Scandinavians. Recruited from the agricultural lands of the Midwest, they, too, came
for the promise of high wages.[60]

Wardell brought in too few Scandinavians to fill the mines. In fact, the
miners of British ancestry remained in the majority. Wardell needed to keep

as many old miners as possible because the new arrivals had no coal-mining experience. Nevertheless, he hoped the new, inexperienced men might disrupt the mining traditions and the work culture. In addition, he thought their ethnicity might keep them from mingling with the British miners. The mines did quiet down, but over time the new miners learned the trade, discovered the dangers, and came to understand the work culture. Further, although their different ethnic origins may have deterred them from mingling with other miners off the job, they soon saw the necessity of working together in a union for the betterment of their jobs. Attempting to use unskilled ethnic groups to disrupt workplace solidarity became a standard practice in the western coal mines. In fact, in 1871 the Laramie *Daily Sentinel* presaged the next step in this diversification and replacement policy when it speculated that Wardell's ultimate intent was to "work the mines with Chinamen." Further, Wardell had set a precedent for the Union Pacific coal mines—in the face of labor difficulties, call on the military for support, fire the troublemakers, and bring in new workers.[61]

As Wardell imported new workers, the coal company, with the support of the railroad, began constructing more housing in Carbon and Rock Springs. It built the dwellings to attract and retain the strikebreakers, and as rentals the homes gave the superintendents some control over the occupants. This action can be seen as the next step in the development of company towns. Yet Wardell did not impose any other changes, and these Wyoming towns continued to grow more like frontier communities than full-fledged company towns.[62]

The coal firms operating in Colorado experienced similar labor discord. After opening the mines with well-paid craftsmen, the companies tried to reduce the wage rate and gain control of workers. Just one month after opening, in February 1871, the superintendent of the Boulder Valley operation decided to screen the coal before weighing it. He argued that this step removed the unsalable waste of dust and fine coal. The miners, however, preferred to be paid for unscreened coal. They believed everything in the mine cart should be weighed and counted toward their tonnage rate, since they had skillfully dug the coal. The men saw the screening process as a challenge to their integrity and a backhanded way to reduce their tonnage and income.[63]

As the screening began, the miners demanded an extra allowance for their losses. The company refused and a strike resulted, resembling the 1871 Union Pacific strike. With the walkout, Superintendent H. C. Hill of the Boulder Valley Coal Company decided to bring in strikebreakers. Unlike the Union Pacific, however, Hill sought his labor in Denver. Since the completion of the Denver Pacific and Kansas Pacific Railroads in 1870, Denver had boomed, and Hill found his new workers there.[64]

When the new laborers arrived in Erie, they reportedly met an "angry and fiery" mob of strikers that scared most of the replacement workers away. Hill called on law enforcement officials. He could not ask the military for protection, since this strike did not threaten a transcontinental railroad. Instead he asked local counties for help, and they responded. Sheriffs and deputies from Arapahoe and Weld Counties arrived and arrested twelve protesting miners for disturbing the peace and threatening lives. The arrests broke the strike. Although the court soon dismissed the charges against most of the accused, the company resumed mining without them and with the screens. The men had to accept the new process, and little else changed. Many original miners returned to work, and the company made no attempt to build housing. The workforce remained fairly independent, and many more labor disturbances would follow.[65]

The strikes in Wyoming and northern Colorado had economic elements, and they reflected the miners' desire to control the workplace. The men did not like the infringements company stores and coal screens placed on their traditional rights. The coal firms, however, wanted to reduce their expenses and control their workers. When these actions led to strikes, the operators' tactics were the same: fire the troublemakers, hire replacement miners, and call on law enforcement for support. In each instance the companies prevailed and managed to eliminate some of the most outspoken people. At Carbon this group probably included the union leaders; at Erie those a Denver newspaper called the "ringleaders" were removed. The paper's editor believed a few troublemakers pushed the strike and forced everyone into compliance. That notion, however, ignored the miners' solidarity and tradition of organizing.[66]

Labor relations at Coal Creek also got off to a difficult start. To attract workers, the operators offered the highest tonnage rate in the West: $1.50/ton. But within months they cut the rate by 25 cents. After a brief strike, management prevailed and reduced the rate to $1.25/ton in early 1873, matching the wages paid in the Northern Colorado Coal Field. In this instance no report was made of hiring replacement workers or bringing in armed assistance. Nevertheless, Coal Creek and the other pioneer mining locations, Erie and Carbon, would be the centers of labor traditions and worker strength in the years to come.[67]

By the end of 1872, railroads had brought industrial coal mining to the mountain West. Although steam engines needed the fuel for operation, developers such as Ames and Palmer also saw mining ventures as a means to profit in the risky world of railroad development. To achieve these returns, they created associated companies and pushed to gain coal monopolies along their rail lines. Only the Denver Pacific founders tried a slightly different tactic: they encouraged coal competition in the hope of increasing rail traffic. No matter the method, the West's first coal towns grew along the railroads, and seasoned miners came west to begin the work. The men expected high wages and control of the workplace, enhanced by a tight labor market, but these desires stood in opposition to the promoters' drive for revenue and their wish to run the mines as they saw fit. The miners' and operators' different objectives set the stage for conflict, and in the good economic times after the Civil War, each side struggled for an advantage. But when the Panic of 1873 hit, trouble was assured, as the financial turmoil changed railroad and coal company management and brought problems for the coal miners.

NOTES

1. *Rocky Mountain News*, January 18, 1871.

2. A. Dudley Gardner and Verla R. Flores, *Forgotten Frontier: A History of Wyoming Coal Mining* (Boulder: Westview, 1989), 6; Donald J. McClurg, "Labor Organizations in the Coal Mines of Colorado, 1878–1933" (Ph.D. diss., University of California, 1959), 3; William H. Goetzmann, *Exploration and Empire: The Explorer and the Scientist in the Winning of the American West* (Austin: Texas State Historical Association, 1993), 277–279, 287–288; R. L. Harbour and G. H. Dixon, *Coal Resources of Trinidad-Aguilar Area Las Animas and Huerfano Counties, Colorado, Contributions to Economic Geology*, Geological Survey Bulletin 1072-G (Washington, D.C.: Government Printing Office [hereafter GPO], 1959), 449.

3. Gardner and Flores, *Forgotten Frontier*, 6–7; A. C. Veatch, *Coal Fields of East-Central Carbon County, Wyo., Contributions to Economic Geology 1906*, Geological Survey Bulletin 316 (Washington, D.C.: GPO, 1907), 259; Frank Fossett, *Colorado: Its Gold and Silver Mines, Farms and Stock Ranges, Health and Pleasure Resorts* (New York: C. G. Crawford, 1880; Glorieta, N.M.: Rio Grande Press, 1976), 146; Colin B. Goodykoontz, "The People of Colorado," in *Colorado and Its People: A Narrative and Topical History of the Centennial State*, LeRoy R. Hafen, ed., vol. 2 (New York: Lewis Historical Publishing, 1950), 96.

4. Fossett, *Colorado*, 128; Duane A. Smith, *The Birth of Colorado: A Civil War Perspective* (Norman: University of Oklahoma Press, 1989), 46, 57, 59; Carl Ubbelohde, Maxine Benson, and Duane A. Smith, *A Colorado History*, 7th ed. (Boulder: Pruett, 1995), 67; U.S. Department of the Interior, Census Office, *Population of the United States in 1860; Compiled from the Original Returns of the Eighth Census* (Washington, D.C.: GPO, 1864), 548.

5. Rodman Wilson Paul, *Mining Frontiers of the Far West, 1848–1880* (Albuquerque: University of New Mexico Press, 1974), 111, 115.

6. Fossett, *Colorado*, 143.

7. McClurg, "Labor Organizations," 12–13; ibid., 130, 147; Paul, *Mining Frontiers*, 115; U.S. Department of the Interior, Census Office, *Statistics of the United States at the Tenth Census*, vol. 1 (Washington, D.C.: GPO, 1883), 51.

8. Quoted in McClurg, "Labor Organizations," 7–8, 10; "Coal," *American Journal of Mining* 5, no. 22 (May 30, 1868): 349.

9. McClurg, "Labor Organizations," 11–12; F. V. Hayden, *Preliminary Report of the United States Geological Survey of Wyoming, and the Portions of Contiguous Territories* (Washington, D.C.: GPO, 1872), 324–325; Samuel Franklin Emmons, Whitman Cross, and George Homans Eldridge, *Geology of the Denver Basin in Colorado*, U.S. Geological Survey Monograph, Vol. 27 (Washington, D.C.: GPO, 1896), 317–318;

Lee Scamehorn, *High Altitude Energy: A History of Fossil Fuels in Colorado* (Boulder: University Press of Colorado, 2002), 2–5.

10. Herbert O. Brayer, *William Blackmore: Early Financing of the Denver & Rio Grande Railway and Ancillary Land Companies, 1871–1878* (Denver: Bradford-Robinson, 1949), 145; McClurg, "Labor Organizations," 10; H. Lee Scamehorn, *Pioneer Steelmaker in the West: The Colorado Fuel and Iron Company, 1872–1903* (Boulder: Pruett, 1976), 14; Antoinette V. Cresto, *King Coal: Coal Mining in Fremont County* (Florence, Colo.: Florence Citizen, 1980), 10; *Rocky Mountain News*, May 12, 1870.

11. "Colorado," *American Journal of Mining* 1, no. 18 (July 28, 1866): 274–275; "Colorado," *American Journal of Mining* 2, no. 11 (December 8, 1866): 163; "Colorado," *American Journal of Mining* 6, no. 20 (November 14, 1868): 308; Phyllis Smith, *Once a Coal Miner: The Story of Colorado's Northern Coal Field* (Boulder: Pruett, 1989), 17; U.S. Department of the Interior, Census Office, manuscript census, Weld County, Colorado, 1870.

12. "Colorado," *American Journal of Mining* 5, no. 26 (June 27, 1868): 403; quote in "Colorado," *American Journal of Mining* 5, no. 19 (May 9, 1868): 293; Lyle W. Dorsett and Michael McCarthy, *The Queen City: A History of Denver* (Boulder: Pruett, 1977, 1986), 22–23.

13. Alfred R. Schultz, "The Southern Part of the Rock Springs Coal Field, Sweetwater County, Wyoming," *Contributions to Economic Geology 1908*, Geological Survey Bulletin 381 (Washington, D.C.: GPO, 1910), 250; Dorsett and McCarthy, *Queen City*, 23.

14. William S. Bryans, "A History of Transcontinental Railroads and Coal Mining on the Northern Plains to 1920" (Ph.D. diss., University of Wyoming, 1987), 70–73; T. A. Larson, *History of Wyoming*, 2d ed. (Lincoln: University of Nebraska Press, 1978), 38–39; *History of the Union Pacific Coal Mines, 1868 to 1940* (Omaha: Colonial, 1940), 10; Nelson Trottman, *History of the Union Pacific: A Financial and Economic Survey* (New York: Sentry, 1923; Augustus M. Kelley, 1966), 12–14.

15. Howard R. Lamar, ed., *The New Encyclopedia of the American West* (New Haven: Yale University Press, 1998), 270–271; Trottman, *History of the Union Pacific*, 23–25, 30–32.

16. Maury Klein, *Union Pacific: Birth of a Railroad, 1862–1893* (Garden City, N.Y.: Doubleday, 1987), 328–329; *History of the Union Pacific Coal Mines*, 75–76; Trottman, *History of the Union Pacific*, 42–43.

17. *History of the Union Pacific Coal Mines*, 444–445; Robert B. Rhode, *Booms & Busts on Bitter Creek: A History of Rock Springs, Wyoming* (Boulder: Pruett, 1987), 14, 35; "Brief Outline of Coal Industry in Southern Wyoming," *Wyoming Labor Journal* (August 31, 1917): 5–6; Schultz, "Southern Part of the Rock Springs Coal Field," 273; C. G. Hammond to Oliver Ames, October 26, 1869, SG-2, S-1, Roll 3, Union Pacific Archives, Nebraska State Historical Society, Lincoln (hereafter U.P. Archives, NSHS).

18. "Correspondence," *American Journal of Mining* 6, no. 8 (August 22, 1868): 121; Mrs. Chas. Ellis, "History of Carbon, Wyoming's First Mining Town," *Annals of Wyoming* 8 (April 1932): 633–634; Klein, *Union Pacific: Birth of a Railroad*, 328; Trottman, *History of the Union Pacific*, 43.

19. U.S. Department of the Interior, United States Geological Survey, *Mineral Resources of the United States, 1882*, by Albert Williams Jr. (Washington, D.C.: GPO,

1883), 85; Hayden, *Preliminary Report*, 326; U.S. Department of the Interior, Census Office, manuscript census, Carbon County, Wyoming, 1870.

20. "Wyoming—Progress in the Northwest," *Engineering and Mining Journal* 11, no. 6 (February 7, 1871): 90–91.

21. U.S. Department of the Interior, Census Office, manuscript census, Carbon County, Wyoming, 1870; U.S. Department of the Interior, Census Office, *The Statistics of the Population of the United States*, Ninth Census, vol. 1 (Washington, D.C.: GPO, 1872), 3, 377; Mrs. Roberta Hagood to David A. Wolff, January 14, 1998, transcript held by author.

22. *History of the Union Pacific Coal Mines*, 29, 48–50, 98–99; Gardner and Flores, *Forgotten Frontier*, 40; *Statistics of the Population*, Ninth Census, vol. 1, 296; U.S. Department of the Interior, Census Office, manuscript census, Sweetwater County, Wyoming, 1870.

23. U.S. Department of the Interior, Census Office, manuscript census, Carbon County, Wyoming, 1870; *History of the Union Pacific Coal Mines*, 28–45.

24. *History of the Union Pacific Coal Mines*, 36; Ellis, "History of Carbon," 639; U.S. Department of the Interior, Census Office, manuscript census, Carbon County, Wyoming, 1870; *Statistics of the Population*, Ninth Census, vol. 1, 375.

25. *History of the Union Pacific Coal Mines*, 28–29.

26. James B. Allen, *The Company Town in the American West* (Norman: University of Oklahoma Press, 1966), 7; ibid., 29, 32, 47–49; Rossiter W. Raymond, *The Report of the Commissioner of Mining Statistics, on Mines and Mining West of the Rocky Mountains for the Year Ending December 31, 1871*, 42d Cong., 2d sess., 1872, H. Ex. Doc. (Serial Set 1513), 367.

27. Anonymous eight-page manuscript entitled "Union Pacific Coal Mines," in Union Pacific Coal Company Collection, Union Pacific Historical Museum, Omaha, Nebraska, Box HO 3 (hereafter UPCCC); *History of the Union Pacific Coal Mines*, 49, appendix; United States Geological Survey, *Mineral Resources, 1882*, 88; Gardner and Flores, *Forgotten Frontier*, 23–24, 28; Sharon Fearn Rufi, *Almy Centennial Book, 1990* (Almy, Wyo.: Privately published, 1989), 7; C. P. Huntington to Charles F. Adams Jr., December 23, 1885, MS#3761, Box 25, U.P. Archives, NSHS.

28. Thomas J. Noel, "All Hail the Denver Pacific: Denver's First Railroad," *Colorado Magazine* 50, no. 2 (Spring 1973): 95; Trottman, *History of the Union Pacific*, 117–118.

29. Noel, "All Hail the Denver Pacific," 95, 99, 101–103.

30. *Rocky Mountain News*, January 18, 1871; ibid., 102–103.

31. Kenneth Jessen, *Railroads of Northern Colorado* (Boulder: Pruett, 1982), 14; Noel, "All Hail the Denver Pacific," 105–106; Brayer, *William Blackmore*, 10–11; Herbert O. Brayer, "History of Colorado Railroads," in *Colorado and Its People: A Narrative and Topical History of the Centennial State*, LeRoy R. Hafen, ed., vol. 1 (New York: Lewis Historical Publishing, 1950), 642; *3,000,000 Acres of Choice Farming, Grazing, Coal and Timber Land in Colorado* (Denver: Rocky Mountain New Steam Printing House, 1873), 2, 15.

32. Noel, "All Hail the Denver Pacific," 102, 104; Hayden, *Preliminary Report*, 322, 325; *Rocky Mountain News*, January 18, 1871; Smith, *Once a Coal Miner*, 20, 26; Erie High School Sociology and History Classes, *Erie: Yesterday and Today* (Erie,

Colo.: Privately published, 1967, 1974), 49; Anne Quinby Dyni, *Erie, Colorado: A Coal Town Revisited* (Erie: Town of Erie, 2001), 1–2.

33. Noel, "All Hail the Denver Pacific," 107; *Rocky Mountain News,* January 18, 1871; Hayden, *Preliminary Report,* 324; United States Geological Survey, *Mineral Resources, 1882,* 46, 47.

34. Erie High School Sociology and History Classes, *Erie,* map; Smith, *Once a Coal Miner,* 26, 28–29; Dyni, *Erie, Colorado,* 5, 9.

35. U.S. Department of the Interior, Census Office, manuscript census, Weld County and Boulder County, Colorado, 1880; U.S. Department of the Interior, Census Office, *Statistics of the Population of the United States at the Tenth Census,* 51, 428, 499; Duane A. Smith, *Rocky Mountain Mining Camps: The Urban Frontier* (Bloomington: Indiana University Press, 1967; Lincoln: Bison, 1974), 26–27; Carolyn Connarroe, *The Louisville Story* (Louisville, Colo.: Louisville Times, 1978), 4.

36. Smith, *Once a Coal Miner,* 26, 33–34; Dennis S. Grogan, "Unionization in Boulder and Weld Counties to 1890," *Colorado Magazine* 44, no. 4 (1967): 326; United States Geological Survey, *Mineral Resources, 1882,* 47; Tivis E. Wilkins, *Colorado Railroads: Chronological Development* (Boulder: Pruett, 1974), 9, 11; Fossett, *Colorado,* 578–579.

37. Robert Athearn, *The Denver and Rio Grande Western Railroad* (New Haven: Yale University Press, 1967; Lincoln: University of Nebraska Press, 1977), 3, 15, 29; Scamehorn, *Pioneer Steelmaker,* 8; Brayer, *William Blackmore,* 13–14, 30; George L. Anderson, *General William J. Palmer: A Decade of Colorado Railroad Building, 1870–1880,* Colorado College Publication General Series No. 209, Studies Series No. 22 (Colorado Springs: Colorado College, 1936), 25.

38. Brayer, *William Blackmore,* 12–13.

39. Athearn, *The Denver and Rio Grande,* 8–9, 14–15, 27; Ubbelohde, Benson, and Smith, *A Colorado History,* 117.

40. Brayer, *William Blackmore,* 30, 62; Athearn, *The Denver and Rio Grande,* 15, 28.

41. Brayer, *William Blackmore,* 156–157; Robert Edgar Riegel, *The Story of the Western Railroads: From 1852 Through the Reign of the Giants* (Lincoln: University of Nebraska Press, 1964), 46.

42. Brayer, *William Blackmore,* 120.

43. Anderson, *General William J. Palmer,* 120–121; ibid., 16, 71–72, 98; "First Annual Report of the Board of Directors of the National Land and Improvement Company to the Stockholders, January 1, 1873," 6, Collection #1057, Box #1, Folder #1, Colorado Fuel & Iron Co., Colorado State Historical Society, Colorado Research Library, Denver, Colorado (hereafter CF&I CRL).

44. Quote in Brayer, *William Blackmore,* 66–69; Anderson, *General William J. Palmer,* 61, 121–122; Lucius Beebe and Charles Clegg, *Rio Grande: Mainline of the Rockies* (Berkeley: Howell-North, 1962), 10.

45. Athearn, *The Denver and Rio Grande,* 18–20, 252–256; Scamehorn, *Pioneer Steelmaker,* 14; Nelson Clarke, "The Tertiary Coal Beds of Canyon City, Territory of Colorado," *Engineering and Mining Journal* 14, no. 20 (November 12, 1872): 305; Anderson, *General William J. Palmer,* 66–67; Brayer, "History of Colorado Railroads," 649.

46. Brayer, *William Blackmore*, 93–94, 120; Athearn, *The Denver and Rio Grande*, 23; Scamehorn, *Pioneer Steelmaker*, 10.

47. Scamehorn, *Pioneer Steelmaker*, 10; Anderson, *General William J. Palmer*, 120; Brayer, *William Blackmore*, 94, 239–240; *Rocky Mountain News*, August 3, 1872; "The Central Colorado Improvement Company Second Report of the Board of Directors to the Stockholders and Bondholders," 3–4, Collection #1057, Box #1, Folder #3, CF&I CRL; "First Annual Report of the Board of Directors of the National Land and Improvement Company to the Stockholders, January 1, 1873," 15–16, Collection #1057, Box #1, Folder #1, CF&I CRL.

48. Scamehorn, *Pioneer Steelmaker*, 15; Brayer, *William Blackmore*, 145; *Rocky Mountain News*, September 24, 1872.

49. Scamehorn, *Pioneer Steelmaker*, 15; Brayer, *William Blackmore*, 145; United States Geological Survey, *Mineral Resources, 1882*, 41; G. B. Richardson, "The Trinidad Coal Field, Colorado," in *Contributions to Economic Geology 1908*, Marius R. Campbell, ed., Geological Survey Bulletin 381 (Washington, D.C.: GPO, 1910), 352–353; *Rocky Mountain News*, August 3, December 13, 1872, December 9, 1873, November 9, 1903.

50. *History of the Arkansas Valley, Colorado* (Chicago: O. L. Baskin & Co., Historical Publishers, 1881), 618; "Central Colorado Improvement Company Second Report," 3–4; "Coal Creek and Brookside," *Camp and Plant* 1, no. 9 (February 8, 1902): 129–130.

51. Brayer, *William Blackmore*, 147, 234; "Central Colorado Improvement Company Second Report," 14.

52. Keith Dix, *What's a Coal Miner to Do? The Mechanization of Coal Mining* (Pittsburgh: University of Pittsburgh Press, 1988), 2–3, 13–14; Gardner and Flores, *Forgotten Frontier*, 34–37; Long, *Where the Sun Never Shines*, 41, 61; Carter Goodrich, *The Miner's Freedom: A Study of the Working Life in a Changing Industry* (Boston: Marshall Jones, 1925), 1–100.

53. *History of the Union Pacific Coal Mines*, 52–53, 161; Long, *Where the Sun Never Shines*, 59–64; Frank Julian Warne, "The Effect of Unionism upon the Mine Worker," *Annals of the American Academy of Political and Social Science* 21 (January–June 1903): 20–21; Maier Fox, interview with author, United Mine Workers of America Headquarters, Washington, D.C., June 10, 1990.

54. David Brody, "Market Unionism in America: The Case of Coal," in his *In Labor's Cause: Main Themes on the History of the American Worker* (New York: Oxford University Press, 1993), 138; Maier B. Fox, *United We Stand: The United Mine Workers of America, 1880–1980* (Washington, D.C.: United Mine Workers of America, 1990), 3; Long, *Where the Sun Never Shines*, 88–89, 98; Arthur E. Suffern, *The Coal Miners' Struggle for Industrial Status* (New York: Macmillan, 1926), 19, 25.

55. Suffern, *Coal Miners' Struggle*, 14.

56. John Duff to Oliver Ames, July 21, 1869, SG-2, S-1, Roll 1; C. G. Hammond to Oliver Ames, October 26, 1869, SG-2, S-1, Roll 3; C. G. Hammond to Oliver Ames, August 15, 1870, SG-2, S-1, Roll 4, U.P. Archives, NSHS.

57. *History of the Union Pacific Coal Mines*, 43; "They Are Having Trouble Among the Carbon Miners Again," Laramie *Daily Sentinel*, April 3, 1871; Erma A. Fletcher,

"A History of the Labor Movement in Wyoming, 1870–1940" (Master's thesis, University of Wyoming, 1945), 25.

58. Laramie *Daily Sentinel*, April 3, 1871; "Carbon," Laramie *Daily Sentinel*, April 28, 1871.

59. *History of the Union Pacific Coal Mines*, 43; Ellis, "History of Carbon," 636; Laramie *Daily Sentinel*, April 28, 1871.

60. Al Gedicks, "Ethnicity, Class Solidarity, and Labor Radicalism Among Finnish Immigrants in Michigan Copper County," *Politics and Society* 7, no. 2 (1977): 129; Angus Murdoch, *Boom Copper: The Story of the First U.S. Copper Mining Boom* (Calumet, Mich.: Roy W. Drier and Louis G. Koepel, 1964), 120–121.

61. Laramie *Daily Sentinel*, May 12, 1871.

62. Raymond, *Report of the Commissioner of Mining Statistics*, 367–369; *History of the Union Pacific Coal Mines*, 47–50; Dell Isham, "Ten Years to Atrocity" and "The Chinese Must Go!" in his *Rock Springs Massacre 1885: Two Essays on the Rock Springs Massacre* (Fort Collins, Colo.: Privately published, 1969), 19; Raymond, *Report of the Commissioner of Mining Statistics*, 367.

63. *Rocky Mountain News*, February 25, 1871.

64. Ibid.; David Brundage, *The Making of Western Labor Radicalism: Denver's Organized Workers, 1878–1905* (Urbana: University of Illinois Press, 1994), 10–11.

65. *Rocky Mountain News*, March 1, 1871.

66. Ibid.; *Rocky Mountain News*, February 25, 1871; Grogan, "Unionization in Boulder and Weld Counties," 324.

67. *Rocky Mountain News*, November 22, 1872; "The Coal Properties of Colorado," *Engineering and Mining Journal* 14, no. 12 (September 17, 1872): 63; Pueblo *Chieftain*, January 24, 1873.

CHAPTER TWO

PANIC AND TURMOIL, 1873–1878

THE PANIC OF 1873 HIT THE NATION AND THE REGION HARD, bringing five years of economic hardship. The collapse came when Jay Cooke and Company, the country's most important banking house, overextended itself financing the construction of the Northern Pacific Railroad and had to close. The bank's failure reflected the overspeculation and large indebtedness that had occurred in the nation since the Civil War. Many businesses stood on the verge of bankruptcy. In the wake of the Cooke bank closure, the nation's fragile economic system unraveled: business firms, banks, and manufacturers soon closed. Many railroads went into receivership, and railroad construction practically ceased. In those industries that managed to keep operating, wage reductions followed, and strikes resulted.[1]

In Colorado and Wyoming, the Panic of 1873 seemed much less dramatic than elsewhere in the nation. In Denver the volume of business and value of real estate declined and unemployment grew, but no banks closed, and the city continued to grow. Coal mine production also increased. At Erie the output went flat with the onset of the depression, but it gradually rose over the next four years. Similarly, the new mine at Cañon City showed a general increase during the depression. But these upward trends were deceptive; annual production figures remained small. By contrast, production exploded at the Union Pacific mines, with output increasing over 100 percent between 1873 and 1878. This expansion does not mean the Panic of 1873 missed Union Pacific operations. It did not. But railroad managers quit buying coal from outside mines and made their own mines more efficient.[2]

Increasing production does not demonstrate the dramatic impact the depression had on coal companies in the West. All of them experienced financial difficulties, management turmoil, and labor discord. The mines most closely associated with railroads suffered the most. The Panic caused the railroads to struggle, and their problems filtered down to the associated coal companies. Although traffic remained relatively strong on the Union Pacific, the company's precarious financial state caused the original investors to lose control of the railroad and the coal mines. The Rio Grande's developers hoped the local rail traffic and the support of associated development companies would make them immune to the Panic, but traffic faltered and the land companies could not find settlers. This situation pushed the Rio Grande close to bankruptcy, threatening Palmer's control of the railroad and related companies.[3]

THE PANIC OF 1873 IN WYOMING

As the nation's primary transcontinental carrier, the Union Pacific had little trouble maintaining traffic during the depression years. The road did, however, have a problem with its finances. It had a large debt, which management had a difficult time funding. In addition, overcapitalization caused its stock to fluctuate in value, making the road an easy target for speculators. Between 1870 and 1873, two different ownership groups gained control of the line, and when the Panic came the stock dropped. This decline allowed a new investor, Jay Gould, to acquire the road.[4]

By 1873 Gould had gained national notoriety for his financial machinations. Although he was only thirty-seven in 1873, the secretive and highly ambitious Gould had served as president of the Erie Railroad and tried to corner the nation's gold supply. The negative publicity from these undertakings had made him widely distrusted by the time he became interested in the Union Pacific. His stock purchases began in 1873, and by 1874 he had control of the line. Gould's intentions have long been debated. Some historians say Gould secured the Union Pacific primarily to manipulate its securities for his own financial gain. Others argue that Gould had broader intentions, that he wanted to improve and develop the railroad. These actions would cause the stock to rise in value and allow the company to start paying dividends; thus both the railroad and Gould would prosper. Gould would then sell his stock at the higher value, profiting further. No matter his intent, Gould aggressively took charge of the railroad and its coal mines.[5]

Gould reorganized all aspects of Union Pacific operations. To improve its financial condition, he issued lower-interest bonds. To run the railroad more efficiently, he brought in new managers. To expand its reach, he acquired new lines, including the Utah and the Northern. Traffic and revenue rose, allowing Gould to reward himself and other stockholders. In 1875 the Union Pacific declared its first stock dividend, and the price of stocks surged as a result.[6]

Gould similarly transformed the railroad's coal business. He viewed the coal properties as some of the company's most valuable assets but felt they were badly used because of the contract with Wardell and the Wyoming Coal and Mining Company. He got the railroad's executive committee to repudiate Wardell's contract and create a new Coal Department to manage the mines. He hired D. O. Clark, a former Wardell employee, as superintendent. Gould believed Clark had the tenacity to make the changes he wanted. In fact, the Union Pacific's official history of coal operations describes Clark as "that stern human machine." He served as superintendent until 1890 and retained an active role in the department until his retirement in 1911. Although Clark made the mines more efficient, he still received his instructions from Gould and the railroad's general superintendent.[7]

Gould's swift action won praise from the government-appointed directors on Union Pacific's board. They had criticized the railroad's contract with Wyoming Coal and Mining, and although the contract cancellation pleased them, they saw a new problem. Gould wanted to eliminate all fuel competitors along his rail line. The government directors felt such a monopoly went against the nation's best interest. Gould, however, had no intention of sharing markets or profits with other companies. By 1875 the railroad stopped using or hauling coal from non–Union Pacific mines. These actions closed Wyoming's independent mines, such as the Blair mine at Rock Springs.[8]

Gould also wanted to operate his mines as efficiently as possible. This desire put him face-to-face with the same problem that had confronted Wardell—the recalcitrant British miners. Gould sought a new workforce, one that would be more obedient and work for less pay—a difficult combination. But he had already located such workers in the Chinese immigrants who were prominent in western labor. The Rocky Mountain Coal and Iron Company used Chinese workers in its mines at Almy, and the Union Pacific Railroad had been employing Chinese as section hands in southwestern Wyoming since 1870. Gould ordered the Coal Department to bring these workers in at the first opportunity.[9]

Clark and the Coal Department did not deal directly with the Chinese. They hired a contractor, Beckwith, Quinn and Company of Evanston, Wyoming. The firm supplied the Chinese labor and ran the company stores for the Coal Department. In essence, the Union Pacific established a new third party in the coalfields, and its role would expand over time. The Union Pacific labeled it a "hybrid system": the railroad furnished the superintendent and managing force, and Beckwith, Quinn and Company hired and paid the miners, using the company store as the payroll office. The contractor also employed a person called Ay Say who functioned as a liaison between the Chinese workers and the company. This arrangement clouded the chain of command and diffused the Union Pacific Coal Department's control over the men it ultimately employed. Although the Union Pacific provided the money for wages, the company wanted the miners to think they were in the employ of Beckwith, Quinn. This system provided the cheap labor Gould wanted while giving someone else much of the responsibility for running the mines.[10]

With such split authority, little change was made in the operation of the coal towns. Although Beckwith, Quinn replaced Wardell as operator of the company stores, by this time independent merchants had opened general merchandise stores in the towns, lessening the company stores' importance. Nevertheless, the new contractors still had the advantages of encouraging the men to shop at their stores and of offering readily available credit. Beckwith, Quinn deducted any charges from the payroll. Also, Clark had extra housing built for the Chinese, but overall the coal camps changed little under the combined guidance of Beckwith, Quinn and Company and the Union Pacific Coal Department.[11]

Mining flourished under Gould's mandate of freezing out competition and expanding operations. Production from the company's six mines more than doubled from 1872 to 1877, from over 116,000 tons to more than 275,000 tons per year. Similarly, the number of miners expanded from fewer than 300 in 1872 to over 700 in 1877, bringing real growth to the three coal towns—including more merchants and privately constructed housing. This increased activity contrasted sharply with conditions elsewhere in the nation during the Panic of 1873. Most eastern mines experienced declines or stagnation during this period. For Gould, the Panic presented an opportunity: he gained control of and transformed the Union Pacific Railroad and its coal resources.[12]

THE PANIC OF 1873 IN COLORADO

In Colorado the Panic of 1873 dramatically changed market dynamics. The seven or so operators in the Northern Colorado Coal Field had hoped to be supplying an exploding market. Instead they found themselves constrained by low demand. Coal production grew slowly during the Panic years. The Denver Basin mines produced about 88,000 tons in 1878, an increase of less than 20,000 tons over the 1872 yield. In particular, the original Boulder Valley Mine struggled in this environment. As the Denver Basin's first mine, it had hoped to dominate the market; but the competition cut into its production, and with the hard times it had to cut its workforce. The *Rocky Mountain News* counted 100 men working at the mine in early 1872 and only 50 in late 1874.[13]

In addition to the fact that the markets failed to develop as hoped, the coal companies' biggest customers—the Colorado railroads—failed during the Panic. The Kansas Pacific had struggled since the day it opened because of poor management and bitter competition with the Union Pacific. In 1873 the Kansas Pacific began defaulting on interest payments, and by 1874 it was in the hands of a receiver. Similarly, the Denver Pacific was chronically insolvent. To compensate and try to survive, both operations sought to lower the cost of coal. At the beginning of the recession, the companies paid $2.40 per ton for coal, but they soon pushed the cost down to $2.00 a ton. In 1877 these prime customers demanded a further cut to $1.75 per ton. The *Rocky Mountain News* reported that the railroad companies were the "heaviest customers of the Erie mines" and that the Denver Basin operators had little choice but to agree with the companies' demands. In fact, the competition among the numerous mines forced the coal companies to accept the demands. If a mine refused to provide coal at the reduced price, the railroads took their business to another operator, thereby ruining the one left behind.[14]

The competition, lack of growth, and financial crunch put a strain on the Denver Basin mines. They operated only part-time; and as the railroads demanded cheaper fuel, the companies lowered the wage scale. With cuts and reduced work, upheaval followed. Workers struck, superintendents quit in protest, and—as in Wyoming—coal company managers considered hiring a new workforce. The British miners in the independent towns of Erie and Canfield stood ready to resist. The Panic of 1873 thus brought economic turmoil to the mines and miners of the Denver Basin.[15]

In southern Colorado, Palmer and his colleagues in the Rio Grande hoped in vain that their recently opened railroad and associated development companies would allow them to avoid the Panic. Instead they soon saw the effect of the downturn. In the 1873 Annual Report, railroad officials declared that the Panic had seriously damaged the transportation business and associated activities. The Cañon City coal mine did show a modest increase in production during the downturn, but as in the Denver Basin, this growth was limited. In 1872 the mine had produced a little over 6,000 tons. In 1876 that amount had grown to about 20,000 tons. Unlike Jay Gould and the Union Pacific, Palmer and the Rio Grande promoters lacked the deep economic resources and a transcontinental connection to maintain prosperity.[16]

Palmer and his associates wanted their railroad to advance, secure more traffic, gain access to the precious metal camps in the mountains, and maintain the monopoly over central Colorado coal. This course seemed all the more pressing since the Kansas Pacific and the Atchison, Topeka and Santa Fe

Railroads were advancing toward the Rio Grande's domain. But Palmer's lack of assets caused him to abandon plans to extend track south of Pueblo in the first years of the Panic.[17]

Not only did construction stop, the Panic also forced the Rio Grande to find ways to survive. One method was to increase freight revenue by charging as much as traffic would bear, and another was to co-opt the coal business of the Central Colorado Improvement Company (CCI). Jones and Burdess had originally opened the Cañon City mines for CCI, but as the Panic started, the company ended the contract and turned operations over to the Rio Grande. The CCI technically owned the mines and should have sold coal to the railroad and on the domestic market itself. The new understanding allowed the Rio Grande to operate the mines directly. Although CCI received a royalty of twenty-five cents a ton, the railroad benefited the most from this arrangement. It did not have to purchase coal, and it profited immediately from the sales.[18]

These survival techniques did have problems. Palmer left himself and his railroad open to criticism. When CCI stockholders complained, he tried to mollify them by arguing that the arrangement would make the coal more competitive in the Denver market and return more in the end. Nevertheless, the stockholders felt Palmer had sacrificed their interests for those of the railroad. Those who felt the railroad's hauling charges were excessive started referring to the line as the "Narrow Gouge." Despite angering many, Palmer and his associates managed to navigate the first years of the recession without significant financial difficulties.[19]

As the hard times continued, Palmer decided to take a chance on expansion. If he advanced the railroad south and west, securing the Santa Fe Trail trade as well as that of San Juan country, he could gain more markets and win needed traffic. This development might help the Rio Grande weather the depression. Further, it would be a preemptive strike. With the Kansas Pacific and the Santa Fe threatening, the Rio Grande could capture the markets and perhaps convince other railroads not to advance. In late 1875 Palmer pushed the railroad south from Pueblo, running one line into the San Luis Valley and another toward Trinidad and the Santa Fe Trail.[20]

In anticipation of the move south, men associated with Palmer's operations started acquiring choice property along the proposed route from Pueblo to Trinidad. Then as the railroad began construction, Palmer, Jackson, and other Rio Grande insiders organized another land development company, the Southern Colorado Coal and Town Company. Similar to the Central Colorado Improvement Company, this new company bought the land from the original purchasers. The investors not only made a profit by selling the land to themselves, but some of the land had been obtained inexpensively through liberal use and abuse of land laws. Gaining nearly 14,000 acres, the Southern

Colorado Coal and Town Company made plans to develop town sites and coal lands along the Cucharas and Purgatoire Valleys in Huerfano and Las Animas Counties.[21]

These two counties contained the extensive Trinidad coalfield, which ran along the eastern base of the Front Range, extending east from the mountains for as much as forty miles and running from just north of Walsenburg to the southern Colorado border—a distance of about sixty miles. This coal-bearing formation continued on into New Mexico, but the name changed to the Raton Field. Palmer and his associates recognized that good-quality bituminous coal existed in the Trinidad field and made plans to exploit it. They anticipated selling the fuel from the northern part of the field on the Denver domestic market, whereas that to the south had gained a reputation as some of the best industrial coal in the state. The Denver Gas Company had experimented with that coal and found that it could be converted into a superior illuminating gas. Also, the coal had been successfully tested for its coking abilities. In 1875 Palmer claimed that the field contained the "only deposit of coking coal yet positively known in the western half of the American continent"—the perfect adjunct to the new precious metal smelting business developing in Colorado and Utah. Plus, he still dreamed of starting an ironworks, an operation that would require coke.[22]

Besides developing coal deposits, the Southern Colorado Coal and Town Company provided assistance to the railroad. To help the Rio Grande's finances, the company's operators contributed half a million dollars in fully paid stock to the railroad and encouraged their investors to purchase railroad bonds. In return, the railroad gave the operation a 20 percent reduction in freight rates for a twenty-year period. Despite these efforts, few investors could be found during the Panic years, and Palmer's efforts to build south strained the railroad financially. Yet the Rio Grande built on, heading directly toward financial trouble.[23]

As construction progressed, Palmer and his associates in the Southern Colorado Coal and Town Company began establishing towns and opening mines. Fifty miles south of Pueblo they decided to develop a coal seam and lay out the town of Cucharas. They soon abandoned this location, relocating a little to the west near Walsenburg, where better coal lands existed. Originally called La Plaza de Los Leones when founded in 1862, the village changed its name to honor its most prominent citizen, Fred Walsen. He had arrived in 1870 and established a trading post; two years later the community became the county seat of Huerfano County. At this location, Palmer's Southern Colorado Company avoided building a new town and contracted with Hunt and Allen to develop the Walsen Mine.[24]

Farther south, Palmer wanted to locate a railroad town near Trinidad. Although Trinidad served as a commercial center on the Santa Fe Trail, was the seat of Las Animas County, and had over 600 residents, Palmer decided not to build directly into town. Just as years before the railroad had stopped seven miles east of Cañon City at Labran, here the Denver and Rio Grande ceased building five miles north of Trinidad. In both cases Palmer alienated the residents of the established communities. He gave excuses, such as a lack of money or the fact that Trinidad's location along the Purgatoire River made it unsuitable for growth. In reality, the company wanted to benefit from town site development. The Rio Grande arrived north of Trinidad in April 1876 and established an end-of-track town called El Moro. The developers placed El Moro along the Santa Fe Trail, hoping it would soon replace Trinidad as the local mercantile center.[25]

Two miles south of El Moro lay the coal banks owned by the Southern Colorado Coal and Town Company. To reach the property, Palmer and his associates again resorted to their well-established system of associated companies and formed the El Moro Railway Company. Then, to open the El Moro Mine, the company turned to contractors Hunt and Allen who also had control of the Walsenburg operation. Although the Coal and Town Company lost money by letting Hunt and Allen sell its coal, the contract saved the company the cost of putting the mine plant together. Hunt and Allen, however, only operated the mines from December 1877 to March 1878, when the Southern Colorado Coal and Town Company took them over.[26]

The move south during the depression did not solve the Rio Grande's financial difficulties; in fact, it caused significant new problems. The project had been expensive. The construction costs exceeded available revenue, and the extension brought little new traffic. To pay for the expansion, Palmer appropriated money intended for interest payments on bonds. Defaulting on the interest payments caused the bondholders to become restive, and they began demanding that a receiver be appointed. Palmer initially deflected these demands, but his troubles deepened. The railroad's expansion did not stop the advance of the Atchison, Topeka and Santa Fe (also referred to as Santa Fe). Despite Palmer's efforts to outmaneuver the Santa Fe and discourage it from building into Colorado, the railroad decided to enter the state. The Santa Fe went after the traffic and markets Palmer wanted. As Robert Athearn describes it, the Atchison road was a "traffic raider."[27]

After hesitating in the early years of the recession, the Santa Fe Railroad built from Kansas to Pueblo in 1876, and under the aggressive leadership of general manager William Strong and chief engineer Albert Robinson, it moved south toward Trinidad in 1878. The Santa Fe was not in better financial condition than other railroads. It had received a federal land grant across Kansas but had no grant for its Colorado expansion. It relied on the same techniques other rail lines used for financing its construction. Multiple companies, including a construction company, sold securities to raise necessary funds. The

Santa Fe, however, had three advantages that allowed it to expand during hard times. First, the Kansas cattle business gave the road badly needed revenue during the mid-1870s. Second, by not building into Cañon City or Trinidad, the Rio Grande had alienated the residents of those towns, thus motivating the outraged citizens to give financial and physical aid to the Santa Fe so it would build into their communities. Third, Strong and Robinson moved ahead with expansion because they ignored financial problems. Whereas Palmer had to deal constantly with financial concerns, Strong and Robinson saw the issue as someone else's matter. They were more concerned with the extension and construction of the road to protect what they thought could be critical trade. And to this end they watched the troubled Rio Grande road and found encouragement.[28]

Palmer was besieged on all sides. He feared the advancing Santa Fe. The bondholders, angered by the Rio Grande's default on interest payments, wanted a change in management. In late 1878 Palmer gave in. The bondholders took control of the railroad and in December signed an agreement leasing the Rio Grande to the Santa Fe for thirty years. The investors saw this move as the best possible method for guaranteeing a return on their investment.[29]

Just as Palmer lost control of the Rio Grande, the Panic of 1873 came to an end. By the end of 1878 he could only look back on financial frustrations and a network of companies that seemed to be in peril. He had tried to outmaneuver the hard times, but instead he pushed the railroad into default. Palmer, however, did lay the groundwork for expansion of the associated companies. His land companies had opened two new coal mines, the Walsen at Walsenburg and the El Moro at Trinidad. Although these operations did little during the last years of the depression, producing only 52 tons in 1877 and combining for a little under 30,000 tons in 1878, they would become much more important in the future.[30]

LABOR RELATIONS DURING THE PANIC

Three factors influenced labor relations from 1873 to 1878: the depression, corporate action, and worker responses. First, the economic depression brought on labor turmoil. It caused some coal companies to falter, and those businesses tried to pass their problems on to the miners—often in the form of wage cuts. Further, the depression undermined workers' positions. It made labor more plentiful, threatening miners' jobs and wage levels. Second, corporate actions affected labor relations. For example, Gould's Union Pacific mines did not falter during the depression, but in the name of profit and efficiency they, too, cut wages and sought a less expensive labor force. Third, the workers hoped to set the course of labor-management interaction. They wanted to maintain control of their work and sustain a living wage, and they did not easily accept threats to their well-being.

The Denver Basin miners felt the drive to cut wages during the depression more strongly than any other group of miners. The Kansas Pacific and Denver Pacific Railroads demanded cheaper coal, and the Denver market failed to expand significantly. As many as seven mines existed in the region, yet production for 1874 barely increased over that in 1873 and lagged behind what had been produced in 1872. In response to low demand, the coal companies began cutting wages, hoping to gain a competitive edge over other producers.[31]

The most important mine in the field remained the Boulder Valley. It had the most employees, produced the most coal, and as the depression started, paid higher wages than its neighbors. Its size allowed it to operate more efficiently and cheaply than the smaller companies. But as the downturn continued, the Boulder Valley Mine tried to cut wages. In November 1874 the manager announced a reduction in wages from $1.25 to $1.00 per ton. The miners and their families stood united to resist the change. The labor troubles three years earlier had caused some turnover at the mine, but many current employees were the skilled craftsmen who had opened the mine at Erie and had worked there since the beginning. Fully steeped in the mining heritage, they had a sense of solidarity and pride, and several owned their own homes and property in the independent town. When they heard about the wage cut, they formed a lodge of the Miners' National Association, a national union recently organized in the eastern coalfields. It became the main agent of solidarity in Colorado and the nation in the early 1870s as the coal miners attempted to stop depression-driven wage erosion. In Colorado the union counted 242 members, most of them at Erie. The union ordered a strike to stop the Boulder Valley wage reduction.[32]

The Boulder Valley miners rapidly won a settlement. Within one day the company backed down from the cut, and on November 11, 1874, the *Rocky Mountain News* reported that eighty men "marched into the mine and went to work." In addition, the paper quoted J. E. Bates, one of the owners, praising the men for their moderation and good conduct. After the turmoil that had occurred with the 1871 strike, the workers' solidarity and potential volatility apparently worried the mine owners. Further, the owners undoubtedly feared losing their market share to the mines still operating. In a weak market a long suspension could permanently damage a company's market share.[33]

The one-day suspension had other ramifications. It inspired miners to walk off the job in at least three other Denver Basin mines. The men initially did so in sympathy with the Boulder Valley strike, but soon they made demands of their own. The smaller operations had already instituted a wage cut, and when the Boulder Valley men held fast, these other workers wanted an increase, although they failed to gain one. The recently opened mines had little capitalization and limited market concerns, so they could outwait the men.[34]

The victory at the Boulder Valley Mine proved short-lived. As the depression continued, the Boulder Valley operators renewed their effort to drive down wages in early 1875. The impetus for the cut came not only from local market pressures, such as the railroads, but also from the national trend. By 1875, coal companies across the country had cut wages and laid off miners because of reduced demand, and in January of that year a prolonged strike had begun in the anthracite regions of Pennsylvania.[35]

With the Boulder Valley wage cut, the men again went on strike. Months before, miners from neighboring Denver Basin mines had joined in the first walkout. This time the Boulder Valley men gained support from miners at the Rio Grande's Coal Creek operation. According to the Pueblo *Chieftain*, these men were not striking over wages; instead, they belonged to the "coal miner's league" and intended to make "coal scarce in Denver . . . to help their striking brethren in the Erie banks."[36] The sympathy strikes from the Denver Basin to Coal Creek indicate the solidarity that existed among early Colorado coal miners. They came west steeped in time-honored traditions and with a generally shared ethnic background, and these bonds brought the men together in a common cause.

Despite the show of solidarity, their efforts failed. This time the poor economic conditions caught up with the miners. The western workers knew they had been making good wages. The *Rocky Mountain News* even argued that the men were overpaid and attempted to convince the public that this was the case. The newspaper ran stories comparing Colorado wage rates with those in the East. The difference could be as much as fifty cents a ton, and the logic followed that Colorado men should willingly take a cut. Further, the national coal strike had increased the pool of workers. Although the Erie lodge of the Miners' National Association ran newspaper ads requesting miners to stay away, the need to survive inevitably drew some to the Colorado field. The strike failed, and the company dropped wages to a dollar per ton. The Coal Creek managers, who had opened their mine paying $1.50 a ton, followed suit. The Rio Grande's financial turmoil clearly made Palmer and his associates want to cut expenses, and by January 1876 the *Rocky Mountain News* reported that the mine was paying its sixty-two diggers from $1.00 to $1.25 per ton. The variation depended on the amount of impurities in the coal—the greater the impurities, the harder the coal was to mine and the higher the tonnage rate went.[37]

During these events, no stories of violence or worker replacement hit the press. Perhaps the miners accepted the drop in wages as inevitable during the hard times. Not all, however, seemed to accept the changes. In August 1875 eighteen men joined together to operate their own mine in the Erie coal banks. They called their organization the Co-operative Union and let it be known that they planned to be a formidable competitor. The effort makes a statement for worker solidarity and the Erie workers' tenacity, but no production records exist for the mine.[38]

After two years under the new wage scale, the Boulder Valley Coal Company—initially joined by another Erie-area mine, the Rob Roy—moved to push wages down another twenty-five cents a ton beginning April 1, 1877. The Boulder Valley managers justified this action as a necessary response to the Kansas Pacific and Denver Pacific demands. The two railroads had again given notice that they would not pay the old rate for coal and wanted a twenty-five-cent-per-ton decrease. The coal company tried to pass the full cut along to the miners, starting a yearlong labor struggle that affected every mine in the Denver Basin.[39]

In 1877 the Boulder Valley Mine was still the largest in the Denver Basin. At times it employed upwards of 200 men. When the company owners, led by J. E. Bates, made the wage cut announcement, they expected a hostile reaction and a strike. They understood the miners' solidarity, and they knew the men were entrenched; many had families and owned their own land and homes. They also recognized that a second wage cut in two years would not be tolerated. The rapid employment of replacement workers seemed the only way to disrupt the workforce, beat the strike, and cut wages. The owners hoped this tactic would not only bring victory but would allow them to gain control of their operation. The depression made workers readily available. Consequently, just as notices appeared of the wage cut, the company ran advertisements for new men.[40]

The workers and their families saw this effort as a massive affront. They believed seventy-five cents a ton did not provide a living wage. In fact, as craftsmen they expected to receive the "full social value of their product." The cut denied them their just due. Further, they saw the use of strikebreakers as a violation of their right to organize and bargain and in general of their rights as workers and citizens. The men and women of Erie would not stand for this situation. They chose to defend their rights with a strike.[41]

In the first weeks of the struggle, dealing with an obdurate company, the workers and their wives felt it necessary to resort to intimidation and violence. When Bates came to town with new workers, Erie residents crowded around them and made a strong case that they should leave. The *Rocky Mountain News* reported that in one instance a company man had been knocked down and severely kicked and beaten by both men and women, stating that "the latter, if anything, [were] more violent than the men." As Bates and other mine officials continued to bring more replacements, the violence increased. Two weeks after the strike began, somebody blew up the coal chutes, the boardinghouse, and other mine property. More explosions followed.[42]

The violence appalled Bates and the other mine owners, as well as the editors of the *Rocky Mountain News*. The paper wanted Governor John L.

Routt to intervene, but he declined, believing local officials could control the violence. Local law officers did attempt to arrest the guilty parties, but that did little to change the course of the disturbance. The *News* also tried to find someone to blame. Unwilling to accept the notion that local miners could do such damage, the paper consistently denounced suspected "troublemakers." Further, the *News* picked a logical organization to accuse, the Molly Maguires. Whenever violence occurred, the paper labeled it "Molly Maguirism."[43]

The Molly Maguires operated in the anthracite fields of Pennsylvania during the 1860s and 1870s. Composed of Irish mine workers who wanted to keep other foreign-born workers out of the coal mines, the group was a secret, sometimes violent organization. Its members threatened, assaulted, and occasionally murdered mine guards, foremen, superintendents, and owners. When violence occurred in any coalfield, the group became a handy scapegoat. Even the *Engineering and Mining Journal* stated that perhaps some branch of the Molly Maguires had emigrated from Pennsylvania to the West. That seems highly unlikely, however. The residents of Erie committed these actions to defend their rights and maintain control of their jobs.[44]

The spurts of violence went on for about a month, and the dispute went on for a year. During that time the Boulder Valley Mine operated intermittently, with workers successfully maintaining their old wage scale. The workers' solidarity and the competition among the various coal companies prevented the company from prevailing. When the Boulder Valley Coal Company closed, the other six small operators in the Denver Basin saw this as the time to profit. Even Rob Roy—the one company that had originally joined Boulder Valley in cutting wages—returned to the old scale, and its miners went to work. These operations produced more than they ever had and hired all available workers. Some of their new hires had worked for the Boulder Valley Mine, and even as they worked they did not abandon their strike mentality or their notion of solidarity. Whenever the Boulder Valley Mine tried to operate, the old employees made every effort to prevent men from entering the mine without a guaranteed dollar a ton for their coal.[45]

During the course of the labor dispute, all operating coal companies occasionally attempted to cut the wage scale, but any announced reduction would bring a strike. The wage rate bounced back and forth between seventy-five cents and a dollar per ton. The smaller mines seemed especially to fear a lengthy work stoppage. They all competed on the Denver market, along with Cañon City coal, and they worried about losing their market share—especially during hard financial times. In fact, the Denver market proved so brutal and companies were so incapable of permanently reducing wages to gain an advantage that by January 1878 most coal operators attempted to form an association to fix the wholesale price of coal. This organization, they hoped, would allow all operators to keep their share of the market at a consistent price that guaranteed a profit. The association had little chance for success; it outraged Denverites, and not all coal companies were participating. Nevertheless, it showed how dearly the operators wanted to bring order to their industry.[46]

By early 1878 disorder reigned at the Boulder Valley coal mine. The company still paid workers a dollar a ton, but mine superintendents had quit or been fired, and rancor existed among investors. The company's pricing policies angered Denverites, and its efforts to import strikebreakers incensed the miners. Specifically, the company recruited Italian laborers. The Italians, however, would not work as strikebreakers, and the company's efforts stalled. Despite all the trouble, in March 1878 the company made another effort to reduce wages—its last attempt for some time.[47]

Order came to the coal industry and the downward push on wages ended with the return of prosperity in the spring and summer of 1878. The Panic wound down, and the great Leadville silver boom brought statewide prosperity. The years following witnessed new railroads, new coal mines, and explosive growth in Colorado. Demand for coal increased dramatically, and mines could more easily compete. Some of the new and expanding mines in the Denver Basin initially started their miners at seventy-five cents per ton, but pressure was soon applied to escalate the wage scale.[48]

Whereas miners in the Denver Basin waged a yearlong struggle to preserve their tonnage rate, the miners in central Colorado at Coal Creek had a less intense fight. The 1875 Boulder Valley strike had gained some sympathy from the Coal Creek men, and reportedly Coal Creek miners still belonged to the union in 1877. But the Erie strike in 1877 brought no apparent response from Coal Creek. In fact, during some Denver Basin stoppages, Coal Creek coal advanced further into the Denver-area market. The Central Colorado Improvement Company gained a coal contract with the Kansas Pacific, and its 1877 coal production more than doubled that of 1876.[49]

Despite the increase in business, Palmer and the other owners of the CCI and the Denver and Rio Grande knew of the wage cuts going on elsewhere and well understood that a similar move could bring them needed revenue. In June 1877 the Pueblo *Chieftain* reported that the Coal Creek tonnage rate had been cut to seventy-five cents and that the miners had gone out in protest. Little else is known about the strike, but apparently the workers at this one operation outside Cañon City could not resist the company as easily as their colleagues to the north. By the end of June, the Coal Creek mine was operating at the reduced rate.[50]

The miners could not stave off the rate cut because they lacked the solidarity and competition that existed in the Northern Coal Field. With just one operator in the field and a limited number of employees, the miners had no other workers to turn to for help, limiting solidarity. Plus, the Rio Grande not only operated the mine in 1877, but the railroad used most of the coal. The company did not worry about losing market share if a strike closed the mine. In fact, the managers of the mine may have provoked the walkout to reduce expenses. The CCI's 1877 Annual Report states that the mines "were shut down to reduce rates charged for mining" and had "resumed operations under arrangements satisfactory to the operators." No matter the circumstances, a return to prosperity would change labor conditions in these mines. Near the end of the depression, the El Moro Mine near Trinidad opened, paying seventy-five cents per ton of coal mined. By June 1878 the men wanted more.[51]

For the Colorado coal mines, the Panic of 1873 limited growth and threatened their solvency. To save money and remain competitive, the mine operators twice attempted to cut wages—in 1875 and in 1877. The 1875 action caused little turmoil, but Denver Basin miners reacted violently to the second cut. They saw the new lower wage as below their product's accepted social value. They resented this injustice, but the companies threatened their control of the mines by bringing in replacement workers. These actions brought a prolonged strike that came to no definitive conclusion. The companies made ongoing efforts to cut wages, but the cuts never lasted. Two factors helped the men resist a permanent reduction: their solidarity and the marketplace. The miners worked together effectively, even absorbing new arrivals into their cause. Also, the competitive nature of the coal market kept the companies from provoking a lengthy strike. Most companies feared losing their market share permanently with a prolonged walkout. To the south, the Cañon City miners suffered the same travails but resisted less effectively. The Rio Grande company did not fear losing its market share, and the small number of miners limited solidarity. Nevertheless, from these labor struggles emerged a tradition of labor activism. The Denver Basin and Coal Creek miners would continue to be at the center of future labor movements in Colorado.

Whereas miners in Colorado suffered because of the Panic of 1873, miners along the Union Pacific in Wyoming had a different problem. Jay Gould wanted production to be expanded and the mines run more efficiently. This meant reducing the wage scale and bringing the workforce under greater control. Wardell had taken steps in this direction during the 1871 strike and had demonstrated a way to deal with labor difficulties—when faced with a strike, call on the military for support, fire the troublemakers, and bring in new workers. Recurring labor problems, however, revealed a fundamental weakness in that plan. Importing workers to defeat solidarity and unionization worked only for a limited time; the underground workplace functioned as a solidifying force. By 1874 the Scandinavian miners Wardell had brought in had learned the nature of the craft, experienced the independence, suffered its hazards, and begun uniting against the company. In fact, a large majority of coal miners had joined the Miners' National Association. When the Union Pacific took possession of the mines, the workers became as recalcitrant as before. Thus Gould planned to use Wardell's formula for labor control, but he would look for a new type of worker—one who would mix with the other miners less easily and not tend to unionize. Gould decided to hire Chinese workers.[52]

When D. O. Clark and the Coal Department took control in March 1874, the miners were already restless. The company wanted production increased, so it granted some concessions and evaluated the situation. By November, the Coal Department was ready to make its first move. When workers at the Union Pacific's Almy Mine appeared to be organizing again, the company began placing Chinese in the mines. The white miners at Almy walked out in protest, and the workers at Carbon and Rock Springs threatened a general strike in support. The Union Pacific, however, held firm. The Almy strike ended with the miners achieving nothing, and the Carbon and Rock Springs men did not join the strike. Gould had gained control of the mine. The railroad opened a new mine at Almy as part of its expansion policy in early 1875 and filled it with Chinese.[53]

Almy was the perfect location for beginning the new policy. Here, the apparent solidarity among the miners could be most easily challenged. The Central Pacific's Rocky Mountain Coal and Iron Company had been using Chinese in its mines at Almy since they opened, which made Almy a racially divided camp. Plus, the Union Pacific used less Almy coal than it did coal from any other company. A strike there would not damage overall operations, as the railroad could increase production at its other locations. The realities of the situation apparently deterred the Rock Springs and Carbon miners from joining the walkout. They were working steadily, and to this point the company had treated them fairly well. Plus, Chinese had been employed as railroad section hands in southwestern Wyoming since 1870, and the Union Pacific men may have expected their advance into the Almy mines.[54]

Many early coal operators resisted the idea of placing untrained men in the mines. They had respect for the craft nature of the job. They believed only skilled men should be employed and that traditions should be honored. Modern industrialists such as Jay Gould, however, lacked reverence for skilled miners. Certainly, enough old-time miners needed to be employed to train new arrivals, but in general, many late-nineteenth-century industrialists saw miners as laborers. These conflicting notions were beginning to be challenged in southwestern Wyoming and would later lead to intense labor clashes.[55]

After the success at Almy, Gould turned his attention to Rock Springs. Here, the company operated three mines, which had enough capacity to reach the higher production levels Gould wanted. The company just needed more miners. It initially found the men in the neighboring operations the Union Pacific was forcing to close. The company would probably have preferred to hire Chinese, but through much of 1875 they were apparently unavailable. A business out of San Francisco—Sisson, Wallace, and Company—had been the suppliers and general agents for the Chinese employed at the Rocky Mountain company's mines. Sisson, Wallace, and Company, however, had sold its Wyoming operations to Beckwith, Quinn and Company of Evanston in 1875. Because of the sale, neither company seemed prepared to supply the number of Chinese the Union Pacific wanted. Consequently, the Union Pacific expanded production with a traditional workforce.[56]

This did not prevent Gould from trying to reduce wages. Of course, during the Panic of 1873, coal companies across the country were pushing down the tonnage rate. Colorado operators had reduced the rate to $1.00 a ton by mid-1875, and soon after the success in Almy the Union Pacific announced a reduction from $1.25 to $1.00 a ton. The Coal Department defended itself by attacking the traditional prerogatives of the men underground. The railroad's general superintendent, S. H. Clark, argued that the men mined only enough coal to earn the wages necessary to cover their living expenses. He figured they worked only three days a week, which did not keep up with the railroad's demand. Clark explained that he had asked the miners to increase their output by 25 percent, but through their union—the Miners' National Association—they had declined. Clark complained that the miners were dictating to the company and that the only way to increase production was to reduce the piece rate. Naturally, the miners saw this as part of their workplace control. With Chinese workers unavailable, Clark did not want to push the point at this time, so to avoid serious labor discord he promised to reduce the cost of goods sold at the company stores to offset the loss in pay.[57]

Clark left Wyoming to wait for Chinese workers to become available and to develop a plan that would allow them to enter the mines without provoking what the company thought could become a "serious riot." By November 1875 everything seemed ready. Beckwith, Quinn could supply the Chinese required. Also, Clark had recruited the territorial governor of Wyoming, John M. Thayer, to the railroad's cause, warning him of the chance of violence and asking for federal protection. Clark then pushed the miners to volatility by not reducing prices at the company stores as promised. After working under the reduced wage scale for five months, the men at Rock Springs began a work slowdown to protest the unchanged policy at the company stores. Initially, the protesters only requested the promised price reductions, but when the company did not respond, the miners went on strike. At that point they broadened their demands to include a return to the old wage scale.[58]

Clark wanted this opening. He knew he could paint the strikers as villains and induce the governor to call on the military to end the walkout. Replacing a significant number of whites with Chinese could be risky. Most Americans saw the Chinese as interlopers, and during a depression, denying white workers a job could cause trouble. Also, when the railroad used Chinese as section hands, it kept them scattered and used them only in southwest Wyoming. No more than twenty were ever assigned to one location, and they were never placed at the larger population centers such as Green River or Evanston. Bringing a large number of Chinese into one town could be difficult. Consequently, Clark moved consciously and cautiously and hoped to deflect any image of evil to the white miners.[59]

When the strike began, letters promptly appeared in regional newspapers vilifying the miners. Signed only under the name "Justice," the letters called the men "turbulent spirits" and stated that these misdirected souls threatened to take possession of the mines. Public sentiment turned against the miners, and the Cheyenne *Daily Leader* stated that it had always been "the working-man's friend" but that "mob law must be put down at all hazards."[60]

Governor Thayer also responded the way Clark wanted. Whereas Governor Routt in Colorado avoided calls for intervention in the Denver Basin, Wyoming's governor felt responsible for the safety of the transcontinental railroad. The day the strike started, he appeared in Rock Springs with Superintendent Clark. Thayer met with the miners and received pledges of peace and of respect for company property. Indeed, no violence occurred except for a reported lone pistol shot. Despite the peaceful nature of the strike, Governor Thayer ordered four companies of federal troops to Carbon and Rock Springs. The troops were instructed to protect railroad property and keep open the "great overland route," and their presence allowed the railroad to fire the striking miners—as had been done in 1871—and bring in a new workforce.[61]

S. Rouff, president of the local chapter of the Miners' National Association, defended the strikers. Writing to a Cheyenne newspaper, he called for restoring the old wage scale and contended that the miners had been "altogether peaceable." He attacked what he termed the false reports of violence, and he saw no reason for the presence of U.S. soldiers. The correspondent "Justice" retorted that the miners had made a "fatal mistake by striking," and he predicted "quite a change" in the next few weeks.[62]

Clark had the upper hand. With the strike barely two weeks old, a train containing 100 Chinese arrived in Rock Springs, accompanied by Superintendent Clark; Governor Thayer; A. C. Beckwith of Beckwith, Quinn and Company; and Ah Say, manager of the Chinese. The railroad also sent a complete outfit of boarding and lodging cars. The Chinese entered the Rock Springs mines one day after their arrival. The company posted a list of white miners who would be allowed to return to work. It contained about a third of the miners previously employed, the number felt necessary to train the Chinese. Members of the miners' union attempted to meet with Clark, but he refused. He offered free transportation to Omaha for any dismissed miner, undoubtedly to remove the hostile element from town. With the army present, the workers could do little. Reports state that 99 men were fired and 48 reemployed. Plus, 50 more Chinese soon arrived.[63]

The Chinese did what Gould had hoped: they reduced the cost of mining. Whereas the white scale had been pushed down to $1.00 per ton, the Chinese came in at $0.75. Whereas the overall cost of producing a ton of coal stood at $2.13 in 1874, two years later the cost was $1.42. Additionally, the Chinese did not unionize, and stopping the union in Wyoming had been one of Gould's goals. With the strikers routed, Gould congratulated Clark on breaking up a "dangerous labor combination." The Laramie *Daily Sentinel* concurred, reporting that Clark had "broken up and completely annihilated one of the most formidable organizations of strikers."[64]

The miners at Carbon largely avoided the problems at Rock Springs. They had protested the original pay cut and the company's failure to reduce prices at the store, and they had threatened to strike. But they did not walk out with the Rock Springs miners. Perhaps the nearly 150 miles between the two camps hindered communication, or maybe the men adopted a wait-and-see attitude. The arrival of federal troops in Carbon and the introduction of Chinese at Rock Springs undoubtedly subdued the Carbon miners. But because no strike occurred, the railroad had no immediate reason to introduce Chinese laborers at Carbon. The railroad had anticipated employing Chinese there, as it built extra housing to accommodate them. But the Chinese never came.[65]

Beyond no strike at Carbon, the Union Pacific had other reasons for deciding not to employ Chinese miners there. First, the railroad perceived that the white miners had been duly "chastened" by its action in Rock Springs, and it did not need to take further action against them. Second, managers worried about anti-Chinese sentiment and potential violence. Whether the Chinese worked as section hands or in the coal mines, the Union Pacific kept them in southwestern Wyoming—isolated from the territory's largest population centers at Laramie and Cheyenne as well as from the gold-seeking population of Colorado. Since the days of the California gold rush, miners in the goldfields had been notoriously anti-Chinese. The Union Pacific wanted no anti-Chinese violence. Third, Carbon was the company's largest camp. It produced the most coal and supplied the railroad as far east as Omaha. The company needed to avoid a disruption at the Carbon mines. And fourth, Carbon was the company's oldest camp. The company could more easily rout the labor element at Rock Springs because those mines had only recently expanded. Carbon had a history of labor activism, and the men there could have launched a notable fight. Consequently, Carbon remained dominated by traditional white miners.[66]

The railroad soon realized the benefit of not having Chinese in all of its mines. They were not the totally subservient workers the company had envisioned. Although they worked for less pay and took orders more willingly than whites, they, too, caused problems. Coming from a preindustrial environment, the Chinese shared one characteristic with the skilled craft miners: they were accustomed to setting their own pace of work. The Chinese did not want to be driven any harder than the previous miners had. One manager reported that "no Chinaman pretends to work more than four days a week"—similar to the workers before them. Consequently, with Almy and Rock Springs predominantly Chinese, the Union Pacific could balance any production problems that might arise at these two locations with the output from the mines at Carbon. Similarly, problems at Carbon could be offset by more output from the other two locations.[67]

In fact, the Chinese shared some of the same concerns as the workers they replaced and saw some of the same company abuses. In 1878 the Laramie *Weekly Sentinel* reported that the Chinese "were in a state of revolt," as they accused the company of charging them more for goods at the company store than it charged the white miners. Rumors of threatened violence spread through Rock Springs, and the Union Pacific increased the number of guards around its mines. Some people advocated calling on Governor Thayer for protection. Handling the matter in the railroad's standard fashion, the Chinese boss Ay Say discharged "about sixty of the most turbulent spirits," returning them to Beckwith, Quinn at Evanston; he then gathered sixty new Chinese for the mines.[68]

Despite the problems, the Union Pacific had seemingly gained control of the Almy and Rock Springs mines. Combined with the mines at Carbon, the company's production rose dramatically. From 1873 to 1878 it more than doubled, increasing from nearly 130,000 tons to over 275,000 tons a year. But a core of traditional miners remained at Carbon, and some were still present at Rock Springs and Almy. They were retained to train and supervise the Chinese. The men who survived the Union Pacific's replacement policy would become the center of future labor activism, especially at the independent town of Carbon. These miners had suffered wage cuts during the 1870s depression, much as the men in Colorado had. The Union Pacific, however, worked under a different premise. It was not worried about losing markets or solvency; Jay Gould wanted his Coal Department to become more efficient and produce more coal. In the end, he wanted to make more money at the expense of the workers. To do this he brought a new labor force to the Union Pacific coal mines.[69]

Beyond Gould's expansion, the Panic of 1873 nearly ended mine expansion in Colorado. The coal companies and workers in northern Colorado suffered because of the competitive nature of the business. Even though demand remained relatively consistent, customers such as the Kansas Pacific wanted cheaper fuel, and companies lowered their prices to maintain their market share. But with labor accounting for most of the expense in the coal industry, wage cuts followed. These actions precipitated a series of labor disputes, as miners had come to expect high wages in what had been a tight labor market. The Panic changed the workers' world: wage rates fell from their old levels and would not easily rebound, replacement workers became a permanent element in the coalfields, and the workers' earlier solidarity weakened under the pressures.

To the south of Denver, Palmer's operation at Coal Creek and his new Walsen and El Moro Mines felt little of the competitive struggle that went on in the Denver Basin. They were too removed and too small. Palmer's greatest concern was maintaining ownership of his companies. Nevertheless, the Panic and labor strife elsewhere allowed him to reduce wages. More important for Palmer, the associated companies laid the groundwork for major coal development in the future and gave him the opportunity to dominate western coal mining when prosperity returned.

NOTES

1. Riegel, *Story of the Western Railroads*, 127; Arthur Cecil Bining and Thomas C. Cochran, *The Rise of American Economic Life* (New York: Charles Scribner's Sons, 1964), 411–412.

2. Brundage, *The Making of Western Labor Radicalism*, 11; United States Geological Survey, *Mineral Resources of the United States, 1882*, 47; "Fifth Report of the Board of Directors to the Stockholders and Bondholders for the Central Colorado Improvement Company, 1877–78," Collection #1057, Box #1, Folder #3, CF&I CRL; *History of the Union Pacific Coal Mines*, appendix.

3. Robert G. Athearn, "The Denver and Rio Grande and the Panic of 1873," *Colorado Magazine* 35, no. 2 (April 1958): 126, 128–129; Brayer, *William Blackmore*, 237; Klein, *Union Pacific: Birth of a Railroad*, 326; Maury Klein, *The Life and Legend of Jay Gould* (Baltimore: Johns Hopkins University Press, 1986), 149.

4. Trottman, *History of the Union Pacific*, 99–106; Klein, *Union Pacific: Birth of a Railroad*, 307; Riegel, *Story of the Western Railroads*, 161.

5. Klein, *Life and Legend of Jay Gould*, 67, 86, 99, 128, 143; Riegel, *Story of the Western Railroads*, 161.

6. Klein, *Union Pacific: Birth of a Railroad*, 311–312; Trottman, *History of the Union Pacific*, 105, 177.

7. *History of the Union Pacific Coal Mines*, 43, 180 (quote on 43); Trottman, *History of the Union Pacific*, 43–44; Klein, *Union Pacific: Birth of a Railroad*, 330.

8. *History of the Union Pacific Coal Mines*, 43; Trottman, *History of the Union Pacific*, 100; Klein, *Union Pacific: Birth of a Railroad*, 330.

9. Klein, *Union Pacific: Birth of a Railroad*, 330; U.S. Department of the Interior, Census Office, manuscript census, Sweetwater County and Uinta County, Wyoming, 1870.

10. W. A. May to S. R. Callaway, September 28, 1885, SG-2, S-1, Box 28, U.P. Archives, NSHS; D. O. Clark to Isaac H. Bromley, October 28, 1885, SG-2, S-1, Box 21, U.P. Archives, NSHS; Klein, *Union Pacific: Birth of a Railroad*, 482–483; *History of*

the Union Pacific Coal Mines, 92; Elizabeth Arnold Stone, *Uinta County: Its Place in History* (Laramie: Laramie Printing Co., 1924), 96.

11. *History of the Union Pacific Coal Mines*, 76–77; Klein, *Union Pacific: Birth of a Railroad*, 482–483.

12. *History of the Union Pacific Coal Mines*, 75–76, appendix; United States Geological Survey, *Mineral Resources of the United States, 1882*, 66–67.

13. *Rocky Mountain News*, January 18, 1871, January 4, 1872, November 10, November 11, 1874; United States Geological Survey, *Mineral Resources of the United States, 1882*, 47.

14. *Rocky Mountain News*, January 27, 1876, quote in April 7, 1877, April 1, 1885; Trottman, *History of the Union Pacific*, 120–121, 148, 155.

15. *Rocky Mountain News*, January 4, 1872, November 10, 1874, April 15, 1877, April 1, 1885.

16. Athearn, "The Denver and Rio Grande," 126; Brayer, *William Blackmore*, 241; "Second Annual Report of the Board of Directors of the Denver & Rio Grande Railway to the Stockholders for the Year 1873," Collection #49, Box #1, Colorado State Historical Society, Colorado Research Library, Denver, Colorado.

17. Scamehorn, *Pioneer Steelmaker*, 18; Athearn, "The Denver and Rio Grande," 122.

18. Brayer, *William Blackmore*, 236–237; Athearn, "The Denver and Rio Grande," 126; "The Central Colorado Improvement Co. Second Report of the Board of Directors to the Stockholders and Bondholders, 1874," 14, Collection #1057, Box #1, Folder #3, CF&I CRL.

19. Brayer, *William Blackmore*, 236–237; Athearn, "The Denver and Rio Grande," 126, 128–129; "The Central Colorado Improvement Co. Second Report," 14.

20. Wilkins, *Colorado Railroads*, 14, 19; Athearn, "The Denver and Rio Grande," 123, 129; Anderson, *General William J. Palmer*, 71; Athearn, *The Denver and Rio Grande Western Railroad*, 41; John S. Fisher, *A Builder of the West: The Life of General William Jackson Palmer* (Caldwell, Idaho: Caxton, 1939), 245–246.

21. Brayer, *William Blackmore*, 178; Scamehorn, *Pioneer Steelmaker*, 27.

22. Quote in Brayer, *William Blackmore*, 185; "The Central Colorado Improvement Co. Second Report," 14; Ross B. Johnson, *Coal Resources of the Trinidad Coal Field in Huerfano and Las Animas Counties, Colorado*, Geological Survey Bulletin 1112-E (Washington, D.C.: GPO, 1961), 131; Scamehorn, *High Altitude Energy*, 73.

23. Brayer, *William Blackmore*, 191; Scamehorn, *Pioneer Steelmaker*, 31; Athearn, *The Denver and Rio Grande Western Railroad*, 38–39; Fisher, *A Builder of the West*, 249–250; "First Report to the Stockholders of the Southern Colorado Coal and Town Co., 1878," 11, Collection #1057, Box #1, Folder #10, CF&I CRL.

24. Brayer, *William Blackmore*, 192; Scamehorn, *Pioneer Steelmaker*, 30.

25. Brayer, "History of Colorado Railroads," 650; Wilkins, *Colorado Railroads*, 14; Scamehorn, *Pioneer Steelmaker*, 29, 30; James T. Gardner, *Report upon the Southern Coal and Iron Fields of Colorado Territory* (Colorado Springs: Out West, 1875), 8, in Collection #1057, Box #1, Folder #16, CF&I CRL; William Wyckoff, *Creating Colorado: The Making of a Western American Landscape, 1860–1940* (New Haven: Yale University Press, 1999), 206.

26. Brayer, *William Blackmore*, 245–247.

27. Ibid., 248; Athearn, *The Denver and Rio Grande Western Railroad*, 46.

28. Athearn, *The Denver and Rio Grande Western Railroad*, 46; Riegel, *Story of the Western Railroads*, 134; Keith L. Bryant Jr., *History of the Atchison, Topeka and Santa Fe Railway* (Lincoln: University of Nebraska Press, 1974), 36–37; Wilkins, *Colorado Railroads*, 31; Brayer, "History of Colorado Railroads," 653–654.

29. Athearn, *The Denver and Rio Grande Western Railroad*, 65; Fisher, *A Builder of the West*, 249–250, 254; Athearn, "The Denver and Rio Grande," 136–138; "DRG Lease," *Engineering and Mining Journal* 26, no. 17 (October 26, 1878): 297.

30. Brayer, *William Blackmore*, 247.

31. United States Geological Survey, *Mineral Resources, 1882*, 47.

32. *Rocky Mountain News*, November 10, November 11, 1874, February 14, March 3, 1875; Suffern, *Coal Miners' Struggle*, 25–30.

33. *Rocky Mountain News*, November 11, 1874.

34. *Rocky Mountain News*, November 10, November 14, December 6, 1874.

35. Isham, *Rock Springs Massacre 1885*, 9; "Wages in the Anthracite Region," *Engineering and Mining Journal* 19, no. 11 (March 13, 1875): 166.

36. *Pueblo Chieftain*, March 10, 1875.

37. *Rocky Mountain News*, March 3, 1875, January 16, 1876; Scamehorn, *Pioneer Steelmaker*, 61.

38. *Rocky Mountain News*, August 22, 1875; Smith, *Once a Coal Miner*, 33; Emmons, Cross, and Eldridge, *Geology of the Denver Basin in Colorado*, 320–323.

39. *Rocky Mountain News*, March 27, April 7, 1877.

40. *Rocky Mountain News*, March 27, March 29, 1877.

41. *Rocky Mountain News*, April 1, 1877; quote in Suffern, *Coal Miners' Struggle*, 136.

42. *Rocky Mountain News*, quote in March 31, April 15, April 27, 1877.

43. *Rocky Mountain News*, April 15, April 17, 1877.

44. "Coal Items in Utah and Colorado," *Engineering and Mining Journal* 23 (April 28, 1877): 280; Long, *Where the Sun Never Shines*, 110; Kevin Kenny, *Making Sense of the Molly Maguires* (New York: Oxford University Press, 1998), 73–129.

45. *Rocky Mountain News*, April 15, April 17, April 20, 1877.

46. *Rocky Mountain News*, June 8, September 18, September 20, 1877, January 26, January 27, January 30, 1878.

47. *Rocky Mountain News*, January 26, January 27, March 23, 1878, December 21, 1879, March 28, April 1, 1885.

48. *Rocky Mountain News*, March 23, 1878; Ubbelohde, Benson, and Smith, *A Colorado History*, 155.

49. *Rocky Mountain News*, March 27, April 10, April 14, 1877; "Fifth Report of the Board of Directors to the Stockholders and Bondholders for the Central Colorado Improvement Company, 1877–78," 8, Collection #1057, Box #1, Folder #3, CF&I CRL.

50. *Pueblo Chieftain*, June 6, 1877; "Labor Notes," *Engineering and Mining Journal* 25, no. 23 (June 8, 1878): 395.

51. "Fifth Report of the Board of Directors," 8.

52. Suffern, *Coal Miners' Struggle*, 30.

53. Klein, *Union Pacific: Birth of a Railroad*, 331; Stone, *Uinta County*, 125–127.

54. Klein, *Union Pacific: Birth of a Railroad*, 330; U.S. Department of the Interior, Census Office, manuscript census, Sweetwater County and Uinta County, Wyoming, 1870.

55. Klein, *Union Pacific: Birth of a Railroad*, 330.

56. *History of the Union Pacific Coal Mines*, 47–48.

57. Isham, *Rock Springs Massacre 1885*, 9; ibid., 75–77; Rhode, *Booms & Busts on Bitter Creek*, 46; Cheyenne *Daily Leader*, November 18, 1875; Patrick J. Quealy to Frank Manley, March 16, 1917, Box HO 3, UPCCC.

58. Cheyenne *Daily Leader*, November 18, 1875; Omaha *Herald* quoted in Cheyenne *Daily Leader*, December 2, 1875; editorial, Cheyenne *Daily Leader*, November 5, 1875.

59. U.S. Department of the Interior, Census Office, manuscript census, Sweetwater County, Uinta County, and Carbon County, Wyoming, 1870.

60. Cheyenne *Daily Leader*, quote in November 5, November 10, November 18, 1875; Laramie *Daily Sentinel*, November 9, November 27, 1875; Klein, *Union Pacific: Birth of a Railroad*, 331–332; Klein, *Life and Legend of Jay Gould*, 152; Rhode, *Booms & Busts on Bitter Creek*, 46.

61. Isham, *Rock Springs Massacre 1885*, 10–12; Cheyenne *Daily Leader*, November 15, November 18, 1875; Laramie *Daily Sentinel*, November 6, November 12, 1875; John Jackson Clarke, "Reminiscences of Wyoming in the Seventies and Eighties," *Annals of Wyoming* 6 (July–October 1929): 228.

62. Cheyenne *Daily Leader*, November 18, 1875; Laramie *Daily Sentinel*, November 9, 1875.

63. *History of the Union Pacific Coal Mines*, 77–78; Rhode, *Booms & Busts on Bitter Creek*, 46–47; "Miners Strike in Wyoming," *Engineering and Mining Journal* 20, no. 24 (December 11, 1875): 576; Laramie *Daily Sentinel*, November 25, 1875; Cheyenne *Daily Leader*, December 2, 1875.

64. First quote in Klein, *Union Pacific: Birth of a Railroad*, 330–332; Klein, *Life and Legend of Jay Gould*, 152; Laramie *Daily Sentinel*, November 25, second quote in November 27, 1875; Cheyenne *Daily Leader*, December 2, 1875; "Report of the Union Pacific Railroad," *Engineering and Mining Journal* 23 (March 10, 1877): 157.

65. Ellis, "History of Carbon," 639; Laramie *Daily Sentinel*, November 6, 1875; Cheyenne *Daily Leader*, March 15, 1875.

66. *History of the Union Pacific Coal Mines*, 77.

67. Long, *Where the Sun Never Shines*, 202.

68. Laramie *Weekly Sentinel*, March 18, 1878; Cheyenne *Daily Sun*, March 16, 1878; Fletcher, "Labor Movement in Wyoming," 91.

69. *History of the Union Pacific Coal Mines*, appendix.

CHAPTER THREE

COAL MINING COMES OF AGE, 1878-1883

A S THE DEPRESSION OF THE 1870S WOUND DOWN, a new burst of industrial development came to the mountain West and the nation. Although the West had grown during the Panic of 1873, the explosive growth in the years after the Panic transformed the region. New industries opened, more railroads entered, and coal mining flourished. Speculators, settlers, and miners looked to the West for new opportunities. Land companies and railroads encouraged settlers to cross the hundredth meridian and take their chances in an area once thought unsuitable for agriculture, and a new metal rush brought more people to the Colorado mountains. The great Leadville silver boom in the late 1870s ignited a statewide boom, and other camps soon followed, including Aspen, Creede, and Silverton. Colorado's silver mines became the most productive in the nation, and by 1880 Leadville stood at the center of that boom, with 15,000 residents.[1]

Existing businesses and cities prospered with the new western boom, and towns along the railroads grew rapidly. Cheyenne claimed 1,450 residents in 1870 and 3,456 in 1880. The real growth, however, came in the early 1880s.

By 1890 the census recorded 11,690 people in Cheyenne. Even greater growth came to Colorado. Pueblo counted 3,217 residents in 1880 and 24,558 in 1890, and Denver's population rose from 35,629 in 1880 to 106,713 in 1890. Denver's explosive growth came from its multiple rail connections and its status as a regional service and supply center.[2]

Railroads flourished in this new economic environment. Whereas the Denver and Rio Grande (D&RG) fought to survive and struggled to expand during the depression, it gained a new lease on life when the downturn ended. In fact, the D&RG renewed its attempt to capture as much business as possible by building into the mountains and beyond. Similarly, Jay Gould's Union Pacific continued its aggressive push. Gould sought a western transportation monopoly, and to that end he bought and constructed new railroads. Other carriers also tried to exploit the region's opportunities. The Santa Fe continued to advance; the Chicago, Burlington and Quincy Railroad built into Denver from Nebraska; and the newly organized Denver and New Orleans began building south from Denver toward Texas.[3]

Naturally, as railroads advanced and towns boomed, coal mining expanded. Whereas Colorado's annual production had increased to over 100,000 tons during the Panic years, it exploded in the years that followed. In one year alone, 1882, the state's output grew by more than 50 percent over the previous year, yielding more than a million tons. As a result, new coalfields, companies, and mines opened throughout Colorado. Gould's Union Pacific mines already dominated Wyoming production, and they continued to expand in this new era of prosperity. Then, as Gould acquired more rail lines, he purchased more mines, gaining properties in Utah and Colorado. Together with the old locations, the Union Pacific operation reached an annual production of over a million tons in 1884. More than 2 million tons of coal were coming from the earth each year in Colorado and Wyoming; railroads consumed up to two-thirds of that output, and regional towns received the rest. The prosperity of the early 1880s radically and permanently altered the dimensions of the Rocky Mountain coal industry. But the economic expansion was uneven. Although many more coal miners came west, the companies did not want to share their newfound riches, and labor struggles again besieged the coalfields.[4]

GROWTH IN THE DENVER BASIN

In the late 1870s the Denver Basin mines were the first to experience the return of prosperity. Rail connections already existed in the area, and with expanding markets the mines were ready to produce. The recovery also brought new railroads and mines to the region. Two of the new rail lines were the Colorado Central and the Golden, Boulder and Caribou. The Colorado Central originally began construction out of Denver in 1870, with the intention of running lines west to the gold camps and north to Boulder, but it stalled because of the depression. It started building again in 1877, including a line through the Denver Basin coalfields. Once again, an insider capitalized on growth. Charles Welch, vice president of the railroad, leased coal lands in the basin along the path of the railroad. He opened what became known as the Welch Mine, five miles southwest of Erie. Welch moved aggressively, antici-pating selling his coal to the Colorado Central and on the Denver market. Soon he had what the *Rocky Mountain News* reported in September 1879 as the largest coal mine in the state, capable of producing 500 tons a day—more than double the amount of most other coal mines in the area.[5]

The return of prosperity also inspired Denver capitalists to build the Golden, Boulder and Caribou into the Denver Basin. David H. Moffat Jr., a key inves-tor and promoter of the Denver Pacific and the Boulder Valley lines, helped instigate this project. He held an interest in the Caribou silver mine above Boulder, and he wanted a railroad to supply it with coal. He also hoped to supply the burgeoning demand in Denver and Boulder. In March 1878 a six-mile line from Boulder to the Marshall coalfields opened. The Marshall Mine had operated sporadically throughout the 1860s and into the 1870s until it was reorganized as the Marshall Coal Mining Company in early 1878 with the anticipated arrival of the Golden, Boulder and Caribou Railroad. When the road arrived, the mine did well. Thanks to Moffat's influence, it gained a contract with the Kansas Pacific, and by 1879 it was producing one-fifth of the coal coming from northern Colorado. Hoping for similar success, other operators soon opened mines in the immediate area.[6]

The expanded coal-mining activity brought new coal camps to the Den-ver Basin. Around the Marshall Mine, in the valley of South Boulder Creek, the town of Marshall grew as an unplanned camp. With little company direc-tion, it resembled the pattern of other first-generation company towns such as Rock Springs and Coal Creek. As in these earlier locations, the company built a few houses and a store, but it did not dominate the community. At the Welch Mine, the town that developed looked more like the railroad town of Erie than it did a coal camp. Charles Welch apparently did not own the coal or the surface land. Instead he leased the land and the coal from a settler, David Kerr, who had acquired it through the Preemption Act years before. Welch initially paid Kerr a royalty for the coal he removed and eventually bought the vein but not the land. Since Welch had little control over the surface, he did not attempt to build a town.[7]

Nearby, the independent town of Louisville developed. A neighbor of Kerr's—Louis Nawatny—platted the town, sold the first lots, and named it after himself. Nawatny had apparently been in the area only since 1877, but he saw the potential of a town that sat between railroad tracks and a mine. Nawatny sold the first lots in late 1878, and by 1880 Louisville had 450 resi-dents, including 174 miners. The Welch company reportedly operated a store in the "early decades," but the town also had a variety of competing businesses. Like Erie, Louisville served as both a railroad town and a coal town, and the first residents settled closer to the tracks than to the mine.[8]

By 1879, mining in northern Colorado had settled around three centers: Erie, Louisville, and Marshall. Three mines operated near Marshall, one at Louisville, and as many as nine near Erie. From Erie in the northeast to the Marshall mines in the southwest, covering a distance of about eleven miles, the basic outline of production was set in this field. Other mines and towns opened, but these three locations were the pioneer centers. It was here that industrial mining first came to Colorado in 1872, and because of the Denver market and early railroad construction in the area, the region led Colorado in coal production until 1880—producing about 67 percent of the state's total output for that nine-year period. The renewed prosperity, however, undermined the Denver Basin's predominant position. As railroad companies built new lines south of Denver, the southern and central regions of the state soon dominated Colorado's coal business. Nevertheless, new coal mines and ownership groups continued to come to the Denver Basin in the early 1880s.[9]

THE TRAVAILS OF WILLIAM JACKSON PALMER

During the 1870s, William Jackson Palmer had been the preeminent developer of central and southern Colorado. But by the end of 1878 Palmer's position seemed to be in jeopardy and the future of his enterprises in doubt. Palmer had been forced to lease the Denver and Rio Grande to the operators of the Santa Fe, an action that threatened the operations of his associated development companies. The Central Colorado Improvement Company and the Southern Colorado Coal and Town Company depended on favorable railroad connections to prosper; and by 1878 these businesses had barely begun to operate, land sales had been limited, and coal sales remained meager. Prosperity arrived just in time for Palmer to save his enterprises.

Palmer lost control of his railroad in 1878, but that same year ushered in the nation's economic recovery. This transition undoubtedly emboldened Palmer to attempt to regain his railroad, and from the day he turned the line over to the Santa Fe, he sought to cancel the lease. Over the next two years he resorted to everything from litigation—claiming the Santa Fe had violated the lease—to armed intervention to recapture his railroad. Finally, in early 1880 the warring parties reached a compromise, and the Rio Grande gained its freedom from the Santa Fe.[10]

Palmer succeeded not only because of his own actions but also through the intervention of Jay Gould. Since acquiring the Union Pacific, Gould had pushed to consolidate all western railroads. By 1879 he had succeeded in merging the Union Pacific, the Kansas Pacific, and other Colorado roads. In an effort to further control Colorado traffic, Gould decided to help the Rio Grande in its struggle with the Santa Fe. Gould bought bonds, advanced cash, and reinvigorated the Rio Grande's management as he helped break the railroad free of the Santa Fe. Gould further intimidated the Santa Fe by threatening to parallel its rail lines with his own lines unless it left the Rio Grande alone. These actions helped make the Rio Grande an independent railroad once again. For his efforts, Gould and his interests gained two seats on the Rio Grande's board of directors, making Gould a sweeping presence in the mountain West.[11]

Although Palmer regained control of the railroad, his struggle with debt and the Rio Grande's lease to the Santa Fe signaled the beginning of what became a permanent separation of his coal operations from the parent railroad. The Central Colorado Improvement Company (CCI) and the Southern Colorado Coal and Town Company had been created to help support railroad operations, including mining coal, developing land, and acquiring railroad bonds to assist in construction. When the railroad began defaulting on its interest payments, the associated companies' close connection to the railroad caused them to suffer, too. The CCI depended on the railroad bond interest to help make its own debt payments, and when the railroad defaulted, CCI defaulted. Just as investors had challenged Palmer's control of the railroad, his direction of the associated companies could have also been threatened.[12]

Further problems for the associated companies accompanied the Santa Fe lease. The agreement stated that the Santa Fe would continue to handle coal from Palmer's companies at discounted rates. The Santa Fe, however, decided to use coal as a lever. It wanted to pool traffic with the Kansas Pacific and Union Pacific Railroads, and it refused to ship coal north to those lines until an agreement was reached. Although this had little practical effect on the two northern railroads, it did cause shipments of Cañon City and Trinidad coal to practically cease, hurting those operations. In addition, Palmer and his associates understood that with their railroad under lease, the Santa Fe would not enter the coal business, but in October 1878 the Santa Fe organized the Cañon City Coal Company with the full intent of competing with Palmer's coal operation.[13]

Palmer and his associates sought to stabilize the land and coal companies by reorganizing them. Out of the Central Colorado Improvement Company, the Southern Colorado Coal and Town Company, and the recently formed Colorado Coal and Steel Works Company, they formed the Colorado Coal and Iron Company in late 1879. This action provided three beneficial results. First, a new consolidated company allowed Palmer to cancel the old companies' outstanding bonds and issue new ones in exchange. This solved the problem of missed interest payments and removed the specter of default. Second, Palmer and the other primary investors wanted tighter control of operations. By including the Colorado Coal and Steel Works certificates in the swap, they could accomplish that goal. They held the company's stocks and bonds, and including its certificates in the exchange enhanced their holdings in the new company. And third, the operatives wanted to avoid losing land in southern Colorado, some of which had been acquired from the federal government through fraudulent activities. By transferring the titles, organizers of the new enterprise could claim they were innocent purchasers of any disputed claims and that the titles should be proved valid. The merger accomplished all three goals.[14]

The organizers also wanted to create a new industry and market for their resources. By 1879 they had constructed a number of coke ovens near El Moro in the Trinidad coalfield, and the product had become important to the growing silver-smelting business at Leadville and in Utah. But beyond just providing coke to these markets, Palmer envisioned a new integrated business for himself and Colorado. He planned to finally fulfill his dream of an iron and steelworks and to build a plant in Pueblo. He chose Pueblo because it had access to the necessary coke and to a recently acquired iron ore deposit. The timing seemed right for such a project. Prosperity had returned, and railroad construction was starting to flourish in the West; Palmer wanted to provide the rails. He believed these activities would stimulate the company's coal output while building a new industry.[15]

The Colorado Coal and Iron Company consolidated the operation of three coal mines: CCI's Coal Creek Mine and the El Moro and Walsen Mines of the Southern Colorado Coal and Town Company at Trinidad and Walsenburg, respectively. By the time of the takeover, the Coal Creek Mine was well established. It had produced for eight years, but its output had only begun to rise significantly in 1878 and 1879, reflecting the new era of prosperity. The mines at Trinidad and Walsenburg had only worked for two years before the corporate change in 1880, part of that time under the direction of a contractor. Nevertheless, the Southern Colorado Coal and Town Company had set the course of its coal operations.

In terms of community development, the camp at the Walsen Mine adjoined the town of Walsenburg. As the mine expanded, the town developed in two sections: the coal company's area, where it built some homes and facilities; and the independent town a little distance away, where a large number of men who worked in the mines lived and owned homes. In the Trinidad coalfield the Southern Colorado Coal and Town Company's coal camp next to the El Moro Mine took on a much different appearance. The mine was removed from the town of Trinidad and the railroad community of El Moro. While the contractors—Hunt and Allen—operated it, little community development took place, only mine work; but under the direction of the Southern Colorado Coal and Town Company (and then the Colorado Coal and Iron Company), this situation changed. The camp became known as Engleville,

3.1 Walsen, Colorado, a coal town originally developed by the Colorado Coal and Iron Company near Walsenburg in 1878. The company expanded the mine and town over the years, and it became a substantial community as seen in this circa 1910 photo. Courtesy, Colorado Historical Society X5014, Welborn Collection.

or more generally Engle, after its first prominent mine superintendent, George Engle. Under his skilled direction the camp of Engle became the first nearly complete coal company town in Colorado. The company built most of the structures—laying them out in an orderly grid pattern—and opened a company store.[16]

Engleville differed greatly from Palmer's other mine camps. Coal Creek had little direction and grew up mostly free of company control. The Walsen Mine abutted the independent town of Walsenburg, and the company paid little attention to it. At Engleville, it developed a full company town. Three reasons explain these differences: the timing of the development, the need for workers, and the director of the operations. First, Engleville came to life in the era of renewed prosperity, and an ever-increasing demand for coke kept the mines busy. In September 1878 the *Engineering and Mining Journal* reported that the company was producing 100 tons of coal a day and had fifteen coke ovens in operation, and that was just the beginning. Second, the increasing demand meant miners were in short supply. Attracting and keeping miners

3.2 *Walsen Mine tunnel entrance as it appeared circa 1910.* Courtesy, *Colorado Historical Society* X6654, *Mazzulla Collection.*

concerned management at the time because several new coal mines were opening in the region, and the expanding metal mines at Leadville continually attracted workers. Consequently, the company housing at Engleville was designed to lure and retain men in southern Colorado. And third, George Engle played a critical role. As a trained civil engineer who would be involved at the location for years, he heavily influenced the creation of Colorado's first company town. He understood that the housing could not only attract workers but could bring order and stability to the community. Engle's activities exemplified a maturing business philosophy within the western coalfields.[17]

By forming the Colorado Coal and Iron Company, Palmer and his associates were prepared to advance when prosperity returned. The steel plant at South Pueblo—known as the Bessemer Works—began production in early 1882, but the Denver and Rio Grande Railway was still the key. It connected all of their dreams: it carried the coal, the iron ore, and the finished products, and it opened the mountains for development they hoped to coordinate. Once Palmer regained control of his railroad, he feverishly built lines, not only to expand its reach but also to capture markets before other railroads arrived. Beginning in 1880 he constructed lines to Leadville for the silver mining, south into New Mexico for the Santa Fe trade, down to Durango for the San Juan business, and then west across the mountains—reaching Utah in 1882.

In the process, Palmer and his associates organized another railroad to build the Utah section, the Denver and Rio Grande Western Railway Company, known as "the Western." By 1884 the Colorado portion of Palmer's railroad empire measured 1,679 miles, compared with 346 in 1880.[18]

The Rio Grande's advance dramatically expanded the demand for coal. The railroad consumed more, and it opened new markets, especially in the new silver areas. In addition, the expanding cities and newly connected locations caused domestic demand to increase. From 1879 to 1883, the Colorado Coal and Iron Company's production went from a little over 120,000 tons to nearly 600,000 tons a year. And the coal company achieved this growth primarily by expanding output at its three existing mines at Cañon City, Walsenburg, and Trinidad. The company did open two new mines known as Oak Creek #1 and #2 at its Cañon City site in 1881. Also, when the railroad crossed the mountains, it gave the coal company access to coal seams in central Colorado and on the Western Slope. The company opened its first mine outside the Front Range in 1881 at Crested Butte, but output there remained small in the early 1880s.[19]

Despite the significant advance in production and an increase in the number of miners the company employed, the Colorado Coal and Iron Company did not modify its coal towns to resemble Engleville. Its Annual Reports do not indicate construction of new company-owned homes. For the most part, the newly arriving men and their families chose where they wished to live. When the Oak Creek mines opened, a new town known as Williamsburg developed next to the coal camp of Coal Creek. Williamsburg grew off of company property and consequently developed as a completely independent town. Crested Butte existed before the railroad and coal company arrived, allowing it to function independent of coal company control. The only innovations the company made during this era involved the operation of company stores. The Colorado Coal and Iron Company first reported returns from company stores in 1881.[20]

Palmer's rapid expansion did not yield the markets or success he had anticipated. Rather, he had pushed his railroad's finances to the limits once again, and by the fall of 1883 his fortunes started to sour. This failing reflected the boom-and-bust nature of the western economy coinciding with a regional downturn. Palmer's first problem came with a slowing of the silver boom. Although silver production remained high, the era of speculative growth ended, dampening what had been a lucrative market. Then, when Palmer's railroads finally reached Ogden in 1883 and could compete directly with the Union Pacific, the latter initiated a rate war that further hurt revenue. These difficulties again brought financial distress to the Rio Grande. Investors and the board of directors expressed intense concern over the railroad's expansion and financial status. Under increasing pressure, Palmer resigned as president of his

3.3 Main Street, Williamsburg, Colorado. Williamsburg in the Cañon City coalfield developed as an independent town in 1882. It grew over the years as coal companies expanded nearby operations, and it sat among the coal camps of Coal Creek and Rockvale. Courtesy, Denver Public Library, Western History Collection X-14161.

railroad in 1883, with New York capitalist Frederick Lovejoy as his successor. Feeling wronged, Palmer later lashed out at those who had forced his resignation. He said their interests were "purely wild and speculative," and he particularly blamed those investors also associated with the Union Pacific.[21]

Palmer's ouster ended his career with the Rio Grande and completely separated the operations of the Colorado Coal and Iron Company from the railroad it once supported. Those who forced Palmer from the Rio Grande presidency claimed ironically that Palmer's outside activities interfered with his running of the railroad. In particular, they claimed his interests, such as the Colorado Coal and Iron Company, took precedence over the Denver and Rio Grande. In reality, the reverse was probably true, but still, the companies had been mutually dependent. Through all of the expansion, the railroad relied on the coal company's product not only as fuel, but it shipped more coal than any other product. The two companies also had a mutually beneficial contract. When the railroad bought coal, it paid a dollar a ton for Walsenburg and El Moro coal and two dollars for the Cañon City product. In both cases the Rio Grande paid little above the actual cost of mining. In return the Rio Grande guaranteed to ship coal for the Colorado Coal and Iron Company at the best possible rates. The splitting of the companies eliminated this mutually beneficial alliance.[22]

Just as Palmer lost control of his Colorado railroad, his operation of the Colorado Coal and Iron Company became troubled. Since its formation in 1880, the company's fortunes had been mixed. Coal and coke sales had been highly profitable since the beginning. These earnings alone paid interest on the bonds and helped underwrite construction of the steel plant at Pueblo. The Bessemer plant produced its first steel in 1882, but the realities of western steel manufacture soon became evident. It cost more to acquire the necessary fuel, labor, and ores in the West than it did in the East. The steel mill could not produce rails at a price that could compete with the eastern product. The regional economic problems in 1883 depressed the iron and steel market further, and in 1884 the mill closed. Early in its history, the steel plant became a drain on the coal operations.[23]

Adding to his concerns, Palmer soon began to clash with the new management of the Rio Grande. The fight began when Lovejoy announced a sharp rise in freight rates. Palmer protested that the escalation violated the contract between the two companies, but Lovejoy defended his actions by stating that the Coal and Iron Company had not only received special rates under the old administration but had also received a rebate. For every six dollars the coal company paid in freight rates, it was given more than five dollars back as part of the rebate. This, Lovejoy argued, brought a heavy loss to the railroad. Also, he did not believe raising the rates violated the contract. After all, it specified a favorable price for shipping coal but not the exact rate the coal company would be charged.[24]

Palmer protested. He knew the most recent contract only promised the best freight rates, but he pointed out that previous contracts signed with the CCI and the Southern Colorado Coal and Town Company had specified set rates. He argued that Lovejoy's actions violated those contracts and that under Lovejoy the railroad was delivering kegs of nails from the East to Salt Lake City for 95 cents per keg, whereas the Coal and Iron Company had to pay $1.45 for the same haul. Palmer contended that this practice violated the contractual guarantee of comparable low rates for his firm. Lovejoy countered that it did not violate the contract, since one was a "through freight" rate and the other was a local rate.[25]

Palmer attempted to apply economic pressure on Lovejoy. Knowing that the Colorado Coal and Iron Company provided about a quarter of the railroad's freight receipts, Palmer began taking his business elsewhere. When possible he shipped freight north to Denver over the new Denver and New Orleans

Railroad. The Rio Grande responded in kind by refusing to haul the coal company's products to Utah.[26]

Palmer was certainly concerned about the higher freight rates cutting into his coal company's revenues, but some observers speculated that the fight constituted a power struggle between Palmer and the new operators of the Rio Grande Railroad. The *Rocky Mountain News* surmised that Palmer wanted to frighten railroad stockholders into believing Colorado shippers would avoid the Rio Grande unless they deposed Lovejoy and returned Palmer to control. On the other hand, the *Engineering and Mining Journal* speculated that Lovejoy might be trying to gain control of the Coal and Iron Company. To confuse the matter further, a faction of the coal company's board of directors wanted a committee to investigate whether Palmer and others in the organization had closed mines and other facilities to make it appear as if the Rio Grande was discriminating against them.[27]

When a national panic erupted in the spring of 1884, the fight proved particularly painful, costing both companies more lost business and money. The Rio Grande, already in trouble, found itself unable to meet payroll or bond interest payments. In July 1884 the bondholders applied to the U.S. Circuit Court in Denver for a receivership. The judge agreed and appointed William S. Jackson, former treasurer of the railroad, as receiver. As a friend of the Colorado Coal and Iron Company, Jackson promised better relations. But it was too late for Palmer. Ironically, at the Colorado Coal and Iron Company's annual meeting in April 1884, a group stepped forward—including several investors from the Rio Grande—to blame Palmer for the coal company's problems. They stated that the optimistic statements that had appeared in Annual Reports had "failed to produce the promised results." They voted Palmer and his associates off the board. Harry Sprague replaced Palmer as president of the Colorado Coal and Iron firm.[28]

The positions seemed reversed. The eastern investors who had removed Palmer from the Rio Grande presidency placed one of his supporters in charge of the bankrupt railroad. Indeed Jackson would become president of the line when it was reorganized in 1886. He brought aggressive leadership to the railroad and understood local problems. Sprague, as the new president of the Colorado Coal and Iron Company, however, knew little about managing a western coal operation. He was an eastern investor who came west with the idea that he could run the company more effectively and make his investment prosper. Sprague found nothing but frustration.[29]

When Sprague took control of the coal company, he made it his mission to find out where the company had gone wrong, see where money had been wasted, and correct the situation. To this end he hired Charles Rolker, a mining engineer, to investigate the holdings of the Colorado Coal and Iron Company and make recommendations for repair. Rolker gave a mixed review.

Reporting in June 1884, he stated that the company had secured the "cream" of Colorado coal properties, and the business looked promising. On the other hand, he pointed out what Sprague should have already known: that, in essence, the iron and steel operations in Pueblo could not compete with eastern works. He believed the company would have to rely on the coal and coke business to carry it.[30]

Frustrations dogged the first years of Sprague's administration. The downturn continued through 1884 and 1885. The steelworks barely operated, and the company's performance backed up Rolker's forecast. The coal and coke business turned a profit, but the iron and steelworks seldom operated because of an inability to make money. To save money, Sprague decided to evaluate the wages paid miners. He concluded that the men in Cañon City made too much, and he ordered a wage cut in October 1884.[31]

Sprague also wanted to resolve the close connections that existed between the coal company and the railroad. He hoped to separate the financial ties between the two, but with mutual investors he found the goal difficult to achieve. As well, he learned just how connected the two companies were. The coal company still held Denver and Rio Grande bonds, and as the railroad defaulted on interest payments in 1884, the coal company lost more money. Then when the railroad workers went on strike in 1885, the company suffered for lack of haulage. But Sprague did make a breakthrough: he managed to gain a traffic agreement not only with the Rio Grande system but also with the Union Pacific that allowed coal and coke to be distributed throughout the West. Nevertheless, Colorado Coal and Iron continued to struggle through the downturn of 1884 and 1885.[32]

THE ATCHISON, TOPEKA AND SANTA FE ENTERS THE COAL BUSINESS

While the Colorado Coal and Iron Company went through expansion and managerial upheaval, a formidable competitor entered Colorado's central and southern coalfields. Just as the Engleville mines began to produce in 1878, the Atchison, Topeka and Santa Fe arrived in Trinidad. The railroad came to Trinidad with the intent of outmaneuvering the Rio Grande and building over Raton Pass to reach the New Mexico market. It succeeded at that venture, but it also wanted to exploit the rich coalfields at the northern base of Raton Pass. In fact, coal was so important to the Santa Fe that when it lost control of the Rio Grande it built another line from Pueblo to the Cañon City coalfields—paralleling the D&RG—with the primary intent of gaining coal traffic.[33]

Unlike the Rio Grande promoters who moved well in advance of the railroad to acquire coal lands, private coal entrepreneurs knew of the Santa Fe's actions and opened coal mines as the railroad neared. At Trinidad, a number of small companies began working coal ground six miles south of

Engleville in the lower reaches of Raton Pass. The Santa Fe initially cooperated with these local operators, contracting with W. G. Riffenburg to furnish coal to the road in September 1878. Six months later the Santa Fe decided to enter the coal business, and it joined with A. G. Starks and J. E. Wicks to charter the Trinidad Coal and Mining Company. In 1881 the company reorganized as Trinidad Coal and Coking Company, with the Santa Fe's William B. Strong as president.[34]

Unlike the Rio Grande coal companies, the Trinidad Coal and Coking Company apparently had no contract with the Santa Fe that gave it preferential rates for coal shipments; and unlike the Union Pacific, the Santa Fe did not want a monopoly. The railroad was interested in maximum railroad traffic. It wanted to haul other companies' coal to market, without prejudice. For Strong and the Santa Fe, the coal business provided the opportunity to put a product on freight cars heading east that otherwise would have been empty. Their coal company did, however, have a distinct advantage. The railroad used its product, promoted the fuel in the commercial markets of Kansas, and provided the resources to build coke ovens. When the Santa Fe reached the Cañon City coalfields in 1880, it took similar steps. The road acquired coal lands, and its previously formed auxiliary, the Cañon City Coal Company, began producing coal.[35]

Loosely configured coal camps formed around the Santa Fe coal mines. At the Trinidad mine the town of Starkville developed, and at Cañon City the camp of Rockvale grew. In terms of organization, these camps resembled the earlier Union Pacific operations; the Santa Fe did not attempt to develop full company towns. At Starkville, the railroad took over an existing operation and shared the town with other area coal companies. The Trinidad Coal and Coking Company added some housing, again to attract key workers, but little else. A few years after opening, a local observer stated that Starkville contained thirty-five houses—seventeen owned by the company—and a large number of "dug-outs." In central Colorado the town of Rockvale sat just west of Coal Creek. The first arrivals hurriedly built shacks, with some miners settling a little distance away from the mine on the banks of Oak Creek. Some miners built houses, with the company adding about ten more. Neither Starkville nor Rockvale apparently had a company store, but several private businesses opened to meet the miners' needs.[36]

Directly connected to the Santa Fe Railroad, the mines of the Trinidad Coal and Coking Company and the Cañon City Coal Company did not experience the ownership or managerial turmoil the Colorado Coal and Iron mines endured. The Santa Fe mines had the advantage of serving a transcontinental carrier, much like the Union Pacific's situation. The opening of the Santa Fe mines and the expansion of Colorado Coal and Iron's operations in central and southern Colorado caused production to expand rapidly.

3.4 Parts of Starkville, Colorado. The coal mines around Starkville opened with the arrival of the Santa Fe Railroad in 1880. Starkville contained a variety of structures and living environments, reflecting the diversity of southern Colorado. The Colorado Fuel and Iron Company acquired the mines here in 1896. Courtesy, Colorado Historical Society A863, Aultman Collection.

Beginning in 1880, more coal came out of central and southern mines than was mined in the Denver Basin. By 1883 the pattern of coal production in Colorado had been established. The southern part of the state produced the most coal, with Engleville and Starkville combining for over 400,000 tons a year and Walsenburg yielding nearly 88,000. The Cañon City mines in the central division followed with 280,000 tons annually, and the Denver Basin mines trailed with just over 222,000. By 1883 the Colorado Coal and Iron and Santa Fe mines had become the dominant operations, accounting for nearly all reported production in the central and southern regions of the state. Coal mining had come of age in Colorado.[37]

GOULD EXPANDS THE UNION PACIFIC

As the Rio Grande and Santa Fe became competitors in the years after the Panic of 1873, Jay Gould attempted to capture all western rail traffic. Through construction and consolidation, he acquired several new lines for the Union Pacific in the late 1870s and early 1880s—including the Oregon Short Line, which connected the Union Pacific to the Northwest and the Pacific Ocean. Gould also tried to obtain any Colorado road that might be a competitor. He gained control of the Kansas Pacific, the Denver Pacific, the Colorado Central, and the Denver, South Park and Pacific. By 1880 the Colorado Central extended from Golden to Cheyenne, crossing through the Denver Basin coalfield and then into the mountains, reaching Georgetown and Central City. The Denver, South Park and Pacific eventually connected Denver to Leadville.[38]

Through loans and stock purchases, Gould also hoped to acquire the Denver and Rio Grande. Although his investment helped save the line from Santa Fe control, Gould was never able to purchase enough of the road to make Palmer follow his dictates. Indeed in the 1880s the Union Pacific and the Rio Grande fought openly over traffic. Nevertheless, Gould had put together an impressive rail system. Before he took control of the Union Pacific, the road had a little over a thousand miles of track; by 1884 the system measured over 5,500 miles.[39]

Gould wanted to control rail transport in the mountain West, but he also hoped for an ever-expanding fuel monopoly—one that would extend from the Pacific Coast through Nebraska. With a much larger railroad, he needed to open new mines to meet the demand; and as the railway expanded, he wanted to acquire any coal mines that might defy his plans for a monopoly. To meet the first challenge, the Coal Department opened seven new mines at its three coal camps in Wyoming between 1879 and 1884. To eliminate competitors and find more fuel for the domestic market, the company began leasing and buying coal mines in Colorado and Utah. None of these mines produced the large tonnages of the Wyoming operations, but they seemed necessary as the railroad sought complete control.[40]

The acquisitions in Colorado included five mines in two different areas: three in the Denver Basin and two in the mountains near Leadville at Como. The railroad had gained access to the Denver Basin coalfield when it took control of the Colorado Central and the Denver Pacific. The Welch Mine at Louisville and the Boulder Valley Mine at Erie had been the main suppliers of these northern Colorado rail lines. After acquiring the railroads, buying their fuel suppliers seemed the next logical step in Gould's plan. Prior to his arrival, these mines had operated independent of the railroads. Consequently, Gould began purchasing them in 1879 and put them under the connecting railroads' direction. For instance, the Welch Mine came under the control of the Colorado Central. Gould also purchased coal mines at Como and Baldwin along his newly completed Denver, South Park and Pacific Railroad. Then, to gain better control of the scattered Colorado coal locations, in 1883 the Union

Pacific formed a new company—the Union Coal Company—to manage them. With a number of new mines, the Union Pacific's coal operations produced close to a million tons of coal in 1883. Of this, 35 percent went to commercial sales, and the railroad consumed the remainder. Still, even with such large production, the 1883 Annual Report claimed demand exceeded the company's supply.[41]

Gould's drive for railroad supremacy seemed wise, as it ensured the strength of the Union Pacific. Some acquisitions helped the Union Pacific, such as the Oregon Short Line; others, however, were unwise. The Kansas Pacific held little value for the Union Pacific. In reality, Gould had reverted to his old trick of manipulating securities. He had personally purchased the Kansas Pacific's nearly worthless securities, pushed up their value, and then had the Union Pacific absorb the line. The Union Pacific did not need this road, but Gould profited handsomely. In another example of Gould's machinations, he purchased the Denver, South Park and Pacific when its connections to the silver districts looked promising. When silver faltered, he pushed the road on the Union Pacific in 1881, knowing it would generate no profit for the parent road. Later, after Gould's withdrawal from the Union Pacific, railroad officials expressed dismay over the way their company had acquired the South Park. Board members called it suspicious and said the South Park was a "serious drag upon the company." Gould, however, did very well from the transaction.[42]

By 1884 Gould had taken full advantage of the increased value of Union Pacific securities and had sold most of his stock to the public. This ended his influence over the road. The change forced the Union Pacific directors to search for new direction, and they chose Charles Francis Adams Jr. as president in May 1884. Great-grandson and grandson of the nation's second and sixth presidents, respectively, Charles saw railroading as his key to success. Prior to becoming president of the railroad, he had served on the Massachusetts Board of Railroad Commissioners and as a government director for the Union Pacific. As a railroad expert and reformer, Adams wanted to transform what he saw as a poorly run and corrupt operation into a modern transportation system. Because Gould had made the railroad's stock attractive, average investors had become the primary owners. Adams saw himself as the trustee for those stockholders, and he wanted to protect their interests.[43]

Adams, however, encountered a multitude of problems: a large debt carried over from construction and expansion; declining traffic because of new transcontinental competition from such roads as the Southern Pacific and the Atchison, Topeka and Santa Fe; a hostile federal government, demanding that more funds be repaid to Washington; a negative public image because the railroad had abused its monopoly by overcharging; and hostile labor relations, especially in the coal mines.[44]

LABOR RELATIONS DURING THE GROWTH

By the end of the Panic in 1877, every coal miner in the West had experienced some hardship. Most had suffered a wage cut. Drawn to the mines by the promise of high wages, the workers saw these wages fall from highs of $1.50 per ton to lows of 75 cents. Others lost their jobs. In Wyoming, the Union Pacific replaced traditional British miners with Chinese as it sought wage reductions and better worker control. But the Denver Basin mines, as well as those at Carbon, Wyoming, remained centers of solidarity and worker resistance. Nevertheless, as the depression of the 1870s wound down and new mines began to open, wages remained depressed. New miners could at best expect 75 cents a ton, with those at Engleville making only 50 cents.[45]

Prosperity changed this scenario. Although the mines at Louisville and Engleville opened with low wages in 1877, the growth in the years after forced the wage scale up. Labor became less available as mines opened at Walsenburg, Starkville, Rockvale, Marshall, and along the Union Pacific. Whereas about 600 coal miners had worked the western mines in 1875, more than 3,000 were counted in 1884. Among these, more Chinese came to the Rock Springs and Almy mines, increasing in number from a little over 100 to about 500 in 1880. Elsewhere, traditional miners from the British Isles continued to arrive. Colorado's largest mine, the Welch at Louisville, had 174 miners in 1880—of whom 87, or 50 percent, were from the British Isles. Those born in the United States numbered 30, or 17.2 percent of the workforce. Similarly, in Trinidad men from the British Isles still constituted a slight majority—44 of 86—among the miners. This ethnic mix contrasted starkly with Colorado's statewide data. Only 10.3 percent of the state's 1880 population had been born in the British Isles, and 79.5 percent of the population was native-born. Much like the situation when the first coal mines opened in the West, many of the mines that opened during this second wave of expansion relied on men with traditional mining skills.[46]

The newly arriving coal miners and those who had persevered through the hard times in the western coalfields understood the labor dynamics that came with the new expansion. The growth of coal mining put miners in short supply. Plus, other industries drew miners out of the coal mines; railroad construction and silver mining, for example, required large workforces. With these conditions, the coal miners soon wanted a wage advance, one that reflected their status as craftsmen and acknowledged their product's social value. The coal companies probably understood the new dynamics also, but they would not voluntarily adjust wages. Palmer and his associates were preoccupied, attempting to end the Santa Fe's lease of the Rio Grande and trying to strengthen their fuel business. The Union Pacific's Coal Department remained confident that the company's use of Chinese workers would prevent any wage demands. Although the Union Pacific's racial diversification stopped potential problems, Palmer and the other Colorado mine owners had a more difficult time subduing their more obdurate workforce.

Colorado labor troubles began in late 1879, just as production began to explode, and they started over a traditional miner prerogative: the decision of who should work in the mines. The difficulties arose at the newly opened coal deposit at Como. It sat in the high mountain valley of South Park, southwest of Denver; and the Denver, South Park and Pacific reached it in 1879 and wanted to exploit it. In a tight labor market, the company undoubtedly used the often-tried tactic of offering the highest wages necessary to attract a crew that could develop the mine. Once accomplished, the wages would be driven down. The South Park managers turned to Chinese workers. Some of the men may have come to the South Park area earlier to work the placer mines, but Jay Gould brought more. He owned part of the construction company building the road, which employed Chinese. Once construction was finished, they became available for coal mine work. Whites at the mine struck in protest, and although there may have been racist overtones, the *Rocky Mountain News* claimed the debate was about employing "cheap labor." Nevertheless, the displaced workers protested, and miners at Coal Creek and in the Denver Basin walked off the job in a show of support.[47]

Although the miners along the Front Range initially struck in solidarity with the Como men and to make a statement about Chinese labor, the men at Coal Creek and those in northern Colorado soon changed direction. They decided to exploit their new market strength, and they turned the strike into an effort to gain a wage advance. In a time of prosperity, the workers could go on the offensive. They knew the Chinese workers did not directly threaten them. Anti-Chinese sentiment ran rampant along the Colorado Front Range, and operators would meet strong resistance from miners—and from Colorado residents in general—if they tried to introduce Chinese into the coal mines there.[48]

Hence the employment of Chinese at Como became a moot issue as the Coal Creek and Denver Basin men pushed for more money. The strikers at Coal Creek felt confident enough not only to ask for more pay but also to fully implement the notion of receiving the full social value of their product. They demanded that wages be based on a sliding scale, with miners receiving more per ton as production increased. The men probably knew they would not receive such an agreement, but the request may have been a bargaining tactic. After a few days, a workers' committee met with the managers of the Coal Creek mines and agreed to a 10-cent-per-ton raise. In the Denver Basin the men went even further and asked for an increase from the current $1.00 to $1.25 per ton of coal. Several mines such as the Boulder Valley initially refused the demand, claiming railroads would not tolerate such an advance. But with other companies accepting the terms, all mines eventually acceded. Beyond their concern for railroad customers, the operators knew they could not be out of the commercial market in Denver for any length of time and maintain their market share. The competitive market forces in Denver prevented coal companies from closing operations.[49]

The 1879 strike was brief because of a number of factors. These coal mines were the oldest in the state and hence had the longest heritage of worker cooperation. Despite earlier efforts to disrupt the solidarity with replacement workers, the locations maintained a solid core of miners steeped in the work culture. In fact, coal companies had recently introduced Italians into the Erie mines in an attempt to weaken solidarity, but such efforts were to no avail as the Italians stood fast with the rest of the miners. The miners at Erie and Coal Creek also had the most experience with unionization of any Colorado coal miners. They had formed locals of the Miners' National Association in 1873, and when the organization folded at the national level, the Erie miners organized the first Knights of Labor Assembly in Colorado in August 1878.[50]

Despite the success of miners at Coal Creek and in the Denver Basin, the 1879 strike was not a rousing victory for organized labor in other Colorado mines. Not only did Chinese workers remain at Como, the Colorado Coal and Iron Company used the strike to thwart labor activism and introduce replacement workers elsewhere. Although Palmer granted a small wage advance at Coal Creek and at the recently opened Walsenburg mines, he made no changes at Engleville in southern Colorado. Plus, Palmer apparently had a plan to defeat any demand for an increase.

The favorable settlement at Coal Creek inspired the Engleville miners to walk off the job asking for more money. Instead of bargaining, the company fired several men and replaced them with Hispanic workers. The old miners did not go quietly, however. The *Engineering and Mining Journal* reported that a "melee ensued" when the discharged workers confronted the new men and that more trouble was anticipated. The *Journal* reported no further violence, however, and Palmer declared in the Annual Report that the company's "prompt" actions had maintained wages at fifty cents a ton for the Engleville Mine. His report further illustrated the company's truly exploitative nature. Colorado Coal and Iron mandated that a miner must produce 2,400 pounds of coal to receive credit for a ton. The extra 400 pounds was supposed to account for unusable material found in the coal, but the company's report declared that there was no waste—"all slack and screenings being sent to coke ovens." Palmer and his company obtained extra profit at the men's expense; that action made real wages about forty-three cents a ton.[51]

The introduction of Hispanic miners at Engleville brought a new variable to labor relations in southern Colorado. Although Palmer and his associates employed few initially, Hispanics made up about 10 percent of the workforce in 1880 and their availability made them an implicit threat. Both Trinidad and Walsenburg had formed around Hispanic villages. Farming and ranching had been the basis of their existence, but with the arrival of the mines, the relatively higher pay drew some Hispanics. They did not, however, rely on mining as a livelihood. Mining's seasonal nature gave them time for farming and ranching in the summer, and the close proximity of the mines allowed for mining in the winter. By 1885 the number of Hispanics employed at Engleville had increased to about 60 in a workforce of 200, or 30 percent. Plus, Colorado Coal and Iron had begun employing Hispanics at Walsenburg.[52]

Much as Gould and the Union Pacific had done in the coalfields of southern Wyoming, Palmer and his associates established a racial and cultural separation between their company's coal towns. At Coal Creek they maintained a traditional workforce, with a majority of miners from the British Isles. The Union Pacific also had one camp with a strong British influence—Carbon, Wyoming. This characteristic caused both locations to have tendencies to organize and to resist company dictates. In southern Colorado Palmer hired Hispanic workers first as strikebreakers, and he enjoyed the fact that they restrained other miners from striking. In a similar fashion, Gould placed Chinese miners in western Wyoming. Neither Palmer nor Gould attempted to place the new coal diggers in all their mines. Landownership undoubtedly deterred some Hispanics from moving elsewhere, but a general hostility toward hiring Hispanics and Chinese as replacement workers also played a part. Just as anti-Chinese sentiment ran high, the advancing white population was often hostile toward the resident Mexican Americans. Trinidad recorded a serious white-Hispanic riot prior to the arrival of coal mining. Keeping the Hispanics and Chinese localized away from major white population centers made sense to company managers. Hence the Union Pacific placed its Chinese miners in Rock Springs and Almy, and Colorado Coal and Iron used Hispanic miners at Walsenburg and Trinidad.[53]

Further, the companies could not necessarily count on the new workers to always do as they wanted, so they continued to employ some traditional miners. Again, the Chinese miners in Wyoming could be as independent as the white miners they replaced. Similarly, the Hispanic miners did not enter coal mining joyfully. As Victor Clark reported in his study *Mexican Labor in the United States*, published in 1909, the coal companies found Hispanic laborers to be "irregular"; they "could not be relied upon to turn out the same amount every day." The mine managers hesitated to count solely on Hispanic miners, claiming instead that they made "good reserve labor, for emergencies and odd jobs." This did not mean the Hispanics were poor workers, but mining was of secondary importance to them. As Clark notes, the Hispanic laborers "usually own a cabin and a small piece of land within walking distance of the camp, or within a day's journey, and therefore are more independent of regular wages."[54] Some traditional miners at Coal Creek also worked the land, but they did so

more as a supplement to their wages. They survived on their wages from digging coal and farmed as a hobby, the opposite of the Hispanic workers. The
Coal Creek miners were thus much more conscious of wage changes.[55]

By 1880 vast wage differences existed from north to south in Colorado.
Miners in the Denver Basin received $1.25 per ton of coal produced, those at
Cañon City earned $1.00, and the men in the southern coalfield were paid
$0.50. Exploitation of Hispanic labor does not alone explain these dramatic
differences. The nature of the coal vein determined in part how much a miner
received. The Coal Creek and Walsen Mines had narrow seams, impurities,
and soft tops. The Walsenburg seam spanned only 3 feet, 3 inches. The miners
were responsible for eliminating the waste and keeping the top solid; this
required time and cut into the amount of coal they could mine. A narrow
seam also required more agility and skill to work. Good miners only removed
usable material, and a 3-foot vein meant they would have to crawl in the work
space. Most diggers, especially the inexperienced, preferred a big vein where
they could stand. The coal at Engleville varied from 10 to 12 feet thick, whereas
mines in the Denver Basin varied from 3 to 12 feet, averaging about 6 feet.
With more difficult mining conditions, miners wanted more pay per ton.[56]

The mines in the Denver Basin were not the most difficult to work in
Colorado, yet these miners still received the highest tonnage rate in 1880.
The high wages can be attributed to three factors: competition among the
mines, the living situation, and the history of labor activism. First, by 1880
at least twelve mines worked this coalfield, most operating independently.
They sold coal to the railroads, but the commercial market was very important, especially in Denver. Competition among operators prevented them from
leaving the market for a long time to break a strike, and the workers benefited.
Second, many workers lived in homes they owned. As demonstrated in the
1872 strike, ownership gave the men and their wives a strong incentive to
fight for what they saw as justice. And third, these miners had a history of
labor activism. Not only did they bring their traditions with them to Colorado, but they had formed local unions as early as 1872. Their backgrounds
and activities helped spawn a movement culture that remained strong in the
Denver Basin.[57]

The mine at Engleville had all the qualities that allowed the Colorado
Coal and Iron Company to keep wages low. The thick seam of coal meant it
could employ less experienced miners. As a new mine it had no history of
labor activism, although some miners came with such a background. Further,
Engleville opened as the most complete company town in the Colorado
coalfields. The town developed as part of a maturing business attitude toward
coal operations, and management initially used low-rent housing to attract
workers. Inexpensive housing could also justify low wages, and it served as a
check on union activity. Men with families might hesitate before going on strike

if it meant losing their home. Without a vested interest in the community, a miner could more easily move on if he did not like the terms of employment.[58]

The thick vein of coal at Engleville held another advantage for the company. With plenty of room to operate, managers placed mining machines in the mine. Miners perceived the machines as a threat; operators saw them as a panacea. These early mining machines cut a swath of coal at the bottom of the seam. Miners traditionally laid on their sides and dug coal out with a pick. With a foot or two of the coal's thickness removed, the rest could be blasted, falling into the space just created. The miner then hand-loaded the coal onto mine carts. The space allowed for a clean explosion, with the coal falling from the face in large chunks. If no cut was made, the coal exploded outward from the front of the face and turned into dust.[59]

Both miners and managers thought mining machines would alter the work and the culture belowground. Instead of workers controlling production, the new technology offered managers the possibility of segmenting production and destroying older traditions. The new process would involve, first, a machine operator cutting the coal, a blaster then setting the explosive charges, and finally a loader removing the coal. Machine advocates saw this change as a chance to eliminate the need for skilled labor, except for a few machine men. Companies could then introduce unskilled labor and lower wages and replace the tonnage rate with a daily wage. For skilled miners who endured the machines, it meant falling to the rank of common laborer.[60]

In early 1881, Palmer and his associates introduced two cutting machines into the Engleville Mine, but they did not work as planned. Sensing the threat, the men did not passively accept the changes in the mining process. Instead of striking, they subtly attempted to defeat the machines. In March, company managers complained that the men were not working very hard with the new machines and that blacksmith bills were excessive because the miners were not taking care of the machines as a sign of quiet protest. The company attempted to train its best men to operate the machines, but once trained, the men took their experience to the silver mines. By May the superintendent at Engleville, George Engle, lamented the lack of qualified men to keep the machines running and worried about putting on more "regular miners."[61]

Despite the difficulties, the Colorado Coal and Iron Company pushed on with mechanization, placing machines in the mine near Walsenburg. The company's 1882 Annual Report praised the machines for providing an economical mining method and for having an "important influence in controlling the miners." The advantages were more hoped for than real, and the company's control remained tenuous. The same Annual Report mentioned that the miners at Engleville had struck in June 1882 over "some of the rules and regulations of the company." The most important rules at that mine dealt with the machines. The company claimed to have successfully resisted the strike, but a strike staged against company policy indicates an independent workforce.[62]

In the end, coal-cutting machines did not revolutionize the workplace or the mining industry. Worker resistance, lack of experienced operators, mechanical problems, and geological limitations combined to stifle change. A coal vein had to be large enough and the slope of the mine flat enough for a machine to work properly. The mines in southern Colorado were some of the few in the West suitable for machine operation. Further, early cutting machines had reliability problems and required intense maintenance. As the system evolved, cutting machines merely became an adjunct to the old process. A machine would be brought into a miner's room and would cut the coal. The miner would then complete all other aspects of the job. Machines made the job easier for the miners, which they approved of, and most men retained their craft status with a tonnage-rate pay scale.[63]

During this era of prosperity and mine development, machines may have been a necessary adjunct to coal mining in the West. Labor remained scarce and small labor struggles continued as the miners felt secure in their positions. For example, soon after the Colorado Coal and Iron Company opened the Oak Creek mines near Coal Creek in 1881, miners went on strike for an advance. Instead of granting a raise, the company closed the mines for two months. This closure caused the miners to disperse and the company to lose revenue, especially as its other mines could barely meet demand. The company prevailed, however, and it reported that its "decisive action . . . prevented a general advance in wages." With coal in short supply, the Denver *Republican* expressed relief when the mines reopened in early December 1881.[64]

Beyond the brief strike in 1879 and occasional flare-ups such as the one at Oak Creek, the years of growth brought few labor problems to the coal mines of the West. Some miners did gain a wage advance, reflecting the need for labor, but the scale did not return to the level of the first years of operation. The miners did not try to attain the earlier peaks, perhaps recognizing that the cost of living had come down and that they still made better wages than most eastern coal miners. When new mines opened, managers generally adopted the wage level that prevailed in that area. The Santa Fe Railroad rapidly became a significant coal producer during this time, and it not only met the established scale but soon began paying its miners a slightly higher wage scale than the neighboring Colorado Coal and Iron mines. This attitude guaranteed general harmony in the Santa Fe mines.

The return of economic prosperity in the late 1870s caused the western coal industry to expand dramatically. The Union Pacific, Colorado Coal and Iron, Santa Fe, and several independent companies all opened new mines. By 1883 the combined output for Colorado and Wyoming exceeded 2 million tons, with almost 3,000 men digging coal. Six years before, the two states yielded just half a million tons, so the 1883 amount represented a fourfold increase. More significant, the operations in Colorado accounted for over 70 percent of the advance. Although Wyoming's output doubled from 1877 to 1883, Colorado's increased by more than six and a half times. In 1883, Wyoming produced nearly 780,000 tons, whereas Colorado yielded over 1.2 million tons—with over 70 percent of the latter amount coming from Colorado Coal and Iron and Santa Fe mines. Most of the remaining production for Colorado came from Denver Basin operations, some of which were controlled by the Union Pacific's Union Coal Company. In Wyoming, the Union Pacific accounted for over 90 percent of the yield. Three companies thus dominated the major Rocky Mountains coalfields after this period of rapid expansion.[65]

The growth in Colorado and Wyoming outpaced that in the rest of the nation from 1877 to 1883. Whereas production in those two states quadrupled, in the nation as a whole it only doubled. And in terms of coal production in the West, in 1883, Colorado and Wyoming produced more than the rest of the region combined. Yet the 2 million tons produced in Colorado and Wyoming in 1883 seems small when compared with the nation's total of over 115 million tons or Illinois's 12 million tons or Ohio's 8 million tons. Nevertheless, output in the two mountain states had grown dramatically.[66]

The workers did not fully share in the renewed prosperity and expansion. Only the men at Coal Creek and in the Denver Basin took advantage of the economic realities to gain an advance after a brief strike. The new arrivals, many of whom came from the British Isles with coal-mining experience, generally accepted the prevailing wage. These western coal mines still paid better than their eastern counterparts, and the introduction of Chinese and Hispanic workers diminished the impulse to strike. Yet traditional mining men still predominated and maintained a strong sense of solidarity.

Western coal mining had seemingly come of age by 1883, but just as prosperity seemed assured, another downturn hit. The coal industry began to feel the pangs of overexpansion as the economy slowed. The newly expanded companies tried to adjust—most often at the expense of workers—and in the process they ushered in an era of labor upheaval.

NOTES

1. Brundage, *The Making of Western Labor Radicalism*, 13; Paul, *Mining Frontiers of the Far West*, 127–129; Trottman, *History of the Union Pacific*, 199.

2. Brundage, *The Making of Western Labor Radicalism*, 13; U.S. Department of the Interior, Census Office, *Report on Population of the United States at the Eleventh Census: 1890*, Part 1 (Washington, D.C.: GPO, 1895), 75, 79, 368.

3. Wilkins, *Colorado Railroads*, 35, 41; Klein, *Union Pacific: The Birth of a Railroad*, 400, 409.

4. *History of the Union Pacific Coal Mines*, appendix; United States Geological Survey, *Mineral Resources, 1882*, 47; U.S. Department of the Interior, United States Geological Survey, *Mineral Resources of the United States, 1887*, by David T. Day (Washington, D.C.: GPO, 1888), 380.

5. United States Geological Survey, *Mineral Resources, 1882*, 45–46; Wilkins, *Colorado Railroads*, 4, 19, 21, 23; Smith, *Once a Coal Miner*, 39; *Rocky Mountain News*, September 30, 1879.

6. Denver *Times*, December 21, 1879; Jean M. Greiner, "The Golden, Boulder and Caribou," *Colorado Magazine* 44, no. 4 (1967): 307–313, 319.

7. Smith, *Once a Coal Miner*, 47; Connarroe, *The Louisville Story*, 3, 4, 11, 31.

8. Connarroe, *The Louisville Story*, 4; U.S. Department of the Interior, Census Office, *Statistics of the Population of the United States at the Tenth Census, June 1, 1880*, vol. 1 (Washington, D.C.: GPO, 1883), 113.

9. United States Geological Survey, *Mineral Resources, 1882*, 45–47.

10. Athearn, *The Denver and Rio Grande*, 71–87.

11. Ibid., 85–90; Brayer, "History of Colorado Railroads," 657–658; Anderson, *General William J. Palmer*, 127, 130; Bryant, *History of the Atchison, Topeka and Santa Fe Railway*, 52; "Railroad Matters," *Engineering and Mining Journal* 26, no. 1 (July 6, 1878): 9.

12. Brayer, *William Blackmore*, 236–237, 240–241; Scamehorn, *Pioneer Steelmaker*, 18.

13. Anderson, *General William J. Palmer*, 143; Athearn, *The Denver and Rio Grande*, 71; "The Central Colorado Improvement Company Fifth Report of the Board of Directors to the Stockholders and Bondholders, 1877–78," 6–7, Collection #1057, Box #1, Folder #3, CF&I CRL; Incorporation Notice of the Cañon City Coal Company, Santa Fe Railway Archives, Kansas State Historical Society, Topeka, Kansas.

14. Scamehorn, *Pioneer Steelmaker*, 34, 44, 45; "First Report of the Colorado Coal and Iron Co., Comprising the Sixth Report of the Central Colorado Improvement Co. and the Second Report of the Southern Colorado Coal and Town Co., December 31, 1879," 10, Collection #1057, Box #1, Folder #3, CF&I CRL.

15. "First Report of the Colorado Coal and Iron Co.," 12; Scamehorn, *Pioneer Steelmaker*, 31.

16. *Camp and Plant* 1, no. 17 (April 5, 1902): 265–256; *Camp and Plant* 1, no. 25 (May 31, 1902): 457–459; M. Beshoar, M.D., *All About Trinidad and Las Animas County, Colorado* (Denver: Times Steam Printing House and Blank Book Manufactory, 1882; reprint, Trinidad: Trinidad Historical Society, 1990), 62–63.

17. *Camp and Plant* 1, no. 25 (May 31, 1902): 457–459; *Rocky Mountain News*, September 14, 1879; "Colorado Coal Mines," *Engineering and Mining Journal* 26, no. 12 (September 21, 1878): 206.

18. Athearn, *The Denver and Rio Grande*, 115, 150; Wilkins, *Colorado Railroads*, 25, 33, 37, 43; Scamehorn, *Pioneer Steelmaker*, 48.

19. "Third Annual Report of the Colorado Coal and Iron Co., December 31, 1881," 9, Collection #1057, Box #1, Folder #17, CF&I CRL; "Fourth Annual Report of the Colorado Coal and Iron Co., December 31, 1882," 8, Collection #1057, Box #1, Folder #17, CF&I CRL.

20. "Third Annual Report of the Colorado Coal and Iron Co.," 10; Cresto, *King Coal*, 14–15; Duane A. Smith, *When Coal Was King: A History of Crested Butte, Colorado, 1880–1952* (Golden: Colorado School of Mines Press, 1983), 25–27; "Williamsburg Centennial Commemorative Edition," *Cañon City Daily Record*, June 18, 1988.

21. Athearn, *The Denver and Rio Grande*, 134–135; Trottman, *History of the Union Pacific*, 200, 202.

22. Athearn, *The Denver and Rio Grande*, 107, 131–133, 135, 150–151; Scamehorn, *Pioneer Steelmaker*, 46; *Engineering and Mining Journal* 37, no. 12 (March 22, 1884): 213; "Official Statements and Reports," *Engineering and Mining Journal* 38, no. 4 (July 26, 1884): 53–54.

23. "Official Statements and Reports," 53; "Official Statements and Reports," *Engineering and Mining Journal* 39, no. 14 (April 4, 1885): 225; Long, *Where the Sun Never Shines*, 189; Scamehorn, *Pioneer Steelmaker*, 48.

24. Athearn, *The Denver and Rio Grande*, 136; *Rocky Mountain News*, March 14, March 15, 1884; *Engineering and Mining Journal* 37, no. 12 (March 22, 1884): 213.

25. *Engineering and Mining Journal* 37, no. 12 (March 22, 1884): 213.

26. Athearn, *The Denver and Rio Grande*, 136.

27. *Rocky Mountains News*, March 14, March 15, 1884; *Engineering and Mining Journal* 37, no. 12 (March 22, 1884): 213; Scamehorn, *Pioneer Steelmaker*, 53.

28. Scamehorn, *Pioneer Steelmaker*, 61; *Rocky Mountains News*, April 8, April 9, 1884; quote in "Sixth Annual Report of the Colorado Coal and Iron Co., for Year Ending December 31, 1884," 5, Collection #1057, Box #1, Folder #18, CF&I CRL; "Official Statements and Reports," *Engineering and Mining Journal* 38, no. 4 (July 26, 1884): 54; Athearn, *The Denver and Rio Grande*, 144–146; Trottman, *History of the Union Pacific*, 200.

29. Athearn, *The Denver and Rio Grande*, 153–154; "Transportation Notes," *Engineering and Mining Journal* 42, no. 3 (July 17, 1886): 46.

30. "Official Statements and Reports," *Engineering and Mining Journal* 38, no. 4 (July 26, 1884): 52–53; Charles M. Rolker, *Report on the Property of the Colorado Coal and Iron Co.* (New York: Jno. C. Rankin Jr., 1884), 8–18.

31. "Report on Coal and Coke Department from Jno. Cameron to A. H. Danforth for Year Ending December 31, 1885," Collection #1057, Box #1, Folder #28, CF&I CRL; "Official Statements and Reports," *Engineering and Mining Journal* 39, no. 14 (April 4, 1885): 225.

32. "Official Statements and Reports," *Engineering and Mining Journal* 39, no. 14 (April 4, 1885): 225; Scamehorn, *Pioneer Steelmaker*, 61.

33. Wilkins, *Colorado Railroads*, 21, 31; Bryant, *History of the Atchison, Topeka and Santa Fe Railway*, 41–53.

34. "Colorado Coal Mines," *Engineering and Mining Journal* 26, no. 12 (September 21, 1878): 206; "Trinidad, Colo.," *Engineering and Mining Journal* 27, no. 8 (February 22, 1879): 130; Beshoar, *All About Trinidad*, 13, 64; *Rocky Mountain News*, March 26, September 28, 1878; "Trinidad Coal and Mining Company," Santa Fe Railway Archives, Kansas State Historical Society, Topeka, Kansas.

35. "Annual Report of the Atchison, Topeka and Santa Fe Railway for the Year Ending December 31, 1884," Santa Fe Railway Archives, Kansas State Historical

Society, Topeka, Kansas; "Annual Report of the Atchison, Topeka and Santa Fe Railway for the Year Ending December 31, 1885," 21, Santa Fe Railway Archives, Kansas State Historical Society, Topeka, Kansas.

36. Virginia McConnell Simmons, *The Upper Arkansas: A Mountain River Valley* (Boulder: Pruett, 1990), 224; Beshoar, *All About Trinidad*, 64; Henry Johns letter in Rockvale file, Historical Collection, Cañon City Public Library, Cañon City, Colorado; Cresto, *King Coal*, 14–15; "Williamsburg Centennial Commemorative Edition," Cañon City *Daily Record*, June 18, 1988.

37. U.S. Department of the Interior, United States Geological Survey, *Mineral Resources of the United States, 1886*, by David T. Day (Washington, D.C.: GPO, 1887), 248; *Second Biennial Report of the State Inspector of Mines of the State of Colorado for the Years Ending December 31, 1885, and December 31, 1886* (Denver: State Printers, 1887), 35, 42.

38. Robert G. Athearn, *Union Pacific Country* (Lincoln: University of Nebraska Press, 1971), 218, 223–224.

39. Ibid., 340; Trottman, *History of the Union Pacific*, 175, 182, 196–197; "The Union Pacific and the Denver & Rio Grande Railroad War," *Engineering and Mining Journal* 32, no. 2 (July 9, 1881): 26.

40. Anonymous eight-page manuscript entitled "Union Pacific Coal Mines," Box HO 3, UPCCC; "Financial," *Engineering and Mining Journal* 24 (December 15, 1877): 446; "The Union Pacific Railroad and the Western Coal Trade," *Engineering and Mining Journal* 31, no. 4 (January 22, 1881): 56.

41. *Rocky Mountain News*, September 30, 1879; Smith, *Once a Coal Miner*, 39–40; "Financial," *Engineering and Mining Journal* 32, no. 19 (November 5, 1881): 309; *Engineering and Mining Journal* 37, no. 10 (March 8, 1884): 184; Klein, *Union Pacific: The Birth of a Railroad*, 515–516; *History of the Union Pacific Coal Mines*, appendix.

42. Isaac H. Bromley to Charles F. Adams, July 2, 1885, SG-2, S-1, Box 15, U.P. Archives, NSHS.

43. Trottman, *History of the Union Pacific*, 203, 210, 240; Athearn, *Union Pacific Country*, 342, 352; Klein, *Union Pacific: The Birth of a Railroad*, 456, 461–463, 490–495; Thomas K. McCraw, *Prophets of Regulation* (Cambridge: Belknap, 1984), 52.

44. Trottman, *History of the Union Pacific*, 201–202, 210, 214–215.

45. "First Report to the Stockholders. The Southern Colorado Coal and Town Co., 1878," 5, Collection #1057, Box #1, Folder #10, CF&I CRL; "First Report of the Colorado Coal and Iron Co.," 6.

46. Connarroe, *The Louisville Story*, 4; United States Geological Survey, *Mineral Resources, 1882*, 48, 89; U.S. Department of the Interior, Census Office, manuscript census, Las Animas County, Colorado, 1880; U.S. Department of the Interior, Census Office, *Statistics of the Population of the United States at the Tenth Census*, 51, 375, 428, 499; *History of the Union Pacific Coal Mines*, 90, 163; *Rocky Mountain News*, December 13, 1879, November 5, December 28, 1880.

47. Trottman, *History of the Union Pacific*, 193; Patricia K. Ourada, "The Chinese in Colorado," *Colorado Magazine* 29, no. 4 (October 1952): 279; *Rocky Mountain News*, December 10, December 16, 1879.

48. Roy T. Wortman, "Denver's Anti-Chinese Riot, 1880," *Colorado Magazine* 42, no. 4 (Fall 1965): 275; Duane A. Smith, *Rocky Mountain West: Colorado, Wyo-*

ming, and Montana, 1859–1915 (Albuquerque: University of New Mexico Press, 1992), 117–118.

49. Rocky Mountain News, December 13, December 14, December 17, December 18, 1879; "First Report of the Colorado Coal and Iron Co.," 6; "The Coal Outlook in Colorado," Engineering and Mining Journal 29, no. 6 (February 7, 1880): 100.

50. Rocky Mountain News, December 21, 1879; First Biennial Report of the Bureau of Labor Statistics of the State of Colorado, 1887–1888 (Denver: State Printers, 1887), 100.

51. "Trinidad, Colo.," Engineering and Mining Journal 29, no. 3 (January 17, 1880): 49; "First Report of the Colorado Coal and Iron Co.," 5, 6.

52. Sarah Deutsch, No Separate Refuge: Culture, Class, and Gender on an Anglo-Hispanic Frontier in the American Southwest, 1880–1940 (New York: Oxford University Press, 1987), 89; Ernest Ingersoll, The Crest of the Continent: A Summer's Ramble in the Rocky Mountains and Beyond (Chicago: R. R. Donnelley and Sons, 1885), 179.

53. Morris F. Taylor, Trinidad, Colorado Territory (Trinidad: Trinidad State Junior College, 1966).

54. Victor Clark, Mexican Labor in the United States, U.S. Bureau of Labor Bulletin 78 (Washington, D.C.: GPO, 1909), 486–488.

55. Report to H. E. Sprague by Joseph Simons, 8, Collection #1057, Box #1, Folder #16, CF&I CRL.

56. United States Geological Survey, Mineral Resources, 1882, 39; Report to E. M. Steck from Geo. S. Ramsay for Year Ending 21 December 1890, Collection #1057, Box #1, Folder #28, CF&I CRL.

57. United States Geological Survey, Mineral Resources, 1882, 45–46.

58. Report to H. E. Sprague by Joseph Simons, 5, 8.

59. Gardner and Flores, Forgotten Frontier, 35–37.

60. "The Foreign Born in the Coal Mines," Reports of the Industrial Commission on Immigration and on Education 15 (Washington, D.C.: GPO, 1901), 399.

61. E. S. McKinlay to Chas. B. Lamborn, March 28, 1881, Collection #1057, Box #2, Folder #30, CF&I CRL; George Engle to Chas. B. Lamborn, April 8, 1881, Collection #1057, Box #2, Folder #30, CF&I CRL; George Engle to Chas. B. Lamborn, May 11, 1881, Collection #1057, Box #2, Folder #30, CF&I CRL; George Engle to Jno. Cameron, May 18, 1881, Collection #1057, Box #2, Folder #30, CF&I CRL.

62. "Fourth Annual Report of the Colorado Coal and Iron Co.," 9–10; Rocky Mountain News, June 6, June 9, 1882.

63. Dix, What's a Coal Miner to Do, 29–31; Fox, United We Stand, 122–124.

64. "Third Annual Report of the Colorado Coal and Iron Co.," 5, 8, quote on 12; Denver Republican, December 3, 1881.

65. U.S. Department of the Interior, United States Geological Survey, Mineral Resources of the United States, 1883 and 1884, by Albert Williams Jr. (Washington, D.C.: GPO, 1885), 35–38, 104; U.S. Department of the Interior, United States Geological Survey, Mineral Resources of the United States, 1885 (Washington, D.C.: GPO, 1886), 25, 73; History of the Union Pacific Coal Mines, appendix; First Annual Report of the State Inspector of Coal Mines for the Year Ending July 31, 1884 (Denver: Smith-Brooks Printing, State Printers, 1884), 57, 64, 75, 87.

66. U.S. Department of the Interior, United States Geological Survey, "Coal Produced in the United States from 1807, the Date of Earliest Record, to the End of 1922," in *Mineral Resources of the United States, 1922* (Washington, D.C.: GPO, 1925), chart.

CHAPTER FOUR

THE GREAT UPHEAVAL, 1884-1885

SIGNS OF AN ECONOMIC SLUMP BEGAN APPEARING IN 1882. In April of that year the *Engineering and Mining Journal* warned of a falling off, and in May it talked of depressed conditions in the coal and iron trades. In November the *Rocky Mountain News* reported a price war among the Denver Basin coal companies, a sure indication of too much supply and too little demand. Further, the paper predicted the price war would last all winter, a time when coal sales and profits should have been the highest. Although the war had started in the Denver Basin, the *News* surmised that "most of the large companies will be forced into it," meaning the Colorado Coal and Iron and the Santa Fe mines.[1]

At the start of 1883, more signs of a sluggish economy appeared. In March the Santa Fe's Cañon City Coal Company suspended work at two of its mines, and the Colorado Coal and Iron Company only ran its mines a few days a week. In reviewing the year, the latter company attempted to be upbeat. Its 1883 Annual Report commented that Colorado had maintained a "fair degree of prosperity." But conditions worsened the next year in what the company called the "spring panic." Similarly, the Union Pacific system found its earnings down 50 percent in the first half of 1884, pushing the company into serious financial straits.[2]

Economic downturns had an immediate effect on coal companies. They depended on railroads as their primary markets, and these carriers cut purchases as soon as traffic began to slump. This situation made coal demand highly sensitive to changes in economic activity, as a small downturn would immediately cut sales. In response, coal operators often attempted to stimulate the market through reduced prices, frequently resulting in a price war—as happened in the Denver Basin in 1882. Lowering prices certainly caused companies to become more competitive, but demand seldom increased. Further, labor costs accounted for as much as 80 percent of the price of coal. Cutting prices generally meant cutting the wage rate, and labor turmoil often resulted.

With less output, more mines existed than were necessary for demand, a condition known as overcapacity. Operators had two choices to counter overcapacity. First, they could close mines, but companies seldom did so. After acquiring the land and developing the mine, operating it entailed limited expense. Consequently, even with less demand, coal companies often kept their mines running. Second, operators could work their mines part-time. Indeed many operations only worked two or three days a week during bad times. Companies often preferred this plan because it gave their men some work, with hopes that they would stick around until better times returned. In all cases workers felt the brunt of economic woes.[3]

The financial difficulties in 1884 brought a number of changes to the Rocky Mountain coal business. William J. Palmer lost control of his railroad and coal company, and Henry Sprague became president of Colorado Coal and Iron. The Union Pacific gained a new president, Charles Francis Adams Jr., as Jay Gould left the system. And the coal miners tried to stave off the machinations of the coal companies. Turmoil and labor discord spread throughout the western coalfields that year. The rest of the nation also experienced labor turmoil in the mid-1880s. This unrest has been labeled the "Great Upheaval." In 1884 and 1885 the Great Upheaval came to Colorado and Wyoming.[4]

BACKGROUND TO THE GREAT UPHEAVAL

In 1884, western coal miners challenged company policies on an unprecedented scale. Four factors contributed to this upsurge of activity. One, a new concentration of traditional miners brought a stronger sense of worker solidarity to the region. Two, a labor organization emerged that appealed to the miners—the Knights of Labor. Three, railroad workers in Denver won a strike victory, inspiring other workers. And four, the coal companies attempted to cut wages and gain control of the mines. This final event crystallized the other factors and pushed the coal miners to act.

The miners had numbers on their side. By 1884 Colorado had over 1,700 miners and Wyoming about 1,000. Many of the new arrivals were of British heritage, trained in mining skills. They believed they should control the mining process, and their numbers and mutual backgrounds enhanced worker solidarity. Coal companies liked to suppress miners with threats of hiring replacement workers, whether Chinese, Italians, or Hispanics. Some of the miners currently working in Wyoming and Colorado had come as replacement workers, but the traditional miners believed their numbers had grown to the point that replacement was no longer a threat. Plus, replacement workers could only stave off unionism for a limited time. Scandinavians and Italians had previously been brought to the mines as strikebreakers, but they soon cooperated with striking miners, as did other scabs in years to come.[5]

The miners also felt an affinity toward the Knights of Labor. Originally formed in Pennsylvania in 1869, the Knights attempted to attract people from nearly all occupations. As a working-class organization, it sought a preindustrial ideal. It believed in small-scale enterprise and equality through economic parity. Coal miners began joining the organization in the late 1870s after the demise of the Miners' National Association. The Knights' vision coincided with coal miners' views of their job and their freedom underground. The egalitarian motives of the Knights led them to welcome most workers as members. They did not recruit unskilled immigrants from southern and eastern Europe, however, and they loathed the Chinese. The Knights led labor's support for the Chinese Exclusion Act in 1882.[6]

The Knights naturally appealed to the miners at the hot spots of western labor activism—Erie, Coal Creek, and Carbon. Each camp formed a local assembly. Joseph Buchanan of Denver was also a fervent booster. He joined the union in 1882 and soon began publishing the *Labor Enquirer*. This weekly publication stressed the principles of the Knights and often published letters to the editor regarding conditions in the coalfields. Many of the epistles came from Coal Creek, where a Knights assembly had organized in 1882. The letters consistently attacked the Colorado Coal and Iron Company. For example, a June 1883 piece damned everything about the company, especially the "iron clad" contract workers had to sign before employment stipulating that the employee would not join a union while working for the company.[7]

Such publicity gained the miners' interest, and the settlement of the Union Pacific Railroad shopmen's strike in May 1884 gave miners faith in the union. Because of the financial crisis, the Union Pacific posted a 10 percent wage reduction at all of its railroad shops on May 1. In Denver, 400 machinists, yard hands, and freight dock workers walked off the job. Initially without organization, they came to Buchanan for advice. With his guidance the strikers quickly organized and spread the strike throughout the Union Pacific Railroad system. Confronted with a massive shutdown, the company restored the old wage scale within four days. A week later the workers formalized their organization as the "Union Pacific Employe's [sic] Protective Association." Its stated mission went well beyond the railroad shopmen. The association planned to "organize all of the employes, [sic] as well as those of other railroads of the state, into local assemblies of the Knights of Labor." This objective seemingly included the company's coal mine workers.[8]

In mid-June an organizer toured the Union Pacific facilities in Wyoming and reported his activities to Buchanan's *Labor Enquirer*. Although he mentioned organizing efforts in most railroad towns, when it came to the coal operations he commented, "I did not slight the coal camps of Carbon and Rock Springs, but lest it might cause trouble in the family I will make no comments at present."[9] The organizer probably deferred regarding the coal camps because Knights of Labor activity had already begun there, and the miners did not necessarily want to be part of the Union Pacific Employe's Protective Association. The Knights included two types of organizations, the trade assembly and the mixed assembly. Trade assemblies were generally composed of workers in a specific craft. The mixed assembly provided an organizational home for workers from a variety of crafts or industries. If organized with railroad workers in the protective association, the miners would probably be placed in mixed assemblies. Coal miners who had union experience wanted to be in their own trade assemblies. When the *Labor Enquirer* announced the organization of a Knights assembly at Rock Springs in July 1884, the reporter did not mention affiliation with the Union Pacific Employe's Protective Association.[10]

THE GREAT UPHEAVAL COMES TO COLORADO

Wage reductions provided the spark that ignited the upheaval in Colorado's coalfields. Despite the Union Pacific's earlier failure to cut railroad wages, both the Santa Fe and the Colorado Coal and Iron Company decided to reduce wages at their Cañon City coal mines in the summer of 1884. In fact, the Santa Fe initiated the action, posting notices of a reduction in June. This initial step, however, did not precipitate a strike. A letter to the editor of the *Labor Enquirer* said the "men took it quietly."[11]

The strike did not occur immediately because the Santa Fe viewed its coal business and employees differently than most other western coal companies did. It had a better relationship with its workers and enhanced the bond by paying them more. Its mines at Rockvale, near Coal Creek, had been paying $1.25 per ton, $0.25 more than the Colorado Coal and Iron Company. In its southern Colorado mines near Starkville, a brief strike in late 1881 brought the men an advance to $0.60 a ton. These miners, then, received a dime more per ton of coal than their neighbors at Engleville. The Santa Fe paid more than the Colorado Coal and Iron Company, and when the former moved for a reduction, it was only to the levels prevailing elsewhere. The higher wages probably attracted the best miners and undoubtedly brought better labor relations. When a mine superintendent left the Santa Fe mines at Rockvale, his former employees presented him with $125 in cash as a "mark of esteem for the kindly and gentlemanly manner in which they were treated." The Santa Fe had a reputation for treating its workers fairly.[12]

The Santa Fe also had a different attitude toward the coal business than most other companies did. The corporate officials saw the mines as good investments, but they considered the coal business of secondary importance. They sold coal along their railroad and needed the fuel for their engines, but they were not strictly driven to produce the cheapest possible product. In 1884 the company reported that its average production cost stood at $1.94 per ton, which it labeled a "low rate." Under the Gould administration the Union Pacific had made every effort to drive down the cost of its coal, and the Carbon mines produced the most costly product at $1.42 per ton. Both railroads essentially enjoyed a fuel monopoly, but Gould had wanted to maximize his profits, whereas the Santa Fe accepted what it could get. Accepting a higher-cost coal allowed the company to pay a higher wage rate and enjoy better labor relations.[13]

One month after the Santa Fe action, Henry Sprague ordered Colorado Coal and Iron to cut wages at its Coal Creek and Oak Creek Mines in the Cañon City coalfield. This action again dropped the company's wages below what the Santa Fe paid at the neighboring Rockvale Mine. Sprague argued that the Coal Creek and Oak Creek Mines were not competitive with other mines in the state and that they operated at a loss. He argued that the company needed at least a 10 percent cut, especially in the hard economic times.[14] But the company's 1884 Annual Report refuted Sprague's contention. It stated that the "coal and coke business is in a very healthy and most flourishing condition." The report acknowledged a high cost of mining at the Cañon City mines but gave reasons that had nothing to do with labor. The Oak Creek Mine had a troublesome roof that necessitated constant repairs, and the Coal Creek slope had lengthy inside roads and heavy grades. To counter these expenses, Sprague decided to cut the cost of labor. He observed that the Coal Creek miners made $1.00 a ton, whereas those at Engleville (or El Moro) only received $0.50. Sprague did not care about the differences between the coalfields; he just wanted to equalize wages and reduce costs.[15]

Sprague's cut ignited an immediate strike in the Cañon City coalfield. About 400 men walked off the job. With the recent success of the Union Pacific shopmen's strike, the growth of the Knights of Labor, and Buchanan's *Labor Enquirer* publicizing their cause, the miners expressed confidence. The Santa Fe men at Rockvale joined the walkout, apparently as a show of solidarity because a railroad washout had already curtailed their work. Nevertheless, the strike gave new life to the local Knights of Labor Assembly. Although the men had begun organizing before, the wage cut strengthened their effort, and the Knights of Labor became their agent of labor solidarity.[16]

The strikers knew the railroad shopmen's strike had been successful because it had spread across the Union Pacific system, and consequently they wanted to close other mines—especially those of the Colorado Coal and Iron Company still working in southern Colorado. A complete shutdown might bring the company to terms. During this time of low coal consumption, a few closed mines had little effect on the company. In fact, the Colorado Coal and Iron Company saw the strike as an opportunity. It moved to introduce Walsenburg coal where Coal Creek coal had previously been consumed. The company's 1884 Annual Report stated, "The benefit derived by this plan is fully shown in the balance sheets."[17]

To close other mines, the striking miners needed to convince the miners there to walk off the job. To do this the strikers called an interstate convention in Pueblo for the end of August. The men who attended came from areas where labor activism already existed: Coal Creek, Rockvale, Walsenburg, Louisville, and Erie. The attendees aired concerns over the wage reductions and complained about the ironclad contract, used not only by the Colorado Coal and Iron Company but also by the Union Coal Company in northern Colorado. They criticized the "truck system" by which coal companies sold miners their supplies, and they denounced the company-mandated medical fund. The miners created the Coal Miners Protective Association of Colorado to secure "just remuneration for their labor," settle trade disputes by "arbitration or conciliatory means," and promote legislation that would carry out and promote these objectives. To gain immediate action, they wanted a general strike of all Colorado coalfields.[18]

Similar in name and function to the protective association formed by the Union Pacific employees just months before, the Coal Miners Protective Association of Colorado functioned as the umbrella organization for the Knights of Labor assemblies and other unions in the coal regions. Most coal towns in the state had formed some type of organization, the majority reportedly associated with the Knights of Labor, but the Coal Miners Protective Association did not want to be exclusive. It welcomed all unions to its cause as it pushed for a general coal strike. Negotiating power for the coal miners fell to the association's executive board.[19]

Joseph Buchanan was away from Colorado at the time and did not lead the new organization. Nevertheless, the miners placed extraordinary confidence in him. He published the *Labor Enquirer* and served on the Knights of Labor National General Executive Board. Each coal mine local had passed a resolution requesting that Buchanan take responsibility for ordering the general strike. When Buchanan returned to Colorado, the executive board of the protective association approached him with the request. Although he initially deferred, claiming he knew nothing about coal mining, Buchanan finally agreed, acknowledging that he did know something about buying and selling coal. He recommended that the strike be delayed until winter approached and the market grew stronger. When the first snow appeared on the foothills, he would call a general strike. The cold weather would raise the demand for coal, exhaust the supply, and bring the operators to the negotiating table.[20]

Four weeks after the conference, on October 25, it snowed. Buchanan ordered the strike for October 27. The men at Cañon City had been on strike since July, but Buchanan's order shut down nearly every other coal mine in Colorado—including mines that did not have representatives at the Pueblo meeting such as Starkville and Engleville in southern Colorado. Only a very few small mines remained in operation.[21]

The success of the strike call caught many by surprise. The *Rocky Mountain News* expressed wonderment that the miners at Louisville and Marshall had walked out without giving a reason except "to help their brethren in the southern part of the state." The paper recognized that the miners belonged to the Knights of Labor and reasoned that they were striking "simply in obedience to orders from the heads of their organization."[22] The *News* did not understand the solidarity that had developed among the miners or the Knights' belief that "an injury to one is the concern of all." John Cameron, superintendent of mines for the Colorado Coal and Iron Company, claimed his company's actions could not have caused a general strike. Since the wage cuts only occurred at Coal Creek, Cameron alleged the miners at Walsenburg and El Moro had no reason to strike. He blamed the operators in northern Colorado, especially the Union Pacific's Union Coal Company, which had recently cut the tonnage rate at Erie. Cameron argued that his workers had been drawn in to assist that struggle.[23]

With the strike call, Buchanan also announced a miners' conference to meet in Denver. Delegates from thirty-five mines met the day the walkout began. According to Buchanan, they came together "to perfect the state organization, to formulate demands, and to provide for official conferences with the mine-owners." To attract more western miners, the conference decided to broaden the union's reach. They replaced the Colorado Coal Miners Protective Association with the Coal Miners' Amalgamation (CMA). Whereas the former had been organized and directed primarily by men from the Coal Creek area, the latter intended to unite coal miners of Colorado, Wyoming, New Mexico, and Kansas. It was important to include these neighboring states since two of Colorado's important mine owners also held properties there— the Union Pacific in Wyoming and the Santa Fe in Kansas and New Mexico.[24]

The new CMA also elected officers. Indicative of the centers of labor activism, the president, William Howells, came from Coal Creek, and the secretary, John L. Lewis, was from Erie. Lewis became a prime force behind the CMA. He had been the recording secretary for Erie's local Knights of Labor Assembly, and he intended to draw the CMA closer to the parent Knights of Labor organization, modeling it after a district trade assembly. Lewis also intended to centralize power within the executive officers. Although never formally sanctioned by the national organization, the Coal Miners' Amalgamation eventually had fifteen Knights of Labor local assemblies as affiliates.[25]

The Denver convention also appointed a committee to invite mine owners to a conference. In anticipation of the meeting, they produced a document entitled "Manifesto" that set forth the causes of the "organized effort," the grievances, and the method for settlement. Although the document spoke of just remuneration, it also delineated a traditional coal miners' objective and a Knights of Labor belief: "Labor being the action, necessary to the sustenance of life, it naturally follows that labor has an unquestionable right to a voice in the distribution of its own products." To achieve the social value of their product, the miners wanted to exert control over the amount of coal produced and sent to market, keeping prices up and wages high. The "Manifesto" closed by calling for a conference of all mine owners in the state to be held in three days.[26]

Only Denver Basin mining companies responded and met with the miners' committee. Together they agreed to form a Conciliation Board, consisting of the executive board of the CMA and five representatives from the attending operators. The board was to act as a mandatory collective bargaining agent on such matters as wages, working conditions, and grievances; and it immediately granted the miners a twelve-and-a-half-cent per ton wage advance. The mining companies also agreed to abolish the "iron-clad contract," the "black list," and the "truck system." The agreement allowed a number of Denver Basin mines to reopen a week and a half after the strike began.[27]

The reopening signaled a major victory for many of the miners in the Denver Basin, but the major companies had not attended the conference. Managers from the Colorado Coal and Iron Company and the Santa Fe refused to participate; and although a Union Pacific representative was present at the conference, he did not comment, deferring to higher authorities. Consequently, the Union Pacific's mines at Erie and Louisville in the Denver Basin, as well as the state's largest producers in central and southern Colorado, remained on strike. These mines produced perhaps seven-eighths of all fuel mined in the state.[28]

The northern coal operators who agreed to the terms did not necessarily do so because they feared the power of organized labor but because they were again worried about losing their position in the Denver market. Along with becoming part of the Conciliation Board, the companies joined the Coal Operators Association of Colorado to set or "fix" prices at which coal could be sold. The prices they chose would ensure a profit and allow for increased wages.

Because its activities affected wages, miners on the Conciliation Board worked with the Coal Operators Association. From the operators' view this cooperation eliminated destructive competition, and from the miners' perspective it in part fulfilled their wish to have some control over prices and production. Both sides, however, recognized that everyone suffered when a price war occurred, and all parties wanted to stabilize prices.[29]

The Union Pacific did not join the Conciliation Board or the Coal Operators Association. The *Labor Enquirer* expressed hope that the company would join as soon as it understood the organizations' purpose, but the Union Pacific had two concerns. First, it did not want to give in to the Knights. The company had already lost ground to the Knights of Labor because of the shopmen's strike, and it fully recognized the coal strike as directed by what the Knights called the "Order."[30] General Superintendent D. O. Clark visited with Colorado miners after the strike began and assured them that if they had "reasonable grounds for complaint, they [those grounds] should be removed." In response, he found the miners were "silent and sulky." The Union Pacific concluded that if it gave in at Erie and Louisville, the organization would spread to the company's other mines, and as Clark reported, "then we will have trouble."[31]

Second, Union Pacific managers took a hostile stance in regard to a wage advance and price fixing. They did not want wages and prices fixed beyond their control. Their greatest anxiety concerned the railroad; they believed a wage advance would push the cost of coal beyond what they were willing to bear. They recognized that other Denver Basin mine operators feared losing the Denver market, but a wage increase would make their Colorado coal more expensive than coal shipped in from Carbon. When it came to "industrial solidarity," the Union Pacific managers felt a greater kinship with the large coal operators in central and southern Colorado than with those in the Denver Basin. One Union Pacific manager stated that if they settled with their miners, it would "complicate matters for the Santa Fe and Rio Grande."[32]

Soon after the northern operators and miners formed the Conciliation Board, officials of the Colorado Coal and Iron Company devised their own plan to end the strike. General Manager A. H. Danforth asked the miners to select two representatives from each of the company's mines to meet with him. Danforth told the miners the company would "use every effort to compromise matters in dispute by amicable conference and mutual concessions; and where differences could not be settled, an effort [would] be made to adjust such differences by arbitration." After this apparent but vague promise of collective bargaining, Danforth and General Superintendent of Mines John Cameron met the miners in Trinidad on November 11, 1884. They agreed to modify the medical plan and to have the miners return to work pending arbitration of the wage issue.[33]

With this understanding, the Colorado Coal and Iron miners in south and central Colorado returned to work, thus violating the solidarity mandated by the CMA. In fact, Danforth had cleverly tried to pass off his meeting with a few employees as collective bargaining. He emphatically wanted to avoid meeting with a union that might carry force. Danforth made concessions to local representatives, fully intending to ignore them. He had no intention of recognizing a true workers' organization. When Lewis and the CMA executive board heard of the supposed settlement, they ordered the miners off the job again. They stated that a settlement would have to come through the union's Conciliation Board, and many of the men did go on strike again.[34]

Offering a settlement they knew the Coal Miners' Amalgamation would probably refuse may have been Danforth's and Sprague's plan all along. In the first place, they had no intention of recognizing any organization. As Sprague told the stockholders, "*Your Company could not permit* any labor association to control its business, which would prevent it from enjoying its natural advantages" (his emphasis).[35] To the public, however, the company proclaimed that it had never refused to arbitrate and that it had agreed to a contract with the miners. It was the miners who refused to be bound by the provisions. When it came to participating with the recently created Conciliation Board, Danforth stated that the Colorado Coal and Iron Company did not have a representative on the board and that the five mine operators on the board were all from the northern part of the state. Danforth insisted "there are only two things that can be done, either give a bill of sale to this Denver board or let the Colorado Coal and Iron Company run their own affairs, and he did not believe the company would do the former."[36]

Such arguments probably made sense to the public, which was initially sympathetic to the miners. Defensive strikes to prevent wage cuts seemed reasonable, especially when their community's prosperity depended on miners' incomes. Backing away from apparent good intentions and arbitration, however, seemed hypocritical. This change of sentiment could be seen in the *Rocky Mountain News*. The paper had never pretended to be a friend of labor, but during the initial strike activities it remained reasonably neutral. But when the miners walked out for the second time, the *News*'s editorials spared no wrath against the union or its principals. It attacked Joseph Buchanan and John L. Lewis. Of Buchanan the paper said, "He is not to be trusted or followed by honest men." On the strike in general, the paper believed the men needed to reconsider their position; a strike was inappropriate "when men are being discharged everywhere by reason of low prices and over worked markets, when wages are being everywhere reduced."[37]

Not only were Sprague and Danforth portrayed as victims, their tactic also began to crack the miners' solidarity. The miners who had initiated the strike at Coal Creek protested the union's order to renew the strike. They argued that they had an agreement with the company that the miners had unanimously ratified. But Lewis proclaimed that the Coal Creek men had "no authority" and demanded the walkout. The Coal Creek miners went on to speculate that the northern coal companies had pushed Lewis and the CMA executive board to renounce the agreement. If southern coal stayed out of the market, mines in the Denver Basin had a virtual monopoly.[38]

The strike, however, did not last much longer. The miners suffered during the November work stoppage. Some left to find employment elsewhere, and others violated the strike order and returned to work. The *Rocky Mountain News* reported in early December that the remaining strikers were on the "eve of starvation." Clearly, the Colorado Coal and Iron Company had no intention of yielding to the miners. The strike had come at a good time. The company had been in financial turmoil, and the strike helped drive down operating costs when some mines closed, especially since it had aggressively worked the open mines before the general strike hit. Further, the financial downturn had closed the steel operation, cutting the company's own demand for coal. Sprague saw the strike as an opportunity to reduce costs and realign the company's finances. He felt no pressing need to come to terms with the miners.[39]

On December 17 the Pueblo *Chieftain* reported that the Santa Fe's Cañon City Coal Company and the miners at Rockvale had arrived at an "amicable understanding," and the next day they returned to work. The Colorado Coal and Iron Company miners followed within a week. The *Rocky Mountain News* stated that the miners at El Moro broke with the "central committee" and the other camps followed. The miners in central and southern Colorado returned to work without the authority of the CMA and the Conciliation Board. In total, about 1,200 miners across central and southern Colorado reentered the mines, with the men at Coal Creek and Rockvale suffering the wage cuts the companies had proposed months before and that had initiated the strike. With the wage reduction in place, Manager Danforth stated that the "prime reason" for the change was to "allay discontent in the El Moro and Walsenburg districts, where the men heretofore could not make as high [a] wage . . . as the average at Coal Creek." Although the men ended the strike under the company-imposed wage scale, they were led to believe other elements of their earlier agreement would be fulfilled, such as changes in the hospital fund. Whereas the Santa Fe seemed to want to return to good labor relations and continued to pay superior rates, the Colorado Coal and Iron Company decided to push the advantage that came with victory.[40]

As discussed in the previous paragraph, when the strike ended, the miners at Walsenburg and El Moro returned to work with no change in their wages and with an apparent agreement on various grievances. Within weeks of the settlement, however, complaints began to emerge that the Colorado Coal and Iron Company had violated the understanding. The company had begun by cutting some day wages at the El Moro and Walsenburg Mines. Despite the company's earlier claims that the wage cut at Coal Creek was necessary to make the mine profitable and to make wages equitable across the system, in truth President Sprague and General Manager Danforth moved to push wages down throughout the system. They knew they had fractured the miners' solidarity; they understood that no united front existed that could bring another general strike. They also concluded that the strike survivors could not endure another work stoppage. About a third of the miners at El Moro and Walsenburg did walk out in protest, but their efforts had little effect. As Sprague and Danforth had hoped, the solidarity had been eroded; Hispanic workers stayed on the job, and some union men—labeled "blacklegs"—rapidly went back to work. In the face of weakened opposition the company took a firm stand: it fired 300 supposed troublemakers, hired guards to protect the mines, and sought new workers who would work on company terms. The company hired replacement workers, more Italians came into the camps, and in February 1885 Danforth brought in African Americans.[41]

Colorado Coal and Iron's importation of black workers caused much controversy. Naturally, the *Labor Enquirer* expressed outrage. It stated that blacks had been freed from slavery and that the Colorado company would again place them in the "yoke of bondage." The paper also insisted that the company had misled the new workers, not properly informing them of the type of work they would do or that a strike was going on. The CMA leaders called for a conference in Pueblo to discuss what they called "the system of serfdom introduced into the state" and what they could do to "stem the tide."[42] The delegates to the Pueblo conference, however, could do little except condemn Danforth and the Colorado Coal and Iron Company and praise their own rational approach to labor relations: "We look upon the introduction of colored labor into the mines at El Moro and Walsenburg as unmistakable evidence of Danforth's intent to reduce labor in the mines of Colorado to the demoralizing condition of things existing in the coal fields of eastern Pennsylvania." They called for "conciliation and arbitration in a practical and effective manner [to] be applied in the adjustment of all labor troubles."[43]

Lewis and the executive board knew they had lost control. As Sprague ran rough over the miners of southern Colorado, Lewis's column in the *Enquirer* continued to call for solidarity: "Noble veterans of Coal Creek do not forget the needy brethren of the south." But Lewis lamented how little he could do: "Several friends from Walsen and El Moro have been at headquarters during the past week, and I am pained in not being able to do all that I wish for them." He recognized the weakness in the great Coal Miners' Amalgamation he had envisioned. At the Pueblo conference he proclaimed the need for a "federation of all trades and vocations," adding that only at that time "can labor ever hope to achieve satisfactory results." He was calling for what the Knights of Labor envisioned—one great industrial union where all workers, no matter their task, would stand together and defeat organized capital.[44]

Although the CMA counted fifteen Knights of Labor locals within its jurisdiction at the time of the Pueblo convention, they could do little. The coal companies that dominated the fields in central and southern Colorado acted at will. The Colorado Coal and Iron Company added more mining machines at the El Moro Mine, "thereby somewhat reducing the cost of mining and lessening the liability of strikes and labor troubles."[45] When mining expert Joseph Simons—hired as a consultant—inspected the properties for Sprague in 1886, when prosperity had returned to the country, he commented on the low wages at the company's mines and credited the living situations. He believed the company housing kept wages down at Engleville, whereas at Coal Creek he believed the low wages could be attributed to the fact that "most of the laborers live in their own houses and through irrigation near Cañon City living there has become cheap and pleasant." Simons did not acknowledge or perhaps understand that the wages had been beaten down by aggressive management action.[46]

Over the next several years major strikes did not recur in the Colorado coalfields. Minor strikes took place, but major wage walkouts did not. Prosperity returned to Colorado soon after the Great Upheaval—a new era of coal mine development and production would occur—but the coal miners would not benefit. During the 1884 economic downturn the Colorado Coal and Iron Company argued that a miner should be willing to share in a general depression by reducing his wage. Certainly, if a miner should voluntarily take a cut during hard times, the employer should reinstate his wages during good times, but that would not be the case.[47]

THE GREAT UPHEAVAL AND THE UNION PACIFIC SYSTEM

As the Coal Miners' Amalgamation and the large coal operators in Colorado grappled for position in November 1884, the Union Pacific attempted to stem the Knights of Labor tide throughout its system. The Union Pacific Employe's [sic] Protective Association, the agent of the Knights of Labor, had taken root among railroad workers; and local Knights trade assemblies had organized in the coal camps of Rock Springs and Carbon. These organizations initially fell under the purview of the CMA. The smallest Wyoming camp of Almy did not organize, possibly because of the preponderance of Chinese; and the union at Rock Springs probably caused the company little concern. A Chinese workforce also dominated there, and the Union Pacific knew the Knights would not recruit them.[48]

The Union Pacific Coal Department had a much greater concern at Carbon where a more traditional workforce existed. The majority of the men were steeped in the mining culture, and many had a history of labor activism. Plus, the men at Carbon had reason to organize. Not only had the railroad workers' success inspired them, but the company had recently pushed their wages down. Before the economic downturn of the 1880s, Union Pacific miners reportedly earned between $0.90 and $1.15 per ton of coal mined. During the recession years the company stated that the "standard price" for mining coal stood at $0.74 a ton. The miners lost between sixteen and forty-one cents a ton.[49]

When the strike came to the Denver Basin in late October 1884 and closed the Union Pacific's mines at Louisville and Erie, the company counted on the Carbon mines to continue working and to replace the lost production. Carbon provided an element of stability, but the settlement in the Denver Basin gave the company other concerns. Although the Union Pacific did not accept the terms, the agreement put Denver Basin wages above those at Carbon, and the managers feared the labor unrest would spread north into Wyoming. The company took the defensive action of firing every man it "suspected of [belonging to the] Knights of Labor."[50] But the tactic proved ultimately unsuccessful, and the Carbon miners struck on January 13, 1885. A few days later John L. Lewis proclaimed in the *Labor Enquirer*, "We now have Carbon, Wyoming, in our lines."[51]

This move, however, did not come until the strike in central and southern Colorado collapsed. With the CMA surviving only in the Denver Basin, the strike at Carbon seems to have occurred at an odd time—particularly since the Carbon mines had been providing coal to Colorado, undermining the strikers at the Union Pacific's mines at Louisville and Erie. The men at Carbon had felt the influence of the Knights since May 1884, but they had hesitated to strike. Perhaps the movement lacked strength until 1885, or the miners may have suffered another wage cut. Although wages had gone down, the timing seems unclear. Lewis and the executive board clearly needed a victory at Erie and Louisville to hold the CMA, the Conciliation Board, and the related Coal Operators Association together. The losses in southern and central Colorado not only threatened them, but in January 1885 Cañon City coal began hitting the Denver market below established prices. The reduced rate could have disrupted the Coal Operators Association and killed the Denver Basin's higher wage scale. Consequently, Lewis and the Denver-area Knights put more emphasis on Carbon and the other Union Pacific mines: unionize those mines, and the Conciliation Board and Operators Association would survive. Success with the Union Pacific could put pressure on the Colorado Coal and Iron Company and the Santa Fe to recognize these labor-backed organizations.[52]

When the strike came to Carbon in January 1885, the Union Pacific had little idea what to do. Officials who investigated the strike reported that the "men were all out on a strike because we will not discharge the foreman and every one else that suits them," including "all Finlanders and Chinese." They expressed great concern about the Knights of Labor spreading throughout the railroad system, and they feared a possible general strike. The general manager reported to President Adams that "one thing is certain[:] this road cannot run very long under existing conditions."[53]

The work cessation at Carbon did the trick. Fearing the strike would spread and worried about a shortage of coal, the Union Pacific decided to yield. The company ended the eleven-week walkout at Erie and Louisville by granting the men a wage rate comparable to the high levels paid in other Denver Basin mines. The contract also stated that all future demands would be "adjusted by the mining operators and operatives conciliation board, it being understood . . . that the Union Coal Company shall have a representative upon said board." This specification gave Lewis and the CMA the apparent security they wanted. Lewis stated, "This makes the state board of conciliation a firmly established tribunal."[54]

When the Union Pacific sent word to the managers at Carbon to end the walkout, the miners responded that company officials needed to meet with a union board member. The company agreed, and Lewis and Howells conferred with representatives from Beckwith, Quinn and Company and the Union Pacific in Omaha soon after. The Carbon strike ended after about two weeks. Each side felt it was the victor. The company believed it had won the terms it originally wanted: the miners dropped the demand over foreign labor, and the local would not become part of the Colorado Conciliation Board. For their part, the miners gained an arbitration committee to discuss wages, which they thought should function like the Colorado Conciliation Board, and the union gained informal recognition.[55]

After the settlement had been reached, the Union Pacific did not know what to do next. Managers expressed great concern over the union's growing strength. Some feared a general strike, and others wondered how they could deal with disloyal men. They did agree that they would never let the Denver board establish a selling price for their coal. Just two weeks after they signed the contract ending the northern Colorado strike, the Union Pacific announced it would not honor the schedule of coal prices the Coal Operators Association had established. Lewis called the Union Pacific's new prices "war rates." He accused the railroad of attempting to "foster a monopoly and crush small enterprises." Further, Lewis argued that the Union Pacific was attempting to break down "every arrangement of the Conciliation Board."[56] The railroad's actions led to another strike by its miners in the Denver Basin in February 1885. As General Manager S. R. Callaway told President Adams, the "Colorado miners all went out today and are trying to get the Carbon and Rock Springs men to join them—they now want to name the price at which we are to sell coal at Denver."[57]

The new strike demonstrated the weakness of the Coal Miners' Amalgamation. Lewis made a veiled threat to Union Pacific officials: either the company would agree to the selling price of the coal, or "I shall be compelled to take further unpleasant steps."[58] The company anticipated a possible systemwide general strike, but it never came. After two weeks the Colorado men began to return to work. As this last-gasp effort wound down, Lewis lamented, "The situation had become very perplexed by reasons of certain facts operating against us, and over which we have not absolute control."[59] Lewis did not explain what problems the union had, but at least two problems apparently existed. First, the Carbon mines continued to operate because of their separate agreement with the company, and their operation undermined Lewis and the Conciliation Board. And second, the CMA needed the help of the Union Pacific Employe's Association to gain a systemwide general strike, and the organization would not agree to help. The Employe's Association feared a walkout would only hurt the organization.[60]

Although a general strike did not happen and the Union Pacific did not follow the Conciliation Board, Lewis and the CMA still felt they had some strength in Wyoming. Knights of Labor locals existed at Carbon and Rock Springs, and the railroad workers had developed a fairly solid organization. As the CMA faltered in Colorado, Lewis began to pay more and more attention to the Union Pacific coal camps. If the Coal Miners' Amalgamation was going to survive, it needed to expand its reach. This necessity became evident in Lewis's weekly reports to the *Labor Enquirer*. Tensions already existed because of the Chinese laborers at Rock Springs, and Lewis made conditions worse. In March 1885 he began reporting that the Union Pacific, through the agency of Beckwith, Quinn and Company, planned to introduce Chinese at Carbon. Further, he speculated that the company anticipated provoking a strike so it would have the necessary openings to hire new workers, much as had happened in 1875. Lewis stirred up enough anger and concern at Carbon that General Superintendent D. O. Clark asked him to stop printing the rumors. Clark also rebuked the notion of hiring new workers by stating that as long as the miners "do their work satisfactorily, there will be no changes made."[61]

Clark's assurances caused Lewis to use a more moderate tone, but it did not ease the hostile feelings. Problems intensified as the coal business slumped further in the spring of 1885. When the Union Pacific closed one of its mines in Rock Springs for lack of business, it gave the Chinese preferential treatment, concentrating them in the open mines while laying off white miners. The Chinese had become a mobile labor pool for the company. If the railroad needed section workers in the summer, they would take Chinese from the coal mines. When the weather turned colder, Chinese—sometimes different ones from the former group—would be pulled from the line and placed in the Rock Springs mines. The white workers saw new Chinese laborers getting preference over their fellow workers. Lewis protested this practice based on the agreement he had signed with Beckwith, Quinn, but Beckwith responded that the understanding only applied to Carbon. By late August, 331 Chinese and 150 whites were working inside the mines at Rock Springs.[62]

On August 28 Lewis sent letters to Beckwith, Quinn and to General Superintendent D. O. Clark. He again complained about Chinese workers being hired instead of whites and about the Rock Springs mines working regularly while the Carbon mines sat nearly idle. He warned of a brewing "storm" and stated that the company needed to do something to "avoid this calamity."[63] Lewis proved prophetic. On September 2 two white miners claimed a Chinese crew was working a room assigned to them. The quarrel turned into a fight, which rapidly spread onto the streets of Rock Springs and developed into a riot. Throughout the town, whites unleashed their hatred of the Chinese—killing 28, chasing 600 others into the desert, and burning 100 homes to the ground. A few days later white miners also took possession of the mines at Almy and at Grass Creek, Utah, a small operation acquired by the railroad in 1880. Violence did not occur at those locations, but whites prevented the Chinese from entering the mines.[64]

With the onset of violence at its most important mines, the Union Pacific management set about to quell the disorder, get the mines operating, and dissipate hostility directed at the company. To company officials, stemming the outbursts took priority. Knowing that local law enforcement agencies and the citizenry sympathized with the white miners, the Union Pacific turned to its traditional allies—the territorial and federal governments. The railroad appealed to Wyoming's territorial governor, Francis E. Warren, for assistance. Warren wired U.S. president Cleveland that "unlawful combinations and conspiracies exist among miners" in Wyoming and that "open insurrection" required sending federal troops. Within days the government had dispatched 250 soldiers to Rock Springs and Evanston under the pretext "to prevent any interruption to the United States mails or the routes over which they are carried."[65]

The troops brought peace to the southern Wyoming coalfields. With that, the company wanted to attain its second goal: get the Rock Springs mines running again. The company gave the order to pay off all white miners who "in any manner participated in the riot." A Rock Springs newspaper estimated that sixty or seventy men had actually taken part in the riot, and they alone would not be allowed to return to work. With the help of the military, the company soon brought a number of Chinese back to Rock Springs. On September 11 the Rock Springs mines reopened with about a hundred Chinese and a few white surface workers and laborers.[66]

Ten days after the riot, the situation in the Union Pacific coalfields seemed tenuous. The company had closed the Almy mines and partially reopened the

Rock Springs mines with a primarily Chinese crew, while at Carbon the mines continued to work. Company officials worried about the next step. Even before the riot they had believed the Knights of Labor fully intended to block the employment of any Chinese laborers. In the weeks after the riot, rumors circulated that the Knights would order a general strike for the entire Union Pacific Railroad system. This would force the company's hand. Then, in September, white workers still at Rock Springs began a work slowdown, interfering with the movement of coal around the mines.[67]

The management wasted no time seeking possible solutions to its problems. To better control the miners and protect the Chinese, the managers decided to concentrate the Chinese in Rock Springs. To take their place at Almy, the Union Pacific found replacements among the Mormons in Utah. Bishop Sharp from Utah promised he could have 50 to 100 men available "upon a few hours notice." Mormon leaders believed the ideals of the Knights of Labor went against church teachings and that the union threatened loyalty and cohesion. Consequently, they wanted to help the Union Pacific. Finally, the company had ordered its first coal-cutting machines. All of them had potential problems, however. So the situation was thus: relying on Chinese workers had become problematic because of the 1882 Chinese Exclusion Act; despite Bishop Sharp's promises, Mormon workers could not come to the mines until they had finished their farmwork; and the lay of the coal in the company's mines made coal-cutting machines difficult to use. The company would inevitably have to come to an understanding with its traditional workforce.[68]

The Union Pacific administration wanted to diminish the hostility many people felt toward the corporation. The workers, customers, and federal government representatives on the board of directors all observed that the company was poorly run. One company official reported that the "sympathy of the entire community west of the Missouri River seems to be with the men against the company," and the *Engineering and Mining Journal* stated that because of the railroad's rate policy, it had "deprived itself of any sympathy in the question of its right to employ the labor it prefers."[69]

All of this anger hurt the Union Pacific's performance, and Charles Francis Adams, a reformist president, wanted to turn the tide. He authorized an immediate investigation of the Rock Springs Massacre, and he chose his investigator wisely. Adams selected Isaac H. Bromley, a government appointee on the Union Pacific board of directors. The federal directors had long felt ignored in the operation of the road, and this selection brought their influence to the forefront. Adams hoped the appointment might relieve some of the government hostility toward the company and allow the public to believe a fair and unbiased report might be made.[70]

Bromley toured the area and held hearings in Rock Springs. He heard many complaints from the white miners, from improper weighing of coal to the operation of the Beckwith, Quinn and Company stores. Bromley concluded that most of the grievances had been an afterthought, that none had led up to the disturbance. He saw the complaints as workers' justifications for what had happened. Bromley could find no "immediate cause of the outbreak." He knew that at the heart of the matter lay the employment of Chinese, but he felt the incident began without premeditation "except in the most vague and general way . . . partly the effects of passion and impulse." Bromley knew the Knights of Labor had not ordered the riot, but he did implicate its anti-Chinese sentiment as a factor. In fact, Bromley was distressed by the Knights' leadership. During the investigation, in Bromley's opinion, the leaders badgered and interfered with witnesses. He complained to Adams that the Knights of Labor "fosters jealousy, distrust and suspicion, and in all matters proceeds upon the assumption that the company is greedy, avaricious, and tyrannical, with no interests in common with its employes [sic], but determined to oppress and crush them."[71]

As the Union Pacific attempted to gain control and restore full production, the Knights of Labor attempted to use the situation to its advantage. The union initially needed to distance itself from the killings, but then it hoped to use the Union Pacific's vulnerable position to have the Chinese removed from the mines and to strengthen the union. The riot itself was not part of any strike activity, nor did the union call a strike on the heels of the violence. In fact, the union remained publicly silent in the days immediately after the outbreak. When eventually questioned about the killings, union leaders responded that they "abhor the action taken by these outraged miners as much as any one."[72]

Within a week the union began taking a more visible stand. The union officials who spoke out were not Lewis and Howells of the CMA but the leaders of the Union Pacific Employe's Protective Association. Organized in 1884 during the Union Pacific shopmen's strike, by 1885 the association had become District Assembly 82 of the Knights of Labor. Its membership included not only the shopmen it had initially organized but also members of the various railroad brotherhoods, such as engineers and firemen. Led by Thomas Neasham, a man raised in English collieries, and J. N. Corbin, the group saw the events at Rock Springs as an opportunity to strengthen the Employe's Protective Association and eliminate the Chinese not only in the coal mines but systemwide.[73]

Their actions put the Employe's Protective Association at odds with the CMA. To this point the latter had been the primary Knights of Labor force in the coal camps. Although it had never gained an agreement for the Rock Springs miners, people such as Lewis had worked on their behalf, and the organization had achieved an understanding with the Union Pacific for the Carbon miners. Despite the existence of the CMA, the leaders of the protective association took charge of union activities at Rock Springs. They may have done so because the Chinese issue went beyond the coal camps, or perhaps they concluded that the CMA had too little leverage to bring the railroad to terms. Nevertheless, this decision caused a conflict to develop between the two umbrella organizations.

The Employe's Protective Association first addressed the dismissal of miners at Rock Springs. Corbin protested that the company was driving white men away, but the railroad's general manager responded that "no loyal law abiding employee has anything to fear."[74] To make its point, the union had little recourse except to strike, and rumors of a "general strike" began circulating nine days after the riot. At the same time, the white workers still employed at Rock Springs began their work slowdown, and others attempted to frighten the Chinese away from the mines. With these problems and rumors, the company considered a lockout. The officials felt this move might force the miners to account for their actions. Or, as one official said, the "odium" would then rest with the strikers. The company did not see the men as legitimate union members but as a "lot of lawless ruffians."[75]

The white miners who had been working at Rock Springs and Almy did strike in the third week of September, but Carbon and the other Union Pacific coal properties kept working. The strike apparently came at the behest of the Employe's Protective Association as it began to consider a systemwide walkout. Members of the CMA, however, did not join the effort; nor did any railroad employees. A number of fractures apparently existed within the Knights of Labor, including one between the CMA and the Employe's Protective Association and another between the railroad workers and their union. As the railroad's general manager reported, "There is apparently some hitch. I think the men on [the] east end are inclined to rebel against the order." Indeed, Neasham had great concern about his union's integrity.[76]

Neasham's frustrations with the CMA and the Employe's Protective Association caused him to lash out. In late September he became very aggressive toward Bromley and his investigation of the riot. Bromley reported that Neasham was attacking the "integrity and honesty of the managers of the road" and accused him of sending "lying, mischievous and malicious reports to the press." Another company official labeled Neasham's tactics as trying to "bull dose" a settlement.[77]

By the end of September traditional Wyoming coal miners were losing ground. Union men refused to work in Rock Springs, but the company kept bringing in more Chinese and production continued to increase. The miners needed a boost, and on October 1 the men at Carbon and Louisville quit work, agreeing not to resume until the company dismissed the Chinese. Other demands soon emerged that included reinstating men not guilty of participating in the Rock Springs riot and severing connections with Beckwith, Quinn and Company. Ignoring the protective association, Lewis and the Coal Miners' Amalgamation directed the strike, and they wanted the settlement handled by their Conciliation Board.[78]

This action fully indicated the break that existed between the CMA and the Union Pacific Employe's Protective Association. Striking independently of the latter, the CMA angered the association's leaders and lost their aid. A general strike or at least a boycott of coal imported into the system had been discussed, but these ideas also died. The CMA tried to gain support from other coal miners in Colorado, especially Colorado Coal and Iron miners. The union wanted these men to strike because their mines had begun supplying the Union Pacific's fuel needs. The miners, already soundly beaten, would not join the effort.[79]

After about three weeks, the Carbon strike began to disintegrate. Some scabs came in under the protection of Pinkerton detectives, and some miners just wanted to return to work. With the strike falling apart, Neasham and Lewis tried to salvage what remained, and both went to Carbon to brace up the men. Terence Powderly, national leader of the Knights, appealed to Charles Francis Adams, assuring him that Knights members had not been involved in the Rock Springs riot and requesting that he restore the union members to their former positions. But the company had no desire to reconsider its position and made no concessions to the striking miners. On November 11 the Carbon strike ended. A company official reported that 250 men had resumed work and were "glad to get back to work."[80]

The collapse of the Union Pacific coal mine strike highlighted the animosity that had developed between the Coal Miners' Amalgamation and the Employe's Protective Association. Neasham blamed Lewis and his tactics for the failure, and Lewis blamed Neasham. J. N. Corbin, the executive secretary of the Employe's Protective Association, wrote to the general manager of the Union Pacific attempting to explain his organization's position during the latest Carbon strike. He stated that the miners went out "contrary to our wish and advice; and we endeavored to show their representatives wherein we believed this would be a mistake." He added that "we do not believe the men at Carbon and Louisville really understood the circumstances connected with the trouble at Rock Springs. . . . [T]ake this into consideration, and allow the miners to return to work."[81]

By this time most of the Carbon miners were working. The loss did not kill the Knights of Labor assemblies in the Union Pacific's Wyoming coal camps, but they were no longer part of the CMA. They officially became part of the Union Pacific Employe's Protective Association. This move mortally wounded the CMA. John L. Lewis issued his last public report in December 1885, resigned as executive secretary, and became a salesman for a retail coal dealer in Denver.[82]

The affairs of 1885 also convinced Union Pacific management that something needed to be done with the mines in northern Colorado. The miners there had fought the company and its policies ever since the Union Pacific had acquired the mines. In considering their options, the Union Pacific managers debated how getting rid of the mines might affect coal sales along their system, how they feared the mines might fall into the hands of bitter competitors, how the mines might be kept operating despite a hostile labor force, and how their sale would affect the railroad itself. After some failed negotiations, the Union Pacific management decided to sell the mines to David H. Moffat Jr. of the Marshall Coal Company, someone they thought was a friend in northern Colorado. He promised to help supply their customers, to provide coal if the Wyoming mines went on strike, and to put in mining machines to end the labor problems.

The Marshall Coal Company took control of the mines in November 1885 and soon attempted to reduce wages. At the Louisville Mine the men rioted and drove away company representatives. At the original Marshall mines near Boulder, the miners set fire to all the buildings and the coal on the dump. The Marshall Company then notified the Union Pacific that it would abandon the Louisville Mine. Incapable of gaining control, the Union Pacific closed its holdings in the Denver Basin, and the miners moved on to other mines. After years of frustration, the miners and their families in the Northern Colorado Coal Field remained ardent spirits. They had driven a major coal producer from the field. Nevertheless, other mines within the Denver Basin would remain highly competitive and would constitute a seat of labor activism.[83]

By the end of 1885 the regionwide coal miners' movement had died. Two years before, conditions had seemed right for success. Expansion had brought a number of traditional miners west, and an organization existed that seemingly could tie them together: the Knights of Labor. But the Great Upheaval of western coal miners began at the local level. Miners at Coal Creek, one of the earliest coal locations in the West, initiated the rebellion by calling a defensive strike in response to a Colorado Coal and Iron wage cut. This inspired the regional movement that generated the Coal Miners' Amalgamation. An umbrella organization for the Knights of Labor locals, the CMA coordinated the general strike in October 1884.

Success came rapidly for the miners in the Denver Basin. All of the companies operating there—except the Union Coal Company—feared losing their markets and undoubtedly feared the miners' solidarity, and they agreed to the workers' terms. Under the direction of Henry Sprague, Colorado Coal and Iron would not deal with the union, however. In fact, he had no intention of dealing with his workers honestly; he deceived them and reneged on supposed understandings. Plus, he beat down wages, fired suspected troublemakers, and brought in replacement workers. Sprague moved with confidence because he welcomed the opportunity to realign his company's finances, and he did not fear the market. For the markets he served, the only potential competition came from the Santa Fe mines, and those miners had walked out with his. Beyond that, Colorado Coal and Iron could still count on a monopoly along most of the Rio Grande Railroad. If other coal came into his market during a strike, Sprague knew that after the strike he could beat out the competition with lower prices and a superior product. With such ability and determination, worker solidarity and organization meant little.

After the Coal Miners' Amalgamation's defeat in central and southern Colorado, labor activity developed in the Union Pacific coal mines of Wyoming. Certainly, the traditional miners there had reason to complain. They had suffered wage cuts, and a mobile Chinese workforce challenged the workers' control, but the CMA began to raise the level of excitement. Ultimately, the increased tension and white miners' racism exploded into the Rock Springs Massacre. The CMA and the railroad workers' union, the Union Pacific Employe's Protective Association, unsuccessfully tried to turn the disaster into a union victory. Much like the Colorado Coal and Iron Company, the Union Pacific had a coal monopoly, one the company knew it could only lose voluntarily. It did not worry about market shares, and with the support of the federal government, the Union Pacific could deal with labor as it wished.

In the end, the Coal Miners' Amalgamation collapsed. Only the miners in the Denver Basin maintained any power. Elsewhere, the major coal companies had conquered their workers. No longer would traditional miners dominate the workforces; no longer could the miners unilaterally think they could control the process of mining and the mines. Through oppressive tactics and worker replacement, the companies prevailed. Workers would rise up against coal companies in the years to come, but the men recognized that their skills were not unique and that they could be easily replaced. They accepted company control. Whereas miners once talked about controlling the means of production and receiving full social value for their work, future labor disputes would revolve around demands for respect, fair play, and representation. The workers had to accept a strong capitalist presence.

Beyond the companies' actions, the economic downturn of the 1880s helped defeat the workers. Not only did a labor surplus exist, but the large companies could well afford to ride out the strikes. They had the resources, and they controlled their markets. Only the small companies in the Denver Basin could not wait for fear of losses and competition. The Colorado Coal and Iron, Santa Fe, and Union Pacific companies pushed the misery of the 1884 and 1885 recession onto the workers. Prosperity would return, but the companies would resist sharing their good fortune.

NOTES

1. *Engineering and Mining Journal* 33, no. 16 (April 22, 1882): 205; *Engineering and Mining Journal* 33, no. 21 (May 27, 1882): 270; *Rocky Mountain News*, November 28, 1882.

2. *Labor Enquirer*, March 24, 1883; "Fifth Annual Report of the Colorado Coal and Iron Co., December 31, 1883," 5, 7, Collection #1057, Box #1, Folder #17, CF&I CRL; Trottman, *History of the Union Pacific*, 203.

3. Morton Baratz, *The Union and the Coal Industry* (New Haven: Yale University Press, 1955), 3–6, 18, 19; Suffern, *Coal Miners' Struggle*, 13–14.

4. Foster Rhea Dulles and Melvyn Dubofsky, *Labor in America: A History, Fifth Edition* (Wheeling, Ill.: Harlan Davidson, 1993), 108.

5. United States Geological Survey, *Mineral Resources of the United States, 1883 and 1884*, 38; United States Geological Survey, *Mineral Resources of the United States, 1885*, 25, 73.

6. Long, *Where the Sun Never Shines*, 141–144.

7. Dulles and Dubofsky, *Labor in America*, 132; *Labor Enquirer*, August 2, 1884; "To Coal Miners," *Labor Enquirer*, June 9, 1883.

8. *Labor Enquirer*, May 3, May 10, 1884; Gene Ronald Marlatt, "Joseph R. Buchanan: Spokesman for Labor During the Populist and Progressive Eras" (Ph.D. diss., University of Colorado, 1975), 73–77.

9. *Labor Enquirer*, June 14, 1884.

10. Ibid., July 26, 1884; Isham, *Rock Springs Massacre 1885*, 26; Shelton Stromquist, *A Generation of Boomers: The Pattern of Railroad Labor Conflict in Nineteenth-Century America* (Urbana: University of Illinois Press, 1987), 63; Stephen Brier, "The Most Persistent Unionists: Class Formation and Class Conflict in the Coal Fields and the Emergence of Interracial and Interethnic Unionism, 1880–1904" (Ph.D. diss., University of California–Los Angeles, 1992), 50–51; Sharon Lynne Reitman, "Class Formation and Union Politics: The Western Federation of Miners and the United Mine Workers of America, 1880–1910" (Ph.D. diss., University of Michigan, 1991), 44–45.

11. *Labor Enquirer*, June 12, 1884.

12. *Engineering and Mining Journal* 32, no. 28 (December 3, 1881): 377; quote in *Rocky Mountain News*, May 22, 1884; James T. Smith, *Eighth Biennial Report of the Bureau of Labor Statistics of the State of Colorado, 1901–1902* (Denver: Smith-Brooks Printing, State Printers, 1902), 149.

13. "Annual Report of the Atchison, Topeka and Santa Fe Railway for the Year Ending December 31, 1884," 23, Santa Fe Railway Archives, Kansas State Historical Society, Topeka, Kansas; "The Coal Mines of the Union Pacific Railroad," *Engineering and Mining Journal* 32, no. 12 (September 17, 1881): 187.

14. *Labor Enquirer*, September 13, 1884; Scamehorn, *Pioneer Steelmaker*, 61.

15. "Sixth Annual Report of the Colorado Coal and Iron Co., for Year Ending December 31, 1884," 8, 10, 11, 20, Collection #1057, Box #1, Folder #18, CF&I CRL.

16. Ibid., 8; *First Biennial Report of the Bureau of Labor Statistics of the State of Colorado, 1887–1888*, 100, 126–127; "Coal Trade Notes," *Engineering and Mining Journal* 38, no. 14 (October 4, 1884): 233; *Labor Enquirer*, July 19, 1884.

17. "Sixth Annual Report of the Colorado Coal and Iron Co.," 8–9.

18. "Labor and Wages," *Engineering and Mining Journal* 38, no. 11 (September 13, 1884): 178; *Rocky Mountain News*, August 25, 1884; quote in *Labor Enquirer*, September 13, 1884.

19. Marlatt, "Joseph R. Buchanan," 81–82; Joseph R. Buchanan, *The Story of a Labor Agitator* (New York: Outlook, 1903), 110.

20. Buchanan, *Story of a Labor Agitator*, 110–113.

21. *First Biennial Report of the Bureau of Labor Statistics of the State of Colorado, 1887–1888*, 120–121, 139; Buchanan, *Story of a Labor Agitator*, 114; Scamehorn, *Pioneer Steelmaker*, 62; "Labor and Wages," *Engineering and Mining Journal* 38, no. 18 (November 1, 1884): 302; *Labor Enquirer*, November 1, 1884.

22. *Rocky Mountain News*, October 28, 1884.

23. Stromquist, *A Generation of Boomers*, 62; Marlatt, "Joseph R. Buchanan," 90; "Coal Trade Notes," *Engineering and Mining Journal* 37, no. 26 (June 28, 1884): 485; Pueblo *Chieftain*, November 9, 1884.

24. Buchanan, *Story of a Labor Agitator*, 114.

25. Marlatt, "Joseph R. Buchanan," 93; *Labor Enquirer*, November 1, December 27, 1884, March 14, 1885. John L. Lewis was not related to the later leader of the United Mine Workers.

26. *Labor Enquirer*, November 1, 1884; Kenny, *Making Sense of the Molly Maguires*, 116.

27. "Sixth Annual Report of the Colorado Coal and Iron Co.," 9; *Labor Enquirer*, November 8, 1884; Marlatt, "Joseph R. Buchanan," 94.

28. "Sixth Annual Report of the Colorado Coal and Iron Co.," 9; *Labor Enquirer*, November 8, 1884; Marlatt, "Joseph R. Buchanan," 94.

29. *Labor Enquirer*, February 7, 1885; Thomas Kimball to S. R. Callaway, November 27, 1884, SG-2, S-1, Box 7, U.P. Archives, NSHS.

30. Thomas Kimball to C. F. Adams, November 6, 1884, SG-2, S-1, Box 9, U.P. Archives, NSHS; *Labor Enquirer*, November 8, 1884; Marlatt, "Joseph R. Buchanan," 94.

31. First quote in Thomas Kimball to S. R. Callaway, November 27, 1884; second quote in Thomas Kimball to C. F. Adams, November 6, 1884, SG-2, S-1, Box 9, U.P. Archives, NSHS.

32. Quote in Thomas Kimball to S. R. Callaway, November 27, 1884; Thomas Kimball to C. F. Adams, November 6, 1884.

33. Scamehorn, *Pioneer Steelmaker*, 62; quote in "Sixth Annual Report of the Colorado Coal and Iron Co.," 9.

34. Scamehorn, *Pioneer Steelmaker*, 62; *Labor Enquirer*, November 29, 1884.

35. "Sixth Annual Report of the Colorado Coal and Iron Co.," 9.

36. Quote in *Labor Enquirer*, November 29, 1884; *Rocky Mountain News*, November 23, 1884.

37. *Rocky Mountain News*, second quote in December 4, first quote in December 19, December 22, 1884.

38. *Rocky Mountain News*, December 4, 1884; Pueblo *Chieftain*, November 27, 1884.

39. *Rocky Mountain News*, December 4, 1884; Buchanan, *Story of a Labor Agitator*, 116; "Sixth Annual Report of the Colorado Coal and Iron Co.," 9.

40. Pueblo *Chieftain*, December 17, 1884; *Labor Enquirer*, January 24, February 7, 1885; *Rocky Mountain News*, December 18, quotes in December 23, 1884; "Labor and Wages," *Engineering and Mining Journal* 38, no. 8 (August 23, 1884): 130; *First Biennial Report of the Bureau of Labor Statistics of the State of Colorado, 1887–1888*, 120–121.

41. *Rocky Mountain News*, December 23, 1884; *Labor Enquirer*, January 17, January 24, January 31, February 7, February 21, 1885; Pueblo *Chieftain*, January 17, 1885; Scamehorn, *Pioneer Steelmaker*, 63.

42. *Labor Enquirer*, February 21, quotes in February 28, 1885.

43. *Labor Enquirer*, March 14, 1885.

44. *Labor Enquirer*, February 21, March 14, 1885.

45. *Labor Enquirer*, March 14, 1885; "Seventh Annual Report of the Colorado Coal and Iron Co., for Year Ending December 31, 1885," 18, Collection #1057, Box #1, Folder #18, CF&I CRL.

46. Report to H. E. Sprague by Joseph Simons, 8, Collection #1057, Box #1, Folder #16, CF&I CRL.

47. "Sixth Annual Report of the Colorado Coal and Iron Co.," 10.

48. Brundage, *Making of Western Labor Radicalism*, 56–60.

49. United States Geological Survey, *Mineral Resources, 1882*, 89; C. F. Adams to I. H. Bromley, October 28, 1885, SG-2, S-1, Box 21, U.P. Archives, NSHS.

50. Quote in *Labor Enquirer*, January 17, 1885; Klein, *Union Pacific: Birth of a Railroad*, 482; D. O. Clark to C. F. Adams, November 6, 1884, SG-2, S-1, Box 9, U.P. Archives, NSHS; S. R. Callaway to J. M. Bromin, November 12, 1884, SG-2, S-1, Box 9, U.P. Archives, NSHS.

51. Quote in *Labor Enquirer*, January 17, 1885; Long, *Where the Sun Never Shines*, 196.

52. *Labor Enquirer*, January 17, 1885.

53. S. R. Callaway to C. F. Adams, January 16, 1885, SG-2, S-1, Box 21, U.P. Archives, NSHS.

54. *Labor Enquirer*, January 24, 1885.

55. S. R. Callaway to C. F. Adams, January 29, 1885, SG-2, S-1, Box 21, U.P. Archives, NSHS; S. R. Callaway to C. F. Adams, August 19, 1885, SG-2, S-1, Box 28, U.P. Archives, NSHS; *Labor Enquirer*, January 24, 1885.

56. A. J. Poppleton to J. F. Dillon, February 6, 1885, SG-2, S-1, Box 21, U.P. Archives, NSHS; S. R. Callaway to C. F. Adams, February 14, 1885, SG-2, S-1, Box 21, U.P. Archives, NSHS; quotes in *Labor Enquirer*, February 7, 1885.

57. S. R. Callaway to C. F. Adams, February 7, 1885, SG-2, S-1, Box 21, U.P. Archives, NSHS.

58. S. R. Callaway to C. F. Adams, February 10, 1885, SG-2, S-1, Box 21, U.P. Archives, NSHS.

59. *Labor Enquirer*, February 21, 1885.

60. S. R. Callaway to C. F. Adams, February 12, 1885, SG-2, S-1, Box 21, U.P. Archives, NSHS; T. M. Orr to C. F. Adams, February 23, 1885, SG-2, S-1, Box 21, U.P. Archives, NSHS; Thomas Kimball to C. F. Adams, February 25, 1885, SG-2, S-1, Box 28, U.P. Archives, NSHS; T. Neasham to T. V. Powderly, October 31, 1885, Terence V. Powderly Papers; Klein, *Union Pacific: Birth of a Railroad*, 482.

61. *Labor Enquirer,* March 7, March 28, April 18, quote in April 25, 1885.

62. *Labor Enquirer,* April 25, 1885; Klein, *Union Pacific: Birth of a Railroad,* 482; D. O. Clark to I. H. Bromley, October 28, 1885, SG-2, S-1, Box 21, U.P. Archives, NSHS; *History of the Union Pacific Coal Mines,* 79.

63. Quoted in *History of the Union Pacific Coal Mines,* 79–80.

64. Gardner and Flores, *Forgotten Frontier,* 47; Rhode, *Booms & Busts on Bitter Creek,* 50; Crane and Larson, "Chinese Massacre," 49; S. R. Callaway to C. F. Adams, September 3, September 4, September 8, 1885, SG-2, S-1, Box 21, U.P. Archives, NSHS.

65. First quotes in S. R. Callaway to C. F. Adams, September 5, 1885, SG-2, S-1, Box 21, U.P. Archives, NSHS; last quote in R. C. Drum to C. F. Adams, September 9, 1885, SG-2, S-1, Box 21, U.P. Archives, NSHS.

66. Quote in S. R. Callaway to C. F. Adams, September 8, September 11, 1885, SG-2, S-1, Box 21, U.P. Archives, NSHS; *History of the Union Pacific Coal Mines,* 81; Gardner and Flores, *Forgotten Frontier,* 52.

67. S. R. Callaway to C. F. Adams, September 4, September 11, September 15, 1885, SG-2, S-1, Box 21, U.P. Archives, NSHS.

68. I. H. Bromley to C. F. Adams, September 26, 1885, SG-2, S-1, Box 21, U.P. Archives, NSHS; S. R. Callaway to C. F. Adams, September 17, September 22, October 9, October 19, 1885, SG-2, S-1, Box 21, U.P. Archives, NSHS; Klein, *Union Pacific: Birth of a Railroad,* 486–487.

69. S. R. Callaway to C. F. Adams, October 2, 1885, SG-2, S-1, Box 21, U.P. Archives, NSHS; "Mining News," *Engineering and Mining Journal* 40, no. 16 (October 17, 1885): 272.

70. Klein, *Union Pacific: Birth of a Railroad,* 452, 483–485.

71. D. O. Clark to I. H. Bromley, October 28, 1885, SG-2, S-1, Box 21, U.P. Archives, NSHS; Report to C. F. Adams, September 26, 1885, SG-2, S-1, Box 21, U.P. Archives, NSHS.

72. T. Neasham and J. N. Corbin to General Manager, September 26, 1885, SG-2, S-1, Box 21, U.P. Archives, NSHS.

73. Stromquist, *A Generation of Boomers,* 68–69.

74. S. R. Callaway to C. F. Adams, September 12, 1885, SG-2, S-1, Box 21, U.P. Archives, NSHS.

75. S. R. Callaway to C. F. Adams, September 11, September 15, quote in September 16, 1885, SG-2, S-1, Box 21, U.P. Archives, NSHS; D. O. Clark to S. R. Callaway, September 15, 1885, SG-2, S-1, Box 21, U.P. Archives, NSHS.

76. S. R. Callaway to C. F. Adams, September 14, September 17, quote in September 21, 1885, SG-2, S-1, Box 21, U.P. Archives, NSHS; T. Neasham to T. V. Powderly, October 31, 1885, Terence V. Powderly Papers.

77. S. R. Callaway to C. F. Adams, September 22, 1885, SG-2, S-1, Box 21, U.P. Archives, NSHS; I. H. Bromley to C. F. Adams, September 23, 1885, SG-2, S-1, Box 21, U.P. Archives, NSHS.

78. S. R. Callaway to C. F. Adams, September 29, October 1, October 2, October 9, 1885, SG-2, S-1, Box 21, U.P. Archives, NSHS.

79. S. R. Callaway to C. F. Adams, October 15, 1885, SG-2, S-1, Box 21, U.P. Archives, NSHS; *Rocky Mountain News,* October 28, 1885.

80. S. R. Callaway to C. F. Adams, October 9, October 19, October 26, 1885, SG-2, S-1, Box 21, U.P. Archives, NSHS; T. Powderly to C. F. Adams, October 26, 1885, SG-2, S-1, Box 21, U.P. Archives, NSHS; quote in T. N. Orr to C. F. Adams, November 12, 1885, SG-2, S-1, Box 21, U.P. Archives, NSHS.

81. Quoted in *History of the Union Pacific Coal Mines*, 89–90.

82. S. R. Callaway to C. F. Adams, November 27, 1885, SG-2, S-1, Box 21, U.P. Archives, NSHS; Marlatt, "Joseph R. Buchanan," 100–101.

83. S. R. Callaway to C. F. Adams, March 11, September 21, October 1, December 5, 1885, SG-2, S-1, Box 17, U.P. Archives, NSHS; T. M. Orr to C. F. Adams, December 30, December 31, 1885, SG-2, S-1, Box 17, U.P. Archives, NSHS; David Moffat to C. F. Adams, September 5, September 10, 1885, SG-2, S-1, Box 17, U.P. Archives, NSHS; Thomas Kimball to C. F. Adams, March 8, 1885, SG-2, S-1, Box 17, U.P. Archives, NSHS; Smith, *Once a Coal Miner*, 61; *First Biennial Report of the Bureau of Labor Statistics of the State of Colorado, 1887–1888*, 101; Emmons, Cross, and Eldridge, *Geology of the Denver Basin in Colorado*, 320–323.

CHAPTER FIVE

PROSPERITY, COMPETITION, AND CONSOLIDATION, 1886-1892

A S THE TURMOIL OF 1884 AND 1885 CAME TO AN END, the nation's economy rebounded once again. Except for a slowdown in 1889 and 1890, good economic health continued until 1893 when another depression hit the nation. The economy during the last half of the nineteenth century alternated between periods of boom and bust, although growth did occur. Economic downturns did little to derail economic expansion, especially in the West where expansion slowed during bad times and then boomed in good times. The region's population continued to increase as it acquired more industries, railroads, and coal mines.[1]

Western coal production increased significantly from 1886 to 1893. Wyoming and Colorado combined for more than 2 million tons of coal in 1886, and output escalated in the following years. In 1893, Colorado's output exceeded 4 million tons, and Wyoming's was just under 2.5 million tons. In the period 1886–1893, annual coal production tripled in both states. This explosion brought new mines, new companies, and more miners to the region. For instance, in 1886 the Colorado Coal and Iron and Santa Fe companies dominated the Colorado coal business, operating thirteen mines and producing nearly 70 percent of the state's output. By 1892 six Colorado companies were producing over 200,000 tons a year. Colorado Coal and Iron still led, but a new competitor—the Colorado Fuel Company—was ranked second. The six Colorado companies together operated twenty-seven mines, accounting for 79 percent of the state's output. That percentage would not last. Too much competition had come to Colorado, and in 1892 three of the companies would combine to form the West's largest coal company: the Colorado Fuel and Iron Company.[2]

Coal competition also increased in Wyoming in this era of prosperity. Coal production tripled in Wyoming between 1886 and 1893, and the Union Pacific lost its near monopoly. Output from the railroad's mines increased 50 percent to nearly 1.5 million tons a year, but the railroad's share of the state's coal production dropped from 88 percent in 1886 to 58 percent in 1893. For the first time since the road's completion, the Union Pacific began cooperating with competing coal companies, and Wyoming's coal industry advanced off the railroad's property. This development brought new mines to southern Wyoming. Nevertheless, the Union Pacific Coal Company was still the second-largest coal operation in the West, trailing only the newly formed Colorado Fuel and Iron Company.[3]

The expansion also encouraged more coal miners to come to the West, but not in the same proportion as the increase in coal. Coal production tripled, but the number of miners did not. Wyoming and Colorado counted 4,600 coal workers by the end of 1886 and over 10,500 in 1893, more than double. This statistic indicates that the mines and miners worked more efficiently and regularly. The miners undoubtedly enjoyed the steady work, yet they did not benefit from the general prosperity with a wage advance. In fact, with the heightened competition, the coal companies attempted to gain a competitive edge by holding the line on wages. The men could do little. Most had no effective labor organization to help their cause. After the Great Upheaval, only a few locations in Colorado still had union activity, and they were the usual hot spots in the Denver Basin and at Coal Creek. In Wyoming, the Union Pacific Employe's [sic] Protective Association represented a minority of the coal workers, and it lacked the strength to increase their wages. With limited organization, the miners did not benefit significantly from the renewed prosperity.[4]

THE END OF THE COLORADO COAL AND IRON COMPANY

Henry Sprague became president of Colorado Coal and Iron in 1884 with the intent of making a profit. He wanted first to cut the cost of labor, and after the strikes in 1884 he succeeded. Then, as prosperity returned in 1886, Sprague decided to strengthen the coal company, especially in the face of rising competition. He hired a consultant, Joseph Simons, to evaluate the operation, point out flaws, and make recommendations for expansion. Simons saw many problems in the coal operations. For instance, he felt the antiquated equipment hurt the company, stating that the coal cars were "extremely primitive and faulty." In addition, he reported that the old mines had long haulages, driving up the cost of mining coal.[5]

Simons believed the company would have to operate more efficiently in order to prosper. It needed to open new mines with easy access and good coal, which he said would "defy the opposition." Although he believed the wage scale was generally appropriate for Front Range mines, he complained about the superintendents and their hiring practices. Superintendents, he argued, had risen from the position of workmen; they preferred to employ experienced miners from their own country, primarily Wales. These men wanted higher wages and more control of the workplace. The superintendents did not want to instruct local unskilled men who might apply. Simons noted the coal company's problems with the Colorado Trading Company, which operated the company stores in the coal camps and had an informal relationship with Colorado Coal and Iron. The coal company benefited primarily through the rent it received, and Simons argued that the rents were too low. In addition, he expressed concern about excessive store prices and declining revenues. Finally, he talked about the steel mill and its dependence on the Rio Grande Railroad. Simons argued that the long distance the iron ore, coal, and coke had to be hauled to the Pueblo mill nearly doubled the product's cost, greatly hindering profits. In essence, much of the coal company's revenue went to the railroad. The company, in sum, had "too many irons in the fire."[6]

Sprague may have asked for advice, but he had his own solutions for improving the company. He wanted to increase production but did not want to spend money doing so. Sprague opened new mines only when absolutely necessary. In 1886 the company had to abandon the recently opened Oak Creek mines in the Cañon City field. The pits had been troublesome since they opened, requiring much work and repair. To replace them, the company purchased an operating mine near its Coal Creek property, naming it Coal Creek No. 2. And in the Walsenburg field the company developed a new opening at the Walsen Mine. Despite these necessary expansions and improvements, the company preferred to spend just enough money to push production at the old locations. The coal company had no desire to develop a major new mine. In fact, the state inspector of coal mines warned in his 1887–1888 report that for the Colorado Coal and Iron Company to keep pace with its competitors, "it must open new mines and equip them with improved and modern machinery."[7]

Sprague instead advanced into areas that distracted the company from its primary mission of mining coal. First, he purchased new coal ground along the

Western Slope. From the Yampa River in northwestern Colorado to south of Glenwood Springs, the company acquired more coal lands—not because it needed them but because Sprague feared losing the region to competitors. He explained to the stockholders that these coal lands sat closer to Utah, Nevada, and the West in general; and with them the Colorado Coal and Iron Company could control those markets. The coal properties, however, were not yet reached by a railroad. Sprague and his associates next organized a railroad—the Aspen and Western Railway Company—to retrieve the coal. Then, despite the steelworks' gloomy past, Sprague bought new iron ore deposits and improved the plant, putting it in full blast in 1887. The plant reached peak production that year as it produced rails for the region's expanding railroads.[8]

Sprague mimicked Palmer; he advanced aggressively to defeat competition without considering what the market would bear or what such moves would cost. Whether by a western developer—Palmer—or an eastern investor—Sprague—the Colorado Coal and Iron Company was primarily involved in speculation. It was concerned more about potential threats and profits than about tending to the business at hand and improving the coal operation. Sprague's aggressive actions, however, inspired public confidence. In April 1887 the Engineering and Mining Journal forecast future prosperity for the company and said it looked "forward to dividends in the not very distant future."[9]

The Colorado Coal and Iron Company, however, did not prosper. Despite increased steel output, the 1888 Annual Report declared that the Iron and Steel Department had been unprofitable, showing a net loss of just over $5,000. The report blamed the "general depression and unprofitableness of this industry in all sections" of the country. Coal production had declined. The report stated that the "loss of coal output was because of lack of consumption by 'your' company." Development work on the coal mines south of Glenwood Springs had to be abandoned in 1888 for lack of funds and the lack of an operating agreement with the Denver and Rio Grande Railroad.[10]

The investors and stockholders once again took a dim view of such failings, and they forced a change in management. The general manager resigned in November 1888, the general superintendent of mines resigned in January 1889, and Sprague left the presidency in February of that year. Sprague stated that he departed because "there were elements in the directory with which I could not agree."[11] The board named Edward J. Berwind as president, a man the Engineering and Mining Journal described as having "a long practical experience in the coal business in Pennsylvania"—implying that the company needed a practical mining man over a speculator. Berwind had made a name for himself in the eastern coal business, most recently organizing the Berwind-White Coal Mining Company.[12]

Berwind concluded that the basic problem in Colorado lay with the past management. As his administration started to take charge in November 1888, a committee on reorganization reported that the company had been run in the interests of its managers. They had gained "benefits and commissions" on the business's transactions, showing little concern for the success of Colorado Coal and Iron. Palmer and Sprague had profited by speculation, and the general manager and superintendent of mines had formed their own land and coal company and personally invested in mining property—an apparent conflict of interest. Berwind wanted, the *Engineering and Mining Journal* reported, proper "business methods adopted."[13]

The Coal and Coke Departments had traditionally supported the company, but the Annual Reports for 1889 and 1890 exposed new problems. The 1889 report noted that the Coal and Coke Departments had operated at a loss, something the new board could not understand. The company had apparently lost some of its market. Also the business had a floating debt of over $600,000. Sprague's expansion had denied the company capital and profits without protecting its share of the coal market.[14]

When Berwind took control, his assistant general manager and general superintendent immediately saw problems that stemmed from years of limited investment in improvements. In their judgment, the mines had not been maintained to allow them to operate at capacity. The Walsenburg mines were in the "worst condition" of any the superintendent had seen—the "machinery and everything" was worn out. The general manager stated that the coal chutes needed to be rebuilt, and El Moro's mine chute contained "rotten and unsafe timbers."[15]

Berwind wanted every department of the company to be made competitive. He ordered procuring the necessary equipment and making the improvements that would allow for production of 5,000 tons of coal a day, a significant increase over the 1,200 tons produced daily in 1887. Berwind even made specific recommendations for changes at the mines, such as where to place new mine openings to allow for maximum capacity. The company also acquired new property, not for speculative purposes but because the managers wanted to produce more coke. Near the El Moro coke ovens, the coal company acquired the Road Cañon Mine for its coking coal. Renamed after President Berwind, the Berwind Mine began producing in 1890. Although the changes did not bring immediate results, with coal production continuing to drop and the Coal and Coke Departments reporting a loss in 1889, by 1890 Colorado Coal and Iron recorded its largest production ever.[16]

The company's attempt at efficiency went beyond the coal operations. At the steel plant it rebuilt furnaces, brought in machinery to replace manual labor, and redid the rail rolling mill. To support the changes, the company closed a rail rolling mill in Denver and sold property it held at South Pueblo.

5.1 Berwind, Colorado. The Colorado Coal and Iron Company opened Berwind in 1890 north of Trinidad. It was named after Edward J. Berwind who became the company's president in 1889. He wanted full company towns, and Berwind's regularity reflected his desire. Courtesy, Colorado Historical Society X5002, Welborn Collection.

In 1891 the *Engineering and Mining Journal* reported that the Pueblo plant was finally ready to operate at full blast.[17]

The Berwind administration's practical business orientation also extended to the coal camps. The various company reports reflected as much concern about the conditions of these towns as they did about the mines. In early 1889 the assistant general manager gave a rundown on the number of homes the company owned at each site: five at the original Coal Creek Mine, thirty-eight at the two Walsenburg mines, fifty-four at El Moro, and two at the newly acquired Coal Creek No. 2 Mine. Miners owned seventy houses at Coal Creek No. 1 and forty at Coal Creek No. 2. As the company reorganized its coal activities, it became more involved in the business of company towns. It built twenty-five houses at the Walsen Mine and twenty-eight "double houses" at the new Berwind Mine, and it anticipated building more. The general superintendent recommended that three boardinghouses and ten blocks of houses be constructed at Berwind and "additional houses as we will need them."[18]

The concerns over the company towns mirrored the new business philosophy Berwind brought to the coal company. Berwind saw company towns as a natural adjunct to coal mining. Colorado Coal and Iron had previously built Engleville and added some housing at other camps to attract personnel. Berwind decided company towns could provide many other benefits, including revenue from renting company-owned houses. Moreover, only workers in good standing could live in the housing. Workers often had to sign a contract with a no-strike pledge to live in a company house. If a worker struck or quit, he and his family would be evicted within days.

Even with Berwind's efforts, the company still struggled as demand fell below capacity. By June 1892 a third blast furnace, at a cost of $1.5 million, had been added to the Pueblo plant. Yet the plant was still not operating at full capacity; the 1891 Annual Report reported that the iron and steel operation had been "practically idle during the year." The coal capacity had been considerably expanded, and although coal sales increased, demand did not meet the company's potential. Company officials had to close the Walsen Mine to concentrate production at the other locations, thus saving operating expenses.[19]

The problems arose from two sources. First, another economic slowdown had hit the iron and steel business as railroad construction slowed in the West. The metallurgical plant in Pueblo once again proved to be the company's Achilles heel. Second, competition prevented expansion of the coal business. New coal companies had recently come to the West. Colorado Coal and Iron investors became restless once again. One claimed the company had misled them with "clever bookkeeping and artificial strengthening of the stock." By the end of April 1892, after less than four years as president, the board of directors removed Berwind and placed C. H. Meek at the helm.[20]

Meek was an odd choice to take control of the Colorado Coal and Iron Company because he had no experience in the coal industry. As general manager of the Denver, Texas and Fort Worth Railway, however, he had turned a latecomer among Colorado railroads into a competitive force. Investors may have hoped he would repeat that success, but he had also led the railroad into consolidation with the Union Pacific in 1890. Just two and a half months after he became president of the Colorado Coal and Iron Company, Meek helped negotiate an agreement with its primary competitor, the Colorado Fuel Company. The companies consolidated to form the Colorado Fuel and Iron Company.[21]

THE RISE OF THE COLORADO FUEL COMPANY

John C. Osgood and his associates had created the Colorado Fuel Company. A relative latecomer to Colorado, Osgood first came west in 1882—the year the Chicago, Burlington and Quincy Railroad built into Denver from Nebraska. The Burlington Railroad sent Osgood slightly ahead of construction to examine the state's coal deposits. Osgood did not work for the railroad, but he was

5.2 John C. Osgood. Osgood came to Colorado in 1882 and established the Colorado Fuel Company. He first worked reselling coal and then began leasing and buying mines, concentrating on the Trinidad coalfield. He organized the Colorado Fuel and Iron Company in 1892, operating it until he lost control in 1903. Courtesy, Denver Public Library, Western History Collection, Lewis-Smith Z-131.

intimately involved with its operation because he handled some of its coal business. In Illinois and Iowa, he operated the Wapello and Whitebreast coal companies for the benefit of the Burlington. Although independent of the railroad, these coal companies and the Burlington worked closely together. The officers of the Burlington did not want the railroad to be involved in the coal business, so they loaned money and gave preferential rates to selected coal entrepreneurs. They selected Osgood for Colorado.[22]

During his first years in the state, Osgood did not buy any coal properties. Rather than just plunge in, as so many others had, he studied the situation. Osgood first worked as a coal reseller, purchasing coal from Denver Basin mines and selling it to the Burlington Railroad. In 1883 he decided to broaden his reach, and with a group of associates from Iowa he formed the Colorado Fuel Company. The new company had a sweeping mission: to acquire, work, lease, and sell coal lands; to produce and market coal; and to manufacture and retail coke. Despite its mission, Osgood's firm expanded slowly. He first acquired a product unique to the West—a vein of anthracite coal, the hardest of all coals. Generally found only in Pennsylvania, anthracite was valued as a high-energy, clean-burning fuel. Osgood leased this mine near Crested Butte in 1884 and the next year built a coal elevator in Denver to handle and store the specialized product. He also expanded his dealings in bituminous coal. In 1883 and 1884, Colorado Fuel began purchasing coal from the Colorado Coal and Iron Company, buying most of the product from the Walsenburg mines.[23]

The economic slump in 1884 and 1885 apparently limited Osgood's activities, but with the return of prosperity in 1886 he moved aggressively into the western market. Each year for the next six years, Osgood expanded his coal holdings until he became the dominant coal entrepreneur in Colorado and the West. Beginning in 1886—working with a variety of investors from the Burlington Railroad and Denver—Osgood formed a number of auxiliary companies to explore, mine, and reach the coalfields. The new companies allowed Osgood to raise more capital and spread the risk. For example, he organized the Crystal River Toll Company to build and operate wagon roads in the coal region of the Crystal River Valley on the Western Slope south of Glenwood Springs. Osgood and his associates also formed the Denver Fuel Company, which bought coal land near Trinidad from Elbridge Sopris and developed the Sopris Mine. The Colorado Fuel Company then purchased the Mitchell Mine near Erie from the Burlington Railroad.[24]

Osgood and associates reorganized the Colorado Fuel Company in 1888, increasing its capital to expand further and absorb its offspring. It acquired the Denver Fuel Company and its property at Sopris and purchased the Rouse Mine near Walsenburg. In 1890, Colorado Fuel purchased the property of two other independent development companies, the Southern Land Company and

© Colorado Historical Society

5.3 Miners at Sopris. John C. Osgood's Denver Fuel Company developed Sopris in 1887 near Trinidad. It eventually became part of the Colorado Fuel and Iron Company and one of Colorado's largest coal producers. Courtesy, Colorado Historical Society X4906, Trinidad Collection.

the Southern Coal Company—acquiring in the process the Pictou Mine near Walsenburg.[25]

Osgood continued to create and absorb new companies. In 1888 he organized the Elk Mountain Fuel Company to purchase coal lands in Pitkin and Garfield Counties. Just eight months later, Colorado Fuel took over Elk Mountain Fuel and its mine at Coalridge on the Western Slope. Osgood also formed the Huerfano Land Association, bought into the Yampa River Coal Company, and resurrected the Denver Fuel Company to purchase more land in western Colorado as well as in Carbon County, Wyoming. Colorado Fuel Company's 1890 Annual Report explained that Denver Fuel needed to be reborn because the parent company had reached its limit in issuing bonds and stocks. Osgood nevertheless worked in the manner of earlier speculators. He and a few associates would buy coal lands, then form an auxiliary company that would buy the land from them and thus receive stock and cash. The company would then be absorbed by the parent Colorado Fuel Company, generally through another stock transaction. Colorado Fuel thus acquired the recently reborn Denver

Fuel property in a stock exchange in 1892. At each step the value of the property increased, allowing Osgood and his associates to gain more securities and profits. To the smaller stockholders Osgood explained that the consolidations would add to "the strength and earning power of the Colorado Fuel Company."[26]

Expansion did not ensure profits, but Osgood planned well. He acquired his properties during the time of renewed prosperity and dramatic western growth. In 1889 he assured the stockholders of 7 percent dividends, as he claimed to have markets from Texas to California and nineteen different railroads that shipped and used his fuel. Other annual reports expressed more caution, professing that light demand and increased competition had hurt the selling price and net earnings; but the company still paid dividends, and production increased. From producing little of its own coal in 1887, the company increased its holdings until it had six mines in 1891 that combined for over 700,000 tons that year. Plus, the Colorado Fuel mines at Rouse (near Walsenburg) and Sopris (near Trinidad) had equaled the Colorado Coal and Iron's mine at Engleville as the largest in the state.[27]

With its rapid advancement and acquisition of existing properties, Colorado Fuel moved gradually into the development of company towns. Like other coal camps in the West, Rouse and Sopris contained houses of mixed construction and ownership. In 1890 the company owned twenty homes in Rouse, but over the next year it constructed fifty more. This increase demonstrated the greater importance coal companies were placing on company towns. The 1892 Annual Report stated that the houses not only facilitated securing miners but also returned "a good revenue in rentals." Osgood and his associates also understood the advantage of company stores. As they advanced into Sopris and Rouse, they organized the Colorado Supply Company in 1888 to "establish, own and carry on stores for the purchase and sale of general merchandise." The Colorado Supply Company opened its first two stores that year in Sopris and Rouse.[28]

By the end of 1891, Colorado Fuel was Colorado's second-largest coal producer and was challenging Colorado Coal and Iron to become the state's leading coal company. In addition, during the first half of 1892, Colorado Fuel acquired Colorado's sixth-largest coal producer, Grand River Coal and Coke, making it an even larger force in western coal production.[29]

The creation and sale of Grand River Coal and Coke revealed the problems coal companies experienced operating on Colorado's Western Slope. Grand River Coal and Coke had been organized in 1886 with the hope of exploiting the deposits of coking coal found along the Grand River (the Colorado River) and its tributaries. Its promoters believed they could supply the coke market of western Colorado and Utah more economically than other operations in the state. By 1889 the company operated a number of coke ovens at Cardiff, a few miles from Glenwood Springs, and produced coal from four mines.[30]

Attempting to mine coal profitably on the Western Slope proved problematic. Mining there was much more expensive than elsewhere in the state because of the steep angle of the coal, faults in the seams, and the need to pay higher wages in these conditions. Acquisition of all available coal lands also strained the company financially. Land purchases were intended to stop the advance of other companies, but they did not prevent market competition. Grand River Coal and Coke wanted to service the mountain mining towns, but Front Range coal companies were already established in these locales. The resulting price war hurt revenue flow. The managers looked to eastern Colorado and beyond as other possible outlets, but they found railroad freight rates priced their coal out of the market.[31]

Profits remained elusive for Grand River Coal and Coke despite an increase in production. In 1892 the investors wanted out and made the properties available to Osgood. After Osgood sent chief geologist R. C. Hills and close associate J. A. Kebler to examine Grand River Coal and Coke's properties, he decided to eliminate the competition, and Colorado Fuel absorbed the company.[32]

With this purchase Osgood became the strongest force in the Western Slope coal industry. The Front Range still dominated the Colorado coal industry, however, and Osgood's mines there still produced less than Colorado Coal and Iron. Osgood then made himself the largest coal producer in the West by reaching an agreement with President Meek of Colorado Coal and Iron to consolidate the two companies into the Colorado Fuel and Iron Company in August 1892—a consolidation in which Osgood would dominate.[33]

Osgood's activities in 1892 brought nineteen mines under the control of the new Colorado Fuel and Iron Company. Six of these operations were from his Colorado Fuel Company, which produced over 700,000 tons in 1891. The Rouse Mine near Walsenburg and the Sopris at Trinidad combined for nearly 550,000 tons of that total. Other Colorado Fuel mines included one in the Denver Basin, one on the Western Slope, and another near Walsenburg. The Colorado Coal and Iron Company brought nine mines into the merger, including two at Coal Creek, four near Walsenburg, two at Engleville, and one at Crested Butte. The mines at Engleville produced the most coal, yielding slightly more than 400,000 tons in 1891. Each of the other three areas produced less than 200,000 tons. Colorado Coal and Iron's annual output exceeded 800,000 tons for 1891, making it the largest coal company in the state prior to the consolidation. Osgood had also acquired the four mines of Grand River Coal and Coke in 1892. These four Western Slope operations yielded nearly 300,000 tons in 1891, making a combined production potential of 1.8 million tons for the Colorado Fuel and Iron Company. This amount represented more than half of Colorado's total production in 1891, giving the new company a commanding presence in the western coal business.[34]

Osgood had achieved success at the right time. As he and Colorado Fuel prospered, Colorado Coal and Iron faltered because of speculation, poor management, and a steelworks that seldom operated at a profit. In contrast, Colorado Fuel flourished because it focused on coal mining. If properly run, coal operations could generally make a profit, even in an economic downturn—wages could be cut, miners laid off, and mines closed. Although the workers suffered, the company could still profit and survive. The Colorado Fuel Company pursued property wisely, mixing its resources from north to south along the Front Range and on the Western Slope. It also owned a mine in southern Wyoming. Consequently, it could effectively offer its customers any type of coal and challenge its competitors at every front. At Colorado Fuel, Osgood focused on the coal business, and a comparatively small number of persons held the majority of stocks and bonds—creating a tightly run operation with a strong business orientation.[35]

Osgood and his associates were critical factors in the success of Colorado Fuel. They worked as developers on the ground in Colorado, studied the business, and moved with the intent of making it last and prosper. Conversely, eastern investors who only sought profit dominated Colorado Coal and Iron. Osgood wanted to make money, but he also wanted the company to do well. Timing also helped Osgood succeed. When Palmer originally created the Denver and Rio Grande and associated companies, he advanced into undeveloped country—areas that could not support a rail line or large coal production. When he defaulted on interest payments, Palmer lost control to the eastern investors he relied on for financial support. By the time Osgood came to Colorado, the state and region had grown. Whereas Palmer had to create industry and markets, Osgood just needed to capture the business. His company recorded large profits and paid regular dividends. Osgood seemed prepared to dominate Colorado and western coal production for years to come.

OTHER COLORADO COAL COMPETITORS

As Colorado Coal and Iron and Colorado Fuel battled for dominance over the state's fuel trade in the late 1880s and early 1890s, two other companies also produced significant amounts of coal. The Santa Fe Railroad had developed its mines in the Cañon City and Trinidad coalfields. In the 1880s Santa Fe president William Strong had aggressively pushed the expansion of his railroad, including a new line from Pueblo to Denver. This extension required more coal. The state mine inspector reported in 1887 that the Santa Fe's Cañon City Coal Company had expanded its mines at Rockvale, sparing no expense for improvements. He predicted that "in the near future, this company must monopolize the coal mining operations" in Fremont County. Although the railroad slipped into a financial crisis in 1888 and 1889 and Strong resigned as president, the coal operations remained viable. By 1892 the railroad's coal operations ran two mines at Rockvale and one at Starkville in southern Colorado, yielding over 550,000 tons of coal—an increase of more than 200,000 tons from 1886.[36]

Another important coal operation was found in the most unlikely place—the Denver Basin. This coalfield had been highly competitive ever since it opened. In 1890 it contained twenty-five mines, with most operating independent of each other and locked in bitter competition. To stabilize prices, the operators occasionally tried to form operators' associations, as they did in 1884, but these arrangements did not last. The 1884 association broke apart when prosperity returned in 1886. John H. Simpson—a longtime resident and mine entrepreneur from Louisville—decided that consolidation could end the destructive competition, guarantee profits, and control labor costs. In 1891 he formed the United Coal Company, which brought together four of the larger mines in the Denver Basin. Simpson also acquired two mines in the Cañon City field, and by the next year he held eleven mines across the state. His eight mines in the Denver Basin produced 63 percent of that coalfield's output in 1892, yielding over 350,000 tons of coal. This made United Coal the state's fourth-largest coal company, and it became the state's third-largest producer with the consolidation of Colorado Coal and Iron and Colorado Fuel. Going into the depression year of 1893, United Coal's future seemed secure as its production neared half a million tons.[37]

THE UNION PACIFIC UNDER CHARLES FRANCIS ADAMS

Adams followed Jay Gould as president of the Union Pacific during the downturn of the 1880s. He had to deal with a number of problems, including the Rock Springs Massacre, long-term debt, declining traffic, and a poor public image. Adams responded by bringing in new managers, imposing every possible means of economy, pleading with Congress for a loan extension, and developing a more aggressive company. He also stopped paying dividends and began applying that money to the debt and to physical improvements of the property. To expand traffic, he continued the railroad's policy of building and buying new feeder lines. This activity included creating new corporations such as the Union Pacific, Denver and Gulf Railway. The line consolidated a number of smaller lines owned by the Union Pacific, and the company built an extension from Denver to the Gulf of Mexico in 1890.[38]

Adams also changed the direction of the coal operations, forming a new subsidiary company known as the Union Pacific Coal Company in 1890 after a five-year examination of his options. When Adams first took control of the railroad, he was concerned with the turmoil in the coalfields. He did not know how to deal with the situation, especially in the aftermath of the Rock

Springs Massacre. Soon after that incident he considered returning the operations to a contractor and buying coal at a fixed price. In the end, he decided to keep the coal properties under railroad control and to deal with the labor situation by finding the "proper man to take charge." Whereas managers often wanted maximum profit and would even provoke strikes to drive wages down, Adams wanted more harmony in labor relations. He understood labor to be an important element of a business enterprise, and he wanted peace in the coalfields without losing control of the workers. In sum, Adams wanted to balance toughness with compromise.[39]

Adams reorganized the coal operations in other ways as well. The new auxiliary company did not resemble the earlier auxiliary companies that had operated in the West. Rather than being designed to let investors prosper at the expense of efficient operations, the company had an independent management to deal with problems more effectively. The company was to run an efficient and economical operation while handling labor relations and competition. Adams pushed the coal operation to operate as a modern business—establishing full company towns, providing the mechanism for renting tenements, and running company stores. Prior to this time the company had owned few houses, and the company stores had been operated initially by Wardell and later by Beckwith, Quinn and Company. If administered correctly, these activities could net the coal company significant profits and lead to better control of the workers.[40]

The company's coal mines, however, were located next to independent towns, and it could not easily change their operations. In Rock Springs the company made an effort by opening a store and building more housing, but to fully implement the policy the coal company needed to open new mines and develop new towns. The company started the process near Carbon when it began searching for a new mining location in 1888. The Union Pacific officially announced that the pending depletion of the Carbon coal basin necessitated the investigation. Carbon, however, produced more coal in 1888 than it had any previous year and would remain open until 1902. Carbon, of course, had been one of the hotbeds of union activity and was a location the company wanted to abandon. The search paid off, and the Union Pacific located the coal camp of Hanna seven miles northwest of Carbon in 1890.[41]

Hanna offered what the Union Pacific wanted. It had excellent steam coal in extremely thick beds, allowing for economical mining with the use of the latest techniques. The company introduced large electric shovels to scoop out the coal in massive quantities. The shovels allowed the company to eliminate skilled miners and employ only what it called "miners' helpers." The new location also permitted the creation of a full company town. The Union Pacific constructed all the houses and the company store and placed them in an orderly scheme of streets, close to the mine openings. The company only

5.4 Hanna, Wyoming. Developed around two mines in 1889, Hanna began producing coal in 1890. The Union Pacific Coal Company built this full company town to replace the independent coal town of Carbon. Company towns brought a new sense of order to coal communities. Courtesy, Wyoming State Archives 19873.

allowed one independent business to open in Hanna. The superintendent served as landlord, mayor, and the law enforcement officer. Adding a community hall and a hospital, the coal company had created the first in what became a series of new company towns along the Union Pacific. The company hoped the new town and modern mining process would bring more revenue and a more pliable workforce.[42]

Adams and the new coal company also changed the long-standing policy toward competition. Congress and regional coal consumers had strongly criticized the Union Pacific for its monopolistic practices. By 1888 the company began allowing other mines to open in the Rock Springs area, and eventually three new companies entered the coalfield. These new concerns did not have an easy time surviving, and some failed as the Union Pacific still dominated the coal business. One of the new operators, Patrick J. Quealy, described it as a "strong and vigorous competition," but the stigma of monopoly had been reduced.[43]

Soon after the creation of the Union Pacific Coal Company, Adams lost control of the railroad. The railroad was ridden with debt, and Adams exacerbated the problem with his expansion program. Heavy competition continued from other railroads, and the government still threatened action for repayment of its loans. The price of Union Pacific stock declined, and it again became attractive to speculators. In November 1890 Jay Gould regained control of the railroad and its coal operation. Adams resigned from the presi-

5.5 Hanna, Wyoming, street scene. Hanna's order contrasted starkly with the more randomly built town of Carbon. Courtesy, Wyoming State Archives 24614.

dency, but he had laid the groundwork for the expansion of the coal business. The Union Pacific Coal Company continued to operate, and its mines continued to expand. In 1892 the company's mines yielded over 1.6 million tons, a record the company would not match until 1901. This production came from thirteen mines, including ten along the railroad's main line in southern Wyoming. Five Union Pacific mines operated at Rock Springs, yielding just under 950,000 tons. The two mines at Hanna ranked second in company production with nearly 250,000 tons. This output served the Union Pacific system's 8,000 miles of track that in 1892 extended from Nebraska to Washington and Oregon and down to Texas.[44]

LABOR IN THE NEW ERA OF PROSPERITY

By the end of 1885 the coal miners' Great Upheaval had ended, leaving only remnants of the former labor movement. Along the Union Pacific system the Knights of Labor still operated as the Union Pacific Employe's Association and remained a factor in labor relations into the 1890s. In the Denver Basin the Coal Miners' Amalgamation (CMA) had disintegrated, but its influence

5.6 Hanna, Wyoming, company store. The Union Pacific Coal Company store dominated the town's business activities and was the center of daily life. Courtesy, Wyoming State Archives 12631.

lingered; scattered assemblies of the Knights persisted, and a new Coal Miners' Federation would replace the CMA. In central and southern Colorado the major coal operators, especially the Colorado Coal and Iron Company, had essentially killed the labor movement. Although pockets of labor activism continued, the companies dominated, and the miners had lost control of their jobs. When prosperity returned in 1886, most western coal miners were not in a position to push for higher wages. In fact, beyond working regular hours, coal miners experienced little benefit from the new economic conditions.

This situation brought relative peace to the coalfields from 1886 to 1893. As the *United Mine Workers' Journal* described it, "The relations between the employers and employes [sic] in the mines of Colorado are not friendly, but peaceable."[45] The Great Upheaval had shattered solidarity and thwarted labor organizations. Where unions still existed—such as in the Denver Basin or along the Union Pacific—they generally worked for defensive causes, trying to prevent further losses by labor. In addition, companies instituted new poli-

5.7 Company store interior. The company meant to satisfy all miners' and their families' needs at its store. Here five clerks are ready to serve customers in a Union Pacific Coal Company store. Courtesy, Collection of Joseph R. Douda.

cies that limited workers' power to protest, such as building company towns and hiring new workers without mining experience. Finally, the steady work and regular pay diminished the coal diggers' desire to organize or push for higher wages. During this era, labor peace meant mining companies remained in control.[46]

Working from a position of weakness, the miners could not take advantage of the labor shortage. The new mines and greater production put labor in short supply. In fact, when opening mines, coal companies often had to offer higher wages to attract workers. The Colorado Coal and Iron Company did so when it opened the Berwind Mine in 1890, offering a ten-cent-per-ton inducement to gain workers. That stipulation, however, did not bring demands for a wage advance from other area miners, and the company soon eliminated the wage differential.[47]

The most significant labor disturbance during this era occurred in the Denver Basin the year after the Great Upheaval. In November 1886 the

5.8 Hanna, Wyoming, miners and mules after a day's labor. Courtesy, *American Heritage Center Collections 11657, American Heritage Center, University of Wyoming.*

northern Colorado operators moved to lower the wage rate the CMA had secured in 1884. The timing seemed opportune. The CMA no longer existed, coal miners had just failed in strikes in Wyoming and Louisville, and the Union Pacific was closing mines in the Denver Basin—which implied that unless the miners gave in, other mines might close. Solidarity seemed on the wane, and since these mines paid the highest wages in Colorado, the operators wanted to bring them in line with the other coalfields.[48]

The CMA may have folded, but the miners in the Denver Basin remained united. In July 1886 the men of Boulder and Weld Counties organized the Coal Miners' Federation to replace the CMA. The new federation was designed to handle grievances and maintain a "fair rate of wages," and the men saw it as the necessary agent to carry on the 1884 contract they had signed with the coal operators. The federation operated with little central organization or control, however. When the coal companies attempted to bring down wages in November 1886, about 750 miners struck, but they went out on their own. The federation did not order the strike but served more as a symbol of unity. With little direct coordination, the mines closed at various times throughout November and reopened at different times. Nevertheless, the miners prevailed, maintaining the 1884 contract and receiving some of the highest wages in the Colorado coalfields.[49]

The Coal Miners' Federation remained active into 1889, earning praise from the Colorado Bureau of Labor Statistics and later from the United Mine Workers for its success in controlling trouble, maintaining fair conditions, and helping fix prices. The defunct Coal Miners' Amalgamation had attempted to maintain coal prices in the Denver market, and the federation tried to do the same. But expansion made this difficult. Whereas the Denver Basin had fifteen mines in 1885, by 1891 it had twenty-five, and that number overwhelmed the federation's influence.[50]

Prosperity and competition also undermined the federation. Steady employment caused some men to lose interest in the organization and allowed others to change jobs if they did not like their working conditions. Sharp competition also caused operators to find ways to evade the 1884 contract. When new mines opened at Lafayette in 1888, the operator decided to reduce costs by replacing pick miners with machines and laborers. The Lafayette miners struck, but they stood alone. The federation lacked enough strength to fight, and the new operator refused to give in. By the end of 1889 the federation had disappeared.[51]

Even without an umbrella organization, the Denver Basin mines still constituted a center of coal labor activism. A number of the miners still understood the traditions of their trade and defended their rights. When pressured, these operators feared losing their share of the Denver market and worked with the miners to ensure stability. The prosperity of the late 1880s made both the miners and the companies feel more secure and made organizational cooperation less important. But a delicate balance still existed between miners and operators in this coalfield. They had a history of organization, and the conditions that had fostered ferment in the past were only laying dormant.

Beyond the Denver Basin, a labor organization continued in the Union Pacific coal mines. After the Great Upheaval, the Union Pacific coal miners and the CMA appeared defeated in Wyoming. The Carbon miners went back to work with no concessions from the company, the Rock Springs mines opened with a predominantly Chinese workforce, and the company counted on an antiunion Mormon workforce at Almy. But labor activism and the Knights of Labor did survive. The CMA and the Union Pacific Employe's Protective Association had fought over jurisdiction during the events of 1885, but after the CMA collapsed, the Employe's Association stood paramount. The unionized coal workers became affiliated officially with the association, also known as District Assembly 82 of the Knights of Labor. District Assembly 82 encompassed the entire Union Pacific system and operated a successful industrial union. Because of the union, railroad workers received better wages than employees on other railroads, and coal miners' wages never fell to the low levels of those in southern Colorado. When an official from the Colorado Coal and Iron Company investigated the Rock Springs mines in 1890, he expressed surprise at the "very high wages" paid.[52]

Local assemblies of the Knights of Labor existed at Carbon, Rock Springs, and Almy. When the Union Pacific opened the Hanna mines in 1890, a local assembly soon followed, even though the company tried to avoid hiring traditional miners with activist proclivities. At all locations except perhaps Carbon, the Knights represented only a minority of the men, but their influence went beyond their actual numbers. When the Knights at Rock Springs went out to protest a new method of weighing coal in November 1889, the Chinese workers went out with them. The Knights of Labor newspaper reported that the company managers tried to "scare the Chinese to work," and when that failed they complained to the "China boss." The boss replied, "[A]s long as the white man stayed out the China boys would stay out."[53]

On several occasions the company worked with the Knights to satisfy their demands. When members wanted a reading room at Carbon, the superintendent provided a six-room house "for their use as a library and a reading room." When the company wanted to bid out certain jobs in the Rock Springs mines, the superintendent worked with a Knights committee to ascertain the proper procedure. And when concerns went beyond individual mining camps, the Knights of Labor district leader negotiated with the Union Pacific hierarchy to solve the problems. Plus, the Knights and the company still talked about wages. As the mines at Hanna developed, the superintendent met with Knights representatives to set the prices paid.[54]

The Union Pacific Knights' assemblies were influential beyond the size of their memberships in part because of a favorable attitude on the part of management. President Adams believed treating workers fairly would bring harmony and a more efficient workforce. Further, when Isaac Bromley investigated the Rock Springs Massacre, he expressed the hope that a reasonable accord could be reached with a labor organization, and General Manager S. R. Callaway instructed the mine superintendents to be "just and fair" in all dealings with workers. Adams attempted to cooperate with the Knights of Labor as long as their requests seemed reasonable. In 1889 the company signed a "Memorandum of Understanding" with employees that related to wages and mine conditions. This sentiment endured even when Jay Gould regained the railroad. In 1891 the general manager received a letter from the Knights of Labor expressing their appreciation for his "kindly spirit."[55]

The coal camp assemblies also had power beyond their numbers because of the superstructure and operation of District Assembly 82, which provided the strength behind the industrial union. The organization extended throughout the Union Pacific system, and it helped the local assemblies survive. Knights leaders preached that trade unions failed because of their individual nature and that power came from concentration. The District Assembly also furnished strong leaders, such as Thomas Neasham who served as the district's first master workman; and it offered an effective means of communication. The monthly *Union Pacific Employes' Magazine* offered support, advice, and space for correspondence. Its columns regularly featured letters from the coal camps in Wyoming.[56]

District Assembly 82 lasted until 1894, and during its tenure labor relations in the Union Pacific coal mines remained fairly cordial. Similarly, peace generally reigned in central and southern Colorado, but the miners there had no general labor organization to defend their cause. After the collapse of the Coal Miners' Amalgamation, no regionwide organization existed. According to the *United Mine Workers' Journal*, attempts were "repeatedly made to reorganize the miners" in central and southern Colorado between 1888 and 1892, but they failed. When protests did occur, they happened at individual mines, generally in response to specific grievances; and each movement collapsed when the problem was resolved. The efforts did not reach beyond the specific location, leaving the companies in command of the coalfields.[57]

Some of the mining camps in central Colorado still had characteristics that fostered labor activism, similar to those of the independent camps in the Denver Basin and at Carbon, Wyoming. For instance, Coal Creek had many traditional miners of British heritage who had participated in past labor movements. Many of these men owned their homes and wanted a secure existence. Colorado Coal and Iron soundly defeated their organized effort in 1884, but the men still sought unity. In 1885, immediately after their defeat, the Coal Creek miners continued to support a local assembly of the Knights of Labor.[58]

The workers in central and southern Colorado lost the 1884–1885 strike because the two primary operators were able to dominate the workers. In particular, the directing officers of the Colorado Coal and Iron Company needed profit above all else, and they sought it through reduced wages and a non-union workforce. They would allow no organization to assume "unwarranted power." The miners sought arbitration of differences, but the company insisted it would negotiate with them only on a one-on-one basis. To give itself an image of credibility, in 1888 the Colorado Coal and Iron Company established contracts each miner had to sign that specified pay rates and work conditions.[59]

The 1884–1885 coal strike illustrated why the miners faced hurdles in their efforts to organize and win a labor struggle. First, owning mines at a number of locations gave the companies an advantage. Colorado Coal and Iron had mines at four locations, with significant distances in between. The separation hindered solidarity and prevented the spread of strikes. In 1884 the company fomented the Coal Creek strike by cutting wages. It took time, however, to spread those miners' concerns to other mine sites. In the meantime, the company's other mines aggressively produced coal, undermining the strike effort. Second, the Santa Fe and the Colorado Coal and Iron Company did not see themselves as bitter competitors that feared one might gain a market advantage over the other. Instead, although they had different labor philosophies, they worked together against strikers. Both companies developed blacklists and exchanged information about suspected "labor agitators." Since these two coal companies dominated the central and southern coalfields, they effectively squashed labor activism and controlled disputes.[60]

When Colorado Fuel and its many associated companies entered the coalfields and stimulated competition, the workers could potentially have benefited. Colorado Coal and Iron could not afford to have its mines shut down if Colorado Fuel threatened its markets. Nevertheless, no strikes occurred. By this time most of the major coal companies were adopting practices that dampened labor activism. Whereas racial and ethnic mixing had been tried in the past to calm labor strife, after 1885 it became standard procedure. The Union Pacific brought in Chinese, the Colorado Coal and Iron Company employed Hispanics, and in 1885 the latter introduced African Americans. After these initial efforts the major operators decided to make workforce diversification a continuous policy. They wanted to make sure no single racial or ethnic group predominated at one location.

Despite the Union Pacific's open dealings with the union and the apparent worker harmony, it moved aggressively to diversify the workforce. The company had concentrated its Chinese workers at Rock Springs in 1885, but the Chinese Exclusion Act of 1882 made the availability of Chinese workers problematic. The company next brought in a number of African Americans to work the Hanna mines when they opened in 1890. The company also recruited natives of Finland, believing Finns did not associate with other ethnic groups and did not organize. In 1896 the Union Pacific Coal Company produced a table entitled "Nationality of Mine Employes, December 1896." The company broke its mine workers into twenty-three nationalities, showing the number employed at each camp. Of the 1,969 men counted, Finns constituted the largest group at 517 employees, whereas Chinese numbered 201.[61]

Mines throughout Colorado tried a similar policy. The Colorado Bureau of Labor Statistics reported a strike in the Denver Basin over the importation of "foreign labor" in 1891. Not understanding the threat the miners and their families felt, the labor commissioner seemed amused. He reported that "a romantic feature of the strike was the fact that the wives of some of the strikers assisted their husbands in taking possession of the mine." He further reported that they armed themselves with clubs and stones and "drove the imported miners from the mines." He concluded vaguely that a compromise had ended the difficulty. The Colorado Coal and Iron Company and the Colorado Fuel Company also looked to new European groups to supplement their workforces.

Besides employing Hispanics and African Americans, the companies hired Italians and Austrians. The Colorado Fuel Company made a specific effort to hire a variety of nationalities. At Rouse, its new camp, one observer reported that out of a workforce of 400 he counted 55 Italians, over 100 Slavs, nearly 100 blacks, and the "rest are all kinds." All of the companies hoped to deter organization and reduce costs through diversity.[62]

Ethnic and racial diversity only hindered labor solidarity for a time. But as an adjunct, the coal companies looked to their company towns. Companies initially started building housing without firmly defined goals. Some company officials saw the facilities as a means to attract new labor or to stabilize the workforce. The great majority of workers, however, lived in their own homes. The camps that developed in the post-1885 era became more concerned with controlling labor. Three of the major companies opened new locations between 1885 and 1893. The Colorado Coal and Iron Company developed Berwind; the Colorado Fuel Company expanded Sopris, Rouse, and Pictou; and the Union Pacific Coal Company built Hanna. In each instance the company made a greater effort to construct housing and incorporate elements that made these camps resemble full company towns. The idea of attracting workers remained, and gaining some revenue from the towns was a goal, but the control factor also became an issue. The Union Pacific demonstrated these concerns at Hanna when it issued leases stipulating that miners had to vacate their homes within days of notice.[63]

In Colorado, new workers, new towns, and general prosperity diminished coal miners' opportunity and desire to organize. To counter this, the newly formed United Mine Workers of America (UMWA) entered the coalfields in the early 1890s in an effort to rekindle solidarity. The UMWA was formed in Columbus, Ohio, in 1890. In that year two unions that had been competing for coal miners' allegiances—the National Trade Assembly No. 135 of the Knights of Labor and the National Federation of Miners—decided to merge. The organizers recognized that their dual unionism had been destructive, and they sought to bring all of the nation's coal diggers—including those in the West—into one union. The new union still advocated the idea of gaining the full social value of the mines' product for the miners, but it also recognized the realities that existed in the coalfields. The union wanted respect and fair play from the operators. Since the companies had diminished the miners' status, the workers needed UMWA's help.[64]

In 1892 Vice President P. H. Penna of UMWA came to Colorado to organize the men. He reported to the *United Mine Workers' Journal* that only Coal Creek had a miners' organization—a Knights of Labor assembly. Beyond Coal Creek the men in Colorado had "no communication between places, no knowledge of each other['s] terms or conditions." Penna had two goals: to create interest in the union and form new locals and to establish a Colorado district.

In an effort to accomplish the former, Penna went from north to south in the state, pointing out what long-term Colorado miners should have known: that prices for mining had declined and conditions of employment had changed to the detriment of employees. To perfect a district organization, Penna called for a convention to be held in Pueblo in August. The delegates organized District 15, selecting William Howells of Coal Creek as president. Howells, a longtime labor activist and former leader in the Knights of Labor organization, had also served as president of the CMA. Penna spoke highly of Howells but complained about the indifference of Colorado coal miners. An observer in southern Colorado recorded that the men "questioned the intentions of eastern-based union heads." Penna grew frustrated and accused the miners of engaging in organized opposition to the union.[65]

Over the next several months Vice President Penna kept the national organization informed of progress in Colorado. The extent of District 15's strength was demonstrated in January 1893 when the union called another convention. Penna reported that only 17 delegates attended. He claimed 800 men had joined the union and perhaps as many as 2,500 supported its cause, but he lamented that it was "not so good a showing as could be desired or even expected." A few months later Penna estimated that Colorado had 1,000 UMWA members. He stated that the greatest drawback to union organizers was "the great number of Italians and Mexicans who work in the mines, and with whom they cannot converse." Penna did not accuse the men of antiunionism; he merely verified what the operators had hoped for—the language barrier prevented solidarity.[66]

With limited organization, the coal miners of Colorado and Wyoming confronted the new economic turmoils in 1893. During the years of prosperity, the labor movement's weakness and the coal companies' actions had prevented miners from benefiting. From 1887 to 1893, no significant change occurred in the miners' wages as workers could mount no major offensive strikes to demand an improvement. In 1887 the average tonnage rate reportedly stood a little above seventy cents per ton, and at the beginning of 1893 it had dropped below seventy cents. The president of Colorado Coal and Iron complained in 1884 that miners were not willing to share in the general depression, but the coal companies obviously did not want to share in the general prosperity. In fact, Colorado Coal and Iron fomented a serious labor struggle at Crested Butte in 1891 in an attempt to reduce the wage scale. The miners could not stop the decrease, and they gained no assistance from miners elsewhere in the state. The coal miners of Colorado had no effective organization. The miners in Wyoming had an organization, but it had little real power.[67]

From 1885 to 1892, economic prosperity reached unprecedented levels in Colorado and Wyoming. Western cities grew dramatically. Denver exceeded

100,000 people in 1890, and its population increase exceeded that in most other cities. Whereas the populations of Chicago and Milwaukee had doubled since 1880, for example, Denver's had nearly tripled. Other western cities expanded as well; Pueblo went from about 3,000 to nearly 25,000 residents in that ten-year period, and the populations of Colorado Springs and Cheyenne more than doubled. Part of the expansion came with railroad development. By 1892, seventeen routes had built into Denver, including such major carriers as the Atchison, Topeka and Santa Fe and the Chicago, Burlington and Quincy.[68]

Coal production naturally boomed with the prosperity. Nationally, coal production increased over 60 percent from 1885 through 1892; in Colorado and Wyoming the growth exceeded 200 percent. At least thirty major mines opened in the two states during this era, bringing the total number of mines to almost seventy. Despite the growth, three companies still dominated the business. The Union Pacific, the Colorado Fuel and Iron, and the Santa Fe companies accounted for over 67 percent of the region's output in 1892, down from 79 percent seven years earlier. Although their percentage of production dropped, the big three combined to deliver over 4 million tons of coal in 1892—an increase of over 2.3 million tons since 1885. Their closest competitor accounted for only 450,000 tons of coal in 1892.[69]

Although three companies controlled the business in 1892, this generalization hides the dramatic changes that occurred in the years after 1885. New companies had entered the western coal business, including Grand River Coal and Coke, Denver Fuel, and Colorado Fuel. In fact, the post-1885 prosperity brought competitive turmoil to the Colorado coal business, causing the collapse of the Colorado Coal and Iron Company. John C. Osgood returned order to the industry by consolidating several Colorado coal companies into the Colorado Fuel and Iron Company. Superficially, the nature of the industry in 1892 looked much as it had in 1885, but one of the main players had changed. Not only did Osgood absorb the largest coal producer in Colorado when he formed the Colorado Fuel and Iron Company, but he also replaced the Union Pacific as the largest coal producer in the West. Nevertheless, the companies seemed well prepared for future growth. That did not happen, however, as another economic panic came in 1893. The downturn sent a shock wave through the industry, and the coal miners—who had not benefited during the good times—suffered even more in the bad times.

NOTES

1. Bining and Cochran, *Rise of American Economic Life*, 412; Brundage, *Making of Western Labor Radicalism*, 14–15; "Eleventh Annual Report of the Colorado Coal and Iron Co., for the Year Ending December 31, 1889," 7, Collection #1057, Box #1, Folder #19, CF&I CRL; "Colorado Fuel Annual Report, June 30, 1890," 4, Collection #1057, Box #3, Folder #53, CF&I CRL.

2. U.S. Department of the Interior, United States Geological Survey, *Mineral Resources of the United States, 1893*, by David T. Day (Washington, D.C.: GPO, 1894), 255, 412; *Fifth Biennial Report of the State Inspector of Coal Mines of the State of Colorado for the Years 1891 and 1892* (Denver: Smith-Brooks Printing, State Printers, 1893), production charts.

3. *History of the Union Pacific Coal Mines*, appendix; U.S. Department of the Interior, United States Geological Survey, *Mineral Resources of the United States, 1901*, by David T. Day (Washington, D.C.: GPO, 1902), 367, 449; "Coal Trade Notes," *Engineering and Mining Journal* 42, no. 12 (September 18, 1886): 206.

4. United States Geological Survey, *Mineral Resources of the United States, 1901*, 367, 449; United States Geological Survey, *Mineral Resources of the United States, 1886*, 250, 377.

5. Report to H. E. Sprague by Joseph Simons, 5, Collection #1057, Box #1, Folder #16, CF&I CRL; "Eighth Annual Report of the Colorado Coal and Iron Co., for the Year Ending December 31, 1886," 5–6, Collection #1057, Box #1, Folder #18, CF&I CRL.

6. Report to H. E. Sprague by Joseph Simons, 5; Long, *Where the Sun Never Shines*, 189.

7. "Sixth Annual Report of the Colorado Coal and Iron Co., for the Year Ending December 31, 1884," 8–9, Collection #1057, Box #1, Folder #18, CF&I CRL; "Eighth Annual Report of the Colorado Coal and Iron Co.," 14–15; "Ninth Annual Report of the Colorado Coal and Iron Co., for the Year Ending December 31, 1887," 18, Collection #1057, Box #1, Folder #18, CF&I CRL; Scamehorn, *Pioneer Steelmaker*, 69; *Engineering and Mining Journal* 44, no. 27 (December 31, 1887): 490; *Third Biennial Report of the State Inspector of Coal Mines of the State of Colorado for the Years 1887 and 1888* (Denver: State Printers, 1889), 71.

8. "Eighth Annual Report of the Colorado Coal and Iron Co.," 5–6, 9; "Ninth Annual Report of the Colorado Coal and Iron Co.," 12; United States Geological Survey, *Mineral Resources of the United States, 1887*, 213; Scamehorn, *Pioneer Steelmaker*, 64–65; *Engineering and Mining Journal* 46, no. 5 (August 4, 1888): 89.

9. *Engineering and Mining Journal* 43, no. 16 (April 16, 1887): 271.

10. "Tenth Annual Report of the Colorado Coal and Iron Co., for the Year Ending December 31, 1888," 8, Collection #1057, Box #1, Folder #19, CF&I CRL; Scamehorn, *Pioneer Steelmaker*, 65; "Colorado," *Engineering and Mining Journal* 46, no. 15 (October 13, 1888): 311; "Colorado," *Engineering and Mining Journal* 45, no. 22 (June 2, 1888): 403.

11. Quote in *Engineering and Mining Journal* 47, no. 6 (February 9, 1889): 146; "Personal," *Engineering and Mining Journal* 46, no. 23 (December 8, 1888): 485.

12. *Engineering and Mining Journal* 47, no. 6 (February 9, 1889): 146; Mildred Allen Beik, *The Miners of Windber: The Struggles of New Immigrants for Unionization, 1890s–1930s* (University Park: Pennsylvania State University Press, 1996), 9.

13. Minutes of the Colorado Coal and Iron Board of Directors, November 15, 1888, Collection #1057, Box #2, Folder #41, CF&I CRL; Scamehorn, *Pioneer Steelmaker*, 85–86; "Mining Stocks," *Engineering and Mining Journal* 48, no. 2 (June 13, 1889): 37.

14. "Eleventh Annual Report of the Colorado Coal and Iron Co.," 7–8, 10; "Twelfth Annual Report of the Colorado Coal and Iron Co., for the Year Ending December 31, 1890," 5–6, Collection #1057, Box #1, Folder #19, CF&I CRL.

15. Report to E. M. Steck from Geo. S. Ramsay dated January 1, 1890, Collection #1057, Box #1, Folder #28, CF&I CRL; Report on Coal Mines to T. H. DuPuy from J. I. Miller, January 24, 1889, Collection #1057, Box #1, Folder #28, CF&I CRL.

16. Report to E. M. Steck from Geo. S. Ramsay dated January 1, 1890; "Ninth Annual Report of the Colorado Coal and Iron Co.," 13; Scamehorn, *Pioneer Steelmaker*, 58; "Colorado Coal and Iron Co.," *Engineering and Mining Journal* 51, no. 2 (January 10, 1891): 71.

17. *Engineering and Mining Journal* 48, no. 11 (September 14, 1889): 228; *Engineering and Mining Journal* 48, no. 21 (November 23, 1889): 456; "Colorado," *Engineering and Mining Journal* 47, no. 5 (February 2, 1889): 123; *Engineering and Mining Journal* 52, no. 6 (August 8, 1891): 169.

18. Report on Coal Mines to T. H. DuPuy from J. I. Miller, January 24, 1889.

19. "Thirteenth Annual Report of the Colorado Coal and Iron Co., for the Year Ending December 31, 1891," 6, 8, Collection #1057, Box #1, Folder #19, CF&I CRL; "Colorado Coal and Iron Co.," *Engineering and Mining Journal* 53 (June 11, 1892): 624.

20. "Colorado Coal and Iron Co.," *Engineering and Mining Journal* 53 (April 9, 1892): 407; "Colorado Coal and Iron Co.," *Engineering and Mining Journal* 53 (April 30, 1892): 479.

21. "Memorandum of Agreement, 16 July 1892," Collection #1057, Box #2, Folder #43, CF&I CRL; Frank Hall, *History of the State of Colorado,* vol. 4 (Chicago: Blakely Printing, 1895), 511–522.

22. "General Mining News," *Engineering and Mining Journal* 46, no. 5 (August 4, 1888): 90; *Coal Age* 1, no. 27 (April 13, 1912): 884–885; *Rocky Mountain News,* August 22, 1884; H. Lee Scamehorn, "John C. Osgood and the Western Steel Industry," *Arizona and the West* 15, no. 2 (Summer 1973): 134.

23. Scamehorn, *Pioneer Steelmaker*, 77, 82, 83; "Coal Trade Notes," *Engineering and Mining Journal* 39, no. 21 (May 23, 1885): 357; "Coal Trade Notes," *Engineering and Mining Journal* 39, no. 9 (February 28, 1885): 145; *Rocky Mountain News,* August 22, 1884; United States Geological Survey, *Mineral Resources of the United States, 1883 and 1884,* 32–33, 35.

24. Scamehorn, *Pioneer Steelmaker*, 83; U.S. Department of the Interior, United States Geological Survey, *Mineral Resources of the United States, 1888,* by David T. Day (Washington, D.C.: GPO, 1890), 226; Record Book of Denver Fuel Co., starting September 10, 1887, Collection #1057, Box #3, Folder #55, CF&I CRL.

25. Scamehorn, *Pioneer Steelmaker*, 85; "Annual Report of Colorado Fuel for Year Ending June 30, 1889," 3, 5, 6, Collection #1057, Box #3, Folder #53, CF&I CRL; "Colorado Fuel Annual Report, June 30, 1890," 5, 6, Collection #1057, Box #3, Folder #53, CF&I CRL; "Colorado," *Engineering and Mining Journal* 47, no. 9 (March 2, 1889): 219.

26. Scamehorn, *Pioneer Steelmaker*, 84–87; "Annual Report of Colorado Fuel for Year Ending June 30, 1889," 3, 5; "Colorado Fuel Annual Report, June 30, 1890," 8;

quote in "The Colorado Fuel Co., Annual Report for Year Ending June 30, 1892," 6–7, Collection #1057, Box #3, Folder #53, CF&I CRL.

27. "Annual Report of Colorado Fuel for Year Ending June 30, 1889," 4, 9–10; "Colorado Fuel Annual Report, June 30, 1890," 4; "The Colorado Fuel Co., Annual Report for Year Ending June 30, 1892," 7; Lois Marguerite Gaynor, "History of the Colorado Fuel and Iron Company and Constituent Companies, 1872–1933" (M.A. thesis, University of Colorado, 1936), 30, 72; Sylvia Ruland, *The Lion of Redstone* (Boulder: Johnson, 1981), 15; *Fifth Biennial Report of the State Inspector of Coal Mines of the State of Colorado for the Years 1891 and 1892*, production chart for 1891.

28. "Colorado Fuel Annual Report, June 30, 1890," 7; "The Colorado Fuel Co. Annual Report for Year Ending June 30, 1891," 5, Collection #1057, Box #3, Folder #53, CF&I CRL; "The Colorado Fuel Co., Annual Report for Year Ending June 30, 1892," 6; "Sopris," *Camp and Plant* 1, no. 15 (March 22, 1902): 230; quote in "The Colorado Supply Company," *Camp and Plant* 5, no. 11 (March 26, 1904): 241–242.

29. Scamehorn, *Pioneer Steelmaker*, 90; *Fifth Biennial Report of the State Inspector of Coal Mines of the State of Colorado for the Years 1891 and 1892*, production chart for 1891.

30. Scamehorn, *Pioneer Steelmaker*, 88; United States Geological Survey, *Mineral Resources of the United States, 1888*, 233–234; "Coal Trade Notes," *Engineering and Mining Journal* 41, no. 23 (June 5, 1886): 414; "Colorado," *Engineering and Mining Journal* 46, no. 13 (September 29, 1888): 267.

31. "Grand River Coal and Coke Co., Annual Report to the Stockholders for Year Ending December 31, 1891," 3–4, Collection #1057, Box #4, Folder #64, CF&I CRL; "Minutes of the Trustees of Grand River Coal and Coke, December 28, 1886," 11–12, Collection #1057, Box #4, Folder #68, CF&I CRL; "Colorado," *Engineering and Mining Journal* 45, no. 25 (June 23, 1888): 460.

32. "Grand River Coal and Coke Co., Annual Report to the Stockholders for Year Ending December 31, 1891," 3–4, 11–12; "Minutes of the Trustees of Grand River Coal and Coke, September 13, 1892," Collection #1057, Box #4, Folder #68, CF&I CRL; Report from J. A. Kebler to J. C. Osgood, May 21, 1892, Collection #1057, Box #4, Folder #66, CF&I CRL; J. J. Thomas to B. S. Fitch, October 26, 1887, Collection #1057, Box #4, Folder #64, CF&I CRL; Scamehorn, *Pioneer Steelmaker*, 89; "Colorado Fuel Co.," *Engineering and Mining Journal* 54 (July 23, 1892): 85.

33. Scamehorn, *Pioneer Steelmaker*, 92; *Engineering and Mining Journal* 54 (August 13, 1892): 159.

34. *Fifth Biennial Report of the State Inspector of Coal Mines of the State of Colorado for the Years 1891 and 1892*, production chart for 1891.

35. Scamehorn, *Pioneer Steelmaker*, 90–91; Report on the Iron and Steel Plant from F. A. Delano to J. C. Osgood, Collection #1057, Box #4, Folder #90, CF&I CRL; "Memorandum on Consolidation," by Strong and Cadwalader, February 26, 1892, Collection #1057, Box #4, Folder #90, CF&I CRL; "Colorado Coal and Iron," *Engineering and Mining Journal* 53 (June 11, 1892): 622.

36. *Second Biennial Report of the State Inspector of Coal Mines of the State of Colorado for the Years Ending December 31, 1885, and December 31, 1886*, 92–93; *Third Biennial Report of the State Inspector of Coal Mines of the State of Colorado for the*

Years 1887 and 1888, 66; *Fifth Biennial Report of the State Inspector of Coal Mines of the State of Colorado for the Years 1891 and 1892,* production chart for 1891; Bryant, *History of the Atchison, Topeka and Santa Fe Railway,* 123, 140–153.

37. *Fourth Biennial Report of the State Inspector of Coal Mines of the State of Colorado for the Years 1889 and 1890* (Denver: Smith-Brooks Printing, State Printers, 1891), production charts; *Fifth Biennial Report of the State Inspector of Coal Mines of the State of Colorado for the Years 1891 and 1892,* production charts.

38. Trottman, *History of the Union Pacific,* 210, 212, 221, 237–238.

39. H. Underwood to C. F. Adams, October 20, 1885, SG-2, S-1, Box 28, U.P. Archives, NSHS; S. R. Callaway to C. F. Adams, October 23, 1885, SG-2, S-1, Box 28, U.P. Archives, NSHS.

40. Klein, *Union Pacific: Birth of a Railroad,* 334, 518–519; Bryans, "A History of Transcontinental Railroads," 92–94; Trottman, *History of the Union Pacific,* 137–138; United States Geological Survey, *Mineral Resources of the United States, 1888,* 390; Anonymous eight-page manuscript entitled "Union Pacific Coal Mines," Box HO 3, UPCCC.

41. *History of the Union Pacific Coal Mines,* 113, 120–121; Klein, *Union Pacific: Birth of a Railroad,* 517; U.S. Department of the Interior, United States Geological Survey, *Geology and Coal and Oil Resources of the Hanna and Carbon Basins, Carbon County, Wyoming,* by C. E. Dobbin, C. F. Bowen, and H. W. Hoots (Washington, D.C.: GPO, 1929), 6, 80–81.

42. *History of the Union Pacific Coal Mines,* 113–119; Klein, *Union Pacific: Birth of a Railroad,* 517–518.

43. United States Geological Survey, *Mineral Resources of the United States, 1888,* 390; Anonymous eight-page manuscript entitled "Union Pacific Coal Mines," Box HO 3, UPCCC; Letter to editor of Chicago *Times Herald* by P. J. Quealy, September 20, 1895, Box 18, Kemmerer Coal Collection, American Heritage Center, Laramie, Wyoming.

44. Trottman, *History of the Union Pacific,* 238–239, 243; Bryans, "A History of Transcontinental Railroads," 95, 102; Gardner and Flores, *Forgotten Frontier,* 71.

45. *United Mine Workers' Journal,* April 27, 1893, 4.

46. "Eleventh Annual Report of the Colorado Coal and Iron Co.," 7; "Thirteenth Annual Report of the Colorado Coal and Iron Co.," 5; "Colorado Fuel Annual Report, June 30, 1890," 4.

47. Report to E. M. Steck from Geo. S. Ramsay for year ending December 21, 1890, Collection #1057, Box #1, Folder #28, CF&I CRL.

48. *Third Biennial Report of the State Inspector of Coal Mines of the State of Colorado for the Years 1887 and 1888,* production charts; "Labor and Wages," *Engineering and Mining Journal* 42, no. 20 (November 13, 1886): 351.

49. *First Biennial Report of the Bureau of Labor Statistics of the State of Colorado, 1887–1888,* 82, 122–123, 128.

50. Ibid., 82; *United Mine Workers' Journal,* April 27, 1893; *Second Biennial Report of the State Inspector of Coal Mines of the State of Colorado for the Years Ending December 31, 1885, and December 31, 1886,* 46, 71; *Fifth Biennial Report of the State Inspector of Coal Mines of the State of Colorado for the Years 1891 and 1892,* production chart for 1891.

51. James D. Hutchison, *Survey and Settlement: Lafayette, Colorado* (Lafayette: Morrell Graphics, 1994), 107; *Rocky Mountain News*, August 26, 1889; "Colorado," *Engineering and Mining Journal* 47, no. 19 (May 11, 1889): 440; "Colorado," *Engineering and Mining Journal* 48, no. 17 (October 26, 1889): 365.

52. Stromquist, *A Generation of Boomers*, 67; Report to E. M. Steck from Geo. S. Ramsay, July 1, 1890, Collection #1057, Box #2, Folder #37, CF&I CRL.

53. *Union Pacific Employes' Magazine*, December 1889.

54. *Union Pacific Employes' Magazine*, June 1887, March 1890, August 1891; "Memorandum of Understanding Between W. H. Holcomb and Thomas Neasham," December 27, 1889, Barrett Collection, Folder 78, American Heritage Center, Laramie, Wyoming.

55. I. H. Bromley to C. F. Adams, September 26, 1885, SG-2, S-1, Box 21, U.P. Archives, NSHS; S. R. Callaway to D. O. Clark, November 15, 1885, SG-2, S-1, Box 21, U.P. Archives, NSHS; Stromquist, *A Generation of Boomers*, 68; Klein, *Union Pacific: The Birth of a Railroad*, 493–495; Long, *Where the Sun Never Shines*, 198, 201.

56. Stromquist, *A Generation of Boomers*, 68–69; *Union Pacific Employes' Magazine*, February 1891.

57. Stromquist, *A Generation of Boomers*, 69; *United Mine Workers' Journal*, April 27, 1893, 4.

58. *Biennial Report of the Bureau of Labor Statistics of the State of Colorado* (Denver: Smith-Brooks Printing, State Printers, 1887–1913), 59.

59. "Sixth Annual Report of the Colorado Coal and Iron Co.," 9; quote in Howard K. Wilson, "A Study of Paternalism in the Colorado Coal and Iron Company Under John C. Osgood: 1892–1903" (Master's thesis, University of Denver, 1967), 35.

60. *First Biennial Report of the Bureau of Labor Statistics of the State of Colorado, 1887–1888*, 488–489.

61. *History of the Union Pacific Coal Mines*, 120; *Union Pacific Employes' Magazine*, March 1890, November 1891; "Nationality of Mine Employes, December 1896," Hist. Doc. 101, Box HO 3, UPCCC.

62. *Third Biennial Report of the Bureau of Labor Statistics of the State of Colorado, 1891–1892*, 176, 177; *Rocky Mountain News*, March 3, 1885; *United Mine Workers' Journal*, May 31, 1894.

63. Report to E. M. Steck from Geo. S. Ramsay dated January 1, 1890; "The Colorado Fuel Co., Annual Report for Year Ending June 30, 1891," 5; "The Colorado Fuel Co., Annual Report for Year Ending June 30, 1892," 6; *Union Pacific Employes' Magazine*, May 1891.

64. Long, *Where the Sun Never Shines*, 150–151; Suffern, *Coal Miners' Struggle*, 136.

65. *United Mine Workers' Journal*, quote in August 4, 1892, 1; August 11, 1892, April 27, 1893; Patrick L. Donachy, *United We Stand* (Trinidad, Colo.: Inkwell, 1990), 7.

66. *United Mine Workers' Journal*, January 26, April 27, 1893.

67. *United Mine Workers' Journal*, January 26, 1893; *Third Biennial Report of the Bureau of Labor Statistics of the State of Colorado, 1891–1892*, 175–179; "Sixth Annual Report of the Colorado Coal and Iron Co.," 10; Smith, *When Coal Was King*, 20–24.

68. Trottman, *History of the Union Pacific*, 239; Brundage, *Making of Western Labor Radicalism*, 13–14, 17; Wilkins, *Colorado Railroads*, 58; Census Office, *Report on Population of the United States at the Eleventh Census: 1890*, 75, 76, 79, 367.

69. U.S. Department of the Interior, United States Geological Survey, *Mineral Resources of the United States, 1900* (Washington, D.C.: GPO, 1901), 371, 457; *Second Biennial Report of the State Inspector of Coal Mines of the State of Colorado for the Years Ending December 31, 1885, and December 31, 1886*, 35, 36, 42; *Fifth Biennial Report of the State Inspector of Coal Mines of the State of Colorado for the Years 1891 and 1892*, production charts; *History of the Union Pacific Coal Mines*, appendix.

COLLAPSE AND RECOVERY, 1893–1900

W ITH SOLID ECONOMIC GROWTH AND CONSOLIDATION in the West's coal business, prosperity seemed assured as 1893 began. But in May 1893 another Panic hit the nation, sending repercussions throughout the West. In fact, some western businesses had faced the prospect of failure even before the Panic. The Santa Fe and the Union Pacific had purchased and extended lines beyond what business required, and the opening of the Great Northern Railway brought more competition. Both companies failed with the onset of the Panic. The Union Pacific had a receiver appointed in October and the Santa Fe in December 1893.[1]

The Panic's effects went well beyond pushing the two railroads into bankruptcy. Overall, sixty-five U.S. railroads went into receivership, as did many other businesses. People in the West felt the distress acutely. In July 1893 twelve Denver banks went out of business, and an estimated 14,000 workers— perhaps a quarter of Denver's workforce—were out of work. Silver collapsed again as Great Britain closed the Indian mints to free silver coinage, and Congress repealed the Sherman Silver Purchase Act. Four thousand unemployed silver miners journeyed to Denver looking for jobs.[2]

With business distress and railroad failures, the western coal industry suffered. For the newly created Colorado Fuel and Iron Company, the Panic came at a less than propitious time. Although the company did well during the first half of 1893, its second Annual Report, dated June 30, 1894, showed a production drop of nearly a million tons of coal—about a 42 percent decrease. The report blamed the general business depression and the collapse of silver, but the company did not fail. After suffering the huge drop in production from June 1893 to June 1894, it successfully weathered the economic storm. After 1894 its output slowly increased, and by the end of 1897 the company's coal production had increased by over 700,000 tons since 1894. In 1898 the Colorado Fuel and Iron Company's mines yielded a corporate record of over 2.5 million tons.[3]

The region's second-largest producer, the Union Pacific Coal Company, had a harder time. With the failure of the parent railroad, Union Pacific's production dropped 9 percent in 1893, the beginning of a decline that continued for four years. From 1893 through 1897, the company recorded less coal production each year. The drop not only reflected the general economic distress but also resulted from the actions of the company's receiver. In an attempt to make the system more efficient, the receiver severed auxiliary lines from the Union Pacific Railroad. The system's total mileage declined from 8,000 miles in 1893 to fewer than 5,000 in 1894. With less demand, the Coal Company closed mines and worked partial weeks. The Union Pacific did not emerge from receivership and see coal production again begin to rise until 1898.[4]

The Santa Fe's subsidiary coal companies also struggled while their parent railroad attempted to reorganize. In 1893 the Santa Fe controlled three coal operations: Trinidad Coal and Coke, Cañon City Coal, and a recently started Western Slope mine known as the Vulcan Coal Company. The combined production from the three companies declined 18 percent with the onset of the depression, dropping from 605,000 tons in 1892 to 495,000 in 1893. In December 1895 a new management team purchased the Santa Fe's assets and attempted to revitalize the road. Whereas the old Santa Fe executives had praised the coal businesses and been pleased with their performance, the new managers decided to get out of the business. In August 1896 the Santa Fe leased its Colorado coal operations to the Colorado Fuel and Iron Company (CF&I).[5]

The new managers of the Santa Fe apparently decided to lease out their mines for two reasons. First, they grew tired of competing in the commercial market. Soon after taking control of the company, the new managers tried to stimulate production by becoming more aggressive in the Denver market. This stance did not bring dramatic increases, however, and the managers decided to leave the frustrations of the domestic market to the CF&I. Second, the railroad wanted to try oil in its steam engines. The Santa Fe had recently acquired oil properties in California and was starting to see oil as a more advantageous fuel than coal. This action allowed the railroad to relinquish control of its coal operations without worrying about future fuel supplies. With the leasing of its coal operations at Trinidad and Cañon City and on the Western Slope, the Santa Fe left the Colorado coal business forever in late 1896.[6]

The 1893 depression also brought change to the Denver Basin. The numerous operators there had traditionally struggled with stiff competition that only intensified during economic downturns. Two years before the depression hit, John H. Simpson began consolidating mines into the United Coal Company, hoping to keep the competition in check. By 1893 Simpson controlled eight mines in the basin, producing 63 percent of the coalfield's output. But the depression took a heavy toll. With a drop in demand, intense competition, and a high wage scale, United Coal began to collapse. The Denver Basin's total output went from nearly 600,000 tons in 1892 to under 400,000 tons in 1894. Simpson's United Coal took the biggest hit; his market share went from 63 percent to 36 percent. In 1896 the United Coal Company went into receivership, unable to meet its bond payments. Simpson blamed the high cost of labor, but all mines in the region paid about the same wage. Obligations on his funded debt prevented Simpson from dropping the price of his coal to meet the competition. A higher-priced product caused United Coal to lose its market share and ultimately to fail. Simpson experienced the same problems the Union Pacific had faced ten years before. The Union Pacific had tried to operate multiple mines in the Denver Basin, but it found the cost of labor too high and the competition too keen and had to pull out. Simpson had believed he could solve these problems, but he could not.[7]

MINERS AND THE PANIC OF 1893

As they had in past economic downturns, the coal companies passed the misery along to the workers. Companies traditionally used wage cuts to reduce costs and lower the price of coal. The coal operators cut wages during the 1890s depression, but other issues also became relevant to labor during that time. Irregular work, lack of pay, and the use of scrip all caused problems between the miners and the companies.

With the onset of the depression, slightly more than a thousand western coal miners lost their jobs, but the number could have been higher. Coal production in the first few years of the downturn decreased 19 percent, whereas the thousand laid-off miners reflected only a 9.5 percent decrease in the total workforce. This discrepancy revealed that the mining companies kept more men on than they needed during downtimes. In fact, this standard practice created an available force so companies could rapidly increase production if necessary. In slack times, however, they only worked their mines and men part-time. This practice allowed all men some work, but irregular work did not provide a living wage, so companies extended credit at their stores and delayed the rent on company housing. The miners sank deeper into debt, but the coal companies benefited by keeping extra men employed.[8]

Early in the depression the CF&I began working its mines half-time, as did most other companies in the state. This decision caused Colorado miners to lose an average of 74 working days a year. Whereas the men had worked 229 days in 1892, they put in only 155 days in 1894. Wyoming miners lost only 41 workdays.[9]

Inadequate and irregular work strained labor relations, and a second problem arose when several coal companies failed to pay their miners. As the Santa Fe system struggled to stay solvent, it began missing paydays. In March 1893 the company failed to pay its miners at Rockvale. After a brief strike, the Santa Fe paid the past-due wages but then announced a 20 percent wage cut. That decision fomented another strike. It had little effect, however. The company had little money to pay the miners. In January 1894 more reports emerged that the company had not paid its miners for two months. Finally, the Santa Fe began to close its Rockvale mines.[10]

Most western mining companies shared the Santa Fe's problems. Despite trying to balance working time with the demand for coal, they had no money to pay their miners. In lieu of cash, the operators issued scrip. Scrip had been used in the mining industry before, but usually only when a miner wanted a pay advance. This happened frequently, since the coal companies paid workers only once a month. But on paydays, companies generally paid wages due in cash. This situation changed during the Panic of 1893, and scrip became the basic currency. One huge problem with scrip was that it could only be redeemed at the companies' stores.[11]

Irregular work, lack of pay, and the scrip system weighed heavily on western coal miners. Even during a downturn, labor activists believed organized labor could help bring order to the industry and correct the problems. They had faith that employer and employee associations could eliminate destructive competition, raise the price of coal, and bring a living wage for everyone. No effective organization existed to make these changes, however. By 1893, only a minority of Wyoming miners still worked with the Union Pacific Employe's [sic] Protective Association; and although many men in the Denver Basin had a history of labor activism, little remained of the Coal Miners' Federation. In the years prior to the depression, the United Mine Workers had created District 15, which included Colorado, but recruiting efforts met with limited success. Miners at Coal Creek—led by William Howells—joined the union, but few elsewhere did so. On the whole, western miners were ill prepared to confront the problems before them.

With such splintered and limited organization, the motivation to strike on a broad scale needed to come from outside the region. Miners across the nation had suffered irregular employment and wage cuts, and the United Mine Workers of America (UMWA) met in national convention in early April 1894 to discuss the problems. The members decided that only a nation-wide strike would redress the wrongs, and they ordered a stoppage for late April. The national union had only 13,000 members before the strike, but 100,000 men walked off the job on the announced day. No Colorado delegate had attended the convention that ordered the strike, and Colorado operators felt confident that their miners would not heed the call. In fact, the CF&I stated that it had not cut wages and that the miners had "presented no griev-ances." But an estimated 450 miners in Fremont County—especially at Coal Creek, the state's most active location and the center of District 15—stopped work.[12]

The strike spread unevenly through the coalfields. At some of the older camps and in places like Engleville, where the UMWA had been active before the depression, miners went out. At the newer coal camps, those with heavy ethnic and racial mixing, the strike had a mixed effect. Some of the men at Sopris eventually left their jobs, but the Hispanic miners continued to work. At Rouse, union activists made little progress. The *United Mine Workers' Journal* blamed Rouse's mix of Italians, Slavs, and blacks. The journal also recognized that the company had hired armed guards to keep organizers out.[13]

To make the strike successful, Colorado's UMWA organizers concluded that more men had to leave work and that the operators needed to meet with them in joint conference. To bring the strike to Rouse, Pictou, and other operating camps, the strikers tried what has been called "collective persua-sion."[14] This meant taking their message directly to the workingmen. In late May 1894, strikers from the Coal Creek area marched the nearly eighty miles to Walsenburg to convince their colleagues to lay down their shovels. Simi-larly, striking miners walked from camp to camp in the Trinidad area to spread the strike. Their actions met with some success. Miners who had earlier re-sisted the call, such as some at Pictou and Rouse, joined the marchers. The state inspector of coal mines estimated that between 4,000 and 5,000 miners eventually participated in the strike, about three-fourths of Colorado's coal mine workers—mostly from the central, southern, and Western Slope coalfields.[15]

With the strike spreading, District president Howells called for a June 20 conference with the mine owners at Pueblo. The operators said they would not participate unless the miners first returned to work, which they refused to do. At an impasse, the conference delegates issued a manifesto demanding an adjustment of their basic grievances—the abolition of scrip and the institu-tion of semimonthly pay periods in "lawful money."[16]

The Colorado strike, however, had taken too long to develop. By the time Howells called for the Pueblo conference, the national office had already ended the strike in the East. Nationally, the UMWA settled with mixed results. Some operators rescinded wage cuts and guaranteed semimonthly pay periods, but others made no changes. The national union ended the strike without a uniform agreement because it feared the strike would soon be lost, as coal production had been increasing and the depression showed no signs of ending. Those mining companies that settled with the union feared losing their market share as other mines opened, and the union worried that those that did not settle would remain permanently closed.[17]

With the national strike over and the Colorado operators refusing to meet with Howells and his district organization, the striking miners began drifting back to work; but the coal walkout suddenly became enmeshed with the Pullman strike in 1894. The strike started at the Pullman Palace Car Company in Chicago, and the American Railway Union called for a nationwide sympathy strike. The nation's railroad workers stopped handling trains containing Pullman railroad cars, including those in Colorado. Railroad strikes had a history of violence, and the justice of the U.S. District Court in Denver ordered that deputy marshals be sworn in to protect railroad property currently in the hands of federal receivers. In essence, they were to guard the lines controlled by the U.S. courts. When violence erupted on the Santa Fe line at Trinidad, deputies arrived to arrest those involved.[18]

The railroad strike added a new element to the already frayed labor relations in southern Colorado. With train haulage uncertain, the coal companies had less incentive to settle the strike. Plus, the miners felt sympathy with the protesting railroad workers. John C. Osgood of the CF&I reported that the railroad strike "completely paralyzed business."[19] Years later Osgood would mistakenly testify before a congressional committee that the entire 1894 coal strike had been part of the national Pullman strike. He was wrong. Nevertheless, the Pullman affair did prolong the Colorado coal strike, as miners continued their walkout.[20]

By early August the strike was over. The railroad strike ended on July 11, 1894, and the mines not operating gradually reopened. The CF&I reported its "principal mines" had resumed work by July 23. Plus, the company stated that the miners had gained no concessions, adding that those who had been "active threatening and intimidating those who wanted to work have been refused employment."[21] Always less likely than Osgood to bludgeon their workers, the Santa Fe managers met with their miners and offered to take as many back as possible. The company reinstated the old wage rate, annulling its previously announced 20 percent reduction. Sensing a slight victory, Howells declared the strike at an end, but the basic causes remained: irregular paydays and the scrip system.[22]

Osgood came out of the 1894 strike defiant and smug. After explaining his actions to Colorado Fuel and Iron stockholders, he predicted that "judging from past experience . . . the Company will have immunity from another such general strike for a long time to come." He fully believed aggressive action in squashing a strike discouraged similar activities for years. Osgood did not see strikes as necessarily bad. They allowed the company to sell stockpiled coal, and despite employing mine guards and maintenance workers, the company lost little revenue. In fact, Osgood had developed a system whereby he charged these expenses to the miners. For every ton of coal mined, Osgood placed a small amount of money into what he called a "strike fund"—a reservoir of funds with which he fought strikes. Ironically, if he had paid his miners that reserve, he may have had fewer labor problems. After the 1894 strike, CF&I miners made from fifty to sixty cents a ton. Regardless of where a miner worked within the system, Osgood had made all tonnage rates roughly the same.[23]

The 1894 strike did not affect the mines in the Denver Basin or those along the Union Pacific. If any labor solidarity had existed among the different coalfields, it had completely broken down. A number of local organizations still functioned in the mines of northern Colorado, but they did not join the United Mine Workers' effort. The United Mine Workers had not effectively organized that field. The Denver Basin men had a long tradition of local organization, but they may have questioned the intentions of an eastern-based union. Many western miners initially doubted UMWA's intentions. Consequently, despite their movement culture, they did not go out.

Basic economic concerns may also have affected the men in northern Colorado. Denver and the surrounding area acutely felt the ongoing depression. Coal output dropped almost 50 percent in the region during the early years of the downturn (1893 to 1895). Work was thus already irregular, and with an estimated 14,000 unemployed workers in Denver—including 4,000 silver miners—a labor walkout could have been devastating. In good times, coal miners sometimes looked for better jobs in the metal mines. In these bad times, the coal miners could see the displaced silver miners as a threat. Staging a strike in a falling market with a readily available labor supply probably seemed silly to many. Also, the long-established coal miners in the area often raised farm crops, which helped them survive when work slowed and allowed them to wait for better economic times.[24]

The Union Pacific coal miners also did not join in the strike. The UMWA apparently made no effort to recruit members in Wyoming in the early 1890s, perhaps because of the Union Pacific Employe's Protective Association. Since 1886, that organization had existed in the southern Wyoming coalfields, but it folded in 1894. Railroad workers had been the biggest faction in the organization, and many of the men had been attracted to the new railroad union, the American Railway Union (ARU). By the end of 1893, Union Pacific Railroad employees had made the ARU their union of choice. In fact, when ARU president Eugene Debs asked members to help the Pullman strikers in

1894, Union Pacific employees promptly sidetracked Pullman cars, paralyzing the railroad.[25]

The railroad workers' defection left the Union Pacific coal miners without broad-based representation or organization, and they were mostly powerless. Yet an uneasy balance characterized labor relations during the 1893 Panic. With the onset of the depression, the railroad's coal demand dropped dramatically. By the end of August 1893 the company's mines were shipping only two-thirds as much coal as they had the previous year. To cut expenses, the Union Pacific Coal Company moved selectively. It reduced the tonnage rate at Almy, Hanna, and Carbon, stating that the men there had been better paid than those at Rock Springs. The miners expressed dismay, and when one of the Almy mines caught fire, some suspected an "incendiary" placed by an upset worker. But no strike followed. In fact, the company hoped to maintain fairly congenial labor relations. When Carbon miners complained about working conditions in December 1893, the company still met with a miners' committee to make the rate adjustment. A general wage cut did not occur until 1896. Again, all the workers could do was complain. A labor surplus, ethnic diversification, a tighter company town policy, and an ongoing exchange of concerns helped keep the workers in check. This labor philosophy served the Union Pacific Coal Company well for the next ten years.[26]

THE 1896 DENVER BASIN STRIKES

Although the Denver Basin mines missed the strike of 1894, they experienced their own labor troubles in 1896, just as conditions seemed to be improving. The struggle for a competitive edge again fomented the difficulties. Competition had always been intense among the Denver Basin mines, but during most of the 1893 depression the operators seemed to have cooperated. They did not try to undercut their neighbors' prices, and although the mines worked fewer days, miners' tonnage rates remained among the highest in the western coalfields. Just as economic conditions began to improve, however, the Denver Basin mines were thrown into a price war, resulting in a wage cut and a labor dispute.

The Santa Fe mines in central Colorado started the price war. After new managers took over the Santa Fe in late 1895, they decided to change the course of the coal business. The old executives had been pleased with the mines' performance, but the new directors wanted more aggressive marketing, especially in Denver. Operators in central and southern Colorado had traditionally priced their coal at least seventy-five cents more a ton in Denver than the cost of the lignite coal from the Denver Basin. The difference reflected the better grade of coal, the greater distance for transport, and a marketing agreement with the northern operators. The Santa Fe decided to end the agreement and make market inroads by dropping the differential to fifty cents.

The decision outraged the northern coal mine owners, and a price war ensued. The outcome did not necessarily represent bad news for the miners. A correspondent for the *United Mine Workers' Journal* reported that the low prices improved sales and made work "brisk" in the Denver Basin, but he also observed that the operators were "not making any money."[27]

The coal war raged from January into April 1896. After four months of heated competition, the UMWA *Journal* noted that the lignite field in the Denver Basin had "received almost a mortal blow" because of low prices, and the Santa Fe soon decided to leave the coal business and lease its mines to the CF&I.[28] But the firms in northern Colorado sought ways to survive. The United Coal Company and the Marshall Coal Company, two of the region's largest companies, attempted to reduce expenses by placing new screens in their coal tipples. Screens separated marketable coal from waste before the coal was weighed. In this instance the screens had a larger mesh and allowed more coal to slip through the holes as supposed waste. The miners received less pay, and the companies profited by selling "waste."[29]

The change in work rules reawakened workers' activism, not only at the two affected mines but throughout the coalfield. The men had not been thoroughly organized before the rule change, but they knew how to organize. They promptly held mass meetings to consider the new impositions and air other grievances. They soon drafted a proposal that called for the companies to remove the screens and increase wages. The workers also wanted to meet with the Denver Basin mining companies. Many operators agreed and promptly settled with the miners. When the Marshall and United Coal Companies refused, the men struck. Apparently caught by surprise and afraid of losing their market shares, the companies quickly settled.[30]

This brief flare-up had ramifications that went well beyond the companies yielding to new terms. The labor activity reawakened the spirit of organization in northern Colorado and attracted a new union to the field, the Western Federation of Miners (WFM). In fact, the miners at Louisville formed a local of the WFM in January when the coal war first began. With the short strike, however, L. W. Rogers, state organizer for the WFM, appeared in the coalfield and, according to the commissioner of labor statistics, successfully established "his order in all the mines."[31]

Metal miners at Butte, Montana, organized the Western Federation of Miners in May 1893 to protect their most fundamental interests, such as fair wages and mine safety. They formed an industrial union that was open to all mine occupations, no matter the type of mine; and they welcomed nonmine workers as well. For Colorado coal miners the WFM came at the right time. UMWA's early efforts had disintegrated; District 15 did not even have a representative at the UMWA national convention in 1895. Several mining camps, however, still had some form of labor organization without affiliation with one another. The WFM filled the void. From their Knights of Labor days, the coal miners understood broad-based industrial unionization, and they could well identify with the WFM's policies and goals. Some western coal miners went back and forth between metal and coal mines, so joining a union that encompassed all types of mining made sense. The UMWA focused on coal miners, ignoring the metal men. The WFM attracted western coal miners because of its inclusive approach and because it developed in the West.[32]

The Western Federation of Miners struggled in its early years because of the 1893 depression and fragmented leadership. By 1896, however, it seemed to be on the move. The depression had abated somewhat, and Ed Boyce became president that year. His aggressive leadership caused the union to grow to more than 200 locals over the next five years, including advances in the Denver Basin. Other local coal unions joined the WFM, including those at Rockvale, another of the state's labor hot spots; and when the Anaconda Copper Mining Company of Butte, Montana, opened coal mines at Diamondville, Wyoming, those men joined the WFM. Even with this promising start, most coal miners' locals in the region remained independent of the WFM.[33]

The WFM failed to organize coal miners more effectively because it remained preoccupied with metal miners and because Boyce and his fellow leaders began moving the union toward more radical stances. For instance, in 1896, the year the WFM first came to the Colorado coalfields, it became heavily involved with a strike in Leadville. Further, by 1898 the WFM leadership had rejected the use of long-term trade agreements between operators and unions. Whereas coal miners traditionally saw trade agreements as ensuring stability and cooperation in the industry, the WFM perceived them as sellouts to capitalists. Most coal miners, in the East and the West, tended to agree with the United Mine Workers' more conservative notion of labor relations. When the UMWA and the WFM encountered each other, relations remained relatively cordial; and as the UMWA gained strength in the West, it eventually absorbed the WFM locals in the coalfields.[34]

Despite its earlier setback, United Coal decided to challenge the new union openly. Losing market share and in financial trouble, United Coal never implemented the agreement reached earlier, thus angering its employees. In addition, the company ordered its men to work the day of a union picnic. As expected, the men disobeyed and attended the picnic. The company immediately replaced them. The outraged miners struck.[35]

L. W. Rogers of the WFM conducted what became a general strike—a strike the majority of mine operators did not want because they feared the loss of their recovering business and production. By 1896, coal production had returned to within 90 percent of its level before the depression. Consequently, soon after the strike began, several operators agreed to terms, and their mines reopened. The United Coal Company, the largest producer in the district, remained unmoved and began putting nonunion men in its mines. The basin's miners suspected some of the other coal companies were secretly helping United Coal in its fight against the union, and another general strike ensued.[36]

In the end, most Denver Basin companies signed a formal contract with the Western Federation of Miners. Although United Coal did not sign, it decided to follow the terms of the contract, which established a tonnage rate of seventy-five to eighty cents a ton and specified the screen size for measuring coal. The men gained a wage advance throughout the field. United Coal, however, would not recognize the union.[37]

The end of the 1896 coal war and strike brought changes to the Colorado coal industry. First, the labor turmoil drove United Coal into receivership and eventually out of the coal business. Second, the Santa Fe, the instigator of the coal war, decided to lease its Colorado coal operations to the Colorado Fuel and Iron Company. And third, the Denver Basin miners managed to come out of the depression with an advantage. They gained a wage advance while all other coal workers in the West suffered cuts. The men in the north earned seventy-five to eighty cents per ton; CF&I miners made only fifty to sixty cents.

Wages, however, had not been most coal miners' main complaint. The men worried more about irregular work, lack of pay, and the use of scrip. The 1894 strike had tried but failed to redress some of these issues. By the 1890s the largest coal companies in the West had developed programs that greatly hindered labor activism. In fact, worker solidarity among the different coal camps was practically nonexistent. The men needed the help of an outside union to counter the companies' power. The WFM initially offered hope, but its preoccupation with metal mining issues increasingly encouraged western coal miners to look to the United Mine Workers of America.

SUSTAINED GROWTH COMES TO WESTERN COAL MINING

In June 1897 John C. Osgood told the stockholders of Colorado Fuel and Iron that it would soon be "reasonable to expect an improvement in the earnings of the Fuel Department." The depression ended in 1897. Coal production grew significantly in the following years, especially at the end of the nineteenth century. In 1900, Wyoming produced over 4 million tons of coal and Colorado yielded over 5 million tons, a combined increase of 64 percent over 1897.[38]

Beginning in 1897 and extending beyond 1910, the western coal industry experienced sustained expansion. Up to 1897 the industry had been very unstable. Periods of prosperity were followed by nearly equal periods of economic depression. Although the coal industry had continued to grow through these ups and downs, the growth had been inconsistent. Growth now became consistent, with western coal production reaching a peak in 1910 when Colorado yielded 12 million tons of coal and Wyoming produced 7.5 million tons. The combined number of workers in those coalfields exceeded 23,500. The levels of output made Colorado the seventh-largest coal producer in the nation, and Wyoming ranked ninth. But the two states were first and second among western states.[39]

The main companies behind this growth continued to be the Colorado Fuel and Iron Company and the Union Pacific Coal Company. They remained the largest and second-largest coal operations in the West. Despite their size, however, they did not dominate the coal business. In 1910 the CF&I produced over 4 million tons of coal but only accounted for 34.5 percent of Colorado's total output. Although the CF&I had consolidated most of its competition, new companies emerged to share in the prosperity. None was nearly as big as the CF&I, although some did produce large tonnages. For example, the Victor-American Fuel Company yielded 1.6 million tons in 1910. In Wyoming the Union Pacific easily led the state, with 46.1 percent of production in 1910. Other companies developed in Wyoming as well. Beginning in 1897, the Kemmerer Coal Company and Diamond Coal and Coke worked alongside the Union Pacific in southern Wyoming, and the two companies became increasingly important operations.[40]

When this era of growth began, the coal companies seemed well prepared to ward off any attempts by workers to share in the prosperity. They had diversified the workforce, built company towns, and subdued worker solidarity. In addition, the miners had no effective labor organization in the West to help their cause. Operators such as Osgood believed they had soundly beaten the miners. The confidence proved ill founded. The United Mine Workers of America became more active in the West, and the workers still wanted the old wrongs redressed. They wanted scrip eliminated and an eight-hour day implemented; they wanted a measure of respect and fair play from the companies. Ultimately, the men believed justice would only come through union representation and recognition. The era of sustained growth therefore ushered in a series of intense labor clashes.

EXPANSION IN WYOMING

The Union Pacific Coal Company spearheaded expansion in Wyoming after 1897. The Union Pacific Railroad had failed at the start of the 1893 Panic, and its reorganization brought a different business philosophy to the company—one that would lead to prosperity. In early November 1897 a syndicate that included Edward H. Harriman and the banking house Kuhn, Loeb and Company purchased the portion of the rail line from Omaha to Ogden and created the new Union Pacific Railroad Company. Serving as president of the executive committee, Harriman had firm control of the corporation and became the architect in rebuilding the rail empire. Under his direction the company began purchasing the branch railroads the receiver had cut away, such as the Oregon Short Line. By 1902 the system nearly equaled the mileage it had claimed in 1890, and the company purchased a controlling interest in the Southern Pacific Railroad. The Union Pacific now held lines in California and the Southwest, as well as the Central Pacific line from Ogden to San Francisco. Harriman also helped organize the Northern Securities Company with the hope of controlling the Northern Pacific, the Great Northern, and the Burlington. Although the venture did not succeed, Harriman's efforts had dramatically increased the Union Pacific's mileage and traffic. By 1905 the Union Pacific Railroad Company had become one of the strongest railroad corporations in the country.[41]

Harriman made the Union Pacific a firm financial and business proposition. The railroad confronted other storms, such as the Supreme Court order for the removal of the Southern Pacific in 1912, but the road endured. Its prosperity would continue to reflect the nation's economic cycle; when business fell off nationally in 1914, the road suffered. But in 1916 the Union Pacific reported the largest gross operating revenues in company history. Thus, beginning in 1898 the Union Pacific enjoyed the stability and growth of a mature business enterprise.[42]

The Union Pacific Coal Company prospered along with the railroad. The coal company reported in the early 1900s that the railroad's coal requirements had increased about 60 percent since 1898. Coal demand on the commercial market grew at a similar pace. The expansion surpassed the company's ability to produce, so it turned to independent operators for help in meeting the demand and reinitiated a program of opening new mines. For example, the company sought a location to replace the aging mines at Almy. A site near Almy called Spring Valley proved unsatisfactory, and ultimately the coal company located a mining camp called Cumberland thirty miles northeast of Almy. Producing its first coal in 1901, Cumberland was the first in a series of mines and camps the Union Pacific established in the early twentieth century. The town and mines of Superior, twenty miles east of Rock Springs, opened in 1906; and in 1911, Reliance, just north of Rock Springs, commenced production. These locations replaced some of the older, expensive mines at Rock Springs.[43]

At each of these new places, the Union Pacific demonstrated what it had learned about the business of coal mining. The company built full company towns. It owned all the homes and operated the only general merchandise stores allowed. Coal company managers fully recognized the advantages of these company towns. They saw their "tenements" as good investments and always expected to make money at their company stores. They also understood the advantage company towns gave them with labor. These communities attracted new employees and stabilized the old hands if a strike threatened.

6.1 Cumberland, Wyoming, coal mine and tipple. The Union Pacific Coal Company opened Cumberland in the extreme southwest corner of Wyoming in 1900. The company built a full company town, but in the distance beyond the coal tipple can be seen South Cumberland, a small independent community built just off the company's land. Cumberland closed in 1930. Courtesy, Wyoming State Archives 3512.

Company towns included a mix of ethnicities and nationalities. In 1906 Finns still constituted the majority in the camps, with a significant number of Italians and Austrians also present. Unlike ten years before, however, the Union Pacific towns also included Japanese miners, some African Americans, and a number of men from several Balkan countries.[44]

The new philosophy Harriman brought to the Union Pacific and the vigorous prosperity after 1897 attracted new coal companies and coal mines to southern Wyoming. In particular, coal entrepreneurs eyed the coal lands north of Evanston along the Union Pacific branch railroad known as the Oregon Short Line. The Anaconda Copper Mining Company of Butte, Montana, made the first move. It had long been buying fuel from the Union Pacific's Rock Springs mines, but in an effort to control all portions of its operations, the copper company bought its own coal land in western Wyoming. Organized as

6.2 Cumberland, Wyoming, coal. Cumberland had an inclined shaft, and a steam hoist pulled the loaded coal cars up the slope. Courtesy, *Sweetwater County Historical Museum.*

Diamond Coal and Coke, the company began development in 1894, forming the new Wyoming coal town of Diamondville. At the same time, Patrick J. Quealy was also acquiring coal property just north of Diamondville. Quealy, a former Union Pacific employee, thought he saw an opportunity to profit from the collapse of the Union Pacific during the 1893 depression. Betting on the separation of the Oregon Short Line from the Union Pacific, Quealy anticipated selling coal to the independent Short Line. He guessed correctly. In early 1897 the Union Pacific receiver sold the Oregon Short Line, creating a new railroad. This action prompted Quealy and his financial backers to organize the Kemmerer Coal Company and begin production.[45]

Quealy had a long history in the Wyoming coal business. He had not only worked for the Union Pacific's Coal Department, but he had tried to compete with the railroad's coal operation. Quealy had opened a coal mine at Rock Springs in the late 1880s. The business failed. Quealy believed he had been crushed by the Union Pacific's predatory practices. With this new endeavor, however, Quealy's fortunes changed. He became a leading force in the Wyoming coal industry. With the help of Pennsylvania industrialist Mahlon S. Kemmerer, Quealy established the coal camp of Frontier, a few miles north of Diamondville. Between Frontier and Diamondville he organized the supposedly independent town of Kemmerer. Frontier was a company town, whereas in Kemmerer merchants and residents could buy property and run businesses beyond company control. Quealy still planned to profit, however. He sold the town lots in Kemmerer, provided the water and power, and maintained a strong presence in the town's government.[46]

Quealy did well selling coal to the Oregon Short Line, but the Union Pacific reacquired the Short Line in 1899. That development could have been trouble for Kemmerer Coal except for the fact that Harriman needed the new company. He was expanding the Union Pacific beyond the limits of its own coal production, and he had to have Quealy's fuel. The railroad also enjoyed the traffic Quealy brought as he sought out the domestic market. Diamond Coal and Kemmerer Coal established a series of mines and coal camps north and south of Kemmerer. Quealy then opened more mines around Rock Springs. Whereas the Union Pacific had previously enjoyed a monopoly over coal mining in southern Wyoming, after 1897 more diversity and competition emerged.

Quealy became very important to the Union Pacific. He not only provided extra coal when needed, but he also became the company's point man in Wyoming. As a coal operator who lived in the Wyoming coalfields and a man who had a vested interest in the business, he had firsthand knowledge of the local scene. If labor troubles developed, the Union Pacific turned to him for advice. If domestic coal became scarce along its line, the road asked Quealy to provide the coal and mollify angry customers. By 1910 Quealy was the acknowledged spokesman for southern Wyoming coal operators.[47]

Even though Quealy played a key role for the Union Pacific, he maintained ambivalence toward the road and its coal company. He remembered the railroad's "trickery" when it ran him out of business in the 1880s. As he operated successfully along the Oregon Short Line, he continually worried about the Union Pacific. Quealy wrote to his business partners that the Union Pacific was a "dictator" when it came to coal prices, and even after a decade of dealing with the coal company, Quealy's associates still characterized the Union Pacific's policy as one of "down with the weak and [gaining] everything for themselves."[48]

By 1904 prosperity had helped bring diversity to the southern Wyoming coalfields. Although the Union Pacific had previously controlled the coal business, two new operators had joined it. The three companies operated sixteen mines in 1904: Quealy ran four, Diamond Coal had three, and the Union Pacific ran nine. Naturally, the Union Pacific dominated production. Whereas the railroad's coal company produced a little under 3 million tons from its

Wyoming mines in 1904, Quealy's operations and Diamond Coal and Coke each yielded just over half a million tons. Over the next two decades all three companies' output would gradually increase.[49]

EXPANSION IN COLORADO

Colorado's coal industry expanded dramatically as the 1893 depression came to an end. From about 3.3 million tons in 1897, the state's output reached 7.4 million tons in 1903. The Colorado Fuel and Iron Company, under Osgood's strong leadership, led the growth. From just over 2 million tons in 1897, by 1903 the company's coal production had almost doubled to nearly 4 million tons. Some of the increase supplied the expanding domestic demand in Colorado and the region, but the general prosperity also brought a demand for iron and steel rails. Consequently, the company's steel plant required more coal and coke. Osgood reported to the stockholders in June 1899 that more than half of the increased coal production had been consumed at the company's mines and steelworks. Contending that the "company's prospects are the brightest in the company's history," Osgood called for an overhaul. He wanted to open new mines, build new coke ovens, and enlarge the iron and steelworks.[50]

To gain the necessary capital, Osgood expanded the company's stock offerings. Whereas the CF&I had been incorporated in 1892 for $13 million with 130,000 shares, in 1901 he offered 400,000 shares for $40 million. Although this initiative brought the money Osgood wanted, the stock offerings also changed the nature of the company. Osgood and his associates initially held much of the company's stock, but the expanded offering put more of the company in the hands of eastern investors such as John Gates, John D. Rockefeller, and Edward H. Harriman. These investors soon gained more say in the company's operations.[51]

The financial enlargement enabled Osgood to build new blast furnaces at the steelworks, open more mines, and construct coke ovens. In late 1899 he developed mines at Placita and constructed coke ovens at Redstone, south of Glenwood Springs on the Western Slope. In early 1901 the mines at Coal Basin replaced the Placita openings, but the real demand for coal and coke remained on the Front Range. Between March 1901 and June 1903, Osgood opened five new locations—four in Las Animas County at Primero, Tabasco, Tercio, and Cuatro, and one called Hezron in Huerfano County. Full company towns accompanied these operations. For instance, the company opened Tercio, about thirty miles southwest of Trinidad, in November 1901 by developing six mines and constructing 600 coke ovens. The first arrivals in camp, which included a large number of Italians, initially built their own homes. But the CF&I wanted a full company town. Soon it replaced the structures with 100 houses the company called "comfortable modern cottages" lining "well planned streets." The CF&I also built the school, the clubhouse, and

6.3 *Tercio, Colorado. Built southwest of Trinidad in 1902 by the Colorado Fuel and Iron Company, Tercio was one of a series of camps John C. Osgood built near the turn of the century. He attempted to make these camps more livable by adding amenities that did not exist in traditional company towns.* Courtesy, Colorado Historical Society F-20925, Trinidad Collection.

the only store. The new camps allowed Osgood to nearly double production from 1897 to 1903, meeting the increasing domestic demand and feeding the growing steelworks.[52]

Osgood was not satisfied to work with just one company. Earlier, he had been involved with the Whitebreast Coal Company of Iowa, the Denver Fuel Company, and the Colorado Fuel Company. He saw such staggered enterprises as a means to increase investment flexibility, limit financial risks, and make extra money. Osgood often bought property under one company's name and then sold it to another for a profit. Similarly, while involved with the expansion of the Colorado Fuel and Iron Company, Osgood and his associates incorporated another company, the American Fuel Company, in 1900. Organized in New Mexico, the operation purchased control of the Crescent Coal Company at Gallup. Osgood apparently planned to merge that firm with the CF&I,

6.4 Hastings, Colorado. Hastings sat north of Trinidad and was developed by Trinidad capitalist Delos A. Chappell in 1890 for his Victor Fuel Company. John C. Osgood eventually gained control of the company and town. This photo shows a mix of activities with company housing in the distance and the more irregular housing built by miners in the foreground. Courtesy, Colorado Historical Society F-37,984, Trinidad Collection.

but the American Fuel mines at Gallup remained independent of the larger corporation's direct control.[53]

The boom that occurred after 1897 inspired other Colorado entrepreneurs to try to capture some of Colorado's coal business. A Trinidad capitalist and promoter named Delos A. Chappell had entered the coal business before the 1893 depression. He formed the Victor Coal Company in 1890 and acquired coal property at Hastings north of Trinidad. To run the operation, Chappell hired former Colorado Coal and Iron superintendent John Cameron. By 1893 the company boasted four mines producing over 300,000 tons of coal a year, as well as a series of coke ovens. The depression, however, hit the company hard. With silver mines closed and coke in little demand, production slumped. Victor Fuel managed to weather the storm, and as the depression ended its output began to surge—topping half a million tons in 1898, or about 20 percent of the amount the CF&I produced. Sensing a good opportunity to compete with the CF&I, the Victor Fuel Company went public in 1899. The new financing allowed it to expand to seven mines by 1902, matching the CF&I at each of its Front Range locations: Cañon City, Walsenburg, and Trinidad. Although the Victor Coal Company never threatened the CF&I's dominance, it developed into Colorado's second-largest coal company.[54]

A third major Colorado coal company was formed in 1897. Although the United Coal Company had tried to bring order to the Denver Basin, its efforts failed. United Coal's managers blamed the high wages, but the economic stringency during the depression was equally to blame. Coal prices had dropped because of the "rate war," and the company could not meet its bonded indebtedness. It went out of business in 1898, but a year earlier a group of Denver capitalists had formed the Northern Coal and Coke Company to replace it.[55]

James Cannon, president of Northern Coal and Coke, believed consolidation and supply restriction would bring stability to the Denver Basin. Cannon first bought United Coal Company bonds and then began purchasing and leasing a number of mines in the area. The company worked rapidly, acquiring several mines in 1897. It did not plan to operate all of the mines but sought to end the ruinous competition and bring order to the coalfield. Cannon tried to gain control of as many mines as possible and then to limit production to just a few locations. He thus hoped to regulate production so the market would never be flooded and the price for coal could be maintained. A concentration of operations would also allow for better control of the workforce. Northern Coal even considered opening company towns at its best mine sites. The company moved aggressively to fulfill its vision of consolidation. By the end of 1898, in just one year, it had gained control of eleven of the twenty-five mines in the Denver Basin and operated only six of them on a regular basis. By 1902 it held fourteen of the twenty-six largest mines in the region, working only eight. Northern Coal and Coke's consolidation policy allowed it to account for 70 percent of the Denver Basin's production, or slightly over 600,000 tons, in 1902. The company had become the third-largest coal operation in Colorado.[56]

COAL LABOR IN SOUTHERN WYOMING, 1897–1901

From the time industrial coal mining came to the West, coal companies had tried to degrade the position of labor. They attempted to reduce wages, eliminate skilled miners, and crush labor organizations. By 1897 most miners' wages had been reduced to all-time lows, and only fragments of labor unions remained. Tension remained high in several of the coalfields. The miners in central and southern Colorado lost a strike in 1894, and Denver Basin workers won a strike in 1896. Nobody was satisfied. With the return of prosperity, both labor and management attempted to strengthen their positions.[57]

Workers moved aggressively to enhance their position at the new mines in southern Wyoming. The primary coal employer in the region, the Union Pacific Coal Company, had pushed wages down during the Panic of 1893. But as the Union Pacific squeezed miners' incomes, the mines at Diamondville and Kemmerer needed men. Some of the employees came from the Union Pacific mines, and they generally received higher wages for opening the new mines. Old-time hands from Almy and other Union Pacific camps flocked to the mines. For instance, Thomas Sneddon, who had worked at Almy and had been a noted member of the Knights of Labor in the 1880s, became the superintendent of Diamond Coal and Coke.[58]

Some of these men brought a tradition of organization to their new jobs. The Union Pacific Employe's Protective Association and the Knights of Labor may have died, but as the men came together in the new camps they gained confidence in the reinvigorated coal business and in their new locations away from the omnipresent Union Pacific. They were also heartened by the growing strength of new labor organizations. The Anaconda Copper Mining Company of Butte, Montana, had started the Diamondville mines, and the Western Federation of Miners had been centered in Butte since 1893. Some miners at Diamondville felt a natural affinity toward that union.

The United Mine Workers of America was also becoming a more national presence. Although stymied by the 1894 strike, it gained new life in 1897. Bituminous coal miners from Pennsylvania to Illinois walked off the job on July 4, 1897. The national union had counted few members before the strike, but because conditions had become so extreme during the depression, miners walked out en masse. The strike lasted until September 1897, when operators in the northern bituminous field agreed to a 20 percent wage increase and promised to meet the miners in a joint interstate conference scheduled for January 1898. The northern mine owners settled with the union because they feared losing their markets. During the strike southern coal producers had made inroads into their markets.[59]

This settlement gave the UMWA a national presence. The agreement yielded a greatly increased membership, including gains in what the union called the "outlying fields" of Alabama and Wyoming. When operators and union members from western Pennsylvania, Ohio, Indiana, and Illinois met in conference, they established a bargaining unit known as the Central Competitive Field (CCF), which represented the heart of coal-mining country. Contracts from the CCF became models for settlements elsewhere. Operators within the CCF saw benefits in working with the union. They looked to it to stabilize wage rates and help eliminate cutthroat competition. Whereas the workers wanted a living wage, the owners in turn hoped a strong union would organize the outlying coalfields that had threatened their markets. They saw a uniform wage rate as an advantage for everyone. The operators agreed to other demands, including the eight-hour day and the checkoff of union dues, wherein employers automatically deducted the monthly dues from every miner's paycheck.[60]

The eight-hour day proved particularly contentious as the union move-ment spread west. The union had talked of a set workday since its organization in 1890, but not without controversy. Men who believed in the traditional miners' freedoms and workplace independence thought they should be able to come and go as they pleased. Often, they worked long hours in the winter to make up for the lack of work in the summer. They also felt that if they had done enough work for one day, they should be able to leave the mine. Mine owners, by contrast, wanted miners to work longer hours during periods of peak demand. The eight-hour day eliminated these prerogatives. During the depression, however, pick miners seldom worked a full day. An eight-hour day thus might guarantee more work. The union hoped such an agreement might bring order to the mines by stabilizing the workforce in good times and bad and ensuring more regular work for all mine workers.[61]

Some miners in Wyoming had a long history of labor activism, and they took notice of the UMWA victory in the Central Competitive Field. In Janu-ary 1898 President Michael Ratchford of the United Mine Workers praised the extension of the union "to the state of Wyoming on the West."[62] But the UMWA had a tenuous hold. Diamondville, previously organized by the WFM, appeared to have the strongest UMWA representation. Out of 280 men, the *United Mine Workers' Journal* reported that the UMWA had 150 members, whereas about 100 belonged to the WFM. In October 1897 the men had successfully struck for a compromise in a wage-scale adjustment, and in early 1898 a *Journal* correspondent claimed the miners were "generally contented and happy" at Diamondville.[63]

Whereas Superintendent Sneddon and Diamond Coal and Coke seem-ingly wanted to work with organized men, Quealy at Kemmerer Coal had no such desire. Soon after he opened his Frontier Mine in November 1897, the miners went on strike to force the recognition of a union committee. When the committee men appeared in his office with their demands, he fired them on the spot. Next he turned the strike into a lockout. He fired all of his miners and posted eviction notices in the coal camp.[64]

Quealy's strong stand worked. The very next day he posted a broadside listing the men he would rehire. "We reemployed all the men we wanted," he wrote in December 1897, "cutting out agitators with a faithful promise that they would not again join the union." He not only called his plan a "grand victory," but he took the opportunity to cut some wages.[65] His success seems all the more surprising given the shortage of miners in Wyoming, but Quealy triumphed because worker solidarity had yet to develop and the national labor organizations offered the miners no help.

Quealy hoped Sneddon and the Diamond Coal and Coke Company would follow his lead because that would mean "we would not be troubled with unions again."[66] His wish came true. When a union committee of Diamondville miners complained of poorly operating coal cars, Sneddon responded by "discharging the committee and all men they knew belonged to the union" and evicting men from their homes.[67] The company then locked out the miners to eliminate the agitators. Apparently, Sneddon did not want to destroy the union but only to reshape it to his liking. By the end of 1898 the UMWA influence had been eliminated, and only a shell of the WFM local remained. Sneddon limited its functions to providing aid to the sick and helping with funeral expenses. Sneddon approved of this type of unionism, and his company soon gave the union two lots in Diamondville on which to build a hall.[68]

When the union went beyond what Sneddon wanted, he acted like other coal company managers and killed it. In late 1899 the men at Diamondville went on strike for a ten-cent-per-ton raise. In response, Diamond Coal and Coke imported workers who a *United Mine Workers' Journal* reporter claimed "could not understand the English language." As these men went to work, they were met by an angry crowd—led by the wives of the strikers—that tried to "appeal" to their sensibilities. The encounter brought the sheriff to the company's aid. Work went on, and the union collapsed. As a correspondent from Diamondville reported, "Our union has struggled for two years or more under the grinding power of great monopolies, and we received no assistance from any place and we had to succumb to these powers because we were alone."[69]

The Union Pacific used similar tactics to head off any attempts at unionization. In early 1898 the miners at Hanna began moving toward joining the UMWA. The company responded by closing the mines, firing the malcontents, and bringing in African American miners. All across southern Wyoming the nascent union movement had been practically eliminated by the end of 1898.[70]

The Union Pacific had pioneered the methods of decisive labor control—building company towns, instituting ethnic and racial mixing, and ruling with a firm hand. When new coal companies came to the coalfield, they used similar techniques. They built full company towns and implemented ethnic and racial mixing to limit solidarity. In fact, their initial ethnic and racial mix resembled that of the Union Pacific, but over time they imported the workers they preferred. In 1902 Kemmerer Coal began relying on Japanese miners. These factors helped keep unions out, even when labor was in short supply.[71]

Lack of competition also undermined any union effort in Wyoming. Fear of losing market shares forced the Denver Basin operators and mining companies in the CCF to accept unionization. In particular, the CCF companies hoped the UMWA could stabilize the industry and end cutthroat competition. The new coal producers in Wyoming did not threaten the Union Pacific's position because they served different markets. The threat of losing markets held no sway in southern Wyoming. In the end, the Union Pacific's dominance allowed it to set the industry standards.

The three southern Wyoming coal operators also worked together to keep unions out. When suspected organizers visited a coal camp in the region, the mine superintendents circulated letters warning each other of the activity. They kept an informal blacklist. When a rumor spread that the UMWA was importing union men to take jobs in the mines, a notice circulated among the mine superintendents: "Be very careful about the men you hire and keep yourselves posted in regard to all your men and their movements. Do not allow idle men or those whom you have refused work to hang around your camp."[72] Coal operators also collaborated on the pay scale. They did not want to lose their men to a neighboring mine or to compete over wages. They kept their wages slightly above those in Colorado, hoping to avoid that state's labor troubles. The Union Pacific had experienced the labor problems of northern Colorado firsthand, and it had no desire to get caught in such turmoil again.[73]

COAL LABOR IN COLORADO, 1897–1901

Similar to their colleagues in Wyoming, Colorado miners did not share in the benefits of prosperity. Colorado Fuel and Iron had adopted corporate practices that allowed it to control its miners. Since the CF&I dominated Western coal markets, it did not fear losing market share. Workers made scattered attempts to challenge the company, but with little effect. In the Denver Basin, however, numerous companies and a rebellious workforce created much labor turmoil, marked by frequent strikes.

Miners with a strong mining heritage still dominated northern Colorado. These men owned homes in the independent towns of the north, and they had the support of the large surrounding communities. The residents of Denver and Boulder resented any attempts to use replacement workers. The United Mine Workers' Journal quoted the sheriff of Boulder County as saying, "Colorado is opposed to cheap labor, and we don't want that class of labor in Boulder County. . . . Outside labor had better stay away." He feared trouble if the mine owners introduced "cheap men," and when asked if he would deputize miners if a situation called for it, he responded, "I might do that very thing."[74]

Seemingly isolated from events occurring elsewhere and organized by the Western Federation of Miners in 1896, workers in the Denver Basin had no apparent response to the United Mine Workers' 1897 strike in the Central Competitive Field. Their greatest concern involved the actions of the newly formed Northern Coal Company. The company consolidated mines to eliminate competition, reduce costs, and—most important to its mission in 1898—get control of the labor force. The company wanted to break the union and eliminate old-time miners. As it closed mines, the company concentrated the workers at its active mines. Although those mines worked full-time, the miners did not. There were too many men for the number of workplaces. The men called a meeting, protested the company's actions, and demanded a wage advance that would provide a living wage in these conditions. The union also ordered a general work suspension for January 18, 1898.[75]

After a week's stoppage and no progress, the two sides turned the dispute over to Colorado's newly formed State Board of Arbitration. Created by the state legislature in 1897, the Board of Arbitration was Colorado's answer to the vast array of labor problems the state had been enduring, not only in coal mines but also in a number of other industries. The legislature empowered the board to act in labor-management disputes whenever requested to do so by both parties. But it had no power to enforce its decisions, a fairly significant weakness. In this case the board found on behalf of the miners and in February approved a wage advance. Fearing lost business and lost markets, the smaller mining companies accepted the settlement and returned to work; the Northern Coal Company did not.[76]

The independent mines operated for a time, with miners from throughout the district sharing the work in the open mines. In a manifestation of solidarity, this plan prevented any miners' families from going completely without incomes. The miners in the district sensed, however, that the owners of the operating mines were working with Northern Coal, even providing it with coal. This concern provoked another fieldwide strike. Although President Boyce of the Western Federation of Miners recommended that the men resume work, given the settlement authorized by the Board of Arbitration, the men refused. They wanted to remain out in support of the Northern Coal Company workers.[77]

The strike moved into August, and both sides continued to hold out. Northern Coal believed it could regain and restore any markets it had lost. A company spokesman told a Denver *Times* reporter that it would fight to "the bitter end." He said the company had the "power to depopulate every village in the whole coal belt, and, if the miners persist in their course we may be forced to do it." He threatened to concentrate the work at three mines and nearby, "erect houses, guard them, and put in 1,000 laborers." By renting the houses and "freezing out the towns," he claimed the company would "gain over $150,000 per annum." If the strikers held "out to the bitter end," the company would begin importing nonunion labor.[78]

With the threats, the strike quickly concluded. In mid-August the miners voted to return to work at a wage rate established by the company, which the *United Mine Workers' Journal* saw as "nearly as much as was awarded by the State Board of Arbitration." The Denver *Times* reported that there was "no contract whatever between the men and the company," yet "both sides are well satisfied."[79] Indeed the miners were glad to get back to work, and the company promised to reemploy all of the strikers. The men gained little in the strike, but they believed they had achieved a tactical victory. Their return to work had blocked the entrance of outside replacement workers, and they had

warded off the company's threat to establish company towns. Company officials expressed satisfaction in keeping wages low. They hoped the other operators in the district would fall in line, thus ending cutthroat competition,
enabling companies to earn bigger profits, and establishing what they called
"legitimate conditions of business." The newly consolidated Northern Coal
Company seemingly had taken the first step to rein in the union forces and
independent spirits among northern Colorado miners, but in reality the miners seethed inwardly over the settlement. They awaited for another opportunity to seize the initiative.[80]

Ever since the burst of organization during the Great Upheaval in 1884 and
1885, labor had been on the defensive in the coal mines of the West. Companies grew stronger, consolidated resources, and adopted more stringent policies to ward off organized labor. Workers consequently suffered, especially
during economic downturns. Operators cut wages and instituted policies such
as using scrip that diminished workers' earnings. When prosperity returned,
mining jobs did not regain their former status in either skill or pay. As the
number of mines increased, company managers became adept at hiring workers with diverse backgrounds. Operators saw mining as nothing more than an
unskilled or semiskilled position, easily taught to any newcomer. The introduction of cutting machines seemed to reinforce this notion, although operating a machine required great skill. Wage levels fell in the West, whether in
good or bad times. Whereas earlier frontier conditions had given western coal
miners some of the highest wages in the country, by 1898 a day worker could
make from $1.35 to $2.50 in a Union Pacific mine. Miners in the Central
Competitive Field made from $1.75 to $2.00 a day. Pick miners in Illinois
made from $0.40 to $0.72 a ton; the same job in Diamondville or Frontier,
Wyoming, brought $0.48 cents a ton.[81]
     Longtime miners who had a heritage of union activism remained, and the
newcomers saw the conditions in the coal camps, the dangers in the mines,
and the coal companies' exploitation. By the turn of the century, however,
organized capital was triumphant, and organized labor was dead. Contemporary observers from all backgrounds seemingly agreed on the state of labor.
John Cameron, superintendent of the Victor Coal and Coke Company, proudly
stated in 1898 that his company shipped coal to nearly all parts of Colorado,
New Mexico, Kansas, and Nebraska—adding that "we have no strikes" in our
mines.[82] President Ed Boyce of the Western Federation of Miners visited the
southern Colorado coalfields in early 1899. Under the banner headline "Cheapest Labor in the Country," he reported in the Rocky Mountain News that he
had never seen such "abject misery as I saw there." He spoke of poor housing,
low pay, company stores, scrip, spies, blacklists, and ethnic diversity—all pointing to the power of Colorado Fuel and Iron. When asked if the WFM would

try to organize the miners, he replied that it would not do any good: "We might organize, but every man would lose his job, and then the federation must support them. If the state of Colorado will take no care of them, it is not our fault."[83]

Others weighed in on the discussion. J. A. Kebler, general manager of the Colorado Fuel and Iron Company, responded to Boyce's charges: "[I]ndeed since 1884, no reduction whatever has been made in the wages of these miners, and the cost of living is much less than it was at that time."[84] The *Rocky Mountain News* countered this response with an editorial that said President Boyce's comments were "probably not overdrawn" and that people "are living in poverty and squalor and their children are growing up in ignorance and discontent." The editor recommended that the state take action by passing an antiscrip law and suggested that the nation should restrict immigration. He believed the elimination of scrip would allow cash to flow more freely for the betterment of the miners and Colorado; and if the nation restricted immigration, coal operators could not "crowd wages down to their present starvation point because they have been able to draw unlimited numbers from Europe."[85]

The editor of the *Rocky Mountain News* turned to Colorado's legislature to solve labor problems because the state government had tried to do so before. Prior to 1899 the legislature had enacted a variety of measures to mitigate troubles within Colorado's workforce, not only for coal miners but in a number of industries. In 1884 the legislature created the office of State Inspector of Coal Mines "to secure the health and safety of persons employed and promote the interests of coal mining."[86] The mine inspector occasionally went beyond just checking mines for safety and tried to find solutions for other coal-mining problems. Following the 1894 strike, the inspector argued that until legislation limited the use of scrip and inaccurate coal weights, more strikes would follow. Ongoing concerns over labor problems throughout the state during the Great Upheaval moved the legislature to create the Bureau of Labor Statistics in 1887. Part of its mission was to investigate labor problems, for if "popular clamor" called for a law, the legislature would need "reliable data" on which to base its decision. One such decision created the State Board of Arbitration in 1897.[87]

Prompted by representatives from coal-mining counties, the state legislature passed laws that specifically addressed coal miners' grievances. It enacted a measure that allowed miners to hire check-weighmen who double-check the weight of coal, and in 1899 the legislature outlawed the use of scrip. Finally, also in 1899 it passed a law to establish an eight-hour workday for mine, mill, and smelter workers. The law, however, did not result in the eight-hour day being instituted. It only started a protracted battle between mine owners and mine workers over the law's constitutionality.[88]

Colorado's legislative activity contrasted starkly with that of Wyoming. In response to coal mine explosions, the Wyoming legislature established the office of Coal Mine Inspector in 1885, but after that action it had little concern with labor issues. Wyoming did not have the industrial complex Colorado had, and after the Rock Springs Massacre, labor relations in the state were fairly harmonious. Part of the reason lies with the Union Pacific's willingness to negotiate with labor, even after the demise of the Knights of Labor. Certainly, the company could take a hard line, as did Diamond Coal and Coke and Kemmerer Coal, but those companies did not generate the animosity Colorado Fuel and Iron and Northern Coal and Coke triggered in Colorado. In fact, Wyoming operators paid a higher wage than those in Colorado. By 1900 the Union Pacific worried less about costs than its Colorado counterparts did. The railroad's concern lay with keeping the ever-increasing number of trains running. It needed a constant, dependable supply of coal. As prosperity continued and the labor market tightened, in 1900 the Union Pacific Coal Company granted its mine workers a significant wage increase. And where the Union Pacific led, other Wyoming coal operators followed. The Colorado operators did not grant an increase, and the resulting animosity and tensions exploded in 1901.[89]

NOTES

1. Bryant, *History of the Atchison, Topeka and Santa Fe Railway*, 149–161; Trottman, *History of the Union Pacific*, 248–249.

2. Brundage, *Making of Western Labor Radicalism*, 117; Bryant, *History of the Atchison, Topeka and Santa Fe Railway*, 162–163; Trottman, *History of the Union Pacific*, 247–250.

3. "Second Annual Report of the Colorado Fuel and Iron Co., for the Year Ending June 30, 1894," 6, 14, Collection #1057, Box #5, Folder #93, CF&I CRL; *Eighth Biennial Report of the State Inspector of Coal Mines of the State of Colorado for the Years 1897 and 1898* (Denver: Smith-Brooks Printing, State Printers, 1899), 45, 117.

4. Trottman, *History of the Union Pacific*, 248–252, 269; *History of the Union Pacific Coal Mines*, appendix.

5. *Fifth Biennial Report of the State Inspector of Coal Mines of the State of Colorado for the Years 1891 and 1892* (Denver: Smith-Brooks Printing, State Printers, 1893), production charts; Bryant, *History of the Atchison, Topeka and Santa Fe Railway*, 168–170.

6. Scamehorn, *Pioneer Steelmaker*, 122; "Colorado Fuel and Iron Company," *Engineering and Mining Journal* 62, no. 10 (September 5, 1896): 228–229; *United Mine Workers' Journal*, April 1, 1897; "Fourth Annual Report of the Colorado Fuel and Iron Co., for the Year Ending June 30, 1896," 8, Collection #1057, Box #5, Folder #93, CF&I CRL; *Atchison, Topeka & Santa Fe Railway System: A Study of Its Progress in the Last Decade and Pertinent Comparisons with Other Transcontinental Carriers* (New York: Wood, Struthers, 1925), 50; "Annual Report of the Atchison, Topeka and Santa Fe Railway for the Year Ending December 31, 1885," 21, Santa Fe Railway Archives, Kansas State Historical Society, Topeka, Kansas.

7. *Fifth Biennial Report of the State Inspector of Coal Mines of the State of Colorado for the Years 1891 and 1892*, production charts; *Seventh Biennial Report of the State Inspector of Coal Mines of the State of Colorado for the Years 1895 and 1896* (Denver: Smith-Brooks Printing, State Printers, 1897), production charts; *Rocky Mountain News*, January 17, 1901; "Colorado," *Engineering and Mining Journal* 64, no. 9 (August 28, 1897): 254–255.

8. United States Geological Survey, *Mineral Resources of the United States, 1901*, 367, 449; *United Mine Workers' Journal*, January 18, February 8, 1894.

9. United States Geological Survey, *Mineral Resources of the United States, 1901*, 367, 449.

10. *Fourth Biennial Report of the Bureau of Labor Statistics of the State of Colorado, 1893–1894* (Denver: Smith-Brooks Printing, State Printers, 1894), 240; *United Mine Workers' Journal*, January 18, February 8, 1894; *Rocky Mountain News*, November 21, 1893.

11. *Sixth Biennial Report of the State Inspector of Coal Mines of the State of Colorado for the Years 1893 and 1894* (Denver: Smith-Brooks Printing, State Printers, 1895), 5–6.

12. Fox, *United We Stand*, 45; *United Mine Workers' Journal*, March 15, 1894; Scamehorn, *Pioneer Steelmaker*, 120; "Second Annual Report of the Colorado Fuel and Iron Co.," 11; Wilson, "A Study of Paternalism in the Colorado Coal and Iron Company," 35.

13. Scamehorn, *Pioneer Steelmaker*, 120–121; Wilson, "A Study of Paternalism in the Colorado Coal and Iron Company," 37–38; *United Mine Workers' Journal*, May 31, September 6, 1894.

14. Scamehorn, *Pioneer Steelmaker*, 120–121.

15. Ibid.; Wilson, "A Study of Paternalism in the Colorado Coal and Iron Company," 39–44.

16. Scamehorn, *Pioneer Steelmaker*, 121.

17. Fox, *United We Stand*, 45–47.

18. Wilson, "A Study of Paternalism in the Colorado Coal and Iron Company," 49; Brundage, *Making of Western Labor Radicalism*, 120; *Fourth Biennial Report of the Bureau of Labor Statistics of the State of Colorado, 1893–1894*, 245.

19. "Third Annual Report of the Colorado Fuel and Iron Co., for the Year Ending June 30, 1895," 3, Collection #1057, Box #5, Folder #93, CF&I CRL.

20. Wilson, "A Study of Paternalism in the Colorado Coal and Iron Company," 49; Brundage, *Making of Western Labor Radicalism*, 120; *Fourth Biennial Report of the Bureau of Labor Statistics of the State of Colorado, 1893–1894*, 245; Senate Committee on Industrial Relations, *Final Report and Testimony*, 64th Cong., 1st sess., 1916, Doc. no. 415 (Washington, D.C.: GPO, 1916), 6423.

21. "Second Annual Report of the Colorado Fuel and Iron Co.," 11; "Third Annual Report of the Colorado Fuel and Iron Co.," 3.

22. Wilson, "A Study of Paternalism in the Colorado Coal and Iron Company," 52.

23. "Second Annual Report of the Colorado Fuel and Iron Co.," 11.

24. Brundage, *Making of Western Labor Radicalism*, 117; *Denver Times*, July 10, 1898; *Fifth Biennial Report of the State Inspector of Coal Mines of the State of Colorado*

for the Years 1891 and 1892, production charts; *Seventh Biennial Report of the State Inspector of Coal Mines of the State of Colorado for the Years 1895 and 1896*, production charts; Donachy, *United We Stand*, 7.

25. Stromquist, *A Generation of Boomers*, 69, 84; Almont Lindsey, *The Pullman Strike: The Story of a Unique Experiment and of a Great Labor Upheaval* (Chicago: University of Chicago Press, 1942), 252; *Union Pacific Employes' Magazine*, January 1894.

26. "Wyoming," *Engineering and Mining Journal* 56, no. 8 (August 26, 1893): 223; "Union Pacific Coal Company," *Engineering and Mining Journal* 56, no. 23 (December 9, 1893): 602; "Union Pacific Coal Company," *Engineering and Mining Journal* 58, no. 22 (December 1, 1894): 519; *History of the Union Pacific Coal Mines*, appendix.

27. *United Mine Workers' Journal*, January 30, February 9, 1896.

28. *United Mine Workers' Journal*, April 2, 1896.

29. Fox, *United We Stand*, 31; *Fifth Biennial Report of the Bureau of Labor Statistics of the State of Colorado, 1895–1896* (Denver: Smith-Brooks Printing, State Printers, 1896), 12–13.

30. Fox, *United We Stand*, 31; *Fifth Biennial Report of the Bureau of Labor Statistics of the State of Colorado, 1895–1896*, 12–13.

31. Fox, *United We Stand*, 31; quote in *Fifth Biennial Report of the Bureau of Labor Statistics of the State of Colorado, 1895–1896*, 14; *United Mine Workers' Journal*, January 30, February 20, April 2, 1896.

32. *Eighth Biennial Report of the Bureau of Labor Statistics of the State of Colorado, 1901–1902*, by James T. Smith (Denver: Smith-Brooks Printing, State Printers, 1902), 384; John H.M. Laslett, *Labor and the Left: A Study of Socialist and Radical Influences in the American Labor Movement, 1881–1924* (New York: Basic Books, 1970), 161, 243–244; John Brinley, "The Western Federation of Miners" (Ph.D. diss., University of Utah, 1972), 48.

33. Vernon H. Jensen, *Heritage of Conflict: Labor Relations in the Nonferrous Metals Industry up to 1930* (Ithaca, N.Y.: Cornell University Press, 1950), 57; Richard E. Lingenfelter, *The Hardrock Miners: A History of the Mining Movement in the American West, 1863–1893* (Berkeley: University of California Press, 1974), 226; Brinley, "Western Federation of Miners," 47; *Seventh Biennial Report of the Bureau of Labor Statistics of the State of Colorado, 1899–1900*, by James T. Smith (Denver: Smith-Brooks Printing, State Printers, 1900), 45.

34. Laslett, *Labor and the Left*, 241–242; Brinley, "Western Federation of Miners," 53–54; *Eighth Biennial Report of the Bureau of Labor Statistics of the State of Colorado, 1901–1902*, 384; Melvyn Dubofsky, "The Origins of Western Working Class Radicalism, 1890–1905," *Labor History* 7 (Spring 1966): 152.

35. *United Mine Workers' Journal*, February 20, April 2, 1896; *Fifth Biennial Report of the Bureau of Labor Statistics of the State of Colorado, 1895–1896*, 12–13.

36. *Fifth Biennial Report of the Bureau of Labor Statistics of the State of Colorado, 1895–1896*, 12–16; *Fifth Biennial Report of the State Inspector of Coal Mines of the State of Colorado for the Years 1891 and 1892*, production charts; *Seventh Biennial Report of the State Inspector of Coal Mines of the State of Colorado for the Years 1895 and 1896*, production charts.

37. *Fifth Biennial Report of the Bureau of Labor Statistics of the State of Colorado, 1895–1896*, 13–16.

38. "Fifth Annual Report of the Colorado Fuel and Iron Co., for the Year Ending June 30, 1897," 9, Collection #1057, Box #5, Folder #93, CF&I CRL; United States Geological Survey, *Mineral Resources of the United States, 1900*, 371, 457.

39. U.S. Department of the Interior, United States Geological Survey, *Mineral Resources of the United States, 1910* (Washington, D.C.: GPO, 1911), 109, 222; U.S. Department of the Interior, United States Geological Survey, *Mineral Resources of the United States, 1913* (Washington, D.C.: GPO, 1914), 824, 925.

40. United States Geological Survey, *Mineral Resources of the United States, 1910*, 110–111, 223–224; *Fourteenth Biennial Report of the State Inspector of Coal Mines of the State of Colorado, 1909–1910* (Denver: Smith-Brooks Printing, State Printers, 1910), 125; *History of the Union Pacific Coal Mines*, appendix.

41. Trottman, *History of the Union Pacific*, 277–280, 297, 302, 306; Athearn, *Union Pacific Country*, 373–374.

42. Trottman, *History of the Union Pacific*, 363, 373.

43. *History of the Union Pacific Coal Mines*, 7, 126, 133, 138, 150; Anonymous eight-page manuscript entitled "Union Pacific Coal Mines," Box HO 3, UPCCC.

44. Anonymous manuscript, "Union Pacific Coal Mines"; *History of the Union Pacific Coal Mines*, 115–116, 163; "Nationality of Mine Employes, December 1906, the Union Pacific Coal Co., Annual Report, 1906," 35, UPCCC.

45. Trottman, *History of the Union Pacific*, 261; Glen Barrett, *Kemmerer, Wyoming: The Founding of an Independent Coal Town, 1897–1902* (Kemmerer, Wyo.: Quealy Services, 1975), 7–8; *Wyoming Labor Journal*, August 31, 1917; Michael P. Malone, *The Battle for Butte: Mining and Politics on the Northern Frontier, 1864–1906* (Seattle: University of Washington Press, 1981), 42.

46. Barrett, *Kemmerer, Wyoming*, 27–28, 46–47.

47. Ibid., 1–21; Glen Barrett, "P. J. Quealy: Wyoming's Coal Man and Town Builder," *Annals of Wyoming* 47 (Spring 1975): 42; "Mr. P. J. Quealy Has Gone from Us," *Employes' Magazine* 7 (December 1930): 518.

48. P. J. Quealy to D. O. Clark, May 29, 1903, Letter Books, Box 6, Kemmerer Coal Collection, American Heritage Center, Laramie, Wyoming; J. L. Kemmerer to P. J. Quealy, February 9, 1907, Box 3, Kemmerer Coal Collection, American Heritage Center, Laramie, Wyoming.

49. "Annual Report of the State Inspector of Coal Mines for Inspection District No. One, Wyoming, December 10, 1904," Wyoming State Archives, Museums and Historical Department, Cheyenne, Wyoming.

50. Gaynor, "History of the Colorado Fuel and Iron Company and Constituent Companies," 91; U.S. Department of the Interior, United States Geological Survey, *Mineral Resources of the United States, 1903*, by David T. Day (Washington, D.C.: GPO, 1904), 447; *Tenth Biennial Report of the State Inspector of Coal Mines of the State of Colorado, 1901–1902* (Denver: Smith-Brooks Printing, State Printers, 1903), 125; "Seventh Annual Report of the Colorado Fuel and Iron Co., for the Year Ending June 30, 1899," 4–5, Collection #1057, Box #5, Folder #93, CF&I CRL; Denver *Times*, November 24, 1899; *Camp and Plant* 2, no. 6 (August 13, 1902): 129–133.

51. "Ninth Annual Report of the Colorado Fuel and Iron Co., for the Year Ending June 30, 1901," 22, Collection #1057, Box #5, Folder #94, CF&I CRL; Gaynor, "History of the Colorado Fuel and Iron Company and Constituent Companies," 95; *Engineering and Mining Journal* 72, no. 8 (August 24, 1901): 244.

52. "Ninth Annual Report of the Colorado Fuel and Iron Co.," 4; "Tenth Annual Report of the Colorado Fuel and Iron Co., for the Year Ending June 30, 1902," 31, Collection #1057, Box #5, Folder #94, CF&I CRL; *Ninth Biennial Report of the State Inspector of Coal Mines of the State of Colorado, 1899–1900* (Denver: Smith-Brooks Printing, State Printers, 1901), 29; Denver *Times*, December 11, 1900.

53. H. Lee Scamehorn, *Mill & Mine: The CF&I in the Twentieth Century* (Lincoln: University of Nebraska Press, 1992), 107; Denver *Times*, April 23, 1900.

54. *Fourth Biennial Report of the State Inspector of Coal Mines of the State of Colorado for the Years 1889 and 1890*, production charts; *Sixth Biennial Report of the State Inspector of Coal Mines of the State of Colorado for the Years 1893 and 1894*, production charts; *Eighth Biennial Report of the State Inspector of Coal Mines of the State of Colorado for the Years 1897 and 1898*, 117; *Tenth Biennial Report of the State Inspector of Coal Mines of the State of Colorado, 1901–1902*, 125; W. H. Whitney, *Directory of Trinidad, Colorado, for 1888* (Trinidad: Advertiser Steam Job Print, 1888), 69; "Colorado," *Engineering and Mining Journal* 68, no. 19 (November 4, 1899): 556.

55. *Rocky Mountain News*, January 27, 1901.

56. "Colorado," *Engineering and Mining Journal* 64, no. 9 (August 28, 1897): 254; *Eighth Biennial Report of the State Inspector of Coal Mines of the State of Colorado for the Years 1897 and 1898*, 13–17; *Tenth Biennial Report of the State Inspector of Coal Mines of the State of Colorado, 1901–1902*, 186, 208.

57. *United Mine Workers' Journal*, October 21, November 11, November 18, 1897.

58. *Wyoming Labor Journal*, August 31, 1917; Unpublished ms. entitled "Western Coal: P. J. Quealy and the Wyoming Mines," by Glen Barrett, n.d., 189, in Barrett Collection, Box 1, American Heritage Center, Laramie, Wyoming.

59. Fox, *United We Stand*, 50–52; Reitman, "Class Formation and Union Politics," 246–248.

60. Fox, *United We Stand*, 52; Long, *Where the Sun Never Shines*, 151–152; Dix, *What's a Coal Miner to Do*, 116; Margaret Mary Hughes, "The United Mine Workers of America as a Social Control" (Ph.D. diss., University of Pittsburgh, 1937), 11, 25.

61. Fox, *United We Stand*, 39–40, 50; Kenny, *Making Sense of the Molly Maguires*, 116; *United Mine Workers' Journal*, April 23, 1891.

62. *United Mine Workers' Journal*, January 20, 1898, 2.

63. *United Mine Workers' Journal*, October 14, 1897, January 5, April 21, 1898.

64. P. J. Quealy to E. E. Calvin, December 18, 1897, Folder 144, Kemmerer Coal Collection, American Heritage Center, Laramie, Wyoming; Notice, December 14, 1897, Folder 144, Kemmerer Coal Collection, American Heritage Center, Laramie, Wyoming.

65. P. J. Quealy to E. E. Calvin, December 19, 1897, Folder 144, Kemmerer Coal Collection, American Heritage Center, Laramie, Wyoming.

66. *United Mine Workers' Journal*, December 2, 1897; P. J. Quealy to E. E. Calvin, December 19, 1897, Folder 144, Kemmerer Coal Collection, American Heritage Center, Laramie, Wyoming; Notice, December 15, 1897, Folder 144, Kemmerer Coal Collection, American Heritage Center, Laramie, Wyoming.

67. *United Mine Workers' Journal*, quote in April 21, 1898, 5; May 5, 1898; *Wyoming Labor Journal*, August 31, 1917.

68. Frank R. Dallezotte, *Oakley, Wyoming: Gone . . . but Not Forgotten* (San Diego: Goodway Printing and Graphics, 1989), 28–29.

69. *United Mine Workers' Journal*, December 7, 1899, quote in January 4, 1900, 3.

70. *United Mine Workers' Journal*, August 18, 1898; "Sweetwater County," *Engineering and Mining Journal* 66, no. 14 (October 1, 1898): 409.

71. H. E. Christmas to P. J. Quealy, August 29, 1902, Box 1, Kemmerer Coal Collection, American Heritage Center, Laramie, Wyoming; "Union Pacific Coal Company," *Engineering and Mining Journal* 66, no. 20 (November 12, 1898): 589.

72. G. F. Black to E. S. Brooks et al., June 13, 1904, Folder 146, Kemmerer Coal Collection, American Heritage Center, Laramie, Wyoming.

73. G. F. Black to P. J. Quealy, June 9, 1903, Folder 146, Kemmerer Coal Collection, American Heritage Center, Laramie, Wyoming; P. J. Quealy to D. O. Clark, January 12, 1907, Box 17, Kemmerer Coal Collection, American Heritage Center, Laramie, Wyoming; Chart titled "Monthly Gross Earnings by Miners in Employ of the Union Pacific Coal Company for the Year 1902," Box 26, Kemmerer Coal Collection, American Heritage Center, Laramie, Wyoming.

74. *United Mine Workers' Journal*, June 30, 1898, 4.

75. Denver *Times*, July 10, 1898; *Eighth Biennial Report of the State Inspector of Coal Mines of the State of Colorado for the Years 1897 and 1898*, 13–17.

76. Denver *Times*, July 10, 1898; McClurg, "Labor Organizations in the Coal Mines of Colorado," 80.

77. Denver *Times*, July 6, July 10, 1898.

78. Denver *Times*, August 3, 1898.

79. *United Mine Workers' Journal*, September 8, 1898, 3; Denver *Times*, August 13, 1898.

80. Denver *Times*, July 10, August 13, 1898; *Engineering and Mining Journal* 66, no. 8 (August 20, 1898): 225.

81. *United Mine Workers' Journal*, March 10, 1898; *History of the Union Pacific Coal Mines*, appendix; "Superintendent Letter Press Book, April 1898," Box 11, Kemmerer Coal Collection, American Heritage Center, Laramie, Wyoming.

82. *United Mine Workers' Journal*, August 18, 1898.

83. *Rocky Mountain News*, January 26, 1899, 1.

84. *Rocky Mountain News*, January 27, 1899.

85. *Rocky Mountain News*, January 29, 1899, 16.

86. *First Annual Report of the Colorado State Inspector of Coal Mines for the Year Ending July 31, 1884*, 3.

87. *First Biennial Report of the Bureau of Labor Statistics of the State of Colorado, 1887–1888*, 3, 11; *Sixth Biennial Report of the State Inspector of Coal Mines of the State of Colorado for the Years 1893 and 1894*, 5; McClurg, "Labor Organizations in the Coal Mines of Colorado," 80.

88. *United Mine Workers' Journal*, February 16, 1899; David Lonsdale, "The Fight for an Eight-Hour Day," *Colorado Magazine* 43, no. 4 (Fall 1966): 340–341; Senate Committee on Industrial Relations, *Final Report and Testimony*, 8020.

89. *History of the Union Pacific Coal Mines*, appendix; Walter Jones, "Coal Mine Explosions at Almy, Wyoming: Their Influence on Wyoming's First Coal Mining Safety Laws," *Annals of Wyoming* 56 (Spring 1984): 54–65.

CHAPTER SEVEN

STRUGGLE AND CHANGE, 1901-1903

THE YEARS IMMEDIATELY AFTER THE TURN OF THE TWENTIETH CENTURY witnessed unparalleled prosperity in the coal business of the Rocky Mountain
West. By 1902 Colorado's coal production had more than doubled since
the end of the 1890s depression, and the relative expansion in Wyoming was
close behind. The six major coal operators in the two states had all successfully advanced, but Colorado Fuel and Iron (CF&I) had become the behe-
moth of western coal producers. It had doubled its production to over 4 million
tons by 1902, opening four new mining towns in the process. Its coal workforce
had increased from a little under 4,000 in 1898 to nearly 5,500 workers in
1902. The CF&I's closest rival in size, the Union Pacific Coal Company, had
also nearly doubled its output by 1902, and it continued to grow in the following years. Even the region's smaller operations had enjoyed similar advances.[1]

The coal miners did not fully share in this prosperity. They enjoyed the
regular work over the intermittent operations during the depression, but when
it came to earning more for the work performed, most saw little difference.
Small advances did come in Wyoming and in a few Colorado locations, but

181

the majority of workers in the mountain West received no extra rewards. Discontent mounted among many of the men. Those in the Denver Basin remembered the bitter strike of 1898, and miners in central and southern Colorado became angry as reports of their horrid living and working conditions spread across the state. The mining men soon took the initiative to gain the fair play and respect they wanted.[2]

The kindling for revolt always seemed present in Colorado. The older locations in the state had long histories of labor activity, and union proclivities remained. Local unions still existed at four towns in the Denver Basin, with the organization at Louisville still associated with the Western Federation of Miners (WFM). Rockvale also maintained a WFM local. The companies' strength and combativeness, however, had left most Colorado miners without organization or representation. In fact, this lack of organization during a time of prosperity surprised Labor Statistics commissioner James Smith. In 1900 he reported that there had been a "rapid formation of craftsmen into unions . . . in Colorado within the last two years," but the "coal miners have lagged behind."[3]

Colorado miners needed the help of the United Mine Workers of America (UMWA). Grassroots movements could not defeat the power of organized capital, and the WFM had proved an inconsistent ally. UMWA's success in the Central Competitive Field of Ohio, Indiana, and Illinois in 1897 had attracted attention. In 1900 the UMWA decided to capitalize on that interest and return to the West. The union reorganized District 15 and called for delegates from Colorado, New Mexico, Wyoming, and Utah to meet in Pueblo in early November 1900. William Howells, the longtime labor activist from the Coal Creek area and in 1900 a national organizer for the union, issued the invitation. The call brought together men ready for action; within three days they affiliated the region's local unions with the UMWA, formulated a plan to expand the union, and issued objectives. The delegates selected John Gehr of Rockvale as president, but they issued no other information about the union. Commissioner Smith explained, "As the new organization has met with much determined opposition upon the part of many operators, its officers do not desire that the names of secretaries or the location of local unions be published at the present time."[4] The *United Mine Workers' Journal* gave an idea of the level of response in early 1901 when it reported that District 15 had 998 members out of 20,000 coal diggers in its four-state jurisdiction. Most of the interest was shown by miners in Colorado and New Mexico.[5]

Union organization became immediately noticeable in the Denver Basin and the Cañon City coalfields. These locations erupted with labor discord simultaneously in early 1901. The men of the Denver Basin wanted to redress the wrongs of 1898, and the UMWA gave them the vehicle to unify their fragmented locals. Similarly, the UMWA tied the locals together around Coal

Creek and gave the men there a vision of solidarity, which they saw as the means to attack the Colorado Fuel and Iron Company. They wanted the union to succeed, and in January 1901 they struck in sympathy for fellow unionists in the mountain West.

THE 1901 COAL STRIKE

Soon after returning to Colorado, the UMWA gained a foothold in the Denver Basin, and labor agitation began. In 1901, 20 percent of the miners there belonged to the United Mine Workers. Although a majority of the men did not join the union, sympathy for organized labor in northern Colorado ran much deeper. By 1901 the UMWA had become popular among western coal miners. Strike victories in the East had given it legitimacy. Plus, the WFM had seemingly given up on Colorado's coal diggers. In early January labor activists decided to move. The time seemed right. Prosperity caused coal to be in short supply, and a strike in the middle of winter would be felt all the more. Showing their independent spirit, in late December 1900 the miners held a mass meeting at Louisville without consulting UMWA officials. They demanded a ten-cent-per-ton wage increase and a decrease in the price of blasting powder. When the operators refused, the men walked off the job.[6]

Soon after the strike started, the mining companies independent of Northern Coal and Coke wanted to settle to protect their markets. With coal in stiff demand, they knew they could pass along any cost advance. At this point the United Mine Workers also become involved. Before deciding whether to accept the independents' offer, the strikers conferred with UMWA president John Mitchell. He advised the men to accept the offer and return to work. UMWA leaders believed they should reward the agreeable companies and let market forces punish the noncompliant ones. With this advice, coal production returned to 25 percent of its former level, but only for a brief time. Fearing that the independents were helping Northern Coal and Coke, the miners reconsidered and again quit work near the end of January.[7]

A few days later a national organizer, Charles Duncan, arrived in the northern field. He sought to take charge of the strike and solidify union membership. Duncan also arranged for a conference to be held with the operators in the office of James Smith, state labor commissioner. Meeting at the end of January, the mine workers laid out their demands, including that the United Mine Workers of America be recognized. James Cannon, president of Northern Coal and Coke, led the charge against the miners. By 1901 he controlled about 70 percent of the Denver Basin's capacity, and he had no time for the rebellious workers or their union. Cannon claimed he "operated at a very small profit and that to grant an increase would entail an absolute loss." As Commissioner Smith reported, "It was evident throughout the entire conference that the miners were anxious to secure a settlement, if they could do so upon any terms that were half way fair and reasonable." Cannon, however, displayed "an obstinacy and stubbornness that would have been commendable if exercised in a better cause," and he "refused to concede anything."[8]

When the conference broke off, the independents quietly negotiated a contract with the union and immediately began shipping coal. These companies recognized the union, granted the wage increase, and allowed for a checkweighman to be paid with the union checkoff that permitted employers to automatically deduct union dues and fees from the payroll. This arrangement constituted a real advantage for the union. To assuage the fears that these operators would assist Northern Coal and Coke, the companies "offered to give bonds not to ship coal to the Northern."[9] Labor Commissioner Smith called the settlement fair and expressed outrage toward Northern Coal. He argued that Northern Coal and Coke could produce coal for less, but it "refused to grant anything." He stated that Northern Coal wanted "unconditional surrender" and that if the miners did not agree, "it would build stockades, import Japanese and work its mines with scabs." Despite its protests about profits, Smith stated that the company's chief objection was recognition of the UMWA.[10]

While the struggles went on in the Denver Basin, other labor difficulties arose over the validity of organization and unionization. In New Mexico, at the Gallup coal mines owned by John C. Osgood's American Fuel Company, the miners organized a local of the UMWA in early January 1901. Osgood refused to have anything to do with the UMWA or any other union, and the American Fuel Company began discharging union members. The move strengthened the men's resolve, and their animosity toward the company grew. Local membership escalated from 259 to 500 in a mine with 550 employees. The miners struck, demanding reinstatement of the discharged men. The *United Mine Workers' Journal* reported that the company tried a variety of tactics to end the strike, from bribing the men with beer to importing "thugs." Every strategy failed.[11]

Labor activists in the Cañon City coalfield moved to help the cause. The miners at Rockvale, Brookside, and Coal Creek—numbering around 1,000— went on strike in mid-January to attack Osgood. All the mines at those locations belonged to the Colorado Fuel and Iron Company. Although American Fuel ran the mines at Gallup, the people in Colorado knew Osgood and his associates owned them. Many assumed the mines were part of the CF&I's operations, but they were not. Nevertheless, Osgood and his antiunion policy remained the target. The UMWA national office only called out CF&I men. Miners at Rockvale asked the union to order out the unionized men in the non-CF&I mines in Fremont County, but the UMWA allowed them to continue to work. As the strike progressed, rumors spread that the union would call out miners employed by the Whitebreast Coal Company in Iowa. Although not actively involved in its management, Osgood held an interest in the company.[12]

The CF&I strike started with the goals of helping the men at Gallup and preserving the nascent union movement within Osgood's operations. Once on strike, the men thought it was an opportune time to have "certain wrongs righted" and make Osgood give at least de facto recognition to the UMWA. The longtime grievances that needed to be corrected varied from camp to camp, but most centered on the system of weighing coal, ventilation in the mines, and the lack of check-weighmen. The local unions also requested adoption of the checkoff. The men, however, did not demand recognition of the union as their bargaining agent. The UMWA leadership seemingly did not want to push for formal recognition until the CF&I had been more thoroughly organized and unionized. Besides, instituting the checkoff would practically guarantee unionization. Everyone would pay union dues whether they wanted to or not.[13]

The miners of the Denver Basin and Cañon City coalfields had moved at the right time to catch the attention of the public and the Colorado state legislature. Coal supplies were already tight, and the threat of a strike in the Cañon City coalfield caused fears of a "coal famine" to spread throughout Denver. Worries increased further as reports surfaced that the UMWA was moving to organize the Walsenburg and Trinidad fields. Concerned about the threatened coal shortage and prompted by representatives sympathetic to labor's cause, in early 1901 the state legislature formed a committee to investigate Colorado's coalfields.[14]

While the strike continued through January, the committee moved quickly through the state's mining camps. At most it heard complaints of dangerous work, poor wages, company stores, and compulsory doctor's fees. Near Walsenburg, however, the committee ran into other problems. When it visited the CF&I's full company town of Pictou, company officials intimidated men to prevent them from testifying. As reported in the *Rocky Mountain News*, the committee soon recognized that it would be "impossible to get any expression of the real feeling of the miners." Fifteen or twenty men who refused to testify were interviewed privately, for they feared that appearing before the committee would cause them to lose their jobs.[15]

The committee returned to Denver to hear the operators' testimony. Cannon and Osgood left no question about their attitude toward the strike or the UMWA. Cannon told the committee that organizations cause strikes and that the strikers always want more than operators can pay. He expressed his willingness to "meet with representatives of the company's men, but merely as individuals." He also labeled the UMWA a "foreign element."[16] Osgood similarly proclaimed his willingness to meet with the men but not the union. He said most grievances could be adjusted, except those dealing with the wage checkoff and unionization. Osgood made his point emphatically clear in an opening statement. He called the coal miners' union a curse and characterized its president, John Mitchell, as "a greater tyrant and autocrat than the czar of Russia." He proclaimed that "no selfish and cold-blooded employer ever exacted the blind obedience, absolute surrender of independence, or contribution of hard-won earnings that he and his organization exacts from his dupes."[17]

While the legislative committee took testimony, union organizers attempted to bring the other CF&I camps into the union fold. Spreading out across southern Colorado, they confronted resistance from a variety of sources. In Trinidad, businessmen met with President Gehr and organizer Howells of the UMWA and asked them to avoid a strike. They argued that they had not yet fully recovered from the 1894 sympathy strike and indicated that although they had contributed to the miners' cause during that walkout, they probably would not do so this time. At the independent town of Starkville, Gehr had rented a hall for a meeting, only to have it refused to him at the last minute.[18]

When the union managed to hold meetings, the gatherings seemed to break apart along ethnic and racial lines. At Sopris the American miners reportedly left the hall shortly after the meeting began, followed by the Hispanic contingent. The Italian miners stayed in session with the union officials for two hours. At Walsenburg the miners' background again seemed to come into play. They did not divide into different groups, but as a local observer stated, "Most of the miners, that is the diggers, are Mexicans and Italians and they are backward in organizing."[19] Many of the foreign-born, most with families, had only recently arrived in the region; they feared losing their jobs and company homes. The CF&I's antiunion policies seemed to be working well.[20]

The company also counted on intimidation to help its cause, especially around Walsenburg in Huerfano County. Commissioner of Labor Statistics Smith reported that coal company representatives and county officials "inaugurated and maintained a reign of terror." Corporate officials subjugated "the miners in these fields with fear of arrest, imprisonment and discharge." The commissioner specifically pointed to Sheriff Jeff Farr and his deputies as spreading abuse and arresting those attempting to organize: "A condition of white slavery almost incredible of belief had been well known to exist in Huerfano county for a number of years, but never before had the outrages upon the rights of citizens been perpetrated so unblushingly and with scarcely an attempt at concealment as they were at this time."[21] President Gehr referred to the situation in Huerfano County as the "worst in any part of the United States."[22]

The company had done its work well; the UMWA achieved only limited success. Intimidation, racial and ethnic diversity, company towns, and lack of experience in organization prevented anything more than preliminary meetings outside of the Cañon City coalfield. Where the union made inroads and a local was formed, such as at Sopris near Trinidad, the CF&I repeated the tactic it had used at Gallup: the company tried to kill the union by locking the men out. The men responded with a strike, and a standoff developed. The miners had to give up their affiliation, or the company would import scabs. At Sopris the local soon disbanded, and the mine reopened. By mid-March American Fuel at Gallup began importing Japanese workers. The UMWA tried to counter the company by warning miners from across the country to stay away from the Colorado coalfields, and it tried to keep the men loyal by providing strike benefits—primarily board. In a protracted work stoppage the union tried to reduce the burden by giving striking miners free transportation to a unionized coalfield where they could find work.[23]

The company proved more powerful and persistent than the UMWA. In early July, seven months after the strike began, the *United Mine Workers' Journal* reported that it had about "3,000 brethren" locked out or on strike in Colorado and New Mexico. For the union, such a protracted assault diminished chances for success. Funds ran low, and local unions that had previously sent assistance lost interest. Further, either through union relocation or by simply drifting away, the number of union members dwindled at the strike locations. After ten months the Gallup local reported only 87 men still receiving strike benefits.[24]

By this time, however, the main struggles had ended. Despite the continued lockout in New Mexico, miners in the Cañon City district returned to work in early April. The sympathy strike had not brought the CF&I to its knees, and any hope for a general strike had disappeared. Although the CF&I's aggressive action had limited solidarity, the company did come to terms on many of the miners' grievances in the Cañon City coalfield. It agreed to change the weighing system to the benefit of the miners, it reduced the price of blasting powder, and it consented to a check-weighman who would be paid through the checkoff of miners' wages. The latter appeared to be a major concession and a step toward company-sanctioned unionization, which the CF&I deplored. But although the company settled on these terms, it had no intention of dealing with the UMWA. In fact, the miners delayed returning to work because the company blacklisted union members who had played a "prominent part in the strike." After a committee met with General Manager Kebler, the blacklist was, as the labor commissioner stated, "ostensibly removed and peace was declared."[25]

The settlement in the Cañon City coalfield reflected a change in policy for the coal company, but it also spoke to the nature of that coalfield. This time the CF&I did not bring in replacement workers or overtly threaten the men in the field. In fact, it reported that its mines reopened with primarily old employees. The company wanted this coal, often called the best domestic coal in the state. But the narrow seams of coal, often mixed with slate, required skilled coal miners to extract it. This situation required that the company keep a core of experienced miners in place. Unfortunately for the company, those men also tended to be the most rebellious.[26]

In the Denver Basin, Cannon also came to terms. He agreed in April to increase wages 10 percent, reduce the price of powder, and recognize an arbitration committee. He did not, however, officially recognize the UMWA as the bargaining agent. Despite this refusal, Cannon met with union members and essentially agreed to union terms. According to Labor Commissioner Smith, "The result was a very decided victory for the United Mine Workers, and impressed the coal miners of the state, as well as many others, with the advantages of organization as a means of securing better treatment." By mid-1901 miners of the Denver Basin were completely organized.[27]

The workers in the Denver Basin and Cañon City coalfields benefited from a healthy economy and a lack of workers. Since the Cañon City mines needed experienced miners, the CF&I could only replace them with other skilled coal miners. In 1901 such men were not readily available. Similarly, Northern Coal and Coke could not get the replacement workers it needed to open its mines; it had to employ its old workers. Good economic conditions were beginning to help the miners and their union.

RAMIFICATIONS OF THE 1901 STRIKE

The UMWA came out of the 1901 strike marginally better than before. A few small operators in Colorado recognized the union—primarily in the Denver Basin—but none of the large producers did. Although Northern Coal did not recognize the union, the UMWA could claim most of its miners as unionized. Further, despite the CF&I's apparent success in beating back organizing efforts around Walsenburg and Trinidad, the UMWA still had members there. But as Commissioner Smith stated, those men did "not wish the fact [of their union membership] to be known to their employers" for fear of immediate discharge. By adopting the checkoff and abolishing the blacklist, unionization in the Cañon City field seemed solid. In October 1901, District 15 held a convention in Trinidad and promised to push its fight in Colorado's southern field, and the Denver *Times* headlined "Outlook for Order Good."[28]

Outside Colorado the 1901 strike gained little for the UMWA. The local at Gallup had been badly damaged, although the men tried to maintain a semblance of the union. In the other two states assigned to District 15, organizers apparently did not make an appearance. Miners in Utah went on strike in early 1901 demanding a wage advance, but the UMWA did not intervene. In Wyoming the men stayed on the job, and the coal companies benefited from Colorado's difficulties. When concerns of a coal famine hit Denver, the *Rocky Mountain News* reported that the "mines of the Union Pacific in Wyoming, in which Chinamen are employed, have assisted in a large degree and have been working double time . . . to meet demands."[29] The UMWA probably made no effort to organize Wyoming in 1901 because it recognized the obstacles to organization, such as the Chinese. Plus, the UMWA did not accept Asians into the union.[30]

More significant than the settlement for the Colorado coal industry was the publicity during the legislative committee's investigation of coalfield conditions. Denver newspapers sent reporters with the committee, and their stories depicted a harsh living and working environment. The headlines read "Struggle for Bread in Coal Miners' Homes" and "Coal Miners Tell Story of Their Hardships."[31] The accounts detailed the conditions in the camps, with the harshest criticism falling on full company towns. At Pictou the committee found company housing with no yards or gardens. The water wells had gone dry, forcing inhabitants to drink from the mine. The papers also carried the committee's findings on the scrip system, company stores, and company policies in general. When the operators responded, the papers also fully covered their remarks. Cannon and Osgood came across as insensitive to their miners' plight and as close-minded toward the problems. After Osgood attacked the UMWA and John Mitchell, he explained to the committee that scrip was "beneficial to the miners." Also, he argued that paying the miners only once a month kept them working more steadily and that Hispanics and Italians preferred to live in shacks rather than houses.[32]

Not only did the publicity go heavily against the coal companies, the legislative committee found the companies culpable for the labor disturbance. The committee endorsed a series of actions to redress the wrongs. It supported measures that would regulate how coal was weighed, eliminate the scrip system, increase ventilation in the mines, and improve the coal mine inspector's enforcement powers. It also recommended amendments to the state constitution that would bring an eight-hour workday and biweekly paydays. Finally, the committee looked askance at the companies' activities and especially found Northern Coal and Coke's efforts to control the price of coal in the Denver Basin onerous. It supported laws to regulate trusts and prevent railroads from cooperating to the detriment of competition.[33]

All of this had a major impact on the Colorado coal industry. The legislature passed laws to ban scrip, institute biweekly paydays, and eliminate screens when weighing coal. Plus, the miners had actively expressed their wish for an eight-hour workday. The Colorado legislature had passed a measure in 1899 that seemingly would have covered coal miners, but the Colorado Supreme Court had ruled it unconstitutional. The legislature responded by proposing a constitutional amendment that would allow the legislature to pass an eight-hour law. The coal miners did not stand alone on this issue. In fact, a vast majority of Coloradans supported the working class, and they passed the amendment in 1902 by a vote of 72,980 to 26,266. The miners hoped for prompt action in implementing the law and looked to the 1903 legislature to fulfill the voters' wishes.[34]

These developments annoyed Osgood. During a time of peak prosperity, when he desperately wanted to expand his operations, he saw the strike cut seriously into company earnings. He blamed the United Mine Workers; without the union, the strike would not have happened. He also saw the state government's incursion as unnecessary. Although Osgood had willingly testified before the committee, he gave the impression of a man who needed to answer to no one. He knew his business, and he knew his men, their wants and desires; and the government did not need to tell him how to run his affairs or where problems existed. The only problems he encountered came from the outside, particularly from the "meddlers" from the UMWA. Throughout his career Osgood always believed he understood his workers and that he was one of them. As an entrepreneur and an individualist, he had worked his way up and felt his men could do the same. But because he had succeeded and become a large employer, he felt he and not the state or the UMWA should have influence over his employees and their conditions.[35]

Soon after the strike ended, Osgood went on the offensive. He wanted to gain better control of his workers and to counteract the negative images planted in people's minds about the Colorado Fuel and Iron Company. In July 1901 the company created a Sociological Department that would develop programs such as kindergartens, libraries, and an educational lecture series to improve the conditions of workers and their families. Osgood did not want these activities to go unnoticed. He enlisted the aid of the Denver *Times* to spread the word of his "philanthropic work." Articles appeared discussing the programs, and the editor of the *Times* added his praise: "Quietly, but withal thoroughly, the Colorado Fuel and Iron company has perfected a fine system of beneficiences for its employes [sic] such as stamps it indelibly as one of the greatest philanthropic corporations of civilization." Osgood would not, the editor thought, eliminate the "possibility of strikes or disputes. . . . But it will unquestionably raise the morals of the employes to such a height that they will reason out their differences with their employers and they will certainly not be so easily misled by agitators."[36]

Osgood wanted not only the general public but also his employees to be aware of his grand efforts. In December 1901 he initiated a weekly publication entitled *Camp and Plant*. Through the magazine Osgood attempted to publicize his programs, educate his workers, and create a new solidarity among his employees. He wanted them to feel a kinship with the CF&I and not the UMWA. Osgood knew that just starting improvement programs did not guarantee success; worker participation needed to be encouraged. He believed highlighting the activities at one camp would stimulate others to imitate that success. Osgood hoped this sharing of activities, along with regular news briefs from the camps, would establish a companywide sense of community and a favorable opinion of the CF&I. In addition, he wanted to educate the workers, to give them what he thought was the necessary background so the United Mine Workers would never "dupe" them again. In sum, Osgood wanted his sense of community to replace potential worker solidarity. Almost in imitation of a UMWA organizer, Osgood hired an assistant to travel from camp to camp to hear complaints, take suggestions, and create enthusiasm.[37]

The timing was critical for Osgood; the 1901 strike came just as he was dramatically expanding the Fuel Department. In March 1901 he opened the town and mine of Tabasco, followed shortly by Primero, Hezron, and Tercio. With such substantial investments, he did not want strikes or a union to interfere with the company's operations or profitability. He attempted to make the new camps "model" communities. From 1901 to 1903 the company built 895 frame "cottages," varying in size from two to six rooms. According to the *Engineering and Mining Journal* the company painted them different colors, laid them out on "wide regular streets," and took care to ensure "general sanitation and drainage." As the *Journal* said, they were not like the "typical company town."[38]

Osgood's grandest experiment in social improvement came on the Western Slope. At Redstone, a location on the Crystal River a few miles south of Glenwood Springs, the CF&I erected new coke ovens for the mines at Coal Basin, and Osgood created his most impressive company town. The *Engineering and Mining Journal* praised Redstone as a true model community, even superior to the new towns he had built elsewhere. In fact, the company claimed it was not a company town at all but a "mountain village." The five-room dwellings had water connections and electricity. A fine boardinghouse called the Redstone Inn was also constructed. "Fitted up in rather elaborate style," it provided accommodations for the "better paid employees."[39]

Osgood had special plans for Redstone. Not only did he build it for his employees on the Western Slope, but he also had big ideas for himself. He built a private mansion at Redstone called Cleveholm. The forty-two-room summer home reportedly cost Osgood millions. The money undoubtedly came from CF&I profits, but Osgood did not make Redstone an official part of the main company. To fund this expansion he had created another auxiliary, the Redstone Improvement Company. In essence, the CF&I invested in the new company and did business with it, but Osgood retained absolute control. As he expanded CF&I's stock offerings, that point became crucial. The new stockholders could be critical of unwise expenditures, and as Osgood well knew, if business turned sour his control of the CF&I could be challenged. The Redstone Improvement Company allowed him to build what he wanted and keep it removed from CF&I affairs.[40]

Along with model towns and new programs, Osgood and associates attempted to head off trouble with a well-planned pay raise. In the summer of

1902 the UMW was fighting for recognition in the anthracite fields of Pennsylvania. By July rumors were circulating that the Colorado miners would lay down their tools in support if UMWA president Mitchell asked them to do so. Mitchell did not ask, but the strike in the East heated up, and by early October the federal government became involved. At that time Colorado Fuel and Iron announced a major wage increase, running from 10 to 25 percent and affecting most employees. The company stated that the cost of living had gone up and that the increasing prosperity allowed it to grant the advance. Plus, CF&I managers claimed they wanted to correct wage "inequalities" among the company's various mining camps.[41]

In fact, the CF&I Fuel Department wanted desperately to avoid another strike that would seriously affect its earnings, as had happened in 1901. Also, the company wanted to reward the camps that had been nonunion and not involved in past labor difficulties. The miners working in southern Colorado received the greatest wage advance. Those men were making less than workers at Cañon City and perhaps deserved more money. But the company was also singling out the unionized miners at Cañon City and giving them less of a raise. The company hoped the raise would placate the men in the south and make everyone question the value of unionization.[42]

Osgood had established two practices most coal producers in the West adopted sooner or later. First, if labor activity threatened, grant a wage increase. Companies saw labor's demands and strikes as nothing more than bread-and-butter issues. More money would wipe away concerns over respect, fair play, or union recognition. Beginning with Osgood's raise in late 1902, this practice became a common feature in coal companies' antiunion policies during this era of prosperity. Second, by building model camps and instituting improvement programs, Osgood became an innovator in welfare capitalism. Whether done to defeat organized labor or to truly help the workers, such betterment activities would become a standard in the West, although not for another twenty years. Osgood brought company towns to full maturity by constructing model communities. In this respect, he was ahead of his time.[43]

Whereas Osgood hoped to keep labor peace with social programs, model towns, and pay raises, the other major operator in southern Colorado—the Victor Fuel Company, under the direction of longtime Trinidad businessman Delos A. Chappell—relied on more traditional techniques: racial diversity and tighter control of camps. Although not targeted in the 1901 labor protest, the Victor Fuel Company decided to root out potential labor activists. An active local existed at the company's Chandler Mine in the Cañon City coalfield in 1901, and a correspondent to the *United Mine Workers' Journal* reported that the camp was "nearly all organized." When the company shipped in Mexican American miners from southern Colorado, the organizers had "little trouble to get them in our local."[44] Chappell wanted to eliminate this solidarity. In early 1902 he began importing workers and selectively firing UMWA members. Chappell brought in Japanese workmen from California and from Rock Springs, Wyoming. In response, 175 miners—mostly Italians—walked out of the mine, asking the miners at Rockvale to join them. Having just recently settled with the CF&I, the Rockvale miners declined. Nevertheless, the Chandler miners persisted, attacking the Japanese and driving them from town. The company closed the mine, stating it would not employ Japanese again. It also argued that it could not find enough Italian workers to operate the mine at a profitable level, so the mine would remain closed. Despite these statements, five months later Chappell reopened the mine with a contingent of 88 African American workers without worker protest. By early 1903 the mine had reportedly returned to full production, with about 120 blacks in a crew of 193.[45]

Victor Fuel still planned to take advantage of the Japanese laborers, however. It had them under contract, and instead of sending them to California as previously announced, Victor Fuel shipped them to Walsenburg. The company employed some of the Japanese in the Maitland Mine and turned others over to the CF&I, which placed them in its operations. As Labor Commissioner Smith explained at the end of 1902, "This county being without effective union labor organization and being absolutely dominated by the Colorado Fuel and Iron Company, the Japs were put to work in the mines and are there yet. The white miners of Huerfano county made an ineffective protest against the action, but nothing came of it."[46]

The operators had two advantages in successfully placing Japanese in the mines near Walsenburg. First, Sheriff Jeff Farr of Huerfano County solidly supported the coal companies. He and his deputies moved aggressively to squelch any protest. The sheriff in Fremont County who had purview over the Cañon City coalfield had more sympathy for the workers' cause. Second, the Walsenburg miners had no effective organization and no history of successfully resisting the companies' activities. The placement of Asians did cause the Colorado state legislature to take action, however. The Colorado House and Senate passed a resolution calling upon the U.S. Congress to "take steps to exclude from this country all of this class of Asiatic labor."[47]

Chappell and Victor Fuel Company further attacked unruly labor by attempting to gain better control of the company's coal camps. At its Hastings camp north of Trinidad the company hired a number of guards to prevent organizational efforts, and at Chandler it decided to incorporate the town in an effort to rein it in. Chandler had been an independent camp, but as the company brought in African American workers it decided to incorporate. In some independent coal camps the residents, mostly miners, would incorporate their village so they could maintain control and run the town themselves. In this instance the miners saw the incorporation as a move by Chappell to

7.1 Chandler, Colorado, near Cañon City. The Western Fuel Company platted Chandler in 1890, but it was then held briefly by the Colorado Fuel and Iron Company before it became the property of the Victor Fuel Company in 1898. This photo shows a well-developed town, circa 1915. Courtesy, Victor-American Collection 7507, 29927, American Heritage Center, University of Wyoming.

dominate the location, "as well as the mines, and everything else around there." The local union fought the incorporation by hiring attorneys and calling upon all union members in Colorado to boycott Victor Fuel products.[48] But Chappell moved ahead with incorporation, and the company built more company houses. Less enlightened than Osgood, Chappell had a more traditional view of company towns and company housing. He believed they could attract workers, bring in revenue, and allow for greater control. Despite these efforts to better control labor, Victor Fuel felt obligated to raise wages in line with the CF&I in 1902.[49]

At the end of 1902 the Colorado coal companies probably sensed success in their assault on unionization. The men had not gone on strike in support of eastern causes, and regional newspapers reported that the "best of relations" existed.[50] The companies had achieved this result through two opposite actions. On the one hand, they rewarded the miners. The major southern op-

7.2 Coal tipple at Chandler, Colorado, circa 1915. Courtesy, Victor-American Collection 7507, 29929, American Heritage Center, University of Wyoming.

erators granted pay increases, and the CF&I made efforts to materially improve working families' lives. On the other hand, the companies introduced potentially disruptive practices: they brought in nonwhite labor and stiffened their opposition to unions, especially in former hotbeds of union activity such as the Cañon City coalfield. The operators there took a toll. The *United Mine Workers' Journal* reported in March 1902 that one of the locals had been "submerged," and the Rockvale local ceased to exist in 1903.[51]

Such actions could seemingly have ended unionization and brought the workers under control, but the miners were still hostile toward the companies—especially because the companies persisted in violating state law. They refused to pay miners every two weeks and continued to use screens when weighing coal. The companies simply chose to evade the laws, believing state lawmakers did not know how the coal business worked. Despite legislation to stop the use of scrip, the companies also continued that practice, although in a slightly altered form. Before passage of the state law, whenever miners wanted an advance on their wages, the companies would issue scrip. Following enactment of the law, the company issued an order for the value of merchandise the miner wanted. If he did not use the entire order, his change was given in scrip. And although the fight for an eight-hour-day law languished in the legislature, the miners felt the voters had spoken and that they should only work eight hours a day. Further, company paternalism did not ensure a happy workforce—not everyone liked living in full company towns or in company houses with company rules and regulations. Finally, Osgood may have tried to change conditions aboveground, but the dangers underground remained the same. When the CF&I mine at Pictou blew up in early 1902, the miners blamed the company for not following the Colorado ventilation law—a state statute since 1883.[52]

OSGOOD LOSES CONTROL OF THE CF&I

Beyond opening more mines, expanding the Pueblo steelworks also figured prominently in Osgood's agenda. Between 1901 and mid-1903 three new blast furnaces had been put into operation, bringing the total to five. The expansion forced the company to issue more stock and bonds. From 130,000 shares of stock in 1892, by mid-1901 the company had expanded its number of shares to 400,000. Replicating western firms' experiences from years before, this rapid expansion created an uncertain value for the stock, and the company could not sell it at face value. The discounted offerings attracted speculators to the business, and in 1901 a struggle for control of the CF&I began. First, John W. Gates, a Chicago financier with a reputation for manipulating corporations for his personal gain, acquired enough stock to gain seats on the board of directors. Although he wanted to work with Osgood, Gates did force him to build new fabrication plants in Pueblo. This move had a huge impact. First, it caused CF&I stock to rise in value, which in turn caused some of the stockholders who had traditionally stood by Osgood to sell their stock at a profit. Second, the new construction forced the company to go into debt. Both developments weakened Osgood's control.[53]

Other investors soon emerged, notably railroad tycoons such as George Gould of the Missouri Pacific and the Denver and Rio Grande, Edwin Hawley of the Colorado and Southern, and Edward H. Harriman of the Union Pacific. All bought large blocks of company stock. Through most of 1902 an intense struggle for control of the CF&I raged. Claim met counterclaim, and countersuits followed suits. Each side accused the other of collusion, bribery, and illegal actions. Osgood tried to protect his financial empire and keep himself in charge. The fight caused the stock to depreciate in value, and Gates had seen enough. He sold his shares at the end of 1902. As Gates got out, John D. Rockefeller moved in. At Gould's urging, Rockefeller paid $6 million for 40 percent of CF&I stock and 43 percent of its bonds, gaining a significant piece of the Colorado company in November 1902.[54]

Although Osgood and his associates lost majority ownership, they remained in control. The company's heavy expenditures brought the next crisis. The company was not producing enough revenue to pay for the improvements, meet dividend payments, and cover everyday expenses. To avert financial disaster Osgood borrowed more money, but receivership seemed near. He ultimately turned to the company's largest stockholders, Gould and Rockefeller, and agreed to step down as manager if they would save the CF&I from insolvency. Osgood continued to serve on the board for a short time, but by September 1903 he had lost all influence.[55]

To some Coloradans Osgood was a local hero trying to protect a homegrown enterprise against marauding eastern capitalists, fighting until he was forced out. But Osgood knew what he was doing. Correspondence to the company's treasurer, John L. Jerome, demonstrated that Osgood was keenly aware of stock market fluctuations and trickery. As early as 1899 Osgood paid attention to who purchased his stock and mentioned vague plans if the company slipped from his control. In 1901 he told Jerome that if Gates reorganized they would all profit, and he speculated freely about the terms under which the company should be sold. At one point in 1901 he asked Jerome to tell his associates that it was the "last chance to buy cheap Fuel stock." Although it appeared publicly that Osgood was at the mercy of stock manipulators such as Gates and Rockefeller, he was fully involved in the process.[56]

Osgood's motives are open to question. In the years before he left the company he had made significant improvements and greatly expanded the CF&I's debt. Were these moves made for the good of the company or to make the company more attractive to outside investors? Osgood profited in the end, but his tactics caused a falling-out among some of his closest and longest allies—all of whom had come to Colorado with Osgood. Alfred Cass, who served as general sales agent, attempted to sue Osgood, but he died suddenly. Two other close associates also died within months of each other during the second half of 1903. Julian Kebler, who had worked as general manager and as president for a time, died of a cerebral hemorrhage, and treasurer Jerome died of a self-inflicted gunshot wound.[57]

Although the men may have been distressed over the circumstances surrounding the CF&I's sale, Osgood proved resilient. After a tour of Europe, he returned to the coal business. Some of his auxiliary companies did not pass to the new operators of the CF&I, including American Fuel and its mines in New Mexico as well as the Redstone Improvement Company. Also, Osgood had acquired an interest in the Victor Fuel Company in southern Colorado. In 1903 he became the active manager of Victor Fuel. The company was Colorado's second-largest coal producer, yielding almost a million tons annually from its eight mines. Although that amount pales when compared with the CF&I's almost 4 million tons a year, Osgood combined his enterprises in

Colorado and New Mexico and formed the Victor-American Fuel Company. Through that company Osgood remained a strong force in the Colorado coal industry.[58]

The events from 1901 to 1903 brought dramatic changes to the coalfields of Colorado. The United Mine Workers became a presence in the state, as it had some success in the Denver Basin and, for a time, at a few CF&I locations. Again, market forces forced some operators to work with the union. A long strike would mean lost profits and market shares. The small operators in the Denver Basin recognized that possibility, and even John Osgood feared missing out on profits and occasionally gave in to the union under pressure. In fact, the union tried to use market forces to punish resistant operators and reward cooperative ones. But concerns over market share did not sway all mine owners. If they adamantly refused to accept a union, owners would ultimately defeat it.

Osgood also brought changes to the coalfields. The 1901 strike hurt his profits when he needed them to support his company's expansion, so in an attempt to ensure that would not happen again, Osgood tried to undermine the union's appeal with kindness. He introduced new social programs, built new towns, and gave pay raises. Osgood, however, continued to use every available method to repress worker solidarity, from workforce diversification to intimidation. Osgood combined new tactics with old in an attempt to maintain control of his workers.

One of the biggest changes came at the end of this era when Osgood lost control of the CF&I. He had assembled the largest coal company in the West, and he seemed to have implemented solid business practices that guaranteed success. Osgood, however, was still a speculator. Like earlier CF&I investors, he wanted to make money. He knew how to make money from CF&I stock, and he knew how to take care of himself. He had the Victor and American Fuel Companies to fall back on when he lost control of the CF&I. The financial integrity of the CF&I continued to be hurt by the steel plant. The company could never count on consistent profits from the steelworks, and more expansion at the plant drained the company financially.

Through these years of turmoil and change in Colorado, the Union Pacific Coal Company and other Wyoming operators enjoyed an era of growth and labor stability. Part of the quietude resulted from the policies of the Union Pacific, which wanted peace among its laborers and implemented a number of policies to gain it. The company pursued labor harmony to keep its trains running. The railroad depended on the coal mines, and railroad officials would not let problems in the mines interfere with their primary mission. The Union Pacific Coal Company had a captive market—the railroad—and that market's needs drove labor relations. Moreover, where the Union Pacific led, other southern Wyoming operators followed. Much to their surprise, however, miners in the West saw a friend in the UMWA, and the union would return to challenge the companies' dominance.

NOTES

1. *History of the Union Pacific Coal Mines,* appendix; *Tenth Biennial Report of the State Inspector of Coal Mines of the State of Colorado, 1901–1902,* 125; *Eighth Biennial Report of the State Inspector of Coal Mines of the State of Colorado for the Years 1897 and 1898,* 114, 117, 150–161.

2. Scamehorn, *Pioneer Steelmaker,* 125.

3. *United Mine Workers' Journal,* December 28, 1899; *Seventh Biennial Report of the Bureau of Labor Statistics of the State of Colorado, 1899–1900,* 44–45, 237.

4. *Seventh Biennial Report of the Bureau of Labor Statistics of the State of Colorado, 1899–1900,* 236–237; *United Mine Workers' Journal,* November 1, November 15, 1900.

5. Fox, *United We Stand,* 63; *Denver Times,* October 25, 1900; *United Mine Workers' Journal,* January 24, 1901.

6. *Eighth Biennial Report of the Bureau of Labor Statistics of the State of Colorado, 1901–1902,* 130–131; *United Mine Workers' Journal,* January 3, 1901.

7. *United Mine Workers' Journal,* January 31, 1901; *Denver Times,* January 22, 1901; "New Mexico," *Engineering and Mining Journal* 71, no. 5 (February 2, 1901): 158.

8. *Eighth Biennial Report of the Bureau of Labor Statistics of the State of Colorado, 1901–1902,* 132–133.

9. *Denver Times,* January 22, 1901.

10. *Eighth Biennial Report of the Bureau of Labor Statistics of the State of Colorado, 1901–1902,* 133–134.

11. *United Mine Workers' Journal,* January 10, January 24, January 31, 1901.

12. *Eighth Biennial Report of the Bureau of Labor Statistics of the State of Colorado, 1901–1902,* 130; *Tenth Biennial Report of the State Inspector of Coal Mines of the State of Colorado, 1901–1902,* 192–193; *Denver Times,* January 22, 1901; *Rocky Mountain News,* January 16, January 23, January 24, 1901.

13. *Eighth Biennial Report of the Bureau of Labor Statistics of the State of Colorado, 1901–1902,* 151; *Rocky Mountain News,* January 18, 1901; *Denver Times,* January 22, 1901.

14. *Rocky Mountain News,* January 17, 1901; "Arizona," *Engineering and Mining Journal* 71, no. 3 (January 19, 1901): 92.

15. *Rocky Mountain News,* January 17, January 20, January 23, quote in January 24, 1901, 2.

16. *Rocky Mountain News,* January 29, 1901, 2.

17. Quotes in *Rocky Mountain News,* January 31, 1901, 1; *Denver Times,* January 31, 1901.

18. *Rocky Mountain News,* January 18, January 20, 1901.

19. *Rocky Mountain News,* January 28, 1901, 1.

20. *Rocky Mountain News,* January 20, January 24, 1901.

21. *Eighth Biennial Report of the Bureau of Labor Statistics of the State of Colorado, 1901–1902,* 156.

22. *United Mine Workers' Journal*, February 7, 1901.

23. *United Mine Workers' Journal*, February 28, March 14, 1901; *Rocky Mountain News*, January 22, 1901; Denver *Times*, March 23, 1901; *Eighth Biennial Report of the Bureau of Labor Statistics of the State of Colorado, 1901–1902*, 156.

24. *United Mine Workers' Journal*, July 4, October 3, 1901.

25. Quotes in *Eighth Biennial Report of the Bureau of Labor Statistics of the State of Colorado, 1901–1902*, 155; *United Mine Workers' Journal*, March 28, 1901; *Engineering and Mining Journal* 71 (April 6, 1901): 441.

26. "Colorado Fuel and Iron Company," *Engineering and Mining Journal* 72, no. 14 (October 5, 1901): 430.

27. *Eighth Biennial Report of the Bureau of Labor Statistics of the State of Colorado, 1901–1902*, 158.

28. *Eighth Biennial Report of the Bureau of Labor Statistics of the State of Colorado, 1901–1902*, 385–386; Denver *Times*, October 9, 1901.

29. *Rocky Mountain News*, January 17, quote in January 24, 1901; Allan Kent Powell, *The Next Time We Strike: Labor in Utah's Coal Fields, 1900–1933* (Logan: Utah State University Press, 1985), 37–50.

30. *United Mine Workers' Journal*, October 3, October 31, 1901; Denver *Times*, October 9, 1901.

31. *Rocky Mountain News*, January 20, January 23, 1901.

32. *Rocky Mountain News*, January 24, January 31, 1901; *United Mine Workers' Journal*, March 7, 1901; *Eighth Biennial Report of the Bureau of Labor Statistics of the State of Colorado, 1901–1902*, 153.

33. *United Mine Workers' Journal*, March 7, 1901; *Eighth Biennial Report of the Bureau of Labor Statistics of the State of Colorado, 1901–1902*, 154–155.

34. Lonsdale, "The Fight for an Eight-Hour Day," 340–348; *Rocky Mountain News*, September 18, 1903; Carroll D. Wright, Commissioner of Labor, *A Report on Labor Disturbances in the State of Colorado, from 1880 to 1904, Inclusive, with Correspondence Relating Thereto*, 58th Cong., 3d sess., 1905, Doc. no. 122 (Washington, D.C.: GPO, 1905), 331.

35. "Ninth Annual Report of the Colorado Fuel and Iron Co., for the Year Ending June 30, 1901," 4, Collection #1057, Box #5, Folder #94, CF&I CRL; Denver *Times*, January 31, 1901; Wilson, "A Study of Paternalism in the Colorado Coal and Iron Company Under John C. Osgood," 56.

36. Denver *Times*, October 15, quotes in October 21, 1901; Scamehorn, *Pioneer Steelmaker*, 149.

37. *Camp and Plant* 1, no. 1 (December 14, 1901): 1; "How One Corporation Helped Its Employees," *Engineering and Mining Journal* 83, no. 26 (June 29, 1907): 1233–1234.

38. *Engineering and Mining Journal* 83, no. 26 (June 29, 1907): 1235.

39. Ibid., 1236.

40. Wilson, "A Study of Paternalism in the Colorado Coal and Iron Company Under John C. Osgood," 105.

41. Fox, *United We Stand*, 89–93; Denver *Times*, July 31, October 16, 1902; *Eighth Biennial Report of the Bureau of Labor Statistics of the State of Colorado, 1901–1902*, 380–381.

42. *Eighth Biennial Report of the Bureau of Labor Statistics of the State of Colorado, 1901–1902*, 380–381.

43. "Ninth Annual Report of the Colorado Fuel and Iron Co.," 4; Denver *Times*, October 16, 1902; Stuart D. Brandes, *American Welfare Capitalism, 1880–1940* (Chicago: University of Chicago Press, 1970), 38–51.

44. *United Mine Workers' Journal*, October 17, 1901.

45. *United Mine Workers' Journal*, March 6, 1902; Denver *Times*, February 12, February 13, February 14, July 24, August 15, October 24, 1902, January 16, February 20, March 11, 1903.

46. *Eleventh Biennial Report of the State Coal Mine Inspector, 1903–1904* (Denver: Smith-Brooks Printing, State Printers, 1905), 150–151; *Eighth Biennial Report of the Bureau of Labor Statistics of the State of Colorado, 1901–1902*, 303.

47. Quote in *Eighth Biennial Report of the Bureau of Labor Statistics of the State of Colorado, 1901–1902*, 303; *United Mine Workers' Journal*, March 6, 1902.

48. *Eighth Biennial Report of the Bureau of Labor Statistics of the State of Colorado, 1901–1902*, 235.

49. Denver *Times*, September 26, October 24, 1902; *United Mine Workers' Journal*, May 8, 1902; Wright, *A Report on Labor Disturbances in the State of Colorado*, 333.

50. Denver *Times*, October 24, 1902.

51. *Rocky Mountain News*, November 11, 1903; *United Mine Workers' Journal*, March 6, 1902, 6.

52. *United Mine Workers' Journal*, February 20, April 3, 1902; *Rocky Mountain News*, September 18, 1903; *Eighth Biennial Report of the Bureau of Labor Statistics of the State of Colorado, 1901–1902*, 150; Wright, *A Report on Labor Disturbances in the State of Colorado*, 331.

53. Scamehorn, *Pioneer Steelmaker*, 98, 100–102, 157–158; Denver *Times*, July 20, 1902; Gaynor, "History of the Colorado Fuel and Iron Company and Constituent Companies," 95, 99.

54. Denver *Times*, August 11, 1902; Gaynor, "History of the Colorado Fuel and Iron Company and Constituent Companies," 97; Scamehorn, *Pioneer Steelmaker*, 158, 163; Athearn, *The Denver and Rio Grande Western Railroad*, 191; Ron Chernow, *Titan: The Life of John D. Rockefeller Sr.* (New York: Random House, 1998), 571.

55. Scamehorn, *Pioneer Steelmaker*, 165–167.

56. J. C. Osgood to J. L. Jerome, April 24, April 26, 1899, quote in May 9, October 17, 1901, Box 1, John L. Lathrop Jerome Collection, Colorado State Historical Society, Colorado Research Library, Denver.

57. Scamehorn, *Pioneer Steelmaker*, 167.

58. *Eleventh Biennial Report of the State Coal Mine Inspector, 1903–1904*, 46; *Rocky Mountain News*, December 21, 1903; *Engineering and Mining Journal* 80 (September 23, 1905): 559; J. C. Osgood to J. L. Jerome, February 2, 1899, Box 1, John L. Lathrop Jerome Collection, Colorado State Historical Society, CRL, Denver; Scamehorn, "John C. Osgood," 147; Ruland, *Lion of Redstone*, 46–54.

CHAPTER EIGHT

UNITED MINE WORKERS IN THE WEST, 1903-1912

DURING 1903 PROSPERITY STILL REIGNED in the coalfields of Colorado and Wyoming. Both states produced record amounts that year, and their outputs continued to rise in subsequent years. In Wyoming the growth allowed the largest coal producers to flourish. The Union Pacific Coal Company, Kemmerer Coal, and Diamond Coal and Coke increased their outputs and enjoyed management stability. In Colorado the situation was different. Although production advanced, Osgood had overextended the Colorado Fuel and Iron Company (CF&I) and lost control of the company. That situation brought a mixed response from Coloradans. Many in the state mourned the loss of a major Colorado company to out-of-state interests. Some company employees, however, hoped new management would bring better labor relations. In reality, the CF&I's operation changed little. Many of the coal operation managers retained their positions and continued the basic policies Osgood had instituted. The new owners, however, were less interested in Osgood's welfare programs. To cut costs, they discontinued some activities, including *Camp and Plant*, which stopped publication in 1904.[1]

Other companies in Colorado also experienced changes in the first years of the twentieth century. The 1901 strike hurt Northern Coal and Coke's financial position and eroded its markets, and the company never fully recovered. Also, change came to the Victor Fuel Company. As discussed in Chapter 7, John Osgood had been buying stock in Victor Fuel since 1899, and by 1903 he held a controlling interest. When he lost control of the CF&I, he asserted his position with Victor Fuel and took charge of the operation. Osgood remained a major force in the Colorado coal industry.

The prosperity of the time inspired the miners to want more. They sought better wages, respect, fair play, and union recognition. The major coal companies of the West, however, had developed a full arsenal of practices to resist what they saw as excessive demands, ranging from rewarding to repressing the men. Some membership in local unions still existed, but as Colorado state commissioner of labor statistics James Smith related, the miners dared not let managers know they were union members for fear of dismissal. Only in northern Colorado did the miners enjoy organization and living conditions independent of company control.[2]

Into this mix of large companies and their policies to control workers entered the United Mine Workers of America (UMWA). The union had made small advances in the West after its organization in 1890, but it retreated after the 1894 strike. Some western miners remained interested in the union throughout the 1890s, but the national office did not actively return to the West until after the turn of the century. In 1901 the union struck the Osgood-controlled mines and those in the Denver Basin. Whereas the competitive nature of the Denver Basin mines allowed for union inroads, Osgood resisted most of the workers' demands. The 1901 strike left only small enclaves of union organization in the western coalfields. As the national union matured, it eventually decided to make another effort to organize the West. Because of the existence of full company towns, ethnic and racial mixing, and compliant law enforcement officials, the coal diggers had little sense of commonality. The UMWA became the agent of worker solidarity.

ORGANIZATION RETURNS TO THE WESTERN COALFIELDS

The national UMWA office put little emphasis on the western fields after the 1901 strike. Although it had success in the Denver Basin and District 15 remained active, the union focused on the East. John Gehr of Rockvale still functioned as District 15 organizer, and he attempted to hold the locals together. Plus, the district's officers kept the national organization informed of its activities. For instance, when Victor Fuel and the CF&I introduced Japanese workers in 1902, the union men sent a flurry of protest articles to the *United Mine Workers' Journal*. They also discussed conditions in the region and ways to expand the organization. In particular, the District 15 officers argued that more attention needed to be directed toward organizing Italians, the largest ethnic group in the southern Colorado coal mines. But the national office offered little support. It was involved in a number of other struggles, such as the 1902 anthracite strike in Pennsylvania. District 15's reach remained limited. By January 1903 it had fewer than 1,500 members out of over 20,000 coal miners under its jurisdiction.[3]

The western coalfields, however, saw a dramatic increase in union activity in 1903 when the UMWA national office again focused attention on the field. The Pennsylvania anthracite strike had ended with an apparent victory for the workers, freeing union resources and motivating western miners to organize. The union announced it would send more organizers to the region in March, and by the end of the month union activists were working throughout the mountain West. In Montana, Wyoming, and Colorado, organizers hoped to encourage men to resist the coal companies' machinations and join the union. In addition, many workers in southern and central Colorado wanted to challenge the new ownership of the CF&I. They hoped it would be more amenable to unionization than Osgood had been.[4]

The Western Federation of Miners (WFM) also encouraged organization. The WFM had tried intermittently to recruit coal miners, but its real interest lay with metal miners. In 1902 the WFM made a push to organize the workers in Colorado's metal reduction plants and smelters. This required efforts across the state, from Denver to Durango; when the plant managers resisted, WFM locals in metal mines began a sympathy strike in 1903. The strike seemed to be winding down when the metalworkers added the demand of an eight-hour workday. This new requirement reinvigorated the walkout and spoke to the frustration of many Colorado workers. The people of Colorado had voted overwhelmingly for an eight-hour day, as discussed previously, but the legislature had failed to enact the measure as law. The new round of strikes soon deteriorated into violence, which caused Governor James Peabody to call for martial law. WFM president Charles Moyer looked to the Colorado coal miners for support. He believed in class solidarity and felt a strike among the coal workers would force the industrialists to recognize the metal miners' demands.[5]

The WFM had many friends in the western coalfields, and a possibility existed that Moyer's call could bring new WFM locals to the coal towns. Some historians argue that the threat of WFM action encouraged the UMWA to try organizing the West in 1903. But the WFM threat only existed in Colorado, and the UMWA sent organizers to other western states. Although union officials often worried about dual organization, UMWA's renewed effort at organization was not made solely to counter the WFM. For the UMWA, the timing was right. It had the resources, the momentum, and the desire to challenge the new ownership of the CF&I.[6]

The UMWA organizers had a huge task before them. With under 1,500 paid members, the union needed to strengthen its ranks. It first tried to achieve greater interethnic solidarity. To this end, District 15 purchased the Italian-language newspaper in Las Animas County and made it "the official organ of District 15." The district officers stated that it had been a labor paper, and through it they planned to "seek the patronage of the Italian people." They further argued that this move was essential as "two-thirds of the population of southern Colorado" was Italian.[7]

As the organizers worked the Rocky Mountain coal regions, they experienced different successes from north to south. In Montana UMWA organizers had a relatively easy time. This coal-mining region had heretofore been left out of any UMWA district organization, and the union had once classified the state's production as insignificant. In 1901, Montana had about 2,150 coal miners and produced only 25 percent as much coal as Colorado. But the coal miners in Montana had been active unionists, with most initially belonging to the WFM. Starting in 1900 the WFM gradually withdrew from the Montana coal mines, and when the UMWA organizers arrived they met a group of willing unionists. By July 1903 the UMWA had organized a new district for the northern Rockies—District 22.[8]

District 22 went beyond Montana. It also included the mines in northern Wyoming, operations formerly considered part of District 15. The inclusion of these mines in District 22 pointed out key similarities between the mines of southern Montana and those in northern Wyoming. First, the mines were fairly close together and shared a common labor market—one influenced by the Montana copper mines. The copper mines paid high wages in 1903, and the coal mines had to follow. The copper mines also recognized a union. To keep their workers, the coal operators had to do the same. Second, these coal mines experienced little competition. Railroads owned or controlled many of the mines, or the mines sold their product in markets with little competitive pressure. The operators could sell more expensive coal without much concern about losing market share. By the end of September, without a disturbance, the coal operators of Montana and northern Wyoming recognized the union as the bargaining agent for the men and agreed to a contract.[9]

In southern Wyoming the UMWA did not have the same success. Companies there had developed a set of tactics that kept unionism at bay. Although the companies wanted to maintain cordial relations with the workers, they did not want the union to enter their mines. Reports to the *United Mine Workers' Journal* from Rock Springs indicated that the Union Pacific was discharging "everybody that sympathizes with the union labor movement." Plus, the company kept enhancing its racial and ethnic mix by hiring miners based on nationality. One correspondent stated that the company hoped "to hold a balance between the nationalities so they can't get together and agree on anything."[10] The full company towns also put the workers at the company's mercy. Reports circulated of evictions coinciding with union activity.[11]

Despite these tactics, a UMWA local apparently formed in Rock Springs in September 1903. At the end of the month the *United Mine Workers' Journal* claimed the miners in southern Wyoming were ready to strike, and it warned of grave consequences. The *Journal* cautioned that another Rock Springs Massacre could occur: "It is said that the white miners will seize upon the opportunity to drive out the Chinese and Japs, and [the result could be] a recurrence of the bloody scenes of fifteen years ago."[12]

The Wyoming men did not walk out, however. Undoubtedly, the companies' firm hold over the miners kept organization weak and the workers in control. Plus, the UMWA had a weakness: it excluded Japanese and Chinese miners. Those men would keep working during a strike, and that reality probably spurred the *Journal's* threat of another Rock Springs Massacre. The exclusion policy disrupted solidarity and deterred other men from striking. Plus, the Wyoming workers did not have the same complaints as the miners in Colorado. Southern Wyoming workers did not like the scrip system, and they wanted institution of the eight-hour day, but the state legislature had not addressed these issues. The miners could not accuse the companies of ignoring the will of the people. The Wyoming workers also had not suffered through the 1901 strike, as many Colorado miners had. The Wyoming miners did not express the same disdain for their employers because of the generally better labor relations maintained by the Union Pacific Coal Company, the Quealy operations, and Diamond Coal and Coke.[13]

Although the *United Mine Workers' Journal* predicted a struggle in Wyoming, the fight came instead in Colorado. When the UMWA sent organizers to Montana and Wyoming, it also worked the Colorado coalfields. After six months of organizing, focusing on southern Colorado, the union could not claim a dramatic increase in membership. It could only report 2,000 paid-up members, most of them in the northern and central parts of the state. The organizers did make inroads at the independent mines in the south, those not controlled by the CF&I or Victor Fuel. At least three locals formed around the independents. The union also counted another 3,000 members who had not paid their dues. In fact, the organizers believed they had the support of the majority of miners and that oppression had kept them from joining.[14]

COLORADO MOVES TOWARD A STRIKE

When financial and managerial turmoil hit the CF&I in 1903, the officers of District 15 thought they saw their chance to bypass the rigors of individual recruitment and put the union in place in one move. The district officers did not know what to expect from Gould and Rockefeller, but the union men made public statements indicating they believed they were "Christian gentlemen."

The district officers were further encouraged when the change in company control caused general superintendent W. J. Murray to leave the CF&I. They claimed he was the "one man who, more than all others, [had] kept the several camps . . . bare of organization."[15] Unfortunately, the union men failed to realize that most other Osgood men remained in place. Nevertheless, the UMWA decided to find out what the changes meant and to test the new ownership. In August 1903 the officers issued a "manifesto" addressed to the governor and the public that listed the miners' numerous grievances and warned of troubles ahead. In reality, the union sought to gain the attention of unorganized miners and operators. The manifesto was meant to inspire the unorganized workers to join, and it asked for a conference with the coal companies.[16]

The manifesto expressed three types of grievances that addressed the miners' craft philosophy, their rights that companies had ignored, and the laws the companies had violated. In terms of the miners' philosophy, the manifesto reflected the craft traditions of coal mining. Miners had long believed they should have a say in the production process, including determining the price of their product. The manifesto complained that workers currently had no voice in fixing the "time value on the commercial traffic of the production of coal." In terms of their rights, the manifesto argued that the coal companies ignored the miners' rights by preventing them from conversing "in open conclave with fellow craftsmen who are employed by the coal operators." Further, the companies denied them the privilege to shop or live where they chose. The manifesto then stated that the companies ignored state laws regulating mine safety and ventilation.[17]

In each case the miners only wanted what they thought the operators had denied them. The miners were provoking a strike to rectify past wrongs. The obscure language in the first grievance hid a demand for higher wages, but the wage issue was put in terms of a grievance. It *was* a grievance in the sense that the miners wanted to regain recognition of their craftsman status. As the manifesto said, the miners wanted a "full and absolute livelihood" that recognized their experience and contribution to the "social and commercial needs of the world."[18]

With the issuance of the manifesto, miners around the state held mass meetings to discuss their own grievances and the possibility of a strike. The miners' complaints varied with their locations and particular circumstances. At most locations, especially those of Victor Fuel, the men decried the prohibition on organization and the discharging of union members. At the CF&I locations at Rockvale and Coal Creek, miners discussed the eight-hour day, recognition of the union, the checkoff, and mine ventilation. Throughout the labor difficulties in 1903 the stated grievances and demands varied depending on who did the talking, but as the strike movement developed, the right to organize and the eight-hour day became the key issues. With this last demand the coal miners paralleled a primary grievance in the ongoing metalworkers' strike.[19]

Although the manifesto requested a conference with the operators, the UMWA organizers fully expected a strike. In fact, part of the manifesto warned that not everything "will be peace and harmony in the future."[20] President Moyer of the WFM wanted the coal miners to strike. Moyer saw his ongoing struggle in the metal mines as much more than a fight for an eight-hour day or union recognition. To him it was an ideological struggle between labor and capital. Soon after the manifesto came out, Moyer asked the UMWA organizers to keep the coal miners out as long as the strike at Cripple Creek continued. He hoped worker solidarity across industrial boundaries would force the capitalists to capitulate. Moyer also wanted assurances that the UMWA would control the coal miners and not allow them to work as strikebreakers in the metal mines.[21]

Despite the apparent inevitability of a strike, Governor Peabody and Labor Commissioner W. H. Montgomery invited the Colorado coal operators to meet with them and "representatives of the coal miners." The invitation stated that they hoped to devise a "means to more fully comply with the present laws relating to the operations of mines, and consider measures to avoid possible friction between employes [sic] and operators." The state officials called for a conference on September 8.[22]

The United Mine Workers soon learned that no changes had come with the new ownership at the CF&I. Despite Murray's departure, old CF&I officials still ran the company—from individual mine superintendents to the general manager—and they continued Osgood's policy of firm resistance to the union. Also, the Victor Fuel Company, influenced directly by Osgood's investments and allied with the CF&I, emphatically refused to attend the conference. Only operators from the Denver Basin responded to the governor's call, and they met with representatives from their mines. When Peabody and Montgomery finally visited with representatives of the southern operators, they met intransigence. The companies would not meet with or recognize the United Mine Workers, and they would only deal directly with their own workers. CF&I officials stated that they intended to continue the "policy that had been so satisfactory."[23]

The failure of the discussions placed the decision regarding what to do with the miners, and not all workers were in agreement. Anxious to take action, miners in the southern mines independent of Victor Fuel and the CF&I decided to strike before negotiations began. In late August 450 men struck the Rugby, Primrose, and Majestic Mines in southern Colorado, asking for the eight-hour day. These miners had been consistently rebellious. The Denver *Times* reported that the men had struck the Majestic Mine fourteen times in the past three years, and the *Rocky Mountain News* stated that "the

miners have always carried their point" at the mine. The independent operators had to keep operating to survive; a work stoppage would dramatically hurt
their place in the market. They needed to appease their workers—including
paying them more—to stay in business. The companies were forced to work
on smaller profit margins than were the CF&I and Victor Fuel. Although the
men had walked out without a districtwide strike order and had been free of
district control, the union saw their actions as relevant to its organizing effort. As soon as they struck, the union began providing support.[24]

With small strikes already on, the large southern operators' refusal to
meet made more miners restive, and the district officers decided they needed
to call a convention. National organizer Gehr hoped the convention would
deflect some of the growing desire for a districtwide strike. Although he had
worked diligently to bring the union to Colorado, Gehr did not want to see a
strike. When the convention met in Pueblo, he submitted a report stating
that a strike at that time would "mean the death of the organization in this
Western field." He believed the small union membership would again be
crushed by the CF&I and Victor Fuel. Whereas Gehr worried about the extent of union membership, he knew the coal strike would be lumped together
with the metal strike. At Cripple Creek, troops had been called out to support the operators, and Gehr felt certain troops would come to the coalfields
"on a moment's notice, should we go out on a strike."[25] Gehr worried that the
coal miners would be unnecessarily drawn into the metal strike and come
under the influence of the WFM. He recognized that the coal miners had
valid complaints, but the timing and the connection with the WFM would be
disastrous.[26]

Indeed, some of Gehr's concerns proved valid. When the convention met
in Pueblo, the miners drifted toward the WFM camp. Early in the meeting
WFM president Moyer called for allies in the strike against the metal companies. Pushing the issue of the eight-hour day, he argued that since the state
legislature would not pass the measure, the coal miners needed to join the
metalworkers in their struggle: "It is my opinion that now is the opportune
time."[27] The convention sympathized with Moyer. The delegates voted to adopt
an interchange card system whereby WFM members would automatically become members of the UMWA, and they adopted a resolution supporting socialism. In the process, they condemned Gehr for his cautious comments.[28]

Although they drew closer to the WFM, the District 15 miners had their
own reasons to strike and would have voted to do so even without the WFM
influence. The change of control at the CF&I, the legislature's failure to act
on the eight-hour law, and the mining companies' continued violation of
state laws motivated the miners to take decisive action. Further, many representatives believed only a strike would reach those yet unorganized. They felt
four-fifths of the miners would respond to a strike call if the national board

endorsed it. The representatives hoped national support would remove uncertainties and attract the miners.

The convention drew up formal demands—including an eight-hour day and a wage advance—and asked again for a conference with the operators. When this failed, the district applied to the national board for permission to strike. Gehr and Montgomery made the board aware of their apprehensions about a walkout, but the pro-strike contingent had more sway with President Mitchell and the national board. They approved a strike for November 9. The order included all of District 15 and inspired miners in Utah to strike, but the focus of the struggle remained in Colorado.[29]

Some historians argue that Mitchell found himself in a dilemma. They claim Mitchell did not want the walkout because it would cause a "desperate and expensive struggle against powerful corporations with little to gain even if victory could be secured." But if he did not support the strike, "the WFM would siphon off coal miners in the West and increase its influence with the radicals within the UMWA." Mitchell may have based his decision "on fear of radical subversion, not on a rational assessment of the situation."[30]

Such an interpretation overlooks UMWA's operations in the mountain West and the realities in Colorado. The strike approval was not just a reaction to the WFM, nor did the union see little to gain from a strike. The UMWA wanted the coal miners of the mountain West in the union, which is why organizers worked the region throughout 1903 and gained recognition in District 22. Plus, the Colorado miners had long-term grievances, and with a change at the CF&I they saw an opportunity for redress. They were ready for a strike. When November 9 came, 95 percent of Colorado's miners answered the call despite low union membership numbers. The *United Mine Workers' Journal* claimed the time was "exactly right for a successful strike." The union had no other strike in progress in the country, and the officials could "concentrate their efforts in this district, which has long been a prospective battleground."[31]

If a dilemma existed, it came from the different goals of the strike supporters. The more radical element, those who condemned Gehr and voted to support socialism, saw the strike more as a class struggle. Perhaps swayed by the WFM or by the long-term oppression in southern Colorado, they expected the strike to continue until all issues were resolved in the coalfields and the metal mines. They believed that only through solidarity would the workers prevail. Mitchell and the more conservative members of the UMWA believed in market unionism. If their terms could be achieved, they were willing to make regional or individual settlements. Coal companies that agreed with them deserved to resume business. Market unionists recognized that coal markets compelled those operators to settle and that they should be allowed to regain their market position.[32]

The market unionists' philosophy became evident early on. Before the strike call, the Denver Basin operators agreed to meet with union representatives. And UMWA officials announced that if they came to a settlement there would be no strike in northern Colorado. The UMWA also hoped to divide and conquer its two most intransigent foes, the CF&I and Victor Fuel. The UMWA claimed Victor Fuel's oppressive attitude toward labor, especially in its operation of company towns, had "precipitated" the general strike. The union argued that if Victor Fuel did not exist, the men could have settled their differences with the CF&I without a strike. The UMWA leadership was counting on a more congenial CF&I ownership group. The union leaders hoped the CF&I would settle and begin returning coal to the market. This would force Victor Fuel to the bargaining table.[33]

Although the UMWA wanted to divide its foes and let the market conquer them, the WFM leaders wanted no agreements until all labor difficulties in both the metal and the coal mines could be settled. Mother Mary Jones—the union's most famous organizer and firebrand—came to Colorado to organize the miners and spread the word of labor solidarity, and President Moyer met with UMWA representatives to convince them of the importance of solidarity. As the 1903–1904 strike started in Colorado, the exact course of action remained much in debate.[34]

THE 1903–1904 STRIKE IN THE DENVER BASIN

The strike call came for November 9, and Colorado miners up and down the Front Range walked out. The *United Mine Workers' Journal* called it the "biggest surprise party in the history of the West." Nearly every man, "union and non-union, white and Mexican, all obeyed the order of President Mitchell and the tie-up is complete."[35] But not all miners initially walked out; those at Chandler continued to work. Victor Fuel had recently introduced a large contingent of African American workers at Chandler, but they left work within a few days—apparently encouraged by the extent of the strike. Miners on the Western Slope also eventually joined the strike effort. As the strike developed, solidarity spread across racial and ethnic lines, as well as across coalfields.[36]

Soon after the strike began, however, disagreements developed over the tactics and meaning of the strike. Within days, some of the smaller Denver Basin mines began to reopen. Those operators were willing to meet the workers' demands, and work resumed with the eight-hour day and wage concessions in place. Northern Coal and Coke and the remaining Denver Basin coal companies followed. They met with miners' representatives and agreed to an eight-hour day—contingent on the outcome of the strike in the south—and a wage advance. If the union failed to achieve the eight-hour day in southern Colorado, then these mines would revert to the longer workday. The men had to vote to accept this settlement, and they narrowly rejected it. No specific reason emerged for the negative vote, but apparently some disliked the "conditional" eight-hour day, whereas others saw a discrepancy in the wage scale. Nevertheless, the smaller mines continued to work while the closed operators and many idle miners expressed dissatisfaction over the outcome of the vote.[37]

The decision of whether to hold another referendum immediately became a major point of contention. At a mass meeting in Louisville in late November, over 1,000 men heard the pros and cons. On the one side stood Mother Jones and District president Howells. Howells argued that the northern miners should not settle with the operators regardless of the terms. Howells's many years of fighting the coal operators in southern and central Colorado had apparently made him a believer in class solidarity. He argued that a settlement in the north would "injure the cause of the South. . . . Should the North go back to work and desert the Southern miners the organization there would be broken up." Mother Jones told the men they had "closed all the mines for the first time by telling the Italians, Mexicans, and Negroes that their brother miners in the North were with them and would stand by them." These men were "not in the habit of fighting for their rights, and were easily discouraged." Neither speaker addressed the terms or conditions on which the miners were voting.[38]

President Mitchell's special representative, John Ream, followed Howells and Jones to the podium. Ream claimed refusing a just offer would be a "blot on the name of the United Mine Workers of America." Further, if the workers continued what appeared to be an unjust strike, they would lose public sympathy, and they would hurt the poor and their fellow laborers in Denver. As the meeting broke up, a hasty vote showed the miners wanted to continue the strike.[39]

The two arguments contrasted starkly. Jones and Howells were asking for a new worker solidarity, one that transcended coalfields and companies. To them, worker solidarity was a prime tool in winning the strike. Of course, President Moyer of the WFM spoke the same message in relation to the metal strike. When a reporter asked Jones if the WFM was "dominating" the coal miners of that district, Jones replied that the WFM had "nothing to do with the action of the miners in the northern coal fields refusing to return to work."[40] The UMWA's traditions stood behind Ream's argument: reward the companies and fields that came to terms. Ream explained to the press that the UMWA policy "has always been to settle, wherever they can get a good proposition," and he felt they had a good offer.[41]

Discouraged, Ream continued to work to gain a settlement for the northern field, but the UMWA national office wanted a stronger hold on the strike. President Mitchell sent more national officials to Colorado, and they began directing the day-by-day affairs. As the *Rocky Mountain News* reported, "This made President Howells, Secretary [John] Simpson and Colorado National Board Member John Gehr merely clerks who do as the Easterners told them to do."[42] Despite the larger national presence, Mother Jones denied that any friction existed between local and national officials.[43]

Considerable dissatisfaction existed in the Denver Basin. Within days of the earlier votes, miners from several locations wanted to reconsider the proposition. Ream continued to work the area, and Howells traveled with him. For an unknown reason, perhaps because of pressure from the national office, Howells had withdrawn his objection to the miners returning to work. The miners soon held another vote, and over 75 percent of the men voted in favor of going to work. On November 30, after a three-week shutdown, the northern mines opened with the eight-hour day and an improved wage scale. When questioned about the ramifications for labor solidarity and for strikes elsewhere, some predicted that the settlement might "force the situation in the Southern fields, and that decisive action might be expected there within a few days."[44] The UMWA's national office had asserted its market union beliefs.[45]

During the strike, managers of the Northern Coal and Coke Company did not resist the settlement. Earlier, in the 1901 strike, Northern Coal had been a fierce opponent of labor and unionization. This time company officials made every effort to settle. They even attended the first meeting called by the governor. Northern Coal still dominated the field, owning eleven mines and producing over 80 percent of the coal coming from the Denver Basin. The company, however, did not want to fight the union. It did not want to risk any of its market share. Several other mining companies in the northern field could easily expand and capture a larger part of the market. Plus, a new competitor was emerging in northern Colorado in 1903. As the strike went on, the Rocky Mountain Fuel Company was sinking two new mine shafts. Rocky Mountain Fuel soon opened mines in the Denver Basin and elsewhere along the Front Range, and it eventually rivaled Northern Coal's production. With a new competitor developing, Northern Coal did not want to close for a strike. Plus, after years of trying, Northern Coal still had little control over its workers. They lived in independent towns, most had worked for the company for years, and many maintained coal mining's strong beliefs and traditions.[46]

The Denver Basin settlement put 1,270 men back to work and gave them the eight-hour day and a wage advance of about 15 percent. The miners did not gain the checkoff, but as the *United Mine Workers' Journal* explained, the workers had not demanded it. This also meant that although the companies met and dealt with union officials, the northern operators still did not recognize the UMWA as the workers' official bargaining agent.[47]

THE 1903–1904 STRIKE
IN CENTRAL AND SOUTHERN COLORADO

The settlement in the Denver Basin had no effect on the strike in central and southern Colorado. Both the union and the operators in those regions took actions that ensured a long strike, and the coal companies moved to turn it into a bitter one. The union entered the walkout pointing to Victor Fuel as the primary antagonist. It took a more conciliatory attitude toward the CF&I, hoping to win favor with the new Rockefeller-Gould directors. Whereas UMWA representatives decried Victor Fuel's mistreatment of the men, Mother Jones and other union leaders stated that the conditions in the CF&I camps "are not as oppressive, but they are bad enough, and must be rectified."[48]

Despite this soft-pedaling, the CF&I did not accept the union. A few CF&I officials had left with the ownership change, as mentioned previously, but many had stayed. John T. Kebler remained as the company's general manager, and he announced early in the strike that the company's past policies would continue. CF&I officials would not meet with the union, and they would do everything in their power to resist the demands. Even with new ownership the CF&I would lead the fight against the union and the striking men.[49]

When Osgood ran the CF&I, he believed labor outbursts were part of business. Tensions would build and eventually explode into a strike, and after the company prevailed, quiet would return. His efforts toward welfare capitalism after the 1901 strike did not change his basic notion about strikes. In fact, the strike fund he had started some years before at the CF&I still existed. For each ton of coal mined, the company set aside a few cents to fight strikes; and according to the *Rocky Mountain News* the fund had grown to "become a large amount" of money by 1903.[50] With Osgood's influence, Victor Fuel undoubtedly had a similar program. The companies used the money to hire mine guards, fund extra deputies for the counties in southern Colorado, and cushion the blow of lost revenue. Sheriff Clark of Las Animas County swore in ninety deputies as the strike began. The coal companies explained that the gunmen were necessary for protection. Without them, they argued, the strikers would destroy the companies' property and prevent miners from returning to the job.[51]

In reality, the companies used the guards to gain tighter control of their coal camps. They closed the towns, allowing only "approved" people to enter. This policy kept out union organizers and striking miners. Victor Fuel's actions again brought the loudest protest. When guards sealed off Delagua and Hastings, they closed the roads that passed through the towns. The union claimed the roads were public highways and could not be closed. The company denied this. By sealing the town, the companies believed loyal men would return to work. That did not happen, but the guards did allow scab labor to be imported.[52]

Failing to control the workers by closing the towns, the companies tried a variety of other tactics ranging from kindness to intimidation. Kebler of the CF&I offered to deal with the men, but as individuals and not through a union. Rumors also circulated that he would offer wage concessions and a contract guaranteeing steady employment for workers who crossed the line. When this failed, he began evicting striking miners and their families from company housing. A loss of shelter as winter approached would make some miners think twice. Then he turned to threats. Stories spread that mine guards sat in the hills above mining towns armed with Winchesters, watching every move of the people below. In conjunction with deputies, the guards would arrest supposed troublemakers and escort them out of the region. Threatening violence, the gun thugs warned the evicted workers never to come back.[53]

The companies also had a new ally in this strike. Citizens' Alliances had formed in Denver and Trinidad. Following a national model, local businessmen organized the alliances, arguing that good citizenship and economic progress were synonymous. The members believed a coal strike would cripple the state's industries, and they wanted to stop that from happening. They accepted the coal companies' arguments that Colorado miners received higher wages than those "in any other state" and that influences "wholly from without the state" had triggered the strike. Throughout the strike the Citizens' Alliances praised the coal companies and admonished the workers.[54]

In response to such weapons, the union was forced to use defensive tactics. The national office sent more organizers to encourage those still working to walk out and to hold the striking miners firm. The union provided food, clothing, shelter, and medical attention for those on strike. The UMWA also undertook a massive relocation program. The union encouraged striking miners to leave the region, promising to find them jobs in union coal mines elsewhere. Notices appeared in local papers announcing 500 openings in Texas and 150 in Iowa, and some miners headed to the eastern coalfields.

The relocation strategy had two goals. One, it saved the union money. Every man working somewhere else was one less person to support. Two, it removed the companies' labor supply. As men left the area, the labor market became tighter, and the union hoped that shortage might make the operators come to terms. After a long strike, too few workers sometimes remained in the field to reopen the mines. The companies countered this tactic by announcing their intention to import more labor. Just days after the strike began, the head of an East Coast employment agency announced that "for every miner deported from the southern fields of Colorado by the United Mine Workers of America there will be two foreigners brought in to take his place."[55]

The union also tried to use worker relocation to affect the coal market. The UMWA just years before had won union recognition in the mines of Texas and Iowa. In the Texas field the union relocated so many workers that the resulting labor shortage had forced the company to yield. With a strike on in Colorado, the companies in Iowa and Texas could be rewarded: they could expand their production to supply coal for the Colorado market. The Colorado strike would boost their sales and profits and perhaps make inroads into the CF&I and Victor Fuel markets. Railroads also helped the midwestern operators meet the Colorado demand. The carriers dropped their rate for hauling coal, bringing great relief to Colorado coal customers.[56]

The union hoped such market threats would motivate Victor Fuel and Colorado Fuel and Iron to settle, but the companies shrugged them off as inconsequential. The operators stated that the men would be back within sixty days and that "every man who went away will return with another miner in his company."[57] The coal companies also knew they could count on the railroads to restore their old freight rates as soon as the strike ended. They would not lose their market shares permanently. The two companies would retain their virtual monopoly on coal sales to many of the West's industrial customers. And ironically, Osgood profited all the more from the strike. Although he had lost the CF&I, he still owned the American Fuel Company in New Mexico, which kept producing during the strike. Unconcerned about coal markets, the CF&I and Victor Fuel could remain intransigent.[58]

With these factors in place, the strike could not be settled and it dragged on, testing the patience of both sides. After two weeks the *Rocky Mountain News* reported that of the 6,500 men who had quit work, about 2,000 had left the coalfield. Those who stayed either lived in "relief camps" or in their homes at Trinidad and other open communities. The paper also stated that the strikers were becoming impatient as they recognized the "confidence of the operators."[59]

The strike continued through December 1903 and into 1904. During this time UMWA president Mitchell came to Colorado to confer with Governor Peabody about a settlement, but to no avail. In the meantime it became a struggle over manpower. Victor Fuel and the CF&I attempted to import workers—reportedly bringing in 4,500 in the first three months of the strike—and the UMWA kept paying their way home. This ploy so annoyed Victor Fuel that it secured an injunction against the union to prevent it from "paying or offering to pay transportation expenses of any person in the employ of plaintiff, or of any persons seeking to be employed by plaintiff, in order to prevent such persons from remaining or entering into service of the Victor Fuel Company."[60]

As the strike continued, the companies grew more impatient than the strikers. The companies had expected a short strike or at least an easy return to full production. After three months this result had not occurred. Output had increased some, but not nearly to the level desired. Although the companies did not worry about markets, they did see their profits slipping away. In February they began lashing out at union organizers and activists. Tensions between the two sides had always been high, and some sporadic violence had occurred, but the companies now stepped up the violence with beatings and deportations. Representatives from the national UMWA office suffered the brunt of the attacks. In one instance three masked attackers beat Financial Representative Chris Evans bloody and unconscious in a passenger car on a train in the Trinidad railroad yards. In total, at least three people were killed and fourteen beaten during the course of the strike.[61]

The violence gave Governor Peabody a reason to impose martial law in the striking coalfields. Working with the coal companies, Peabody knew the troops would allow a return to full production. Although the UMWA protested the call for martial law, the militia did the operators' bidding. It closed the union's Italian newspaper in Trinidad, occupied the union's district office, and deported Mother Jones and four union officials. Militia officers ordered them not to return to Colorado while martial law existed. The operators believed that with those people gone, two-thirds of the strikers would return to work. Ironically, the union had decided to end the strike before martial law had been declared, but these events inspired the miners to continue their stand.[62]

This resolve caused the strike to drift on over the next several months. Although deportations and violence continued, the mining companies gradually attracted men to the mines. In an effort to maintain complete control, the companies registered the workers and recorded their descriptions for future reference. When some miners at Berwind refused to register, the militia arrested them. Other disturbances occurred as well, but production still increased. The union attempted to hold strong. Notices appeared in the *United Mine Workers' Journal* reminding the nation's miners that the strike continued.[63]

Believing the strike was lost, the UMWA national office withdrew support in July 1904. Some miners in District 15 resisted and voted to continue the strike, but the strike could not be won. The companies had returned to full production. Also, by this time the strike in the metal mines had been crushed. Recriminations soon followed the UMWA failure. Some accused the national union of giving up too easily and turning its back on Colorado. But the national office had other problems. By August 1904 coal mining had diminished nationally, and a large number of men lost their jobs. The national officers needed to worry about preserving their union.[64]

AFTERMATH OF THE 1903–1904 STRIKE

Discontent over the handling of the Colorado strike exploded at the UMWA national convention in January 1905. Robert Randall, a delegate who had participated in the 1903–1904 strike, charged that Mitchell had provided insufficient funds to the effort and then withdrawn the funding when it was most needed. He saw the separate settlement in the Denver Basin as another problem. Speaking on behalf of the WFM, Mother Jones, and the socialists who had preached solidarity at the beginning of the strike, Randall argued that Mitchell had forced the northern settlement on the miners against their wishes. Mitchell stated in his defense that the union had supported the strike as long as practical and that he had not forced the settlement on the miners. In the end, he questioned Randall's motives, suggesting that he was an agent of the WFM.[65]

Randall put commitment to a common cause above all else. He believed solidarity would win strikes. But solidarity would have made no difference in this strike. With the CF&I and Victor Fuel acting together and dominating their markets, the companies had little motivation to settle. In fact, the producing mines in northern Colorado could have been a greater threat to the large coal companies than a general strike. The Denver Basin companies might have made inroads into the southern companies' markets and made them consider a settlement. A general strike might have caused more public concern and clamor, but that would not have motivated the companies to settle.

The expectation of a solid front and a unified strike from the miners defies historical trends within Colorado and the West. Certainly, the miners did feel some solidarity toward their fellow coal miners, but by the twentieth century that sense existed primarily among men within one coalfield or among those working for the same company. Solidarity across coalfields existed more in terms of empathy. The miners shared and understood the dangers and problems their work entailed, but every location was different. The miners of Colorado and Wyoming also recognized the differences that existed among employers. Although the miners often had similar desires and demands, they knew companies responded differently. The workers believed market pressures and different managerial attitudes affected the outcomes of their strikes. They tried to evaluate every situation and work it to their advantage. The coal miners of the West did not have a sense of class warfare. They did not see their strikes as industrial worker versus capitalist. By 1903 they accepted the fact that they were a part of the coal business, and they wanted their share of the profits.

After the 1903–1904 strike, unionism remained in the Denver Basin. Although UMWA representatives had negotiated the settlement that year, they did not sign a contract or gain formal union recognition. A strike in 1906 brought the first written contract to the region, and it was renewed in 1908. The miners gained union recognition, and they enjoyed the highest wage scale in Colorado. Despite selling higher-priced coal, the companies in the Denver Basin did not suffer because of unionization. In fact, production increased dramatically. In 1907 the region produced over 500,000 tons more coal than it had in 1903—a 59 percent advance. Northern Coal and Coke remained the predominant company. Each year it accounted for a little more than 70 percent of the region's output. Northern Coal had once been bitterly antiunion, but unionization seemed to cause it little trouble.[66]

Elsewhere in Colorado the union had little representation. A few scattered locals existed, primarily at mines independent of the large companies, but the UMWA had been defeated. To keep it that way, the major companies stepped up their antiunion campaigns. The CF&I and Victor Fuel brought tighter control to their company towns. Guards became a regular fixture in the camps, removing anyone who did not belong. As well, the companies began fencing the perimeters of their fully owned towns, also to limit the coming and going of "strangers." The fences created what were known as "closed" towns. In these towns the companies not only owned the houses and the stores, but they also regulated those with whom the miners associated. The 1903–1904 strike had stiffened antiunionism among southern Colorado coal operators.[67]

While taking new repressive measures to repel unionization, the companies also continued some of the welfare programs Osgood had brought to southern Colorado in 1901. The CF&I Sociological Department continued its educational programs, and a Medical Department ran a company hospital in Pueblo. The *Engineering and Mining Journal* praised the CF&I for its "sociological work" in 1907, claiming such programs caused employees to "do better work, and give less trouble."[68] Nevertheless, the extent of the CF&I's welfare capitalism had diminished. In surveying the company's welfare activities, the *Journal* emphasized the housing projects Osgood had built in 1901 and his efforts to curb worker drinking. The CF&I management had slashed programs to economize and would continue to do so in the years after 1907. That was the year the Rockefeller family gained a controlling interest in the company and named Lamont Bowers chairman of the board of directors to help company president Jesse Welborn cut costs. To this end, Bowers further trimmed the sociological and medical programs and cut back plans for improvements. He hoped repression alone would control labor.[69] Plus, Osgood's influence in Victor Fuel led to camp improvement projects.

UNIONIZATION COMES TO SOUTHERN WYOMING

With unionism thwarted in southern Colorado but present in northern Colorado and northern Wyoming, the UMWA decided to close the gap in between the two areas. At the union's annual meeting in early 1906, members passed a resolution to organize the camps along the Union Pacific. Recognizing that the Chinese miners were a hindrance to organization, a companion resolution called for the "strict enforcement of the Chinese Exclusion Act."[70] In June 1906, organizers appeared in the Union Pacific camps. Some came from northern Wyoming, spreading the word that the contracts in District 22 provided the highest wages in the nation. Others came from the national office, and they overcame the diversity in the audience by translating the speeches into four languages.[71]

The organizers moved at the right time. The Union Pacific Railroad had continued to expand, and its business remained strong. In 1907 alone the company laid 285 miles of double track around the system to handle increased traffic. Such expansion required an ever-larger coal supply. In fact, the company had stopped selling coal on the commercial market. Plus, the company found the labor supply inadequate. The Cheyenne *Daily Leader* reported that at least 1,000 more men were needed to work the mines in Wyoming and Utah. The *Engineering and Mining Journal* echoed the concern. Throughout 1906 and 1907 the *Journal* reported a "scarcity of labor in the West . . . more pronounced at present than at any time during recent years." The combination of a strong demand for coal and a shortage of labor gave the union a solid base for representation.[72]

The UMWA organizers focused on the Union Pacific's Rock Springs mines, the center of the railroad's coal-mining operation. In December 1906 the company produced 54 percent of its coal at Rock Springs and employed over half of its employees—1,699 of 3,014 systemwide. Rock Springs was a mixed town. It had some elements of a company town, including a few company houses and a company store, but many miners lived in housing they owned. Outside of Rock Springs, at Hanna and Cumberland, the Union Pacific operated full company towns—locations more difficult to organize. Rock Springs was the company's oldest location, and a few old-time miners—men who had originally brought the mining traditions west—still lived there. As the company pushed ethnic diversification, these men were joined by men from a variety of ethnic groups. By 1907 a number of Finns, Italians, and Austrians worked at Rock Springs. Nearly every Balkan country was represented. The men seldom spent leisure time together, but they shared work experiences and mutual dangers underground. Over time the men developed a mutual understanding and a common bond. This led to a latent solidarity that came to the surface as unionization became a possibility. Only the Chinese and Japanese seemed removed. They had little choice, as the UMWA did not accept Asians. By 1907 the union did not see that policy as a roadblock because the relative number of Asians had diminished. The 200 Asians at Rock Springs comprised only 11.8 percent of the workforce.[73]

As the organizers worked Rock Springs, the Union Pacific remained intransigent. The company posted notices stating that any miner joining the UMWA could call for his time, and the company began a lockout. It shut down two of its five mines, and a third barely kept operating. Furthermore, the miners living in company housing were notified to vacate. The *United Mine Workers' Journal* quoted a Union Pacific source as stating "we will not in any way help to support such a union at this place."[74] Soon the Union Pacific closed all but one mine in Rock Springs, with over 1,400 men reportedly locked out by the company. The Chinese and Japanese kept one mine operating. The locked-out men rallied in defiance, and each punitive act by the company generated more support for the union.[75]

The company began looking for solutions. Because of the regional labor shortage, the Union Pacific could not easily find strikebreakers. Consequently, the company attempted to duplicate its 1903 tactic, offering an immediate 10 percent wage increase if the miners returned to work. The Union Pacific stated that it would let miners work even if they had signed a membership application with the UMWA, but it still refused to recognize the union as the miners' bargaining agent. The men realized the strength of their position, and they wanted more than wage advances. They wanted union recognition, which they thought would bring fair play, respect, and justice.[76]

The situation rapidly grew critical for the Union Pacific. With the demand for coal at an all-time high and its most important mines closed, the company needed a settlement. The company could not turn to the local commercial market because the men employed by the other coal operators in Rock Springs had also gone out on strike, and a high nationwide demand for coal made other sources unlikely. At one time the Union Pacific considered shipping in coal from Australia. The Union Pacific had never felt a pinch like this one. To keep its trains running and bring stability to the coal business, the Union Pacific management decided to yield to its workers. The company called for a conference with all southern Wyoming coal operators and union officials of District 22. The Union Pacific also announced a change in the company's management. Up to this time, General Manager D. O. Clark controlled labor policy. He had been the architect of the antiunion philosophy. But his viewpoint now stood in the way of coal production, and he was given an assistant—John J. Hart—to deal with labor relations.[77]

Hart not only spoke for the Union Pacific Coal Company, but other operators at Rock Springs gave him power to negotiate for them. Once in charge, Hart immediately contacted UMWA president John Mitchell and asked for help in organizing the conference. Although Mitchell did not attend the conference, the miners still benefited. The southern Wyoming operators formally recognized the UMWA as the miners' bargaining agent. The operators also agreed to carry out the previously offered 10 percent wage increase. With this news the miners in Rock Springs returned to work. The final details of a contract had yet to be worked out, but the negotiators decided to delay that action until Mitchell could participate.[78]

The unionization of Rock Springs ensured the spread of the union throughout southern Wyoming. The other operators, Kemmerer Coal and Coke and Diamond Coal and Coke, knew they had to accept the union if the Union Pacific had done so. They had previously worked together to defy unionization, and they now followed the Union Pacific in accepting it. If they did not do so, they would lose their workforce. Patrick J. Quealy of Kemmerer Coal groused to his Pennsylvania financiers about the imposed union. They responded that after working with it in Pennsylvania, they had come "to rather appreciate the union." The Pennsylvania operators found the union brought stability and ultimately a cost savings. Although Quealy never became completely convinced of the union's advantages, the Union Pacific greatly appreciated the order the UMWA brought to its coalfields.[79]

The final District 22 contract for southern Wyoming was drafted one month after the first conference. On July 15, 1907, John Mitchell met the southern Wyoming coal operators in Denver, and after thirty-four days the union had gained practically everything it requested. The settlement included union recognition, an eight-hour day, and a wage increase of over 20 percent. The most surprising development at the Denver conference was the inclusion of Asian representatives. Even though the UMWA had bitterly opposed Asian labor for years, as had the local miners, both groups put their racism aside and admitted Chinese and Japanese workers to the union. The union was willing to accept the Asian workers to make sure no weaknesses existed in the southern Wyoming organization. The Japanese labor contractors also saw the wisdom of joining the union. They feared the UMWA might force the Japanese out of the mines as it established a closed shop. Working with the union would preserve their positions.[80]

The successful conclusion of the Denver conference inspired an outpouring of superlatives. The *United Mine Workers' Journal* extolled the contract as "one of the best . . . ever entered into by the organization," and the Rock Springs paper heralded Hart as the "great compromiser." Further, the local paper praised the high wages paid in Wyoming—matching those of Montana, the highest in the country. Prior to union organization the pay scale along the Union Pacific had averaged almost 7 percent more than that of the miners in the Central Competitive Field, but with this contract the southern Wyoming miners now averaged 33 percent more than the union miners to the east. Over the next two decades the UMWA actively participated in the coal operations of southern Wyoming. Strikes occasionally occurred, but overall the union brought the stability and order the Union Pacific Coal Company wanted. The railroad's trains continued to run.[81]

LABOR UPHEAVAL RETURNS TO COLORADO

By the end of 1907, unionization seemed to be gaining a tighter hold on the western coal industry. The UMWA had representation in Montana, Wyoming, and the Denver Basin. The next logical move was into central and southern Colorado. Since the union's setback there in 1903 and 1904, organizers had returned to the region, but with little long-term effect. After the victory in southern Wyoming, efforts in central and southern Colorado intensified. Although union membership increased, the UMWA still failed to make significant inroads. The companies remained defiant, discharging suspected unionists. Plus, the union activists became distracted by events in northern Colorado.[82]

In the Denver Basin the coal operators, led by Northern Coal and Coke, had worked with the UMWA since 1903. They had again agreed on contracts in 1907 and 1908. When the contract came up for renewal in 1910 the companies decided not to cooperate, with Northern Coal and Coke leading the way. When the companies rejected a wage hike, the miners struck on April 2, 1910. This move started a protracted labor struggle in Colorado that would spread to the central and southern coalfields and last until 1914.[83]

Northern Coal and Coke led the resistance in the Denver Basin in 1910 in part because of changed market dynamics. One year earlier, the Denver Northwestern and Pacific Railroad had reached a new coalfield across the mountains from Denver in Routt County. David Moffat, the man who years before had built railroads and developed mines in the Denver Basin, was the new line's primary promoter. He wanted a route that ran west from Denver and ultimately connected with Salt Lake City. As the line curved over the mountains, Moffat counted on Routt County coal mines to provide a profitable freight business. He needed to make inroads into the Denver coal market for his line to survive, something he encouraged with favorable freight rates. Five coal companies soon worked the Routt field using nonunion labor. The competition hurt Northern Coal. Its output dropped as its demand declined. Northern Coal blamed the union wage scale and decided to eliminate the union.[84]

A few months after the strike began, companies independent of Northern Coal wanted a settlement. The owner of the Fox Mine appealed to the state labor commissioner. He stated that he had operated without a profit before the strike, and since the walkout "the loss has been very great."[85] He needed to open and was willing to work with the union. In the years before union contracts, the miners would have settled with the Fox and the other independent mines and permitted them to reopen. Such a move would have further punished Northern Coal and perhaps brought it to agreement. Under the terms of the contract, however, the mines could not operate until all operators signed up. Ironically, the UMWA contract prevented it from using market pressures that had worked so successfully before. The independent mines soon looked to strikebreakers.[86]

Northern Coal and Coke had other reasons to be defiant. Since 1903 the company had adopted the antiunion tactics that had served the southern Colorado operators so well. It had built company houses and taken the dramatic step of surrounding them with "stockades or wire fences."[87] The company hoped to shield its workers from the temptation of unionization. Plus, it became apparent to some observers that Colorado Fuel and Iron was providing financial assistance to Northern Coal and Coke. The union organizers believed the southern operators wanted to eliminate the UMWA from Colorado. Although the union's presence in the Denver Basin had been unnerving to the CF&I and Victor Fuel, the UMWA's spread to southern Wyoming and the West's second-largest coal producer scared them. They wanted to remove the union before it could advance.[88]

As the strike progressed, the market displacement rearranged the Denver Basin coal business. Already in financial trouble even with CF&I support, Northern Coal and Coke went out of business, selling its mines to Rocky Mountain Fuel. The new company had previously opened mines in the Denver Basin but had decided to concentrate its operations in southern and central Colorado. By 1910 Rocky Mountain Fuel had become Colorado's third-largest producer, operating eight mines. Working side by side with Victor Fuel and the CF&I in Las Animas, Huerfano, and Fremont Counties, it adopted their wage scale and antiunion mentality. When it acquired Northern Coal's assets in 1911, Rocky Mountain Fuel continued to ignore the union and hired strikebreakers.[89]

A group of independent mine owners also formed a new coal company in the Denver Basin. Known as the American Fuel Company, it brought together seven mines in 1911. The organizers hoped the new company could bring stability and end the strike. The company had never been a party to a union contract and had no restraints. In March 1912, American Fuel signed an agreement with the UMWA. The men received a wage advance, and the mines reopened. Rocky Mountain Fuel, in conjunction with another northern Colorado operator, decided it would not tolerate the new company's union tendencies and decided to eliminate it. The two companies initiated a coal war, cutting prices below the level they felt the union mines could endure. The union miners wanted to maintain their organization and the new company, and they voluntarily cut their wages. The commissioner of labor statistics reported that these were the "old-time miners" who owned "their own homes and have built up their towns." They did not want "any combination to ruin a coal mining company that was favorable to union labor." Nevertheless, American Fuel soon failed. Rocky Mountain Fuel dominated the coalfield, and because of its extensive holdings elsewhere in Colorado, market forces did not force it to recognize the union.[90]

Under assault in the Denver Basin, union organizers knew the threat to their organization came from southern Colorado. Union officials argued that organizing southern Colorado would bring a settlement to northern Colorado and maintain District 15. Further, they felt unionization would protect their organization in Wyoming and Montana. Beyond stabilizing the union, the organizers also wanted to improve the miners' working and living conditions in southern Colorado, but they knew it would be difficult. The last effort to do so had resulted in the strike of 1903–1904, which had been hard and bitter. During its course, the miners experienced the full arsenal of antiunion tactics—including evictions and violence. Since then the owners' attitudes had not changed. In fact, Bowers had joined Welborn to reinforce the CF&I's

resolve. But the union had met success in Wyoming. A formerly antiunion company had yielded there, inspiring the hope that the same could happen in Colorado. Instead, the allied companies of southern Colorado remained intransigent, and the union decided to meet them head-on. The workers' pent-up anger met the companies' hardened resolve, resulting in an explosion at Ludlow.

NOTES

1. Scamehorn, *Pioneer Steelmaker*, 155; United States Geological Survey, *Mineral Resources of the United States, 1903*, 447, 537.

2. *Eighth Biennial Report of the Bureau of Labor Statistics of the State of Colorado, 1901–1902*, 385–386.

3. *United Mine Workers' Journal*, March 6, 1902, January 22, 1903; U.S. Department of the Interior, Census Office, manuscript census, Las Animas County, Colorado, 1900.

4. Denver *Times*, March 12, August 14, 1903; *United Mine Workers' Journal*, March 26, June 18, 1903.

5. Wright, *A Report on Labor Disturbances in the State of Colorado*, 112, 120, 123, 131–132, 151, 167.

6. Craig Phelan, *Divided Loyalties: The Public and Private Life of Labor Leader John Mitchell* (Albany: State University of New York Press, 1994), 212–217.

7. *United Mine Workers' Journal*, May 14, 1903, 4.

8. United States Geological Survey, *Mineral Resources of the United States, 1901*, 226, 297; Fox, *United We Stand*, 66.

9. Fox, *United We Stand*, 66; *United Mine Workers' Journal*, June 18, October 15, 1903.

10. *United Mine Workers' Journal*, May 14, 1903, 4.

11. *United Mine Workers' Journal*, June 11, 1903.

12. *United Mine Workers' Journal*, September 10, quote in September 24, 1903, 3.

13. *United Mine Workers' Journal*, September 24, 1903.

14. *Ninth Biennial Report of the Bureau of Labor Statistics of the State of Colorado, 1903–1904*, by W. H. Montgomery (Denver: Smith-Brooks Printing, State Printers, 1904), 185, 238–239; *Rocky Mountain News*, August 15, 1903; Denver *Times*, August 15, 1903.

15. Denver *Times*, August 14, 1903.

16. *Ninth Biennial Report of the Bureau of Labor Statistics of the State of Colorado, 1903–1904*, 194; *Rocky Mountain News*, August 15, 1903; Denver *Times*, August 14, 1903; *United Mine Workers' Journal*, August 27, 1903.

17. *United Mine Workers' Journal*, August 27, quotes in September 10, 1903, 4.

18. *United Mine Workers' Journal*, September 10, 1903, 4.

19. *Ninth Biennial Report of the Bureau of Labor Statistics of the State of Colorado, 1903–1904*, 184–185; *Rocky Mountain News*, August 14, 1903.

20. Denver *Times*, August 14, 1903.

21. *Rocky Mountain News*, August 15, 1903.

22. *Ninth Biennial Report of the Bureau of Labor Statistics of the State of Colorado, 1903–1904*, 183.

23. Ibid., 183–184; quote in *United Mine Workers' Journal*, September 17, 1903, 1.

24. *Denver Times*, August 15, 1903; *Rocky Mountain News*, August 30, 1903.

25. *Ninth Biennial Report of the Bureau of Labor Statistics of the State of Colorado, 1903–1904*, 185.

26. *Rocky Mountain News*, September 18, 1903.

27. *Rocky Mountain News*, September 26, 1903.

28. *Rocky Mountain News*, September 27, 1903.

29. *Ninth Biennial Report of the Bureau of Labor Statistics of the State of Colorado, 1903–1904*, 185–187; Powell, *The Next Time We Strike*, 51.

30. Phelan, *Divided Loyalties*, 215.

31. *United Mine Workers' Journal*, October 15, 1903, 5.

32. Brody, *In Labor's Cause*, 139.

33. *United Mine Workers' Journal*, November 12, November 19, 1903; *Rocky Mountain News*, November 10, November 12, 1903.

34. *United Mine Workers' Journal*, November 12, November 19, 1903; *Rocky Mountain News*, November 3, November 10, November 12, 1903.

35. *United Mine Workers' Journal*, November 19, 1903, 5.

36. *Rocky Mountain News*, November 9, 1903.

37. *Rocky Mountain News*, November 12, November 14, November 15, November 16, November 17, November 18, 1903.

38. *Rocky Mountain News*, November 22, 1903, 7.

39. Ibid.

40. *Rocky Mountain News*, November 26, 1903, 5.

41. *Rocky Mountain News*, November 23, 1903, 2.

42. Ibid.

43. *Rocky Mountain News*, November 26, 1903.

44. *Rocky Mountain News*, November 30, 1903, 1.

45. *Rocky Mountain News*, November 28, November 29, November 30, 1903.

46. *Ninth Biennial Report of the Bureau of Labor Statistics of the State of Colorado, 1903–1904*, 183; *Eleventh Biennial Report of the State Coal Mine Inspector, 1903–1904*, 44, 46; *Tenth Biennial Report of the Inspector of Coal Mines of the State of Colorado, 1901–1902* (Denver: Smith-Brooks Printing, State Printers, 1903), 36, 38, 123, 125; *Rocky Mountain News*, November 29, 1903.

47. *United Mine Workers' Journal*, December 3, 1903; *Ninth Biennial Report of the Bureau of Labor Statistics of the State of Colorado, 1903–1904*, 188–192.

48. *United Mine Workers' Journal*, November 19, 1903, 1.

49. Ibid.

50. *Rocky Mountain News*, November 10, 1903.

51. Ibid.

52. *Rocky Mountain News*, November 14, November 18, November 19, 1903; *United Mine Workers' Journal*, November 26, 1903.

53. *Rocky Mountain News*, November 14, 1903.

54. *Rocky Mountain News*, November 11, November 14, 1903; Long, *Where the Sun Never Shines*, 214.

55. *Rocky Mountain News,* quote in November 11, 1903, 9; November 16, 1903.

56. *Rocky Mountain News,* November 11, November 12, 1903; Marilyn D. Rhinehart, *A Way of Work and a Way of Life: Coal Mining in Thurber, Texas, 1888–1926* (College Station: Texas A&M University Press, 1992), 88–89; Dorothy Schwieder, Joseph Hraba, and Elmer Schwieder, *Buxton: Work and Racial Equality in a Coal Mining Community* (Ames: Iowa State University Press, 1987), 75.

57. *Rocky Mountain News,* November 14, 1903, 5.

58. *Rocky Mountain News,* November 15, November 19, 1903.

59. *Rocky Mountain News,* November 22, 1903.

60. *United Mine Workers' Journal,* February 4, quote in December 10, 1903, 3.

61. *United Mine Workers' Journal,* March 17, June 30, 1904; Phelan, *Divided Loyalties,* 218.

62. *United Mine Workers' Journal,* March 31, April 7, 1904.

63. *United Mine Workers' Journal,* May 5, May 19, May 26, 1904.

64. *United Mine Workers' Journal,* July 14, August 18, August 25, 1904; Jensen, *Heritage of Conflict,* 148–153.

65. Phelan, *Divided Loyalties,* 222–223.

66. *United Mine Workers' Journal,* September 27, 1906, January 3, 1907, July 16, 1908; *Eleventh Biennial Report of the State Coal Mine Inspector, 1903–1904,* 44; *Thirteenth Biennial Report of the State Coal Mine Inspector, 1907–1908* (Denver: Smith-Brooks Printing, State Printers, 1909), 134; U.S. Department of the Interior, United States Geological Survey, *Mineral Resources of the United States, 1907* (Washington, D.C.: GPO, 1908), 103; *Engineering and Mining Journal* 85, no. 26 (June 27, 1908): 1311.

67. *United Mine Workers' Journal,* January 19, May 4, 1905; Long, *Where the Sun Never Shines,* 242; Senate Committee on Industrial Relations, *Final Report and Testimony,* 8495.

68. Lawrence Lewis, "How One Corporation Helped Its Employees," *Engineering and Mining Journal* 83, no. 26 (June 29, 1907): 1233–1238, 1250; "Sociological Department," *Coal Age* 2, no. 16 (October 19, 1912): 549–550.

69. Scamehorn, *Mill & Mine,* 30–31; Lewis, "How One Corporation Helped Its Employees," 1233–1238, 1250.

70. *United Mine Workers' Journal,* February 1, 1906.

71. *United Mine Workers' Journal,* June 6, 1906.

72. Cheyenne *Daily Leader,* July 12, August 23, 1907; Floyd W. Parsons, "The Fuel Situation in the Northwest," *Engineering and Mining Journal* 84, no. 18 (November 2, 1907): 832; "Abstracts of Official Reports," *Engineering and Mining Journal* 82, no. 8 (August 25, 1906): 364.

73. "Nationality of Mine Employes, December 1906," the Union Pacific Coal Co., Annual Report, 1906, 35, UPCCC; Erika Kuhlman, "'Greetings from This Coalvillage': Finnish Immigrants of Red Lodge," *Montana: The Magazine of Western History* (Spring 1990): 32–45.

74. Kemmerer *Camera,* May 25, 1907; *United Mine Workers' Journal,* June 6, 1907.

75. Cheyenne *Daily Leader,* May 24, 1907.

76. Cheyenne *Daily Leader*, May 24, May 26, June 2, June 4, 1907.

77. Trottman, *History of the Union Pacific*, 275, 297; *History of the Union Pacific Coal Mines*, 180; Cheyenne *Daily Leader*, June 8, July 12, August 23, 1907; Yuji Ichioka, "Asian Immigrant Coal Miners and the United Mine Workers of America: Race and Class at Rock Springs, Wyoming, 1907," *Amerasia* 6 (1979): 10.

78. Ichioka, "Asian Immigrant Coal Miners," 8–9; Cheyenne *Daily Leader*, August 9, 1907.

79. Mahlon S. Kemmerer to P. J. Quealy, June 2, 1909, Box 5, Kemmerer Coal Collection, American Heritage Center, Laramie, Wyoming.

80. Rock Springs *Miner*, August 17, 1907; Ichioka, "Asian Immigrant Coal Miners," 9–17.

81. *United Mine Workers' Journal*, August 15, 1907, 4; Rock Springs *Miner*, August 11, August 17, 1907; Cheyenne *Daily Leader*, August 9, 1907; *History of the Union Pacific Coal Mines*, xli.

82. *United Mine Workers' Journal*, January 23, 1908, August 12, 1909, March 21, 1912.

83. *United Mine Workers' Journal*, March 14, 1912; Long, *Where the Sun Never Shines*, 255.

84. *United Mine Workers' Journal*, February 9, 1911; *Thirteenth Biennial Report of the State Coal Mine Inspector, 1907–1908*, 134; *Fourteenth Biennial Report of the State Inspector of Coal Mines, 1909–1910*, 125; Wilkins, *Colorado Railroads*, 174; Edward T. Bollinger and Frederick Bauer, *The Moffat Road* (Chicago: Swallow, 1962), 94.

85. *Twelfth Biennial Report of the Bureau of Labor Statistics of the State of Colorado, 1909–1910* (Denver: Smith-Brooks Printing, State Printers, 1911), 265.

86. *United Mine Workers' Journal*, July 21, 1910.

87. *Twelfth Biennial Report of the Bureau of Labor Statistics of the State of Colorado, 1909–1910*, 11.

88. *United Mine Workers' Journal*, January 19, 1911, January 18, 1912.

89. Smith, *Once a Coal Miner*, 115; *United Mine Workers' Journal*, January 18, 1912; *Fourteenth Biennial Report of the State Inspector of Coal Mines, 1909–1910*, 125.

90. *United Mine Workers' Journal*, March 14, March 21, 1912, January 23, 1913; *Thirteenth Biennial Report of the Bureau of Labor Statistics of the State of Colorado, 1911–1912* (Denver: Smith-Brooks Printing, State Printers, 1913), 135–138; Smith, *Once a Coal Miner*, 115.

CHAPTER NINE

EXPLOSION AT LUDLOW, 1913-1914

THE FIRST DECADES OF THE TWENTIETH CENTURY had generally been good to the Colorado coal operators. Production had doubled from 1900 to 1910, and thirty-five new mines had opened. The Colorado Fuel and Iron Company (CF&I) and the Victor-American Fuel Company shared in this prosperity. As the second decade of the century began, both operations reported profits, and John C. Osgood complained that he lacked the labor to do more. Yet troubling signs existed: Osgood's production had gone flat at about 1.5 million tons a year, and John D. Rockefeller's enterprise showed inconsistency. The CF&I broke the 4-million-ton mark in 1902 but only occasionally exceeded that amount in the years that followed. The CF&I thus lost some of its market dominance. It produced more than 54 percent of the state's coal in 1902 but just over 31 percent in 1912. This situation, along with conditions at the steel plant, made Rockefeller lament the "unsatisfactory financial returns" from his CF&I investments.[1]

These economic concerns made Jesse Welborn and John Osgood search for ways to save money. First, they kept wages in check. They had granted advances in 1902 and 1907, primarily to ward off unionization; but by 1912 Colorado's Bureau of Labor Statistics claimed coal miners' wages had increased 30 percent in the past ten years while living expenses had grown 60 percent. Second, camp amenities had been curtailed. Whereas Osgood had once been at the forefront of improving living conditions, he was no longer concerned with doing so. A visitor to the southern Colorado mining camps in 1913 claimed the houses were "nearly all shabby, ugly, and small"; that "absolutely no sanitation worthy of the name" existed; and that the unfiltered drinking water came directly from the mines.[2]

The companies also realized some savings by ignoring state laws. As discussed in previous chapters, Colorado had passed laws mandating the eight-hour workday and semimonthly pay periods. Osgood and other coal mine managers did not want their operations constrained by an eight-hour day. They believed that during peak periods miners should work as long as possible and that all parties benefited by receiving more income. Also, Osgood argued that holding the miners' money longer prevented the men from making foolish expenditures. He particularly liked the larger base of working capital. The state had also instituted measures that prohibited mine owners from forcing workers to shop at company stores and that banned the use of scrip. Such practices brought more revenue, so Osgood and Welborn continued them. Although the miners complained, Osgood and Welborn denied any wrongdoing.[3]

Beyond taking steps to save money, Osgood's and Welborn's economic concerns hardened their antiunion stands. Osgood emphatically believed that he alone had the right to set the terms of employment, and Welborn reflected Rockefeller's passionate disdain for unions. At one time Rockefeller claimed he would rather lose the millions he had invested in the coalfields than recognize the unions there. Then, as union activities began again in late 1911, Osgood and Welborn tightened their control of the coal camps. They hired more guards to question everyone who entered and threaten away anyone suspected of being sympathetic to the union. Plus, Osgood and Welborn could count on the support of Sheriff Jeff Farr of Huerfano County and Sheriff Jim Grisham of Las Animas County.[4]

The union organizers countered these obstacles with tactics of their own. Soon after establishing the Trinidad office in early 1912, they discreetly sent men to the neighboring camps who convincingly professed company loyalties. Often they took jobs where they could quietly recruit for the union. In some instances they managed to eliminate miners who showed no union sympathies. If a worker seemed resistant to their overtures, the organizers reported him to the company as a union man, knowing the suspect would soon be dismissed. And the organizers worked slowly, taking two years to spread the word; during that time they did not announce membership numbers, organize locals, or issue membership cards. This secrecy prevented discovery and made Osgood and Welborn mistakenly feel the union had little support.[5]

The organizers, however, found a receptive audience. The miners resented the companies' domination and understood the abuse of state laws. They wanted the eight-hour workday, more frequent paydays, abolition of scrip, and freedom from the company store. Plus, they wanted a check-weighman employed, something also allowed by state law but effective only when supported by union dues because an unbiased check-weighman cannot be on the company's payroll. Further, the workers wanted a wage advance. The United Mine Workers of America (UMWA) had gained the Wyoming men some of the highest wages in the nation, and the Colorado miners wanted that advantage. The initial enthusiasm for the union ran so high that a number of miners sought a strike in the spring of 1912, but the union sought a delay. Some leaders believed the 1903–1904 strike had been called before the organization was ready, and they would not approve another premature walkout. A number of miners ignored the union and walked out anyway. The effort failed, as the national office withheld support.[6]

Despite denying the union's influence, Osgood and Welborn became concerned enough to act, albeit slowly. They needed to rectify some obvious wrongs and change the policies that angered workers the most. In March 1912 they adopted semimonthly pay periods, and a year later they instituted the eight-hour day. The companies also abolished scrip, and the CF&I posted notices encouraging workers to select check-weighmen. Osgood also decided to improve living conditions and had his company houses repaired and painted. Plus, both operations instituted a 10 percent wage advance in April 1912. Although the other measures may have been necessary, the southern Colorado coal operators saw a wage advance as the strongest weapon against unionization.[7]

Much to the coal companies' dismay, the concessions did not satisfy the mine workers. They wanted organization. Many miners had long been frustrated by company domination, some since the failed 1903–1904 strike. Although the wage advance and the other changes encouraged them, they well knew they could not depend on the operators to protect their rights. The miners needed the UMWA to maintain justice and fair play. Without a union contract the companies could easily ignore their promises; they had done so before. As one observer saw it, the push for organization "released a flood of passionate protest, a long pent-up spirit of revolution."[8]

After nearly two years of recruiting, the national union decided to move. UMWA vice president Frank Hayes came to southern Colorado in August 1913 and initiated a multistep process to engage the operators in a dialogue. He asked Governor Elias Ammons to call a conference. The companies refused to meet. Next, Hayes and local union officials drafted a letter explaining the situation and delineating what needed to be considered to avoid a strike.

This, too, gained no response. Then, the miners' union invited the operators to a conference in Trinidad on September 15. Although no representatives from the coal companies attended, the spirited UMWA organizer Mother Jones did attend, and everyone knew the next step was a strike.[9]

Welborn and Osgood saw the union and the Trinidad conference as frauds. They believed under 10 percent of their 6,200 employees belonged to the organization and that few of the 250 people who attended the conference were from their mines. To Welborn and Osgood, the agitators either came from northern Colorado or were on the union payroll. Yet they were concerned. They believed, as most mine managers did, that miners were "somewhat timid," and once a strike began they might readily give in to intimidation.[10]

The Trinidad conference established the workers' grievances and set a strike date of September 23, hoping a settlement could be reached before that time. The delegates put forward seven demands, many of which had already been required by state law and only recently instituted by the operators. Other requests included such things as elimination of the mine guard system and the right to choose their own doctor and place of residence. The two most important points were union recognition and a wage advance that fell in line with the Wyoming scale. Some observers claimed the recent changes made most of the demands unnecessary, but few could solve the dilemma of union recognition.[11]

Welborn, Osgood, and the other southern Colorado operators did not accept the demands, and during the week after the conference, tensions increased further. The operators believed in the power of intimidation, and they hired detectives from the Baldwin-Felts Detective Agency to bolster their mine guards. Some of these men had recently been in a labor dispute in West Virginia, where several people had been killed and considerable property destroyed. They brought arms, ammunition, and machine guns. Not to be outdone, the union responded by arming the coalfield for war, and the killing started early. A month before the strike began a Baldwin-Felts detective killed union organizer Gerald Lippiatt on a street in Trinidad. The potential for greater violence worried Governor Ammons, and he notified the Colorado National Guard to be ready for immediate mobilization.[12]

When the strike day came, the miners and the union showed their strength. Estimates of the number of men who left work vary from source to source. Company officials claimed about 50 percent of the workers walked out, whereas the union estimated 95 percent. Most likely, around 80 percent of the miners quit work in southern Colorado, around 7,200 out of about 9,000 men. But most of Colorado soon became involved, as the strike quickly spread to Crested Butte and Cañon City. Ultimately, the number of strikers exceeded 10,000, with the union claiming 11,232.[13]

The men and their families well knew that striking meant vacating company housing, and they were prepared to move. The union had leased property at fourteen strategic locations around the southern coalfield for tent colonies. Union officials wanted the temporary housing to be as close to roads and mines as possible. Instead of mine guards controlling who could come and go, the strikers wanted to dictate terms of entry. They hoped to shut every mine and keep strikebreakers from opening them. The union built fourteen camps that could hold about 5,000 people, with Ludlow housing the most—between 1,200 and 1,300 men, women, and children. Other strikers found lodging in Trinidad and elsewhere, and some left the coalfield.[14]

With both sides armed and intransigent, violence resumed the day after the strike began. On September 24 Bob Lee, the camp marshal at Segundo, was killed, and from there the killing and destruction continued. At least three battles near Ludlow took place in October 1913, and on October 17 an intense exchange of gunfire that included the use of a company-owned armored car with two machine guns attached occurred at the Forbes tent colony. At least two people died in the exchange, and the killing continued. Whereas some outbursts had broken out during the 1903–1904 strike, the strike of 1913 released a veritable storm. Some of the violence undoubtedly resulted from the miners' pent-up frustrations, but with two sides heavily armed, little else could have happened.[15]

With turmoil in the southern Colorado coalfield, Governor Ammons ordered the National Guard to mobilize on October 27. Soon 1,200 militiamen arrived in the region, and the workers met them with ambivalence. On the one hand, they hoped the killing would end, and they were pleased that the militia would not allow the importation of strikebreakers. On the other hand, the strikers remembered the National Guard's pro-company stance in 1903 and 1904, and they were concerned. Adjutant General John Chase led the guard into the coalfield, and he had no sympathy for the workingmen. Despite some brief outbursts, violence tapered off as the militia restrained the mine guards, taking away their machine guns and sending some away from the territory.[16]

Relations soon turned sour between the miners and the militia, however. General Chase believed the arrival of the National Guard created a state of martial law in the region, and he established a commission to dispense justice under the notion of "military necessity." The commission reviewed charges against strikers and other civilians, holding the suspects in Trinidad's city jail. The greatest outcry came when the commission ordered Mother Jones out of the district in early January 1914 on charges of inciting to riot, and when she returned a week later the militia imprisoned her in a hospital at the edge of town. Her imprisonment sparked a women's protest march through the streets of Trinidad in the third week of January, which General Chase dispersed by ordering a militia charge.[17]

A policy change by the National Guard also worried the strikers. After initially keeping strikebreakers out, Governor Ammons ordered the militia to allow them to enter the mines. Plus, he wanted the National Guard to prevent strikers from intimidating and blocking the path of the new arrivals. Ammons gave the order apparently for two reasons. First, he had helped broker a settlement the union rejected. The union officers felt they had no choice, as the governor had asked them to waive union recognition. But the governor thought the union was ignoring a good settlement. Second, the militia had taken arms from the company guards, and it wanted the miners to turn over their weapons. The strikers relinquished few guns. The union men felt justified in keeping their arms, as they still faced a formidable foe, but the militia and the governor saw their refusal as another example of bad faith. Ammons thus gave the order to protect the strikebreakers, and by early January 1914 the operators reported they were producing about 60 percent of their normal output.[18]

The National Guard retained a significant force in the southern coalfield until early April 1914. During that time violence diminished, but the animosity toward the militia grew. Not only were the troops clearing the way for strikebreakers, but reports emerged of company guards joining the militia. Some original militia members had returned home during the five-month occupation, and their replacements came from the local companies. Also, the state ran out of money and fell four months behind in paying the men. Some sources assert that the coal companies stepped in to supplement the militia's pay, drawing the National Guard even closer to the operators. The strikers believed these reports and rapidly began to suspect that the militia would be used against them. Governor Ammons denied such complicity. He felt the state's soldiers served with "truly commendable devotion."[19]

The apparent calm and the state's poor financial condition caused the governor to draw down the militia contingent. About 200 men remained in early April 1914, distributed between Walsenburg and Trinidad—with about 35 at Ludlow. The militiamen at Ludlow formed Troop A, and a number of the group had only recently enlisted in the National Guard—many from the ranks of company mine guards. Very poor relations existed between the miners and the militia, who communicated with each other mainly with insults and threats. Rumors circulated among both groups that Lieutenant K. E. Linderfelt wanted "to get" Louis Tikas, the leader of the Ludlow colony, and the feeling was mutual.[20]

Violence picked up soon after the majority of state troops had left the coalfield. Governor Ammons stated in retrospect that the miners had carefully planned an extended uprising across the state. Other observers argued that the frustrations merely exploded. Nevertheless, the murder of a mine worker on Sunday, April 19, near Ludlow and the sound of gunfire during the night raised apprehensions. On Monday morning, April 20, Troop A took up a position known as Water Tank Hill above Ludlow. From there they could fire into the tent colony, and the strikers responded by moving for cover away from the colony. In the confusion shooting began, and an all-day battle ensued. At about six o'clock that evening the tent colony began to burn, and in the excitement the militiamen rushed onto the scene. Some say they were saving the women and children, whereas others argue they were spreading the flames. The fire destroyed the colony, and as the struggle went on, Linderfelt captured and killed Tikas.[21]

The battle at Ludlow and the subsequent discovery of eleven children and two women suffocated in a cellar below a burned tent sent rage throughout Colorado. Local UMWA officials issued a call to arms, asking volunteers to organize and fight the assassins in the employ of the coal companies. Angry workers attacked the coal companies wherever and however they could. In northern Colorado strikers imprisoned the sheriff in the Hecla Mine, in central Colorado armed men seized the Chandler Mine, and in southern Colorado protesters destroyed the camp of Forbes, engaged in a large gun battle at Walsenburg, and paraded through the streets of Trinidad. Within two days the strikers controlled an area eighteen miles long and five miles wide in the southern coalfield. As many as ninety people may have died in the outburst (experts do not agree on the exact number).[22]

Ammons rapidly brought in more National Guardsmen, but they could not contain the trouble through negotiations or force. The governor finally requested federal help, and ten days after the Ludlow fight President Woodrow Wilson sent in federal troops. With that action Wilson asked the governor to remove the militia, and he issued a proclamation urging an end to the violence. Wilson also ordered that no strikebreakers be allowed to enter Colorado. The federal presence brought calm, and little more happened except for the flood of recriminations.[23]

Throughout the strike a number of delegations from state and federal agencies appeared in Colorado to investigate and attempt to solve the problems. None succeeded. When Governor Ammons offered a settlement early in the disagreement, the union could not accept the nonrecognition. After the Ludlow turmoil, President Wilson tried to end the standoff by offering a "truce plan." As part of the plan, the president offered to appoint a committee to serve as mediators. The operators rejected the plan, as it implied acceptance of collective bargaining. Also, a number of congressional committees looked into the Colorado situation, and most focused on one supposed villain: John D. Rockefeller Jr., who represented the Rockefeller interests on the CF&I board. Although he had little to do with the strike, his absentee ownership and hands-off approach to business became widely criticized.[24]

On December 10, 1914, the UMWA ended the Colorado strike, both in the southern coalfield and the long-term battle in the north. As *Coal Age*, the journal of the mine owners, bluntly reported, "No concessions were made by the operators to the striking miners to effect this settlement."[25] Yet the union had made some inroads. During the last few months of the strike a number of Colorado's independent operators, employing about 2,000 men, signed an agreement with the UMWA. The companies could no longer afford to resist. The federal troops left in early January 1915. But tensions remained, particularly as a number of strikers sat in jail waiting for trial on a variety of charges. In the end, over 200 people died in a struggle that seemingly accomplished little.[26]

The violence that occurred in southern Colorado was inevitable. Since the 1903–1904 strike, both sides well knew the rules of coalfield engagement. The companies had succeeded in 1904 with evictions, guards, guns, and strikebreakers; and they planned to use those tactics again. The union organizers believed they had to respond in kind. They built colonies that blocked the entries to the mines and brought in their own weapons. In addition, worker frustration added to the potential for violence. For years the companies had ignored state laws and controlled the workers with a firm hand. The companies, for their part, bitterly detested the notion of collective bargaining and would do anything to stop it. With the Wyoming mines 100 percent organized, Colorado operators wanted to make sure the UMWA would not advance.

The workers had little chance to win the 1913–1914 strike. The allied companies dominated the West's most important coalfields. They not only owned the towns, but they also controlled the county sheriffs and gained the support of the National Guard. Just as important, they had little concern about losing their markets for coal. Strikes took them out of business for a time, but they knew their customers would come back. The CF&I also had a steel mill to worry about, but Rockefeller's antiunion stand outweighed any desire to keep it running. The operators did worry about losing money in long strikes, but they tried to counter that concern by rapidly employing strikebreakers and using strike fund reserves they had collected. Thus the companies won because they worked together not only in sharing markets but in defeating unionization.

The Colorado Fuel and Iron Company and the Victor-American Company were seemingly paramount in the southern Colorado coalfield after the 1913–1914 strike, but that situation soon changed. Congressional investigations and the national press heaped criticism on Rockefeller for his absentee ownership and neglect of the CF&I. The attack caused Rockefeller to change course and institute what he believed would be a new era of industrial labor relations. With the help of Canadian labor expert Mackenzie King, he developed the Rockefeller Plan of Employee Representation whereby workers could air their grievances through company unions. The apparent sympathy for workers changed the labor dynamics of southern Colorado and forced Osgood to change as well. Osgood did not try to mimic Rockefeller's plan; instead—with great reluctance—he signed a contract with the UMWA, and other companies followed. In 1910 only 187 people officially belonged to the UMWA; in 1917 the union counted over 5,000 members in Colorado, about half of the state's miners. Although the UMWA lost the 1913–1914 strike, the violence brought a new era in labor relations and company operations.[27]

SUMMARY REFLECTIONS

The violence that erupted in the southern Colorado coalfield in 1913 and 1914 seemed merely to echo the past. From the time coal mines opened in the West, armed conflict seemingly accompanied labor relations. But the cause of the violence had changed over time. In the 1885 Rock Springs Massacre, traditional craft miners saw the Chinese as a threat to their status and their jobs. They lashed out against the Chinese to defend their skilled positions and workplace prerogatives. Over time, most operators gained more and more control over their workers, and some ultimately used violence to maintain order. The Ludlow Massacre resulted from an obsession to control the mines at all costs. In the Rock Springs Massacre the workers wanted to protect their rights; in the Ludlow Massacre the companies tried to assert their dominance.

The evolution of labor violence was just one aspect of this study. In an attempt to better understand these events, it explored the transformation of the western coal industry from its conception in 1868 to full maturity in the early twentieth century. In the process, four aspects of the coal industry were examined: (1) the coal companies and their owners, (2) the workers and their workplaces, (3) the economic cycle and the coal business, and (4) labor relations.

Coal Companies and Owners

Coal development in the West accompanied railroad expansion. Railroads typically opened mines through associated companies. Whether it was the Wyoming Coal and Mining Company or the Central Colorado Improvement Company, these operations were designed to return a profit to the primary promoters. Railroad construction in the West entailed a significant risk, and the developers saw coal companies as one source of immediate revenue. The coal entrepreneurs profited by selling coal to their own railroads and then on the expanding domestic market.

In most instances western coal developers sought a monopoly. For the first thirty years of operation, the Union Pacific ran most competition out of business. Only in the twentieth century, when the railroad needed extra coal, did it willingly work with other coal companies. Similarly, William Jackson Palmer attempted to control the coal ground wherever the Rio Grande advanced. His Colorado Coal and Iron Company bought property throughout Colorado to keep others out. Even after Palmer lost control of the company, his successors continued to buy coal lands, at times straining their financial resources to the point of collapse.

The events in the Denver Basin showed why companies sought a monopoly and feared competition. When the Denver Pacific built into the region it did not attempt to control the mining ground, and a number of other companies opened. From that point on a competitive struggle went on in northern Colorado that pushed most companies to the edge of profitability. The operators tried marketing associations, mine consolidations, and working with unions to eliminate competitive differences and bring order to the field. None of these efforts worked effectively. Instability reigned in the Denver Basin.

The West's largest companies found, however, that monopoly did not ensure stability. Much western industrial development was based on speculation. Few knew what to expect, and most developers wanted a quick profit—hence the associated companies. Many parent railroads had uncertain values. Fluctuating stock prices allowed Jay Gould to buy and sell the Union Pacific twice, as well as other western railroads. Failing revenues for the Rio Grande eventually forced Palmer to yield control of the line. Palmer also lost influence in Colorado Coal and Iron when the company did not perform as the eastern investors wanted. Most early capitalists wanted quick profits instead of long-term growth. Even John C. Osgood, who seemingly brought a keener business sense west, ended his association with Colorado Fuel and Iron for a chance at quick profits.

Rampant speculation did diminish over time. Charles Francis Adams Jr. tried to bring a new business order to the Union Pacific during his short presidency. When Edward H. Harriman gained control of the railroad, he finally ended its speculative past. Osgood ended the tumultuous history of Colorado Coal and Iron when he formed the Colorado Fuel and Iron Company. He brought a new sense of order to the business, but then he left the CF&I for a chance at personal gain.

Although western investment had its ups and downs, a maturing business philosophy can be observed in the development of coal towns. Carbon, Rock Springs, Almy, and Coal Creek were the region's first coal camps. All of them developed as towns independent of company control. They often sat on company property, but the miners built their own houses and organized community activities. Wyoming Coal and Mining did open company stores, and the coal companies did build a few houses, but the towns resembled frontier towns more than company-organized coal towns.

The opening of Engleville in 1877 seemed to indicate the next stage in coal town development. Palmer's Southern Colorado Coal and Town Company developed Engleville as a nearly complete company town. It built housing and a store. For the company, a town might attract workers, return revenue, and allow better control of the workforce. Engleville, however, did not last as a company town. Independent merchants and privately owned housing soon appeared. Plus, when Palmer subsequently opened other coal camps, they resembled the earlier frontier coal towns.

The Union Pacific returned to the idea of full company towns in 1889 when it opened Hanna, and Colorado Coal and Iron did the same when it developed Berwind in 1890. These company towns reflected the business orientation of the companies' presidents: Charles Francis Adams Jr. and Edward J. Berwind, respectively. The towns were laid out in orderly patterns, with all houses built and owned by the company; and the company store monopolized the coal miners' business. The developers hoped the towns would bring revenue and order to the coalfields.

Osgood took the next step in company town development when he began opening new towns in 1901. At Primero, Segundo, Tercio, and Quatro, he provided nicer housing, better schools, and improved sanitation. These new communities were meant to create a more satisfied workforce. Making miners and their families happy would, it was hoped, bring efficiency and end labor disputes. Osgood had started creating what became known in the trade as "model" company towns. His experiment died when he lost control of the CF&I, but his notion of model company towns returned to the West in the next decade.

In all of these instances, the men in charge of the companies fell into two categories: speculators and developers. Some helped the West grow, whereas others only wanted to exploit it. Many have criticized absentee owners as the most nefarious exploiters and the worst owners, with Rockefeller receiving his fair share of blame, but that was not necessarily the case. As westerners, Palmer and Osgood were certainly developers, but speculation drove their business ambition. Stability came to the West through such easterners as Adams and Harriman. In terms of handling labor relations, it made no difference if a westerner or an easterner was setting the policy. Osgood hated unions as much as any eastern industrialist. Individuals made the difference, not where they came from.

Workers and the Workplace

The first miners in the West were experienced. Many had worked as miners in the British Isles or in the East. They came imbued with the skills and traditions of the trade. These men knew how to open mines and dig coal. They did so with little supervision and enjoyed what has been called the miner's freedom. They worked together for their common good and brought a long history of labor activism.

The companies needed these men to open the mines, but they soon tried to disrupt the ethnic and craft solidarity that bound the men. Racial and ethnic diversification became a standard technique used by nearly every coal company in the West. The Union Pacific first used Scandinavian miners, then Chinese workers, and finally any group willing to go into the mines. Colorado Coal and Iron tried first to incorporate Hispanic farmers and then a variety of groups, including African Americans. Companies also introduced mining machines to disrupt the workplace. They wanted to turn the skilled miner into an unskilled laborer. The machines did not have the effect the operators wanted; and no matter who entered the mines, the men soon identified the underground world as their domain. The ethnic and racial differences diminished over time as the men shared skills, dangers, and hostile employers.

The Business of Coal

Coal was a growth industry. Once mines opened along railroad lines, they grew dramatically. The first major activity occurred in southern Wyoming, then in the Denver Basin, followed by central and southern Colorado. From the day they opened, the Union Pacific mines were some of the most important in the West. In Colorado the mines in the southern coalfield gradually increased in importance until they eventually led the West in production. In 1912 they produced 6.6 million tons of coal, 60 percent of Colorado's total output. The Union Pacific mines yielded 3.4 million tons that same year.[28]

Growth, however, was not consistent. Economic downturns significantly affected the demand for coal. Slumps such as those in 1873 and 1893 hurt production and brought cutbacks in manpower, but they never permanently damaged the industry. More often, the economic slumps hurt the coal companies' parent operations. The 1873 slump forced Palmer to lease his railroad to the Santa Fe, and the 1893 depression drove the Santa Fe and the Union Pacific into receivership. When the two companies emerged from insolvency, they took their coal operations in different directions. The Santa Fe leased its mines to the CF&I, and the Union Pacific expanded its coal operations. In one instance Jay Gould demonstrated that a company could use a downturn to its advantage. During the Panic of 1873, Gould consolidated his hold on the Union Pacific and increased coal production.

The economic cycle seldom benefited the miners. Hired at high wages, the miners felt the brunt of slumps as operators, assuming lower-priced coal would increase sales, drove wages down. This tactic seldom worked. The demand for coal was inelastic; sales were determined more by the level of business activity than by the price of coal. Nevertheless, companies cut wages during the 1873 and 1893 downturns and whenever else they felt an economic pinch. When good times returned, wages rarely returned to their former levels.[29]

The almost continuous prosperity in the early twentieth century finally benefited some of the West's miners. As coal demand remained high and labor was in short supply, companies started granting wage advances. This became a favorite tactic as the coal companies tried to head off union organization. Conditions, however, favored the workers. The miners wanted more than just wages. In 1907 the coal workers in southern Wyoming received union recognition and some of the highest wages in the nation. That did not happen in Colorado, where the companies resisted mightily.

Coal markets constituted another important aspect of the business of coal. Most mines in the West opened at the behest of railroads, which consumed much of the product. As the West developed, the market for coal diversified to include domestic, agricultural, and industrial uses. Although the Denver Basin mines produced a lower-grade coal, their proximity to Denver allowed them to dominate that market. Their hold on Denver was tenuous, however. The Denver Basin companies consistently worried about competition undermining their market share. The mines in central and southern Colorado locked up most of the region's other markets south of Wyoming. Central and southern Colorado coal was used from Nebraska to Texas and into the Rockies. The mines near Trinidad also produced coke, which fed the metal smelters and the CF&I's steel plant. The central and southern coalfields were the most important fields in the West; they controlled the western markets. During work stoppages consumers used coal from Texas, Kansas, and New Mexico, but they always returned to Colorado coal.[30]

In Wyoming, Union Pacific coal ruled along the railroad's route, initially supplying the railroad and the commercial market. The railroad's transportation monopoly gave it an immense advantage. As the region developed, the Union Pacific found it could no longer supply both the commercial demand and its own railroad. The Union Pacific allowed competitors to open with no fear of losing its market. In fact, the Union Pacific withdrew from the commercial market so it could focus on railroad consumption. This situation made its mines "captive." The railroad let the other producers in southern Wyoming control the commercial business.

Labor Relations in the Coalfields

Labor relations in the coalfields can be seen as a control issue. The miners who came west established the work environment and received a tonnage rate commensurate with that of skilled employees. From the beginning, coal companies tried a variety of tactics to diminish the miners' status and pay. Some of the first strikes can be seen as strikes over control. In 1871, miners in the Denver Basin and at Carbon, Wyoming, went out to protest company actions. In both instances the miners resorted to threats of violence. They would not tolerate any challenge to their position.

The largest companies proved relentless, however. Through ethnic and racial diversification, they undermined the workers' status. Then, taking advantage of a labor surplus during economic downturns, the companies pushed wages down. The 1884–1885 strike proved a critical turning point. At that time enough traditional miners still worked in the coalfields to share a sense of solidarity based on their work culture. They had a labor organization, the Knights of Labor, that reflected their ideals. When the strike culminated in workers killing other workers in the Rock Springs Massacre, it was a case of traditional miners lashing out at company-imposed labor dynamics. Labor's defeat in 1884–1885 meant employers had gained the upper hand. From that point on, employers asserted control over the workers.

Not all companies treated their workers the same, however. The Union Pacific continued to deal with the men, whereas the CF&I abused its position of power. Regardless of state law or popular sentiment, the CF&I dictated the terms of employment. The company was not challenged until the United Mine Workers of America became involved. The UMWA had the organizational size to counter the largest coal producers. The union tried to bring the diverse workforce together. The UMWA did not want to challenge the companies' control; it simply sought fair play and justice. The union recognized the validity of capitalism. It wanted the miners to share in the profits by receiving wages that reflected their product's full social value. In Wyoming and the Denver Basin the union made inroads. In central and southern Colorado the companies tried a variety of tactics to maintain their control, and they prevailed.

An underlying question remains: Why did some strikes fail and others succeed? Regarding the strikes workers lost, labor historians often damn the coal operators but blame the miners or their union. They argue that the strikers did not maintain a solid front or that the national union handled the strike badly. These points did influence strike outcomes, but two other factors need to be considered. First, the coal market played a role in a strike's success or failure. When workers gained a quick settlement, it often came because mine operators feared losing their market share. The bitter competition in the Denver Basin helped the men there win union demands. The coal companies could not close down long enough to make changes to the workforce for fear of never reopening.

Little competition existed elsewhere in the mountain West. The Union Pacific did not fear market competition, and two coal companies in central and southern Colorado dominated the coalfields. The companies changed over time, yet their cooperative efforts to resist unionism did not. They did not compete for each other's markets, and they had no reason to yield to the miners. The companies could endure a long strike and not fear losing their markets. Long work stoppages became painful because of revenue losses, but Osgood had instituted strike funds to ease the financial damage. The companies could wait for workers to cross the picket lines and gradually reopen their mines.

The second factor that influenced labor relations and strike outcomes was the operators' attitude toward their workers and the coal business. The Santa Fe managers saw their coal mines as secondary to their railroad. Not driven to profit from coal mining, they established a more congenial relationship with their workers. Under the influence of Charles Francis Adams Jr., the Union Pacific also worked more openly with labor organizations. When the Union Pacific accepted the UMWA in 1907, it did so for the sake of the railroad. The company wanted order in the mines and consistent coal production. If the managers could see an advantage in cooperating with their miners or thought it was the right thing to do, the workers benefited. If an operator did not have that motivation, he remained intransigent.

In the clash between miners and operators, worker solidarity was the variable both sides counted on. The mine owners did not believe it existed and were confident that their employees would not heed a strike call or that if they did, they would soon come back to work. Union activists needed solidarity to make organization a success. The meaning of solidarity, however, changed over time. The traditional miners who first came west carried a sense of solidarity that crossed coalfield boundaries and extended regionwide. This philosophy changed as the workforce changed. The new ethnic groups felt a tighter bond among themselves than they did with other workers. Yet they did see the advantage of cooperating with all groups for mutual gain. When a strike call came, they often joined the effort. Because it was not based on an entrenched work culture or shaped through years of struggle, however, such solidarity could diminish quickly.

The United Mine Workers recognized the limitations of solidarity and understood the way the market worked. UMWA officials tried to balance the two, as in the 1903–1904 Colorado strike. Letting the Denver Basin settle while the south remained out allowed union mines to open in Colorado. That decision strengthened the union's position, made the men solid unionists, and brought coal onto the market. Not settling when terms had been offered might have provoked men to cross the picket lines and return to work. Although the men in central and southern Colorado remained on strike and they were coal miners, the Denver Basin workers felt no strong bond of solidarity with them. The coal industry had changed too much. Regionwide worker solidarity had little force. What solidarity existed came at the behest of the UMWA.

In sum, four variables were at work within the western coal industry. Coal entrepreneurs started the businesses, but each operation was different depending on the operator's attitude and what he wanted from the business. Coal miners came to the western coalfields to do one job: dig coal. Depending upon when they arrived, where they worked, and whom they worked for, miners had different ambitions and experiences. The economic cycle and market forces greatly affected both operators and miners, sometimes helping and sometimes hurting them. Labor relations connected and grew out of the other three variables. The way the first three variables came together determined labor relations.

NOTES

1. "Victor-American Fuel Co.," *Coal Age* 5, no. 17 (April 25, 1914): 712; "Colorado Fuel & Iron Co.," *Coal Age* 7, no. 3 (January 16, 1915): 150; Senate Committee on Industrial Relations, *Final Report and Testimony,* 8046; *Tenth Biennial Report of the Inspector of Coal Mines of the State of Colorado, 1901–1902* (Denver: Smith-Brooks Printing, State Printers, 1903), 125; *Fifteenth Biennial Report of the Inspector of Coal Mines of the State of Colorado, 1911–1912* (Denver: Smith-Brooks Printing, State Printers, 1913), 13.

2. W. T. Davis, "The Strike War in Colorado," *Outlook,* May 9, 1914, 70; Witt Bowden, "Two Alternatives in the Settlement of the Colorado Coal Strike," *Survey,* December 20, 1913, 321.

3. "The Colorado Strike," *Coal Age* 5, no. 19 (May 9, 1914): 773.

4. "Editorial," *Survey,* May 2, 1914, 159; "Some Causes of the Struggle," *Survey,* December 5, 1914, 247; "Freedom of Contract," *Survey,* January 2, 1915, 352; Priscilla Long, "The 1913–1914 Colorado Fuel and Iron Strike, with Reflections on the Causes of Coal-Strike Violence," in *The United Mine Workers of America: A Model of Industrial Solidarity?* ed. John H.M. Laslett (University Park: Pennsylvania State University Press, 1996), 348.

5. McClurg, "Labor Organization in the Coal Mines of Colorado," 197–198.

6. John A. Fitch, "Law and Order: The Issue in Colorado," *Survey,* December 5, 1914, 241–258; John A. Fitch, "When Peace Comes to Colorado," *Survey,* May 16, 1914, 205; *United Mine Workers' Journal,* January 18, December 5, 1912.

7. "The Colorado Strike," 773; "Victor-American Fuel Co.," *Coal Age* 5, no. 17 (April 25, 1914): 712; Committee on Industrial Relations, *Final Report and Testimony,* 8020–21.

8. Davis, "The Strike War in Colorado," 73.

9. Fitch, "Law and Order," 251; Long, "The 1913–1914 Colorado Fuel and Iron Strike," 350.

10. "The Situation in Colorado," *Coal Age* 4, no. 13 (September 27, 1913): 456; "Colorado Coal Strike Situation," *Coal Age* 4, no. 18 (November 1, 1913): 664; *First Annual Report of the State Inspector of Coal Mines, 1913* (Denver: Smith-Brooks Printing, State Printers, 1914), 11–12.

11. "The Coal Strike in Colorado," *Coal Age* 4, no. 22 (November 29, 1913): 817–818; Long, "The 1913–1914 Colorado Fuel and Iron Strike," 351.

12. "The Situation in Colorado," 456; Fitch, "Law and Order," 251–252.

13. Committee on Industrial Relations, *Final Report and Testimony,* 6518; *Coal Age* 4, no. 18 (November 1, 1913): 675; "The Situation in Colorado," 456; Elias M. Ammons, "The Colorado Strike," *North American Review,* 1914, 35.

14. Fitch, "Law and Order," 252; Davis, "The Strike War in Colorado," 67.

15. Fitch, "Law and Order," 252.

16. Ibid., 255; Davis, "The Strike War in Colorado," 67.

17. Davis, "The Strike War in Colorado," 68; Fitch, "Law and Order," 256.

18. Davis, "The Strike War in Colorado," 67; "Report from Trinidad," *Coal Age* 5, no. 1 (January 3, 1914): 34; Ammons, "The Colorado Strike," 39.

19. Fitch, "Law and Order," 257; Ammons, "The Colorado Strike," 38.

20. Fitch, "Law and Order," 257; Long, "The 1913–1914 Colorado Fuel and Iron Strike," 356–357; Davis, "The Strike War in Colorado," 68.

21. Fitch, "Law and Order," 253, 257; Davis, "The Strike War in Colorado," 68.

22. Long, "The 1913–1914 Colorado Fuel and Iron Strike," 358–359; "The Colorado Strike," 732; Ammons, "The Colorado Strike," 43.

23. "The Colorado Strike," 732; "Strike Breakers Banned in Colorado," *Survey*, May 16, 1914, 211.

24. Fitch, "Law and Order," 243; "Editorials," *Survey*, December 5, 1914, 261–262; "The President's Colorado Committee Unwelcome," *Survey*, February 27, 1915, 571.

25. "Colorado," *Coal Age* 7, no. 2 (January 9, 1915): 46.

26. *Coal Age* 6, no. 10 (September 5, 1914): 403; "Militia Called out in Colorado," *Coal Age* 7, no. 3 (January 16, 1915): 127.

27. *Coal Age* 11, no. 18 (May 5, 1917): 788; "Union Membership Has Increased Greatly," *Coal Age* 13, no. 5 (February 2, 1918): 249; Howard M. Gitelman, *Legacy of the Ludlow Massacre: A Chapter in American Industrial Relations* (Philadelphia: University of Pennsylvania Press, 1988), 32–67.

28. United States Geological Survey, *Mineral Resources of the United States, 1913,* 823; *History of the Union Pacific Coal Mines,* appendix.

29. Brody, *In Labor's Cause,* 132.

30. United States Geological Survey, *Mineral Resources of the United States, 1888,* 227, 229; U.S. Department of the Interior, United States Geological Survey, *Mineral Resources of the United States, 1912* (Washington, D.C.: GPO, 1913), 119, 120; "Tenth Annual Report of the Colorado Fuel and Iron Co., for the Year Ending June 30, 1902," 9, Collection #1057, Box #5, Folder #94, CF&I CRL.

Table A.1 Coal Production in Wyoming, Colorado, the Union Pacific operations, the Colorado Coal and Iron Company, the Colorado Fuel and Iron Company, and Victor Fuel, 1872–1912 (in thousands of tons)[1]

Year	Wyoming	Union Pacific[2]	Colorado	CC&I/ CF&I[3]	Victor Fuel[4]
1872	221.7	116.6	68.5	6.1	—
1874	219.1	137.4	77.4	17.3	—
1876	334.6	264.8	117.7	20.3	—
1878	333.2	275.8	200.6	66.6	—
1880	589.6	445.1	462.7	221.4	—
1882	707.8	597.6	1,061.5	512.4	—
1884	902.6	823.3	1,130.0	583.2	—
1886	829.4	732.1	1,368.3	616.4	—
1888	1,481.5	1,092.5	2,185.5	739.7	—
1890	1,870.4	1,134.4	3,077.0	790.5	—
1892	2,503.8	1,532.0	3,510.8	1,872.7	201.7
1894	2,417.4	1,218.7	2,831.4	1,338.8	—
1896	2,229.6	959.5	3,112.4	1,968.1	250.7
1898	2,863.8	1,134.5	4,076.3	2,553.2	503.8
1900	4,014.6	1,406.7	5,244.2	2,922.1	749.8
1902	4,429.5	2,018.6	7,401.3	4,032.9	923.1
1904	5,178.6	3,043.6	6,658.4	2,728.4	948.5
1906	6,134.0	3,314.0	10,111.2	4,128.1	1,793.9
1908	5,490.0	3,175.7	9,635.0	3,324.7	1,451.3
1910	7,533.1	3,709.2	11,973.8	4,126.1	1,639.0
1912	7,368.1	3,390.2	10,977.8	3,441.9	1,526.9

Notes: 1. U.S. Geological Survey, *Mineral Resources of the United States, Calendar Year* (Washington, D.C.: GPO, 1883–1922); *History of the Union Pacific Coal Mines, 1868 to 1940* (Omaha: Colonial, 1940), table; Annual and Biennial Reports of Colorado's Inspector of Coal Mines for the CF&I and Victor-American data, 1884–1912.

2. The Union Pacific production figures include only its Wyoming mines.

3. The Colorado Coal and Iron Company became part of the Colorado Fuel and Iron Company in 1892. The production totals given in state and federal documents are lower than the figures released in the companies' Annual Reports. This chart uses the federal and state totals.

4. The Victor Fuel Company became the Victor-American Fuel Company in 1909.

Table A.2 Coal Production in Colorado and in the Denver Basin, Cañon City, and Trinidad Coalfields, 1872–1912 (in thousands of tons)

Year	Denver Basin	Cañon City	Trinidad	Colorado
1872	54.3	—	—	68.5
1874	59.3	18.1—for both coalfields		77.4
1876	97.4	20.3—for both coalfields		117.7
1878	87.8	73.1	37.7	200.6
1880	123.5	136.0	126.4	462.7
1882	270.0	160.0	466.4	1,061.5
1884	159.0	168.0	463.9	1,130.0
1886	239.1	332.0	519.7	1,368.3
1888	343.2	438.8	866.1	2,185.5
1890	472.1	397.4	1,582.5	3,077.0
1892	520.5	538.9	1,712.8	3,510.8
1894	375.3	275.0	1,595.9	2,831.4
1896	453.0	294.8	1,614.9	3,112.4
1898	475.6	426.6	2,287.2	4,076.3
1900	654.3	619.4	2,978.4	5,244.4
1902	880.1	696.0	4,434.6	7,401.3
1904	855.7	256.2	3,996.9	6,658.4
1906	1,117.5	666.0	6,572.7	10,111.2
1908	1,411.4	669.3	5,834.9	9,635.0
1910	1,125.7	722.1	7,935.2	11,973.8
1912	1,545.8	738.8	6,608.2	10,977.8

BIBLIOGRAPHY

MANUSCRIPT SOURCES

Barrett Collection. American Heritage Center, Laramie, Wyoming.

Beckwith-Quinn Collection. American Heritage Center, Laramie, Wyoming.

Colorado Fuel and Iron Company Collection. Colorado State Historical Society, Colorado Research Library, Denver, Colorado.

Denver and Rio Grande Railway Collection. Colorado State Historical Society, Colorado Research Library, Denver, Colorado.

Historical Collection. Cañon City Public Library, Cañon City, Colorado.

John L. Lathrop Jerome Collection. Colorado State Historical Society, Colorado Research Library, Denver, Colorado.

John Lawson Papers. Western History Collection, Denver Public Library, Denver, Colorado.

Kemmerer Coal Collection. American Heritage Center, Laramie, Wyoming.

Santa Fe Railway Archives. Kansas State Historical Society, Topeka, Kansas.

State Inspector of Coal Mines Reports. Wyoming State Archives, Museums and Historical Department, Cheyenne, Wyoming.

Terence V. Powderly Papers, microfilm edition, 1884–1885.

Union Pacific Coal Company Collection. Union Pacific Archives, Nebraska State Historical Society, Lincoln, Nebraska.

Union Pacific Coal Company Collection. Union Pacific Historical Museum, Omaha, Nebraska.

Union Pacific Coal Company Collection. Wyoming State Archives, Museums and Historical Department, Cheyenne, Wyoming.

Victor Fuel Collection. American Heritage Center, Laramie, Wyoming.

GOVERNMENT RECORDS AND PUBLICATIONS

Biennial Report of the Bureau of Labor Statistics of the State of Colorado. Denver: Smith-Brooks Printing, State Printers, 1887–1913.

Clark, Victor. *Mexican Labor in the United States.* U.S. Bureau of Labor Bulletin 78. Washington, D.C.: Government Printing Office (GPO), 1909.

Emmons, Samuel Franklin, Whitman Cross, and George Homans Eldridge. *Geology of the Denver Basin in Colorado.* U.S. Geological Survey Monograph, vol. 27. Washington, D.C.: GPO, 1896.

"The Foreign Born in the Coal Mines." In *Reports of the Industrial Commission on Immigration and on Education* 15. Washington, D.C.: GPO, 1901.

Harbour, R. L., and G. H. Dixon. *Coal Resources of Trinidad-Aguilar Area, Las Animas and Huerfano Counties, Colorado, Contributions to Economic Geology.* Geological Survey Bulletin 1072-G. Washington, D.C.: GPO, 1959.

Hayden, F. V. *Preliminary Report of the United States Geological Survey of Wyoming, and the Portions of Contiguous Territories.* Washington, D.C.: GPO, 1872.

Johnson, Ross B. *Coal Resources of the Trinidad Coal Field in Huerfano and Las Animas Counties, Colorado.* Geological Survey Bulletin 1112-E. Washington, D.C.: GPO, 1961.

Raymond, Rossiter W. *The Report of the Commissioner of Mining Statistics, on Mines and Mining West of the Rocky Mountains for the Year Ending December 31, 1871.* 42d Cong., 2d sess., 1872, H. Ex. Doc. (Serial Set 1513).

Richardson, G. B. "The Trinidad Coal Field, Colorado." In *Contributions to Economic Geology 1908*, Marius R. Campbell, ed. Geological Survey Bulletin 381. Washington, D.C.: GPO, 1910.

Schultz, Alfred R. "The Southern Part of the Rock Springs Coal Field, Sweetwater County, Wyoming." In *Contributions to Economic Geology 1908*, Marius R. Campbell, ed. Geological Survey Bulletin 381. Washington, D.C.: GPO, 1910.

Senate Committee on Industrial Relations. *Final Report and Testimony*, 64th Cong., 1st sess., 1916, Doc. no. 415. Washington, D.C.: GPO, 1916.

State Inspector of Coal Mines of the State of Colorado. Annual and Biennial Reports. Denver: Smith-Brooks Printing, State Printers, 1884–1915.

U.S. Department of the Interior. Census Office. Manuscript census, 1870, 1880, 1900.

U.S. Department of the Interior. Census Office. *Population of the United States in 1860; Compiled from the Original Returns of the Eighth Census.* Washington, D.C.: GPO, 1864.

U.S. Department of the Interior. Census Office. *Report on Population of the United States at the Eleventh Census: 1890*, Part 1. Washington, D.C.: GPO, 1895.

U.S. Department of the Interior. Census Office. *The Statistics of the Population of the United States*. Washington, D.C.: GPO, 1870.

U.S. Department of the Interior. Census Office. *Statistics of the United States at the Tenth Census*, vol. 1. Washington, D.C.: GPO, 1883.

U.S. Department of the Interior. United States Geological Survey. *Geology and Coal and Oil Resources of the Hanna and Carbon Basins, Carbon County, Wyoming*, by C. E. Dobbin, C. F. Bowen, and H. W. Hoots. Washington, D.C.: GPO, 1929.

U.S. Department of the Interior. United States Geological Survey. *Mineral Resources of the United States*. Washington, D.C.: GPO, 1882–1888, 1893, 1900, 1901, 1903, 1907, 1910, 1912–1922, 1925.

Veatch, A. C. "Coal Fields of East-Central Carbon County, Wyo." In *Contributions to Economic Geology 1906*, Marius R. Campbell, ed. Geological Survey Bulletin 316. Washington, D.C.: GPO, 1907.

Wright, Carroll D. *A Report on Labor Disturbances in the State of Colorado, from 1880 to 1904, Inclusive, with Correspondence Relating Thereto*. 58th Cong., 3d sess., 1905, Doc. no. 122. Washington, D.C.: GPO, 1905.

NEWSPAPERS, MAGAZINES, PROFESSIONAL JOURNALS

American Journal of Mining, 1866–1868

Camp and Plant, 1901–1904

Cañon City *Daily Record*, 1988

Cheyenne *Daily Leader*, 1875–1907

Cheyenne *Daily Sun*, 1878

Coal Age, 1912–1915, 1917, 1918

Denver *Republican*, 1881

Denver *Times*, 1879, 1898–1903

Employe's [sic] *Magazine*, 1930

Engineering and Mining Journal, 1871–1911

Kemmerer Camera, 1907

Labor Enquirer, 1883–1885

Laramie *Daily Sentinel*, 1871–1875

Laramie *Weekly Sentinel*, 1878

North American Review, 1914

Outlook, 1914

Pueblo *Chieftain*, 1873–1877, 1884–1885

Rock Springs *Miner*, 1907

Rocky Mountain News, 1868–1903

Survey, 1913–1916

Union Pacific Employes' [sic] *Magazine*, 1887–1894

United Mine Workers' Journal, 1891–1913

Wyoming Labor Journal, 1917

PRIMARY PUBLISHED MATERIAL

Atchison, Topeka & Santa Fe Railway System: A Study of Its Progress in the Last Decade and Pertinent Comparisons with Other Transcontinental Carriers. New York: Wood, Struthers, 1925.

Beshoar, M., M.D. *All About Trinidad and Las Animas County, Colorado.* Denver: Times Steam Printing House and Blank Book Manufactory, 1882; reprint, Trinidad: Trinidad Historical Society, 1990.

Buchanan, Joseph R. *The Story of a Labor Agitator.* New York: Outlook, 1903.

Fossett, Frank. *Colorado: Its Gold and Silver Mines, Farms and Stock Ranges, Health and Pleasure Resorts.* New York: C. G. Crawford, 1880; reprint, Glorieta, N.M.: Rio Grande Press, 1976.

Goodrich, Carter. *The Miner's Freedom: A Study of the Working Life in a Changing Industry.* Boston: Marshall Jones, 1925.

History of the Arkansas Valley, Colorado. Chicago: O. L. Baskin & Co., Historical Publishers, 1881.

Ingersoll, Ernest. *The Crest of the Continent: A Summer's Ramble in the Rocky Mountains and Beyond.* Chicago: R. R. Donnelley and Sons, 1885.

Rolker, Charles M. *Report on the Property of the Colorado Coal and Iron Co.* New York: Jno. C. Rankin Jr., 1884.

Suffern, Arthur E. *The Coal Miners' Struggle for Industrial Status.* New York: Macmillan, 1926.

3,000,000 Acres of Choice Farming, Grazing, Coal and Timber Land in Colorado. Denver: Rocky Mountain New Steam Printing House, 1873.

Warne, Frank Julian. "The Effect of Unionism upon the Mine Worker." *Annals of the American Academy of Political and Social Science* 21 (January–June 1903): 20–35.

Whitney, W. H. *Directory of Trinidad, Colorado for 1888.* Trinidad: Advertiser Steam Job Print, 1888.

SECONDARY SOURCES

Books

Allen, James B. *The Company Town in the American West.* Norman: University of Oklahoma Press, 1966.

Anderson, George L. *General William J. Palmer: A Decade of Colorado Railroad Building, 1870–1880.* Colorado College Publication, General Series no. 209, Studies Series no. 22. Colorado Springs: Colorado College, 1936.

Athearn, Robert. *The Denver and Rio Grande Western Railroad.* New Haven: Yale University Press, 1967; reprint, Lincoln: University of Nebraska Press, 1977.

———. *Union Pacific Country.* Lincoln: University of Nebraska Press, 1971.

Baratz, Morton. *The Union and the Coal Industry.* New Haven: Yale University Press, 1955.

Barrett, Glen. *Kemmerer, Wyoming: The Founding of an Independent Coal Town, 1897–1902.* Kemmerer, Wyo.: Quealy Services, 1975.

Beebe, Lucius, and Charles Clegg. *Rio Grande: Mainline of the Rockies.* Berkeley: Howell-North, 1962.

Beik, Mildred Allen. *The Miners of Windber: The Struggles of New Immigrants for Unionization, 1890s–1930s.* University Park: Pennsylvania State University Press, 1996.

Beshoar, Barron B. *Out of the Depths: The Story of John R. Lawson, a Labor Leader.* Denver: Golden, 1942.

Bining, Arthur Cecil, and Thomas C. Cochran. *The Rise of American Economic Life*. New York: Charles Scribner's Sons, 1964.

Bollinger, Edward T., and Frederick Bauer. *The Moffat Road*. Chicago: Swallow, 1962.

Brandes, Stuart D. *American Welfare Capitalism, 1880–1940*. Chicago: University of Chicago Press, 1970.

Brayer, Herbert O. *William Blackmore: Early Financing of the Denver & Rio Grande Railway and Ancillary Land Companies, 1871–1878*. Denver: Bradford-Robinson, 1949.

Brody, David. *In Labor's Cause: Main Themes on the History of the American Worker*. New York: Oxford University Press, 1993.

Brundage, David. *The Making of Western Labor Radicalism: Denver's Organized Workers, 1878–1905*. Urbana: University of Illinois Press, 1994.

Bryant, Keith L., Jr. *History of the Atchison, Topeka and Santa Fe Railway*. Lincoln: University of Nebraska Press, 1974.

Chernow, Ron. *Titan: The Life of John D. Rockefeller Sr*. New York: Random House, 1998.

Clyne, Rick J. *Coal People: Life in Southern Colorado's Company Towns, 1890–1930*. Denver: Colorado Historical Society, 1999.

Connarroe, Carolyn. *The Louisville Story*. Louisville, Colo.: Louisville Times, 1978.

Cresto, Antoinette V. *King Coal: Coal Mining in Fremont County*. Florence, Colo.: Florence Citizen, 1980.

Dallezotte, Frank R. *Oakley, Wyoming: Gone . . . but Not Forgotten*. San Diego: Goodway Printing and Graphics, 1989.

Deutsch, Sarah. *No Separate Refuge: Culture, Class, and Gender on an Anglo-Hispanic Frontier in the American Southwest, 1880–1940*. New York: Oxford University Press, 1987.

Dix, Keith. *What's a Coal Miner to Do? The Mechanization of Coal Mining*. Pittsburgh: University of Pittsburgh Press, 1988.

Donachy, Patrick L. *United We Stand*. Trinidad, Colo.: Inkwell, 1990.

Dulles, Foster Rhea, and Melvyn Dubofsky. *Labor in America: A History, Fifth Edition*. Wheeling, Ill.: Harlan Davidson, 1993.

Dyni, Anne Quinby. *Erie Colorado: A Coal Town Revisited*. Erie, Colo.: Town of Erie, 2001.

Erie High School Sociology and History Classes. *Erie: Yesterday and Today*. Erie, Colo.: Privately published, 1967, 1974.

Fisher, John S. *A Builder of the West: The Life of General William Jackson Palmer*. Caldwell, Idaho: Caxton, 1939.

Fox, Maier B. *United We Stand: The United Mine Workers of America, 1880–1980*. Washington, D.C.: United Mine Workers of America, 1990.

Gardner, A. Dudley, and Verla R. Flores. *Forgotten Frontier: A History of Wyoming Coal Mining*. Boulder: Westview, 1989.

Gitelman, Howard M. *Legacy of the Ludlow Massacre: A Chapter in American Industrial Relations*. Philadelphia: University of Pennsylvania Press, 1988.

Goetzmann, William H. *Exploration and Empire: The Explorer and the Scientist in the Winning of the American West*. Austin: Texas State Historical Association, 1993.

Hall, Frank. *History of the State of Colorado*, vol. 4. Chicago: Blakely Printing, 1895.

History of the Union Pacific Coal Mines, 1868 to 1940. Omaha: Colonial, 1940.

Hutchison, James D. *Survey and Settlement: Lafayette, Colorado*. Lafayette, Colo.: Morrell Graphics, 1994.

Isham, Dell. *Rock Springs Massacre 1885: Two Essays on the Rock Springs Massacre.* "Ten Years to Atrocity," "The Chinese Must Go!" Fort Collins, Colo.: Privately published, 1969.

Jensen, Vernon H. *Heritage of Conflict: Labor Relations in the Nonferrous Metals Industry up to 1930*. Ithaca, N.Y.: Cornell University Press, 1950.

Jessen, Kenneth. *Railroads of Northern Colorado*. Boulder: Pruett, 1982.

Kenny, Kevin. *Making Sense of the Molly Maguires*. New York: Oxford University Press, 1998.

Klein, Maury. *The Life and Legend of Jay Gould*. Baltimore: Johns Hopkins University Press, 1986.

———. *Union Pacific: The Birth of a Railroad, 1862–1893*. Garden City, N.Y.: Doubleday, 1987.

Lamar, Howard R., ed. *The New Encyclopedia of the American West*. New Haven: Yale University Press, 1998.

Larson, T. A. *History of Wyoming*. 2d ed. Lincoln: University of Nebraska Press, 1978.

Laslett, John H.M. *Labor and the Left: A Study of Socialist and Radical Influences in the American Labor Movement, 1881–1924*. New York: Basic Books, 1970.

Lindsey, Almont. *The Pullman Strike: The Story of a Unique Experiment and of a Great Labor Upheaval*. Chicago: University of Chicago Press, 1942.

Lingenfelter, Richard E. *The Hardrock Miners: A History of the Mining Movement in the American West, 1863–1893*. Berkeley: University of California Press, 1974.

Long, Priscilla. *Where the Sun Never Shines: A History of America's Bloody Coal Industry*. New York: Paragon House, 1989.

Malone, Michael P. *The Battle for Butte: Mining and Politics on the Northern Frontier, 1864–1906*. Seattle: University of Washington Press, 1981.

McCraw, Thomas K. *Prophets of Regulation*. Cambridge: Belknap, 1984.

McGovern, George S., and Leonard F. Guttridge. *The Great Coalfield War*. Boston: Houghton Mifflin, 1972.

Montgomery, David. *Workers' Control in America: Studies in the History of Work, Technology, and Labor Struggles*. New York: Cambridge University Press, 1979.

Murdoch, Angus. *Boom Copper: The Story of the First U.S. Copper Mining Boom*. Calumet, Mich.: Roy W. Drier and Louis G. Koepel, 1964.

Papanikolas, Zeese. *Buried Unsung: Louis Tikas and the Ludlow Massacre*. Salt Lake City: University of Utah Press, 1982.

Paul, Rodman Wilson. *Mining Frontiers of the Far West, 1848–1880*. Albuquerque: University of New Mexico Press, 1974.

Phelan, Craig. *Divided Loyalties: The Public and Private Life of Labor Leader John Mitchell*. Albany: State University of New York Press, 1994.

Powell, Allan Kent. *The Next Time We Strike: Labor in Utah's Coal Fields, 1900–1933*. Logan: Utah State University Press, 1985.

Rhinehart, Marilyn D. *A Way of Work and a Way of Life: Coal Mining in Thurber, Texas, 1888–1926*. College Station: Texas A&M University Press, 1992.

Rhode, Robert B. *Booms & Busts on Bitter Creek: A History of Rock Springs, Wyoming.* Boulder: Pruett, 1987.

Riegel, Robert Edgar. *The Story of the Western Railroads: From 1852 Through the Reign of the Giants.* Lincoln: University of Nebraska Press, 1964.

Rufi, Sharon Fearn. *Almy Centennial Book, 1990.* Almy, Wyo.: Privately published, 1989.

Ruland, Sylvia. *The Lion of Redstone.* Boulder: Johnson, 1981.

Scamehorn, H. Lee. *High Altitude Energy: A History of Fossil Fuels in Colorado.* Boulder: University Press of Colorado, 2002.

———. *Mill & Mine: The CF&I in the Twentieth Century.* Lincoln: University of Nebraska Press, 1992.

———. *Pioneer Steelmaker in the West: The Colorado Fuel and Iron Company, 1872–1903.* Boulder: Pruett, 1976.

Schwieder, Dorothy, Joseph Hraba, and Elmer Schwieder. *Buxton: Work and Racial Equality in a Coal Mining Community.* Ames: Iowa State University Press, 1987.

Shifflett, Crandall A. *Coal Towns: Life, Work, and Culture in Company Towns of Southern Appalachia, 1880–1960.* Knoxville: University of Tennessee Press, 1991.

Simmons, Virginia McConnell. *The Upper Arkansas: A Mountain River Valley.* Boulder: Pruett, 1990.

Smith, Duane A. *The Birth of Colorado: A Civil War Perspective.* Norman: University of Oklahoma Press, 1989.

———. *Rocky Mountain Mining Camps: The Urban Frontier.* Bloomington: Indiana University Press, 1967; reprint, Lincoln: Bison, 1974.

———. *Rocky Mountain West: Colorado, Wyoming, and Montana, 1859–1915.* Albuquerque: University of New Mexico Press, 1992.

———. *When Coal Was King: A History of Crested Butte, Colorado, 1880–1952.* Golden: Colorado School of Mines Press, 1983.

Smith, Phyllis. *Once a Coal Miner: The Story of Colorado's Northern Coal Field.* Boulder: Pruett, 1989.

Stone, Elizabeth Arnold. *Uinta County: Its Place in History.* Laramie: Laramie Printing, 1924.

Storti, Craig. *Incident at Bitter Creek: The Story of the Rock Springs Chinese Massacre.* Ames: Iowa State University Press, 1991.

Stromquist, Shelton. *A Generation of Boomers: The Pattern of Railroad Labor Conflict in Nineteenth-Century America.* Urbana: University of Illinois Press, 1987.

Taylor, Morris F. *Trinidad, Colorado Territory.* Trinidad: Trinidad State Junior College, 1966.

Trottman, Nelson. *History of the Union Pacific: A Financial and Economic Survey.* New York: Sentry, 1923; reprint, New York: Augustus M. Kelley, 1966.

Ubbelohde, Carl, Maxine Benson, and Duane A. Smith. *A Colorado History,* 7th ed. Boulder: Pruett, 1995.

Wilkins, Tivis E. *Colorado Railroads: Chronological Development.* Boulder: Pruett, 1974.

Wyckoff, William. *Creating Colorado: The Making of a Western Landscape, 1860–1940.* New Haven: Yale University Press, 1999.

Theses and Dissertations

Brier, Stephen. "The Most Persistent Unionists: Class Formation and Class Conflict in the Coal Fields and the Emergence of Interracial and Interethnic Unionism, 1880–1904." Ph.D. diss., University of California–Los Angeles, 1992.

Brinley, John. "The Western Federation of Miners." Ph.D. diss., University of Utah, 1972.

Bryans, William S. "A History of Transcontinental Railroads and Coal Mining on the Northern Plains to 1920." Ph.D. diss., University of Wyoming, 1987.

Fletcher, Erma A. "A History of the Labor Movement in Wyoming, 1870–1940." Master's thesis, University of Wyoming, 1945.

Garceau, Dorothy Claire. "The Important Things of Life: Women, Work and Family in Sweetwater County, Wyoming, 1880–1929." Ph.D. diss., Brown University, 1995.

Gaynor, Lois Marguerite. "History of the Colorado Fuel and Iron Company and Constituent Companies, 1872–1933." Master's thesis, University of Colorado, 1936.

Hughes, Margaret Mary. "The United Mine Workers of America as a Social Control." Ph.D. diss., University of Pittsburgh, 1937.

Marlatt, Gene Ronald. "Joseph R. Buchanan: Spokesman for Labor During the Populist and Progressive Eras." Ph.D. diss., University of Colorado, 1975.

McClurg, Donald J. "Labor Organizations in the Coal Mines of Colorado, 1878–1933." Ph.D. diss., University of California, 1959.

Reitman, Sharon Lynne. "Class Formation and Union Politics: The Western Federation of Miners and the United Mine Workers of America, 1880–1910." Ph.D. diss., University of Michigan, 1991.

Suggs, George Graham, Jr. "Colorado Conservatives Versus Organized Labor: A Study of the James Hamilton Peabody Administration, 1903–1905." Ph.D. diss., University of Colorado, 1964.

Wilson, Howard K. "A Study of Paternalism in the Colorado Coal and Iron Company Under John C. Osgood: 1892–1903." Master's thesis, University of Denver, 1967.

Articles

Athearn, Robert G. "The Denver and Rio Grande and the Panic of 1873." *Colorado Magazine* 35, no. 2 (April 1958): 121–138.

Barrett, Glen. "P. J. Quealy: Wyoming's Coal Man and Town Builder." *Annals of Wyoming* 47 (Spring 1975): 31–43.

Brayer, Herbert O. "History of Colorado Railroads." In *Colorado and Its People: A Narrative and Topical History of the Centennial State*, LeRoy R. Hafen, ed., vol. 1. New York: Lewis Historical Publishing, 1950.

Clarke, John Jackson. "Reminiscences of Wyoming in the Seventies and Eighties." *Annals of Wyoming* 6 (July–October 1929): 225–236.

Crane, Paul, and Alfred Larson. "The Chinese Massacre." *Annals of Wyoming* 12 (January 1940): 47–55.

———. "The Chinese Massacre, Part II." *Annals of Wyoming* 12 (April 1940): 153–161.

Dubofsky, Melvyn. "The Origins of Western Working Class Radicalism, 1890–1905." *Labor History* 7 (Spring 1966): 152.

Ellis, Mrs. Chas. "History of Carbon, Wyoming's First Mining Town." *Annals of Wyoming* 8 (April 1932): 633–641.

Fishback, Price. "An Alternative View of Violence in Labor Disputes in the Early 1900s: The Bituminous Coal Industry, 1890–1930." *Labor History* 36, no. 3 (Summer 1995): 426–456.

Gedicks, Al. "Ethnicity, Class Solidarity, and Labor Radicalism Among Finnish Immigrants in Michigan Copper Country." *Politics and Society* 7, no. 2 (1977): 127–155.

Goodykoontz, Colin B. "The People of Colorado." In *Colorado and Its People: A Narrative and Topical History of the Centennial State*, LeRoy R. Hafen, ed., vol. 2. New York: Lewis Historical Publishing, 1950.

Greiner, Jean M. "The Golden, Boulder and Caribou." *Colorado Magazine* 44, no. 4 (1967): 307–319.

Grogan, Dennis S. "Unionization in Boulder and Weld Counties to 1890." *Colorado Magazine* 44, no. 4 (1967): 324–337.

Ichioka, Yuji. "Asian Immigrant Coal Miners and the United Mine Workers of America: Race and Class at Rock Springs, Wyoming, 1907." *Amerasia* 6 (1979): 1–23.

Jones, Walter. "Coal Mine Explosions at Almy, Wyoming: Their Influence on Wyoming's First Coal Mining Safety Laws." *Annals of Wyoming* 56 (Spring 1984): 54–65.

Kuhlman, Erika. "'Greetings from This Coalvillage': Finnish Immigrants of Red Lodge." *Montana: The Magazine of Western History* (Spring 1990): 32–45.

Laslett, John H.M. "Introduction: 'A Model of Industrial Solidarity?' Interpreting the UMWA's First Hundred Years, 1890–1990." In *The United Mine Workers of America: A Model of Industrial Solidarity?* John H.M. Laslett, ed. University Park: Pennsylvania State University Press, 1996.

Long, Priscilla. "The 1913–1914 Colorado Fuel and Iron Strike, with Reflections on the Causes of Coal-Strike Violence." In *The United Mine Workers of America: A Model of Industrial Solidarity?* John H.M. Laslett, ed. University Park: Pennsylvania State University Press, 1996.

Lonsdale, David. "The Fight for an Eight-Hour Day." *Colorado Magazine* 43, no. 4 (Fall 1966): 339–353.

Noel, Thomas J. "All Hail the Denver Pacific: Denver's First Railroad." *Colorado Magazine* 50, no. 2 (Spring 1973): 95–116.

Ourada, Patricia K. "The Chinese in Colorado." *Colorado Magazine* 29, no. 4 (October 1952): 273–284.

Scamehorn, H. Lee. "John C. Osgood and the Western Steel Industry." *Arizona and the West* 15, no. 2 (Summer 1973): 133–148.

Suggs, George G., Jr. "The Colorado Coal Miners' Strike: A Prelude to Ludlow?" *Journal of the West* 12 (1973): 36–51.

Wortman, Roy T. "Denver's Anti-Chinese Riot, 1880." *Colorado Magazine* 42, no. 4 (Fall 1965): 275–291.

■ INDEX

Page numbers in italics indicate illustrations.

261